DEMOCRATIC THEORY AS PUBLIC PHILOSOPHY

For Myra

Democratic Theory as Public Philosophy
The alternative to ideology and utopia

NORMAN WINTROP
The Flinders University of South Australia

LONDON AND NEW YORK

First published 2000 by Ashgate Publishing

Reissued 2018 by Routledge
2 Park Square, Milton Park, Abingdon, Oxon OX14 4RN
711 Third Avenue, New York, NY 10017, USA

Routledge is an imprint of the Taylor & Francis Group, an informa business

Copyright © Norman Wintrop 2000

All rights reserved. No part of this book may be reprinted or reproduced or utilised in any form or by any electronic, mechanical, or other means, now known or hereafter invented, including photocopying and recording, or in any information storage or retrieval system, without permission in writing from the publishers.

Notice:
Product or corporate names may be trademarks or registered trademarks, and are used only for identification and explanation without intent to infringe.

Publisher's Note
The publisher has gone to great lengths to ensure the quality of this reprint but points out that some imperfections in the original copies may be apparent.

Disclaimer
The publisher has made every effort to trace copyright holders and welcomes correspondence from those they have been unable to contact.

A Library of Congress record exists under LC control number: 99076646

ISBN 13: 978-1-138-71335-2 (hbk)
ISBN 13: 978-1-138-71334-5 (pbk)
ISBN 13: 978-1-315-19901-6 (ebk)

Contents

Preface and Acknowledgements   vii

Introduction   1

PART I: DEMOCRATIC THEORY AS IDEOLOGY AND UTOPIA

1. Formalism in Democratic Theory: Democracy as Political Procedures   15

2. Formalism in Democratic Theory: Democracy as Integrated Elites   28

3. Formalism in Democratic Theory: Robert Dahl and Democracy as Political and Social Pluralism   48

4. Utopianism and the Utopian Challenge to Democratic Theory   71

PART II: DEMOCRATIC THEORY AS PUBLIC PHILOSOPHY

5. Walter Lippmann's Call for and Contribution to a Public Philosophy   99

6. Democratic Theory as Public Philosophy: Its Nineteenth-Century Foundations   122

7. The Last of the New Liberals, and Analytic-Philosophic Public Philosophers   149

| 8 | Twentieth Century Natural-Law, Augustinian-Realist and Democratic-Elite-Theory Public Philosophers | 167 |

PART III: CONCLUSIONS

9	Functions of Democratic Theory as Public Philosophy	199
10	Does History End With Liberal Democracy and, If So, What Type?	222
11	Democratic Theory as Public Philosophy: Prospects and Problems	244

Bibliography 267

Index 285

Preface and Acknowledgements

Two of the principal themes and arguments of this book go back to a Flinders University political theory course on the problems of democratic theory which I taught from 1972 to 1992. The first is that the most fruitful way to classify conceptions of modern democratic government and politics is to describe them as *ideological, utopian* or *public philosophic*. The second is that although the ideological and utopian understandings of democracy have for several decades predominated in political rhetoric, political journalism and academic writing in English speaking nations, the public philosophic alternative provides superior insights into modern democratic government and politics, and both their positive potential and their dangers.

What is meant mainly though not solely by *ideological* democratic thought is formal or formalist democratic theory, sometimes described as procedural and/or empirical democratic theory. Such formalism or proceduralism sharply separates the formal institutions of democratic government from their content by reducing democratic government to its decision making procedures, principally free elections, competing parties and representative assemblies. Formalist democratic theory is made ideological (narrowly conservative) by its inherent tendency to act as an apology for and to give democratic credentials to the personnel, beneficiaries and outcomes of democracy's institutional forms and procedures, irrespective of the extent to which they may be manipulative and/or oligarchic. In the 1940s and 1950s this formalism was promoted, primarily, by American behavioural political scientists, many of whom were influenced by Joseph Schumpeter's *Capitalism, Socialism and Democracy* which, in 1942, redefined modern democracy as a system of competitive political elites.

Utopian democratic theory, by contrast, is overwhelmingly normative, and it conceives of democracy as a project; but the norms or standards and the goals of its adherents, it will be argued, are unrealistic, perfectionist and counter-productive. Utopian democratic theory, often described by its adherents as *participatory* democratic theory, became prominent in the 1960s when it was partly a reaction to the prevalent formalism, and partly an attempt to introduce into political theory and practice, and the university and other teaching of politics, the assumptions and objectives of the American New Left. By a *public philosophic* alternative to ideological and utopian democratic theory is meant writing which, like that of utopian democrats, is primarily normative but which, unlike that of the utopians, is characterised by a psychological, sociological, political and historically based realism.

It was during the time I taught the above course on democratic theory that I became convinced that the dominant ideological-formalist and utopian approaches to democratic theory and practice were defective. The main defect of formalist writing was and is its lack of a critical edge, and, as a consequence, its legitimating of entrenched practices, however harmful to democratic politics they and their effects may be. This concealing of deficiencies and abuses is furthered by the lack of realism of utopian styles of thought, a lack of realism which leads to relevant objections to democratic practice being pushed aside by fanciful ones. The necessary corrective to both formalism and utopianism, I have concluded, is a realistic, normative democratic theory which serves as a public philosophy. Moreover, such an alternative does not have to be a created afresh as its fundamentals are to be found in the classic liberal and democratic texts of the last two centuries. These are texts which formalists and utopians usually ignore, travesty or try to mould to their own purposes. But it was not until the 1990s that I began to systematically explore this liberal, democratic and public philosophic alternative to ideology and utopia.

In preparing for and writing the book I have incurred many debts. I was stimulated by the challenge of teaching a university course on the problems of democratic theory, and I am indebted to the many students who in essays and in tutorial and other discussions responded critically and thoughtfully to the topic. A major debt is to three colleagues, Rick De Angelis and Andrew Parkin, who gave me written comments on drafts for all chapters, and George Crowder on some crucial ones. Further helpful comments on chapter drafts were made by staff and postgraduate students at some Flinders University, Politics Department, seminars.

In 1987 I presented to an Auckland annual conference of the Australasian Political Studies Association a paper, 'The Public Philosophy, Democratic Government and Democratic Theory', which foreshadowed some of this book's central arguments. Helpful comments on the paper were made, at the conference, by Jim Flynn of Otago University. A version of Chapter 2, under the title of 'Elite Theory and Neo-Elite Theory Understandings of Democracy: An Analysis and Criticism', was published in 1992 in the *Australian Journal of Political Science*, when constructive suggestions were made by two anonymous referees and the journal's editor, Ian McAllister. A part of my response to Frances Fukuyama's end-of-history thesis, which is discussed in Chapter 10, was first formulated in a June, 1993, *Quadrant* article, 'Fukuyama's Challenge to Leftism'.

I have benefited from the assistance of the Flinders University Library staff, who, under difficult conditions, consistently maintain first-class services. I profited from my use of the University of Adelaide's Library and I enjoyed the hospitality of its Politics Department, on two short study leaves in that department, when I undertook some preparatory work for this book. Without the efforts and good humour of the late Bill Brugger, when he was the head of the Flinders University Politics Department, I would never have embarked on word processing. Secretarial assistance has been given competently and cheerfully by Anne Gabb, Julie Tonkin and Jackie Ansaar, also of this department - now the School of Political and International Studies. Julie also assisted in the completion of the Index. Andrew Parkin, when he was the department's head, enabled me to organise my teaching so as to find time for working on the book. Since my becoming an honorary research fellow, Andrew and now David Plant, the present head of the School, have ensured that the department offers adequate facilities and an encouraging environment. John Cowan located some articles for me. David Mathieson assisted in the completion of parts of the final typescript.

A long-standing debt is to John Dunn whose 1967 Cambridge University lectures on democratic theory made me aware of the political and educational importance of democratic theory and its possibilities as a university subject. John Dunn also commented on a provisional manuscript for the book. Another intellectual debt is to Walter Lippmann. Although I have departed from a central feature of his conception of a public philosophy, I have been stimulated by and have tried to build upon many of the ideas of his 1955 *Essays in the Public Philosophy*.

The patience of my wife, Myra, has been a major support, particularly when it became clear that the project was going to be more refractory than was expected. Myra has also assisted in removing obscurities from the text. Finally I should like to thank Anne Keirby and Claire Annals of the Social Sciences and Humanities editorial staff of Ashgate International Publishing for their assistance in preparing the final manuscript.

For the many inadequacies which remain in the content and presentation of my arguments and discussions, I am responsible.

Norman Wintrop
School of Political and International Studies
The Flinders University of South Australia
September, 1999

Introduction

Democratic Theory as Public Philosophy challenges what have become the dominant conceptions and theories of democratic government in political debate, journalism and academic writing. The challenge is made however not by proposing a new and untried conception or theory but by returning to and building upon a now overshadowed tradition of writing on democratic government.

The literature on modern democracy since the 1830s, it is contended, reveals three opposed conceptions of democracy: the *ideological, utopian* and *public-philosophic*. It will be argued that the public-philosophic tradition, which has been overshadowed since the 1950s, is the soundest of the three, and that it is imperative for democratic nations that it be revived and followed. Its understanding of democracy is both empirical and normative, and it synthesises the insights of *ideological* and *utopian* democratic theories while avoiding their deficiencies and excesses. But what exactly is meant by *ideological, utopian* and *public-philosophic* democratic theory?

Ideological, Utopian and Public-Philosophic Democratic Theory

The distinction between *ideology* and *utopia* has been taken from Karl Mannheim's once influential *Ideology and Utopia* (1936), a selection of his 1920s and 1930s essays in which he turned to intellectuals, whom he thought were capable of distancing themselves from dominant beliefs and prejudices, as the only people who could overcome the distortions of ideological (excessively conservative) and utopian (leftist, revolutionary) thought. He urged intellectuals to transcend class and other social biases by examining political and social issues from different perspectives, expose the sectional interests served by ideology and utopia, and construct a sociology of knowledge - Mannheim's alternative to ideology and utopia. For Mannheim, ideological thought was predominantly that which expressed the interests of feudal or bourgeois ruling classes while utopianism characterised Marxist and other revolutionary thought. I shall use the ideology-utopia distinction, however, to illuminate the character of and the differences between the two main ways in which democratic government and politics are now understood. But the idea of a *public philosophy*, this book's alternative to ideology and utopia, has not been taken from

Mannheim but primarily from Walter Lippmann's *Essays in the Public Philosophy* (1955). All three terms, *ideology*, *utopia* and the *public philosophy* will be given new emphases.

Ideological democratic theory will mean mainly that which defines and conceives of modern democracy in formal or empirical terms as existing institutions and practices irrespective of the standards expressed in or the social effects of these institutions and procedures. Although formal and procedural criteria (principally near-universal adult voting, free elections, and competing political parties and pressure groups) are indispensable for identifying a modern, representative democracy, unless they are supplemented by evaluative criteria which distinguish between, at a minimum, government in the interest of citizens and government which manipulates citizens for the benefit of favoured elites and other sectional interests, they are unable to separate genuine from sham representative democracy. Formal definitions and accounts of democracy point to necessary but insufficient conditions for a democratic community and system of government. By confusing what are only parts, though indispensable parts, of the democratic undertaking with the whole, formal conceptions of democracy are easily corrupted into ideological apologies for a status quo, its power relations and the ends they serve. In common with Mannheim's use, therefore, the word *ideology* will be restricted to thought which is limited and distorted because of its bias towards established social and political conditions, practices and privileges. Apart from an occasional departure from this usage, made necessary and clear by the context, *ideology* will not be used as a neutral word for describing sets or clusters of doctrines and goals, irrespective of whether they are conservative, radical or anything else.

Utopian democratic theory will mean that which admonishes the formalists in democratic theory for their narrow empiricism, and which asserts the need for normative theory, but which offers perfectionist and impractical rather than realistic norms. Utopian democrats make assumptions about human beings and their societies that are naive, and they advocate unattainable goals, the pursuit of which is likely to be counter-productive if not disastrous. They confuse democratic government and politics with unrealistic projects for obtaining new types of society and people, one consequence of which is that attention is diverted from more feasible reform and, when necessary, radical change.

Most utopian democrats are on the political left; explicitly or implicitly they associate democracy with socialist or other egalitarian ends which require social transformations for their achievement. But this is not to say that utopianism is a socialist monopoly, or that all socialists are utopians. An anti-socialist form of utopianism is expressed, for example, in the extreme laissez-faire belief, which had such a remarkable revival in the

Thatcher and Reagan years, that the extension of free-market principles into all areas of social life will cure all social ills. Libertarian utopians who hold this belief, however, unlike socialist and other egalitarian utopians, do not usually mistake their utopian economic and other proposals for an improved conception or theory of democracy.[1] It is because it is the egalitarian left who have been more assiduous than anyone else in introducing utopian goals and styles of thought into democratic theory that they are of particular interest to this study. But what is the public philosophic alternative to both ideological and utopian democratic theory?

Democratic theorists in the public philosophic tradition differ from formalists in that they are concerned about substance and outcome as well as procedural forms. They conceive of democracy as an end or project as well as a means for reaching decisions. They realise that it is when formal procedures are separated from content that democratic theory can become a mask for a manipulative and oligarchic politics, just as it is when ends are separated from necessary social and political conditions, agencies and institutions that democratic theory is likely to become utopian. The work of public philosophers, like that of utopian democrats, therefore, is normative and evaluative; but, unlike utopian work, it offers norms or standards that are based on realistic thinking about the citizens, associations, communities and systems of government of democratic nations. These standards have as their purpose the maintenance and improvement of democratic societies, not their socialist, quasi-socialist, quasi-anarchist, free-market libertarian or other restructuring. Democratic theory as a public philosophy thus combines the formalist emphasis on the need for empirical work with the utopian emphasis on the need for normative standards, while avoiding the defects and excesses of both ideology and utopia.

Public philosophers and political actors who uphold public philosophic standards do not try to reconstruct nations on the basis of one-sided free-enterprise, socialist, environmentalist, feminist or other ideals. No matter how much they sympathise with the exponents of such ideals, they encourage them to better appreciate the responsibilities entailed by democratic politics and government. The public philosophic objective is not to convert people from one vision and set of values to another or to discourage enthusiasm but to encourage political opponents to engage in public debate in an attentive, responsible and tolerant manner. Such toleration is seen as a necessary condition for and one of the chief virtues of a democratic society, while *pluralism* in at least one of its meanings (social diversity) is held to be desirable. Public philosophers accept that, for the foreseeable future, the political actors, intellectuals and other citizens of

---

1   Laissez-faire, libertarian utopianism is John Gray's main target in his *Beyond the New Right* (1994).

modern industrialised nations will have various and often opposed interests, opinions and goals. It is essential, therefore, that the inevitable disputes and conflicts be peaceful and productive rather than cause bitter and rankling social and political divisions.

This public philosophic style of thought will be traced from Alexis de Tocqueville, John Stuart Mill and other classic nineteenth-century democratic theorists to the present day. As these democrats were also leading liberal thinkers who brought liberal principles to a public philosophy for democratic nations, this book will uphold central parts of liberal thought - just as it will support major parts of conservative and democratic socialist thinking. Basic liberal principles, it will be argued, are essential parts of democratic theory and practice, and that it is folly for democrats to treat them as the ideology of the bourgeoisie, an extrapolation of a Hobbesian 'atomistic' individualism, a capitalistic 'possessive individualism', or an emaciated body of individualist thought lacking in adequate conceptions of community life, the common good, statecraft or civic virtue.[2] As it will be maintained that modern democratic government is dependent upon and inspired by liberal principles, for most purposes the terms *modern*, *representative*, *constitutional* and *liberal* democracy will be used synonymously.

This book's threefold classification of democratic theory as ideological, utopian and public philosophic, it should also be noted, challenges not only formalist and utopian democratic theory but the classifying of democratic theory and practice in terms of models or types. One noteworthy example of such a classification was C. B. Macpherson's (1977) study in which four models were constructed: the *protective*, *equilibrium*, *developmental* and *participatory*. Macpherson's *protective* model was a revised version of laissez-faire liberalism, now frequently described as *individualist* liberalism, the primary concern of which was said to be the protection of individuals and their property against other people and the state. His *equilibrium* model sought a balance between competing elites and interest groups. His *developmental* model was said to be that of John Stuart Mill, John Dewey and other late-nineteenth and early-twentieth-century liberals who emphasised democracy's potential for the development of people as human beings, moral agents and citizens but who failed to see the need for radical social reconstruction. The *participatory* model, which

---

2   For an ambitious and wide-ranging leftist critique of the liberal tradition, which makes most of these accusations, see Arblaster (1984); and for a concise and subtle argument on what are alleged to be liberalism and liberal democracy's Western individualist excesses, Parekh (1993). But for an early-twentieth-century pioneering interpretation of liberal thought and history, closer to the present book's, see Guido de Ruggiero (1959).

Macpherson favoured, combined the control of industry by workers, as urged by syndicalists and guild socialists at the beginning of the century, with the neighbourhood politics, radical democratisation of political parties and other direct forms of democracy urged by 1960s New Left activists.

Later, David Held (1987) went further in his model making, constructing no less than nine models of democracy. In common with Macpherson he included a preferred model which was similarly weighted towards socialist change and mass, participatory politics. In the 1990s, however, it has become more usual for types rather than models of democracy to be constructed. In a recent introductory article (Gutmann 1993), for example, six types are outlined: the *Schumpeterian, populist, liberal, participatory, social democratic*, and *deliberative*. Types of democracy are sometimes used for detached analysis, sometimes set up as targets for attack and sometimes to pave the way to a preferred type.

Although models and types of democracy may be enlightening, there are several objections to their being used to classify modern democratic theory and practice. First, there is no limit to the possible number of models, modellers and types; thus, the more popular the approach becomes, the more democratic theory will resemble the Tower of Babel - already a conspicuous tendency. Second, by their nature, most models or types of democracy are partial and unbalanced. They consist of extracting and highlighting selected objectives and components of democratic politics, often at the expense of others that contain necessary complements to them. Consider, for example, such types of democracy as representative and participatory, capitalist and socialist, elitist and populist, liberal and communitarian or classical republican. Third, rival models of democratic theory imply that the task of the democratic theorist or actor is either to select an existing model or construct a new one. What is lost is a public philosophic understanding of democratic politics as a quest for a comprehensive tradition of theory and practice which combines the best of the values, standards and ends of political thinkers, leaders, elites and citizens.

The threefold classification of democratic theory as ideological, utopian and public philosophic, therefore, has advantages over both dual (empirical and normative, conservative and radical, etc.) and multi- model and multi-type classifications. It avoids the unnecessary and politically damaging separation of empirical and normative theory, and affirms that the connections and mutual relations between empirical and normative work are as important as their differences. Without exaggerating the harmony and unity of or ignoring the many tensions in democratic theory and practice, it avoids the fragmentation of democracy into models or types. It enables the full range of empirical and normative thinking about democracy to be assessed and, when possible, synthesised and further developed.[3]

But as the idea of a *public philosophy*, which is central to the above threefold classification, has been given different contents and used for different purposes by various writers, some additional comment is necessary on how in this book it will be used.

The Idea of a Public Philosophy

The term *public philosophy* has no agreed meaning, and sometimes lacks a political content. This occurs when *public philosophy* is substituted for *popular philosophy* to describe epistemological, metaphysical or other largely non-political philosophic work addressed to lay readers rather than to philosophers. But it is more usual and fruitful for *public philosophy* to be given a political meaning as the guiding standards for the life of a political community. In this conception of a public philosophy, the adjectival phrase, *public philosophic* describes both (1) the principles and standards which comprise its contents, and which - whatever the degree of their success - are intended to direct political life, and (2) the work of political actors and theorists who establish and develop these principles. This means that in important respects a public philosophy resembles political philosophy, as whatever the precise intentions of the authors of classic and other political philosophic texts, from Plato's *Republic and* Aristotle's *Politics* to the present century, political philosophers have been among the main creators of public philosophic standards.

But although public and political philosophers have some common interests and a person may be both a public and political philosopher, the functions of a public and political philosophy are not the same. For example, some political philosophy may be a part of a contemplative philosophic system, or an argument and hypothesis intended for philosophic rather than political or other public discussion. By contrast, public philosophic writings or speeches are addressed to political actors and other citizens rather than to philosophers, their language and style are likely to be less technical, and their authors and speakers include not only political philosophers but politicians and other political actors, journalists and academic and other intellectuals. The comparison is returned to in Chapter 9's section on 'Cooperating with Political Philosophy...'.

---

[3] Additional surveys and classifications of democratic theory to those by Macpherson, Held and Gutmann include Rejai (1967); Holden (1974); Lively (1975); Etzioni-Halevy (1989); and Birch (1993).

A public philosophy always seeks and to be successful depends upon widespread support that approximates to unanimity; it is not, however, any kind of consensus. Whereas the root word of consensus is *consent*, and it would be absurd to describe standards as consensual if there were little support for them, the term *public philosophy* may be used, without absurdity, to describe a minority view. The reason is that a public philosophy may consist not of the principles on which there is a consensus but those with which dissenters challenge and seek to replace a dominant consensus. If, however, a public philosophy is to be more than one of several competing sets of doctrines, it has to have at least the capacity to achieve the support of all sections of a political community. In other words, although not all compromises are public philosophic, and on public philosophic terms may be reprehensible, a public philosophy always seeks to become the basis for general agreement. Its principles have to possess at least the potential to unite a political community. Whereas a consensus is any general agreement, irrespective of its content or the interests it serves, a public philosophy, in the way the term will be used in this book, means an actual or potential consensus that is intended to unite and benefit all the citizens of a democratic nation.

A call for such agreement and commitment by governmental personnel, political elites and citizens to the principles that are necessary for civilised, life-enhancing democratic communities was made by Walter Lippmann in his *Essays in the Public Philosophy* (1955), the most systematic, English-language account of a public philosophy. But Lippmann weakened his call by identifying the public philosophy with only one school of political thought, that of a natural law tradition which he traced to classical Greece and Rome and to Christian Europe.

Three decades after the publication of Lippmann's *Essays*, William M. Sullivan's advocacy of a public philosophy (1986) was similarly undermined by a confining of the public philosophy to only one branch of political thought. Sullivan made it synonymous with a republican tradition in Western political thought, but with this republican tradition being remarkably similar to American, 1980s, leftist, participatory and other thinking, the source of which was the New Left politics of the preceding two and a half decades. More recently, Robert E. Goodin (1995) has similarly associated the public philosophy with only one branch of political thought: a modified Benthamite utilitarianism in which governments and public bureaucracies redistribute, in an egalitarian manner, the resources which Goodin believes are required for satisfactory individual lives. His public philosophy, therefore, is more of a tool for politicians and officials than a means for enabling a democratic community and its citizens to check and to achieve mutually responsive relations with their governments.

In comparison with the post-Lippmann books by Sullivan and Goodin, Robert E. Statham, Jr's *The Constitution of Public Philosophy* (1998), the most recent advocacy of a public philosophy of which I am aware, has more in common with the present book. It shares, for example, several of my targets, principally behavioural political science, relativism in moral and political thought, the pursuit of an equality of condition, and the separation of freedom and rights from responsibilities and duties, and its alternative to the ills of American and other democracies consists of public-philosophic inspired political cultures. But there are also some important differences. Like Lippmann, Sullivan and Goodin, Statham overwhelmingly associates the public philosophy with only one school of political philosophy, that of Leo Strauss, his followers and a classical, Socratic natural-rights tradition which they extract from Western political philosophy. For all the many insights in Statham's book on the need for a public philosophy, and his and the Straussian contributions to it, therefore, his failure to see that an effective public philosophy for politically and culturally pluralist nations cannot be monopolised by only one school of thought makes the public philosophy he advocates both sectarian and ineffectual.

A more neutral use of the term *public philosophy* is that of R. Bruce Douglass and David Hollenbach (1994), the editors of a collection of essays intended to stimulate a political dialogue between American Catholics and liberals. Although the essays fail to explore the idea of a public philosophy, the Preface contains a brief but illuminating description of a public philosophy, at least for the United States: 'the philosophy that informs the public life of the United States' (p. xv).[4] Despite the book's authors being confined to Catholics and liberals, this statement, the book's purpose and its sub-title, *Contributions to American Public Philosophy*, all highlight an important function which a public philosophy should perform for a democratic nation: enabling people whose religious, philosophic, political and other fundamental values clash to cooperate in clarifying and confronting the issues which divide their nation.

Another recent revival of the idea of a public philosophy is Michael Sandel's (1996). In Sandel's vigorously argued critique of the dominant assumptions and goals of American political life, he follows Douglass and Hollenbach in using *public philosophy* mainly to describe the standards which do rather than those which should direct a nation's politics. Unlike Lippmann's *Essays in the Public Philosophy*, therefore, his book does not castigate American governmental and public life for not having a public

---

4   Other writers, however, have preferred to describe the ideas which pervade the public life of a nation not as a philosophy but by such terms as 'operative ideals' (Lindsay 1943) and 'operative public values' (Parekh 1994).

philosophy; his contention is that the existing public philosophy is inadequate and should be replaced. He argues that an individualist, rights-based liberal public philosophy should be replaced by a public philosophy which better promotes civic-republican virtues, a conception of the nation's common good, and stronger and healthier local and other communities. But whatever the merits of Sandel's political argument, and they are considerable, his use of the idea of a public philosophy equates it with any set or cluster of political doctrines be they civic republican, communitarian, liberal individualist, conservative, socialist, multicultural or anything else.

By contrast, the conception of democratic theory as a public philosophy which this book develops is not reducible to such partial and divisive doctrines. It is more comprehensive and open, it repudiates the one-sided bias of partial doctrines, and it tries to absorb their insights and those parts of their objectives that are justified and compatible with democratic principles. Such a comprehensive conception of democracy is expressed in a tradition of writing on democratic government that can be traced to Alexis de Tocqueville. Most of the participants in this public philosophic tradition see modern liberal democracy as a new civilisation in which the citizens of democratic nations, by means of their liberties and rights, and by constitutional and representative government, advance themselves, mitigate if not overcome their many social problems and difficulties, and obtain a superior way of life to that of any previous or, for the foreseeable future, different politics and society.[5]

The Book's Purposes and Structure

The first three chapters critically examine influential formalist and ideological work which identifies democratic government with decision making procedures and which, in theory if not always in practice, avoids judgements on the social and political content and consequences of these procedures. This is work which reduces modern democracy largely to representative assemblies and free elections, competing political parties, a means for the integration of elites, and/or social pluralism and pressure-group politics. Part I's fourth and final chapter, however, is on utopian democratic theory. After discussing the origins of utopian thought, it

---

5   The classic study of modern democracy as a new civilisation is Alexis de Tocqueville's (1968). The idea of modern democracy as a civilisation is also expressed in the title and content of Leslie Lipson's (1969) study.

suggests that the American New Left movements of the 1950s and 1960s were the main source of subsequent utopian writing on democracy. The chapter culminates in a critical discussion of writers described as 'utopian democrats', including C. B. Macpherson, Carole Pateman, Anthony Arblaster, Philip Green, Carol Gould and Benjamin Barber.

The four chapters in Part II, the first of which is on Walter Lippmann, survey the public philosophic tradition of democratic thought by focusing on several of its main exponents. The discussion of Lippmann is given precedence because, although in one important respect the present book's conception of a public philosophy departs from Lippmann's - the result of democratic theory taking the place of natural law, which Lippmann made the basis for a public philosophy - this book builds upon both Lippmann's analysis of the public philosophy and his five decades of writing as a public philosopher. Chapters 6, 7 and 8 discuss the work of other major democratic theorists who, despite their diverse backgrounds and often writing from opposed philosophic and political positions, have made distinguished contributions to democratic theory as a public philosophy. They include the nineteenth century founders of the tradition, Alexis de Tocqueville, John Stuart Mill and T. H. Green and his New Liberal successors, and twentieth century theorists who have brought to the tradition the methods and findings of analytical philosophy, neo-Thomist natural-law theory, Augustinian realism, elite theory and other schools of thought.

The remaining chapters (Part III) turn to the functions of and prospects for democratic theory as a public philosophy. Chapter 9 draws conclusions from the previous chapters, it sketches and argues for a public philosophic conception of justice, and it contends that the idea of a *mean* is a central part of democratic theory as a public philosophy. By a public philosophic mean, however, is meant the best principles, standards and courses of action rather than a median point or a compromise for the sake of compromise. A further section in Chapter 9 examines the relations of the public philosophy to the social sciences and other intellectual disciplines. The chapter concludes with an emphasis on the public philosophic function of warning against the dangers and temptations which always accompany the democratic project. Chapter 11 discusses Francis Fukuyama's thesis on the end of history, arguing that the thesis contains important insights and should not be dismissed as little more than a now dated liberal gloating over the collapse of the Soviet Union. The problem for the contemporary world, the chapter maintains, is not how to achieve a postmodern, post-liberal democracy, whatever that might be, but how to avoid the corruptions to which liberal-democratic government is prone. Several possible corruptions of liberal democracy are explored, mainly those which take corporate-capitalist, technocratic, managerial and quasi-totalitarian forms.

The final chapter on the current situation of both democratic government and democratic theory as a public philosophy begins with the problems created by political parties. It is argued that if a nation is to have responsible and respected political parties then more important than its electoral system is whether it has an effective public philosophy. Other major challenges which confront democrats and public philosophers are considered, principally the problems created by electronic and other journalism, and the elusive but fundamental issue of culture. The chapter and book conclude with a summary of the prospects for both democratic government and democratic theory as a public philosophy.

References

Arblaster, Anthony (1984), *The Rise and Decline of Western Liberalism*, Blackwell, Oxford.

Birch, Anthony H. (1993), *The Concepts and Theories of Modern Democracy*, Ch. 4, 'Democracy', Routledge, London.

Douglass, R. Bruce and David Hollenbach (eds), *Catholicism and Liberalism: Contributions to American Public Philosophy*, Cambridge Univ. Pr., Cambridge.

Etzioni-Halevy, Eva (1989), *Fragile Democracy*, Ch. 1, '...Major Theories Reconsidered', Transaction Publishers, New Brunswick.

Goodin, Robert E. (1995), *Utilitarianism as a Public Philosophy*, Cambridge Univ. Pr., Cambridge.

Gray, John, *Beyond the New Right* (1994), Routledge, London.

Gutmann, Amy (1993), 'Democracy', in Robert E. Goodin and Philip Pettit (eds), *A Companion to Contemporary Political Philosophy*, Blackwell, Oxford.

Held, David (1987), *Models of Democracy*, Polity Pr., Cambridge.

Holden, Barry (1974), *The Nature of Democracy*, Nelson, London.

Lindsay, A.D. (1943), *The Modern Democratic State*, Oxford Univ. Pr., London.

Lippmann, Walter (1955), *Essays in the Public Philosophy*, New American Library/Mentor, New York, a paperback edn of a Little, Brown, 1955, hardcover edn.

Lipson, Leslie (1969) *The Democratic Civilization*, 2nd edn, Oxford Univ. Pr., London.

Lively, Jack (1975), *Democracy*, Part Three, 'Theories of Democracy', Blackwell, Oxford.

Macpherson, C.B. (1977), *The Life and Times of Liberal Democracy*, Oxford Univ. Pr., Oxford.

Mannheim, Karl (1936), *Ideology and Utopia*, Routledge, London.

Parekh, Bhiku (1993), 'The Cultural Particularity of Liberal Democracy', in David Held (ed.), *Prospects for Democracy*, Polity Pr., Cambridge.

Parekh, Bhiku (1994), 'Cultural Diversity and Liberal Democracy', in David Beetham (ed.), *Defining and Measuring Democracy*, Sage, London.

Rejai, M. (ed.) (1967), *Democracy: The Contemporary Theories*, Atherton Pr., New York.

Ruggiero, Guido de (1959), *The History of European Liberalism* [1927], 2nd edn, Beacon Pr., Boston.

Sandel, Michael J. (1996), *Democracy's Discontent: America in Search of a Public Philosophy*, Harvard Univ. Pr./Belknap Pr., Cambridge, Mass.

Statham Jr, E. Robert (1998), *The Constitution of Public Philosophy: Toward a Synthesis of Freedom and Responsibility in Postmodern America*, Univ. Pr. of America, Lanham.

Sullivan, William M. (1986), *Reconstructing Public Philosophy*, Univ. of California Pr., Berkeley.

Tocqueville, Alexis de (1968), *Democracy in America* [1835 and 1840], 2 vols, (eds) J.P. Mayer and Max Lerner, 2nd edn, Collins/Fontana, n.p.

PART I
DEMOCRATIC THEORY AS IDEOLOGY AND UTOPIA

So we have really two distinct and developed democratic theories loose in the world today - one dismally ideological and the other fairly blatantly Utopian.

John Dunn,
Western Political Theory in the Face of the Future, 1979

Only a great fool would call the new political science diabolic: it has no attributes peculiar to fallen angels. It is not even Machiavellian, for Machiavelli's teaching was graceful, subtle, and colorful. Nor is it Neronian. Nevertheless one may say that it fiddles while Rome burns. It is excused by two facts: it does not know that it fiddles, and it does not know that Rome burns.

Leo Strauss, 'Epilogue',
in Herbert J. Storing (ed.),
Essays on the Scientific Study of Politics, 1962

From time to time the belief spreads among men that it is possible to construct an ideal society. Then the call is sounded for all to gather and build it - the city of God on earth. Despite its attractiveness, this is a delirious ideal stamped with the madness of logic. The truth is that society is always unfinished, always in motion, and its key problems can never be solved by social engineering.

Thomas Molnar,
Utopia: The Perennial Heresy, 1972

1 Formalism in Democratic Theory: Democracy as Political Procedures

This chapter is on the work of writers who see modern democracy primarily as parliamentary or presidential government, free elections, and competing political parties and leaders. The next two will examine in greater detail further influential versions of formalism in democratic theory, including work which regards modern democracy predominantly as a means for the reconciliation and integration of the elites of modern societies, and the view that it is social pluralism and pressure-group politics which more than anything else characterise modern democracy. Although these formal understandings of democracy are frequently brought together, there are noteworthy differences in their origins, supporting arguments and the conclusions drawn from them. As most formalist democratic theory assumes that modern democracy's central governmental features are parliaments and free elections, this view provides a good starting point.

Democracy as Parliamentary Institutions and Free Elections

Two of the clearest statements of this standpoint are the studies of democracy by Henry Mayo (1960) and Dorothy Pickles (1970). The strengths of their analyses are clarity, a businesslike style and common sense. The two authors bring to their work a healthy scepticism about excessive and unnecessary abstraction, and they are astute in detecting sophistry, pretension, and the smuggling of alien matter into democratic theory. These may be limited virtues, but they are virtues and not vices.

For both authors, to speak of democracy in the modern world is to speak about parliamentary, constitutional, representative and liberal democracy. But what gives their holding of this position and that of their co-thinkers its distinctiveness, separating it from that of writers in the public philosophic tradition, is the insistence that modern democracy is a means rather than an end, and a modest rather than a radical undertaking. Democracy, they declare, is not an end or a set of goals for a political community but a means, a set of procedures for peacefully establishing governments, reforming the law, deciding between policy packages and overcoming conflicts. In a succinct statement of this view, Henry Mayo has written that,

> a democratic political system is one in which public policies are made on a majority basis by representatives subject to effective popular control and periodic elections which are conducted on the principle of political equality and under conditions of political freedom (p. 70).

Dorothy Pickles, who wrote her (1971) introductory study of democracy a decade later was unwilling to offer a definition of democracy. Persuaded by the strictures of analytical philosophers, she declared that definitions of democracy are misleading, unimportant and metaphysical. In lieu of a definition she offered a list of necessary conditions, but conditions which strikingly resembled the components of Mayo's definition. They were 'universal suffrage, political parties, and the organisation of free voting in uncorrupted elections [for parliamentary assemblies] at relatively frequent intervals' (p. 13).

Both Mayo and Pickles were thoughtful in explaining and developing their conception of modern democracy. They argued that in addition to political debate, and majority decisions by voters at elections and parliamentarians in parliaments, representative government also meant a respect for the interests and views of electoral and parliamentary minorities. Free elections, they acknowledged, did not guarantee democratic government; democratic institutions and policy making also required freedom of speech, assembly and association, individual rights, toleration and compromise. Moreover, as Pickles wrote, democratic governments had to keep in touch with and be responsive to public opinion, ensuring that government became 'a dialogue between rulers and ruled' (p. 13).

Most of these propositions about democratic government and the conditions on which it depends are uncontentious; they are the ABC of democratic theory. But Mayo and Pickles attached to them and gave prominence to two additional propositions that are more questionable. The first is that the values of democracy are modest and moderate, and that they are almost entirely political - unconnected to economic or cultural life. The second is that democracy is not an end or a fundamental goal but a means, and because it is a means it may serve many different purposes and ends.

In support of the view that democratic government entails only modest political values, Dorothy Pickles repeated many of the arguments of Isaiah Berlin's (1969) defence of negative against positive freedom. She argued that when people were enticed into seeing modern democracy as an end, a grand objective, ideal society or set of ultimate social values, democracy was likely to be confused with ends that were socially divisive and disruptive. As examples of pseudo-democratic ends, she cited such predominantly leftist projects as economic and social equality, and a classless society. Such ends, she contended, far from being a part of democracy, made democracy impossible; they generated conflicts, fears and hatreds, and they embittered political divisions. They turned society into a battleground for opposed visions and ideals, and for class and other sectional interests. Furthermore, they induced cynicism, frustration and anger in voters by arousing desires and hopes which could never be satisfied. Here, Pickles was contrasting a formal and procedural conception of democracy with what in this book is being called 'utopian democratic theory'. What her arguments failed to establish, however, is that a formal and procedural conception of democracy is the only alternative to and an effective safeguard against utopianism.

The assumption that democracy is not an end but a set of political procedures which can serve different ends leads Mayo, Pickles and other proceduralists to turn away from substantive sociological and cultural issues. The problems which receive most of their attention are the establishing of consensual rules, principally constitutional laws and conventions, for the operation of governmental institutions and the conduct of political affairs; the maintaining of efficient and respected parliamentary and electoral institutions; obtaining political leaders who follow the rules; and achieving a competition between political parties and among diverse private associations which is genuine without being too intense, thus making possible restrained policy debates and a consensus on the limits and fundamentals of policy making.[1] Although the procedural view of democracy is intellectually stronger than what most advocates of greater participation and other critics allow, it does have serious flaws which, as long as democratic government is seen as no more than procedures, cannot be repaired. Richard Wollheim (1958), another exponent of the procedural conception of democracy, acknowledged the presence of one of these flaws when he observed that, 'all these [parliamentary and related] devices are no more than well-tried means of securing democratic control: none of them logically guarantees such control' (p. 126). Neither, it should be added, do they ensure outcomes that are compatible with even modern democracy's more moderate values.

The essential problem with the procedural, commonsense and widely held view of democracy as parliamentary or presidential government, free elections and universal or near-universal adult voting is

---

1   For a brief but thorough and illuminating recent analysis of the necessary conditions for sustaining the procedures of modern democratic government, and one which learns from the experiments in democracy of post-communist nations, but an analysis which never quite escapes the shackles of proceduralism, see Schmitter and Karl (1991).

that these institutions are compatible with a political and social content and product that is oligarchic - rule by small minorities in their own interests. Before further explaining and exploring the weaknesses in the Mayo and Pickles procedural version of democratic formalism, however, it is pertinent to examine the earlier analysis of Joseph Schumpeter, in which similar conclusions were reached but by a different, more complex, sociological route.

Joseph Schumpeter's Theory of Competitive Political Leaderships

Joseph Schumpeter, who constructed what became known as the 'revisionist' theory of democracy, a theory which systematically developed the view that democracy was not an end but a means, grounded his argument on an attempt at a destructive criticism of what he called *classical* democratic theory. This was a theory about democracy's ends and related norms which he traced to Jean-Jacques Rousseau, Jeremy Bentham, James Mill and John Stuart Mill, and Schumpeter's criticism of the theory encouraged Mayo, Pickles and other post-war political theorists and scientists to follow suit in similarly dismissing previous writing on democratic politics. But the acclaim given to Schumpeter's critique is more a reflection of the lack of knowledge and wilfulness of much post-1945 neo-positivist, behavioural-political-science and other hostility to classical, normative, democratic theory than of the quality of Schumpeter's account and objections to it.

Schumpeter's *Capitalism, Socialism and Democracy* (1942) was a more ambitious study than those of Mayo and Pickles. Its main purpose was to examine democracy's relations with both capitalism and socialism, and to this task Schumpeter brought the skills and knowledge of a major economist and economic historian. Whereas most democratic formalists avoid economic and cultural issues, Schumpeter's analysis of democracy was a part of a *tour de force* which was as concerned with economics and culture as it was with politics. It contained, in addition to its redefining of modern democratic politics, a careful comparison of capitalism and socialism, and an extensive criticism of Marx's - among other socialist - thought that was better informed than that of most other criticism of Marx by Schumpeter's contemporaries.[2]

Schumpeter argued that, from the end of the eighteenth century, writers on democracy had disseminated imprecise and misleading

---

[2] For an outstanding study of Schumpeter's life, and his economic and political thought, see Swedberg (1991). See also Heertje (ed.) (1981). For an incisive and thoughtful criticism of his revision of democratic theory, Plamenatz (1973).

definitions of their subject. Because they failed to clearly demarcate democratic from non-democratic government, their definitions and conceptions of democracy were useless. They gave no help to anyone who wished to explore democracy's compatibility with capitalism and socialism or to confront other major issues. To rectify these inadequacies Schumpeter redefined democracy and supported his revised conception of modern democracy with a sociological-empirical critique of the 'classical' definition of democracy, which he summarised as follows.

> [T]he democratic method is that institutional arrangement for arriving at political decisions which realizes the common good by making the people itself decide issues through the election of individuals who are to assemble to carry out its rule (p. 250).

The main part of this alleged 'classical' view of democracy, according to Schumpeter, was the assertion of a common good which entailed a belief in absolute values, and the capacity of ordinary people to construct a general will founded on both universal moral principles and their material interests. This common good, he wrote,

> implies definite answers to all questions so that every social fact and every measure taken or to be taken can unequivocally be classed as 'good' or 'bad'. All people having therefore to agree, in principle at least, there is also a Common Will of the people (= will of all reasonable individuals) that is exactly coterminous with the common good or interest or welfare or happiness (p. 250).

Schumpeter's objections to previous democratic theorists (pp. 250-68) focused on their alleged belief in such a common good. For Schumpeter, however, there was no common good; in democratic societies there were only self interested groups of people and majority decisions. The common good, objective and absolute values, and a rational agreement or will based on them, he declared, were all myths. There were only the different and often opposed values and conceptions of the 'common good' of individuals and groups. More than anything else, it was this appeal to the moral scepticism and value relativism of intellectual life which explains the influence exerted by Schumpeter's reconstruction of democratic theory.

The classical definition of democracy and its common good, Schumpeter argued, exaggerated the rationality of men and women. He accused previous democratic theorists of naively believing that the citizens of democratic nations consistently thought rationally and logically about their goals and the means for achieving them. Democratic theorists, he asserted, had ignored the psychological and sociological evidence that refuted this belief, and which disclosed that most people were emotional and easily misled and manipulated. Politicians, however, were regarded differently; according to Schumpeter, although they appealed to the rhetoric of normative democratic theory, they saw through it, and were aware of and utilised human irrationality. Politicians appreciated and used, for example, the techniques of modern advertising.

Most citizens, however, were irrational, and irrationality was more rampant in their political opinions than in their private lives. This was because, Schumpeter asserted, they had no political experience; they lacked the practical skills which in private life they acquired in their work, family relations and leisure activities. The only rational judgements on political issues which could be expected from them, therefore, were those which they learned as voters and political consumers when choosing between competing parties at elections. It was in fact partly if not largely as a response to Schumpeter's account of the political irrationality of voters - an account which the voting studies of American political scientists in the post-war years gave some support - that several left-wing academics of the 1960s and 1970s constructed theories of participatory democracy. These left-wing academics urged, as the way to give citizens political experience and to overcome apathy, ignorance and political irrationality, such measures as a greater control by employees of factories and offices, and a greater control of their education by students.[3]

But for all the attention given to Schumpeter's critique of previous democratic theory, by both enthusiasts and critics, his critique did little more than attack straw persons. First, from the beginning of the nineteenth century, with few if any exceptions, democratic theorists were well aware of the irrationality in human behaviour. Second, it is unlikely that any major democratic theorist had a concept of a common good which corresponded to Schumpeter's tendentious account of one. Third, the 'classical' definition and theory which Schumpeter constructed bundled Rousseau's concept of the general will with natural-law and philosophic-idealist emphases on the common good, and associated them with Benthamite utilitarianism, despite the fact that the Benthamites shared Schumpeter's hostility to the ideas of a general will and common good. Schumpeter was one of the century's outstanding economists, and a knowledgeable economic historian and critic of Marxist and other socialism - but not a reliable historian of democratic thought. John Plamenatz, who was a leading historian of democratic and other political thought, and usually a courteous critic, began his encounter with Schumpeter's thinking on democracy with the following observation. It was a pity, he wrote

---

3 Several of these theories of participatory democracy will be examined in Chapter 4's discussions of utopian democratic theory.

(1973), that Schumpeter 'ever took it on himself to attack what he called "the classical theory of democracy", for his attack is ignorant and inept, and is worth discussing only because it has been taken seriously' (p. 96). A more interesting topic, therefore, is Schumpeter's alternative to 'classical' theory?

Despite his view that the praising of democratic politics by previous democratic theorists was worthless, Schumpeter was emphatic that democratic government, when properly defined in empirical terms, had considerable merit and was far superior to communist, fascist and other possible government. He argued that, provided democratic theorists discarded myths about human rationality, a general will and the common good, and defined democracy in precise, empirical terms, it was possible for theorists and other scholars to undertake serious comparative and other analyses of democratic government. What he seized upon for redefining democratic government in empirical terms was competing political elites and leaders, a feature of modern democracy previously emphasised in the elite theory of Vilfredo Pareto (1963) and the political sociology of Max Weber (1970). The result was Schumpeter's much quoted redefinition of democracy.

> the democratic method is that institutional arrangement for arriving at political decisions in which individuals acquire the power to decide by means of a competitive struggle for the people's vote (p. 269).

The great merits which Schumpeter claimed for his definition were its realism and honesty. It told the inhabitants of democratic nations exactly what they possessed. In contrast to the alleged woolly and wishful thinking of previous definitions, his definition was factual. It told people that they possessed not popular sovereignty, not equality, not the common good, not justice and not even the will of the majority - but political parties and leaders who peacefully competed for governmental power. Modern democratic government, he asserted, had nothing to do with the original Greek meaning of *democracy* (*demos* = the people and *kratein* = the power of). It did not mean the rule of the people - for democratic like all forms of rule gave governmental power to a small minority. His definition, therefore, did not identify utopia, an ideal democracy or the direct democracy of ancient Athens but, he insisted, the observable and well documented realities of modern democratic nations.

Schumpeter also commended his definition for its moderation, in particular its emphasis on modern democracy being primarily an instrument for establishing and replacing governments, and for reaching decisions. He thus anticipated Mayo, Pickles and other proceduralists in arguing that democratic procedures were compatible with many different goals, and that they were a modest political achievement with modest values rather than an epoch-making project. Democracy's chief virtues, he thought, were political toleration and, until the twentieth century, a limited state and a separation of the state from society. But these modest achievements, he contended, were not insignificant. They gave individuals the maximum possible amount of freedom; they sustained modern capitalism, the most efficient of possible economic systems; and they enabled political and other associations to be independent of the state and to promote rich and diverse cultures. Modern democracies, he thought, should not be judged by the morality of their policies. Because democratic government was a means and not an end, it was compatible with many different goals and policies, not all of which satisfied people with high moral standards. What was important was that modern democracies survived, sustained modest but worthwhile values including the individual liberties of modern liberalism, brought some stability and permanence to their societies, and produced responsible and competent leaders, politicians and administrators.

Although Schumpeter's study of democracy was to be acclaimed by the advocates of value-neutral social sciences for its value-neutral definition of democracy, and for its assault on the unscientific character of previous democratic theory, Schumpeter did not present his work as an exercise in value neutrality. It is in fact full of evaluative and prescriptive propositions. A curious feature of his book's reception, therefore, is that whereas its apparently tough-minded empirical definition of democracy was subsequently given an almost biblical status by advocates of value neutrality, Schumpeter himself was outspoken in recommending values and standards for the leaders and citizens of democratic nations. He was well aware of the differences between defining modern democracy and conducting a serious analysis and evaluation of it, and he had few reservations about offering normative advice.

This normative advice mainly took the form of conditional arguments: that if *a* then *b*. In other words, if the elites and citizens of democratic nations desired stable democratic institutions and competent government then certain political and social conditions were necessary. In arguing for these conditions, an indirect way of recommending standards and values, Schumpeter entered the domain of normative democratic theory and public philosophy. In practice, however, the advice which he offered democrats was aloof and aristocratic, and it glaringly contrasts with the assumptions of most subsequent political science and theory. But it contains a great deal of sense, and the fact that it was his critique of 'classical' normative theory, and the formalism and empiricism of his definitional discussions which proved to be influential, rather than his prudential normative advice, tells us a great deal about the intellectual life of the second half of the twentieth century. The political and social conditions which Schumpeter considered necessary for modern democracies - the main components of his prudential, normative advice - were as follows.

First (my enumeration), he argued that democracy needed 'high quality' politicians and ministers, who were committed to the maintenance of established political institutions and traditions. For the obtaining of such leaders, a 'social stratum' from which they could be drawn was required, which should be neither too exclusive nor too easily accessible to outsiders (pp. 290-91). But, although it was important that democratic nations should find a place for neo-aristocratic ruling and political classes, only Britain, Schumpeter thought, fulfilled this condition. A second condition was that political controversy and processes should be constrained. Opposed doctrines about the fundamentals of social organisation should be transformed into empirical and administrative problems; an 'all-powerful parliament must impose limits upon itself'; governments must not overburden themselves with unnecessary projects and reforms; and ministers must accept the advice of specialists (pp. 291-93). *Specialists*, however, meant not so much technical experts as conservative minded, public spirited, well educated and experienced public servants. A third condition, in fact, was the existence of 'a well-trained [public] bureaucracy... endowed with a strong sense of duty and a no less strong *esprit de corps'* (p. 293).

Fourth, moderation must be practiced by both government and opposition parties, neither of which should raise false hopes in voters by promising too much. Politicians had to put patriotism and a loyalty to parliamentary government before personal ambition and party loyalties. 'In particular, politicians in parliament must resist the temptation to upset or embarrass the government each time they could do so. No successful policy is possible if they do this' (p. 294). Voters, too, had to possess at least a basic capacity for political judgement, distinguishing the demagogue from the responsible politician and spotting the 'crook and the crank' (p. 294). Voters must not think that at elections they could mandate governments, and between elections they should refrain from harassing parliamentarians by 'bombarding them with letters and telegrams for instance' (p. 295). Democratic government demanded a division of labour in which governments, public servants, parliamentarians and voters all knew their place and their responsibilities. Fifth, in addition to the toleration of different religious beliefs, there should be 'a large measure of tolerance for differences of opinion' (p. 295). This political toleration required that people with unpopular views should not be intimidated into silence by politicians, journalists or anyone else, and that criticism of other people be restrained. Political actors should be cautious when objecting to the interests and opinions of others, and patiently tolerate objections to their own. Majorities had to respect minorities, and minorities respect majorities.

These discussions of necessary political and social conditions introduced a tension into Schumpeter's work. On the one hand it assailed previous theorists for confusing the empirical issues of defining and understanding the main features of modern democratic government with the advocacy of ideals and norms while, on the other, it urged the adoption of the values of Central European conservatism. One reason for the apparent anomaly was that nothing of consequence had been changed, for democratic theory, by Schumpeter's empirically based, elite-theory conception of democracy. The long-standing normative questions remained, and Schumpeter had to find answers. For all his dislike of talk about the *common good*, he was unable to dispose of the issues with which the concept dealt. In practice, his book did not dispense with but offered a new version of the common good, at the centre of which was the sustaining of what he regarded as the necessary conditions for democratic government.

Schumpeter's necessary conditions, whatever other insights they contained, acknowledged that democracy depended on much more than the mere existence of parliaments, elections, and competition among political elites and between parties and their leaders. His book demonstrated that whether democracy was defined empirically or normatively, and in elite theory or public philosophic terms, the fundamental normative question remained: what are the standards which leaders, elites and citizens need to follow if modern democracies are to survive, prosper and benefit their members?

Objections to Procedural Democratic Theory

If Schumpeter's slide from empiricism and formalism in his defining of democracy to substantive political-sociological and normative analysis does nothing else, it demonstrates that democracy is more than parliamentary and electoral procedures, and a peaceful competition for governmental power which can be attached to any number of ends. When individuals, groups and nations establish democratic procedures, whatever their other ends, they are committing themselves to a political end (self government in the interest of a political community and its members) and to related political values. Guiding standards therefore are required for the achieving of a *common good*, *general interest* or whatever other concept is used to express a shared interest in a successful, civilised, life-enhancing democracy.

The other main procedural assertion, that democracy is a modest achievement, is as odd as the proposition that democracy is solely a means and not an end. Democracy may not bring a perfect society and individual salvation, or be an adequate substitute for religion, art, literature, friendship and much else, but it is a force which has transformed the modern world. Whether a person likes or dislikes democracy, whether he or she is a radical who wishes to encourage or a conservative who wishes to curb the forces unleashed by democratic institutions and procedures, it is simply historical and political nonsense to see democracy as a modest undertaking. To suppose that placing the final decision on who governs in the hands of tens if not hundreds of millions of people is a modest political undertaking, with few major political, economic and cultural implications, is to display an ignorance about both the history of the last two centuries and present day nations.

Neither can it be said that, though procedural definitions and understandings of democracy may be naive, they are harmless. Unless they are carefully qualified they function as an ideology which legitimates as democratic whatever power relations, laws and policies result from democratic procedures. Provided that they are able to co-exist with and use democratic procedures, forces which turn democratic institutions into the instrument of sectional interests or which cause a drift to chaos are, on procedural terms, simply another empirical part of 'democratic' practice. Procedural democratic theory thus legitimates social relations and political practices which, in their content, may be closer to oligarchic government (government by minorities in the interest of themselves and favoured groups) than they are to self government in the interest of all sections of a political community.[4]

What appears to be procedural formalism's most compelling feature, its demand that democrats and democratic theorists refrain from judging present day representative government on the basis of Athenian citizenship, nineteenth-century bourgeois, classical republican or other historically based experience, is its fatal flaw. It is precisely because power in modern democracies no longer resides with citizens who, as in ancient Athens and other small republics, directly participated in the government of their states, or with the independent civil societies and local communities of eighteenth- and nineteenth-century Western nations, that political life requires more rather than less normative theory and guidance. Meditations on history and the adoption of philosophic perspectives may have their limits, but the complexities of current democratic politics require that citizens and governments be guided by something more than the simplicities of procedural formalism.

---

[4] Chapter 10, 'Does History End With Democracy and, If So, What Type?', examines some of the main oligarchic tendencies in modern democratic politics.

Procedural formalism, by abandoning the quest for shared standards and a clarification of the ends which democratic procedures should serve, expresses not so much the interests of citizens as those of the less responsible members of political elites - people who, to benefit themselves, are or would like to be the decision makers for their societies. Such people do not want to be bound by ends and standards. What they value in democratic government is what procedural democratic theory tells them they have: procedures which enable them to peacefully compete for power, status and other privileges, overcome their conflicts, and seek compromises and consensuses. Procedural conceptions of democracy thus function as a justificatory ideology for whoever obtains or seeks to obtain privileges from the operation of democracy's procedures.

What counts for ordinary citizens, by contrast, is not the presence of procedures that appear to be democratic but their outcomes. What counts is whether the procedures result in citizens receiving greater respect and recognition, security, and opportunities to lead satisfactory lives and to improve their living standards and conditions. Democracy for citizens has to mean more than voting in free elections, and choosing between party leaders and politicians - people for whom, in many nations, citizens have increasingly lost respect. For citizens, democracy has to mean not just form but content. They should be able to believe that democratic government is in their interests, that it is better than any other possible system of government, and that their representatives and leaders, as well as being responsive and accountable to them, are worthy of their trust, and the power and authority they have acquired.

Although procedural accounts of democracy are sometimes supplemented by different authors with normative discussions and prescriptions, procedural democratic theory, by the way it defines itself, can provide only random bundles of norms and criteria for influencing and assessing the content of democratic government and politics. The next two chapters, however, will turn from procedural to other, in some ways more ambitious, formalist accounts of democratic government.

References

Berlin, Isaiah (1969), 'Two Concepts of Liberty' [1958], in *Four Essays on Liberty*, Oxford Univ. Pr., Oxford.

Heertje, Arnold (ed.) (1981), *Schumpeter's Vision: Capitalism, Socialism and Democracy after Forty Years*, Praeger, Eastbourne and New York.

Mayo, Henry B. (1960), *An Introduction to Democratic Theory*, Oxford Univ. Pr., New York.

Pareto, Vilfredo (1963), *The Mind and Society* [1916], 4 vols in 2, A. Livingston (ed.), 2nd Eng. edn, Dover, New York.
Pickles, Dorothy (1971), *Democracy* [1970], 2nd edn, Methuen, London.
Plamenatz, John (1973), *Democracy and Illusion*, Longman, London, Ch. 4, 'Schumpeter and Free Competition for Power'.
Schmitter, C. Philippe and Terry Lynn Karl (1991), 'What Democracy Is...and Is Not', *Journal of Democracy*, vol. 2, No. 3, pp. 75-88.
Schumpeter, Joseph A. (1954), *Capitalism, Socialism and Democracy* [1942], 4th edn, Allen and Unwin, London.
Swedberg, Richard (1991), *Joseph A. Schumpeter: His Life and Work*, Polity Press, Cambridge.
Weber, Max (1970), 'The Vocation of Politics' [1919], in H. H. Girth and C. Wright Mills (eds), *From Max Weber: Essays in Sociology*, 2nd edn, Routledge, London.
Wollheim, Richard (1958), 'Democracy', *Journal of the History of Ideas*, vol. 19, pp. 225-42.

2 Formalism in Democratic Theory: Democracy as Integrated Elites

Vilfredo Pareto and Gaetano Mosca, the founders of what has become known as elite theory, in addition to trying to combat revolutionary socialist ideas and to give political science new foundations, developed novel conceptions of modern democratic politics. Most democratic theorists have considered these elite theories, particularly Pareto's, to be an attack on liberal democratic theory and practice. The reaction of Schumpeter and others, however, has been to incorporate elite theory into democratic theory. More recently, writers whom I shall describe as *neo-elite* theorists have returned the compliment and tried to turn democratic theory into a sub-branch of elite theory.

The present chapter culminates in a critique of this neo-elite theory, a new version of ideological formalism. It will be argued that, although neo-elite theorists present themselves as more sympathetic to democratic government than were Pareto and Mosca, their claim is misleading. Their work contributes less to understanding democratic government, and it has a greater tendency to serve as a legitimating ideology for oligarchic corruptions of democracy. The chapter begins with the issues raised by elite theory for democratic government, and the responses to them by political thinkers of the right, left and centre.

Elites: Issues and Responses

Although the word *elite* is defined and used by elite theorists in many ways, it has some core meanings, and reasonably clear and consistent uses. Originally, *elite* was an approbatory word meaning the best members of a group or the best group of people within a society, in other words those most worthy of respect and emulation. But in Pareto's project of a positivist (entirely factual and logical) political science, in which all societies were held to be ruled and dominated by elites, he strove to use the concept of an *elite* in a detached manner. For Pareto, elites consisted primarily of people whose ability and energy made them the most successful competitors in politics, law, warfare, crime, business or any other occupation.

But he also saw elites as integral parts of political and social structures. A structural view of elites, for example, underlays his concern that a society could be over-supplied or under-supplied with elite individuals. This dual, psychological and sociological, understanding of elites resurfaces in the work of most elite theorists. On the one hand elites are thought to be powerful or esteemed individuals; on the other, they are the products of the structures of military, industrial, democratic and other societies.[1]

Whether or not the word *elite*, a French export, is superior to the English words it displaces, the issues raised by elite theorists are fundamental for democratic theory and practice. They include the roles, rights and duties of citizens and governments; the relations between citizens and their representatives; whether social and economic as well as political equality are desirable and feasible; the extent to which authority and leadership are necessary; and how beneficial power is to be furthered and harmful power constrained.[2] In the literature on democracy six responses to the issues raised by elite theory may be found.

First, for classical democratic theorists from Tocqueville and John Stuart Mill to their present day, public philosophic successors, elites are an unavoidable social fact. They are products of the natural differences among human beings; the division of labour which accompanies social organisation, particularly that of industrialised nations; the need for political leadership, economic management and other forms of authority; and representative democracy itself which produces at elections - at least if the word is used non-evaluatively - an elite. Classical democrats assume that the democratic problem is neither to abolish elites nor to tolerate all forms of power and privilege but to foster the elites and elite functions that are appropriate for democratic nations and to resist those which are not.

A second and opposed conception of the relations between democracy and its elites is that of anarchists and Marxists. They agree with what is usually taken to be Pareto's view, that modern representative democracy is fraudulent, and that it does not lead to liberty, equality and community but to elite domination and rule. More specifically, Marxists and anarcho-communists maintain that modern democracy is based on deception and consists of elite rule on behalf of an exploitative capitalist

---

1   For surveys of elite theories, see Bottomore (1966); Burnham (1943); and Parry (1969).
2   For work on the issues raised by elite theorists but by means of different concepts, see for example Arendt (1961), for 'What is Authority?'; and (1972) for the discussion of power in 'On Violence'; Simon (1951; and 1962); Tucker (1981, esp. pp. 1-30); and Watt (1982).

class. They conclude that if the people and not their elites are to rule then capitalism and, for anarchists, the state must be destroyed.

Third, there is the view which David Spitz (1949) and other critics of elite theory attribute to Pareto and Mosca but which neither of them consistently held. This is the view that because all societies, including post-revolutionary ones, have elite-non-elite divisions, democracy in the sense of the rule of the people or even as an approximation to such rule is impossible. A fourth, widely held, softer version of the above, third, view - that elites make democracy impossible - and one which is closer to that of Pareto and Mosca is Schumpeter's: that the necessity for governmental elites in large nations results in only a minimal amount of democracy being possible, namely, the procedures which permit and encourage peaceful competition for governmental power by rival elites.

Fifth, since the 1960s, purportedly as a defence of classical democratic theory, a soft Marxist and a soft anarchist response has become widespread. It consists of the view, to be found in the work of many academic radicals, that democracy and elites are incompatible, and that contemporary, so-called democratic societies are misnamed because they are dominated by elites. But, unlike Marxists and anarchists, these academic radicals do not urge, at least explicitly, socialist and/or anarchist revolution; they advocate that democratic rights and procedures be used to create new kinds of libertarian, egalitarian, participatory and/or communitarian democracies. Their projects and supporting theories will be examined in Chapter 4's discussion of utopian challenges to democratic theory.

Sixth, neo-elite theorists contend that it is only by concentrating on the role of elites that the origins, histories and character of modern democracies, which they regard as systems of integrated elites, become comprehensible, and they claim that they have constructed an empirical and normative democratic theory that is merged with and improved by elite-theory. This chapter's contention, however, is that their neo-elite theory is formalist and ideological, and that, along with the remainder of the above responses to the problems posed by elites for democratic government, inferior to the first (classical democratic and public philosophic) response. As a preliminary step in the argument, mainly to reveal the distinctive features of neo-elite theory but also to disclose its inferiority to the elite theories of Pareto and Mosca, as a contribution to understanding modern democracies, the original elite theories and their implications for democratic nations will be discussed.

Vilfredo Pareto and Gaetano Mosca: Democracy, Elites, Political and Ruling Classes

Pareto and the Inevitability of Elite Rule and Domination

Most commentators on Pareto's political thought note the acerbity of his references to and his apparent hatred of modern democratic politics. His insistence that all government is oligarchic and that democracy in the sense of rule by the people is a myth are emphasised, and the following and similar statements are frequently quoted. '[W]hether universal suffrage prevails or not, it is always an oligarchy that governs, finding ways to give to the "will of the people" that expression which the few desire' (Pareto, 1963, para. 2183). The meaning of such statements, however, is more subtle and complex than is often realised.

It was in the 1890s that Pareto (1848-1923), already an internationally known economist, turned his attention to sociology and elite-theory. From the 1870s, as a freelance journalist with parliamentary ambitions, he had opposed the economic protectionist and overseas expansionist policies of the parliamentary governments of his native Italy and of other European nations. By the 1890s, when he turned to sociology, he had concluded that only the presence of vested interests could explain why democratic governments preferred protectionist and imperialist to more productive laissez-faire economic policies. One of the main reasons for his turn to social and political analysis, in fact, was to locate these vested interests and the sources of their power.[3]

In early formulations of his elite theory and objections to contemporary democratic practice he argued that most modern democracies were governed by political elites, overwhelmingly in their own interests and those of manufacturers and their employees. Some citizens were advantaged but others were victimised, principally those on a fixed income; Britain and Switzerland, Pareto then believed, were among the few exceptions to this 'bourgeois socialism' and 'pluto-democracy' (Pareto 1963, paras 2208-21, and 2237-78; and 1966, pp 59-62, 64-7 and 117-20). Pareto's hostility to the statism of 'bourgeois', Marxist and other forms of socialism, along with his contempt for pre-1914 Italian and other parliamentary elites explain the anti-democratic invective of his 1916 magnum opus (1963).

Pareto, in his 1916 treatise, made three linked objections to the parliamentary democracies of his day. The first was that the effect of

---

3   For the origins of Pareto's hostility to the democracies of his day, see Bellamy (1987, pp. 12-21); Pareto (1966) for S. E. Finer's Introduction (esp. pp. 10-12); and Powers (1987, pp. 19, 25-6 and 33-4).

parliamentary government and mass voting was ruled by factions and lobbies, in which a 'governing class' appropriated 'other people's property not only for its own use, but also to share with such members of the subject class as defend it and safe-guard its rule...' (1963, para. 2267). Democracy thus became 'demagogic plutocracy', a system of government by sectional interests in the hands of professional demagogues. Second, parliamentarians, journalists and other demagogues disseminated a language of egalitarianism, compassion and popular rule which hid the substance of politics. This 'religion' of humanitarianism and democracy consisted of vague notions of equality, a specious concern for the poor and vacuous slogans of popular sovereignty, all of which were a mask for government by deception and the accumulation of power and privilege by successful elites (Pareto, 1963, paras 1215-28). Third, the successful elites of democratic politics relied on cunning and guile. Elites with a predominance of such 'fox-like' or 'combination' qualities recruited and absorbed into the political system people similar to themselves, and drove into opposition individuals who possessed the more 'lion-like' qualities of courage and persistency in the defence of values and traditions.

The predominance of *foxes* over *lions*, to use Pareto's metaphors, made democracies weak and unstable. 'Predominance of the combination instincts and enfeeblement of the sentiments of group-persistence result in making the governing class more satisfied with the present and less thoughtful of the future' (Pareto, 1963, para. 2178). Either by revolution or military defeats by nations less handicapped by spineless elites and the religion of humanitarianism, democracies would perish. Indeed, in the last years of his life, Pareto believed that the Bolshevik revolution of 1917 and Mussolini's 1922 March on Rome had confirmed this prognosis.

Linked to his objections to the democratic governments of his day was his conviction that most human behaviour was irrational ('non-logical'). Most human acts, he thought, did not derive from the relating of means to ends or of one end to another but from instincts, drives, sentiments and impulses ('residues'). Religions, philosophies, and moral and political codes, he contended, were rationalisations ('derivations') of these residues. Economic activity, however, was less contaminated by 'non-logical' behaviour as it was the means for satisfying wants and goals in the immediate areas of life in which people had some understanding of costs. By contrast, modern democratic politics was rampant with counter-productive behaviour and policies as it encouraged the masses who had no political experience and who were particularly prone to irrational conduct to influence events with their votes.

But there is more to Pareto's analysis of modern democracy than an attempt to expose its irrationality, corruption and rhetoric. A more subtle appraisal of parliamentary institutions and universal adult voting is found if attention is turned from his deriding of the elites and voters of 'pluto-democracies' to other parts of his elite-theory sociology, in particular his criteria for assessing political regimes. For Pareto, the societies which were the most stable and permanent, and which most benefited (maximised the utilities of) their members combined individual liberty and social diversity with security against internal and external aggressors. Strong, endurable societies combined economic prosperity, military strength and a capacity for political and other reform. They balanced the liberties of individuals and of professional and other private associations, including those of university and other intellectuals, with necessary constraints. Pareto argued that the fact that all societies were ruled by elites, and all political and social movements were led and organised by elites did not mean that all elites were equal, or that the results of their conflicts were inconsequential. Whether democratic and other societies flourished or declined depended on the character of their governmental and other elites, a more important consideration than whether their political institutions were democratic or autocratic.

The best societies, Pareto thought, had elites consisting of people who possessed many types of personality and skill. Such variety and optimality required a circulation of elites (a rise and fall of individuals within elites and between elites and the rest of a society) which was neither superficial nor excessive. In particular, successful societies had elites whose members possessed the more positive qualities of both lions and foxes. Political leaders and administrators, Pareto contended, should be fox-like in their ability to speak, write, negotiate, organise and thus rule by persuasion and consent rather than by force. But they should also be lion-like in their steadfastness, their loyalty to - and, when necessary, their willingness to use force to support - values, colleagues and the institutions, traditions and long-term interests of their nations. Pareto's optimal rulers combined knowledge, competence and communication skills with integrity and a desire for honour - the best of modern democratic with the best of traditional aristocratic values. Pareto may have grown increasingly pessimistic about representative democracies obtaining such socially beneficial elites, but he never abandoned these criteria.

Pareto's elite theory was intended to be a tool for separating fact from fiction, and for distinguishing between worthy and corrupt political leaders. Despite the fact that democratic like other rulers ruled in their own interests while appealing to the dominant sentiments of their societies, their interests could parallel and advance those of their country. Countless were the cases, he wrote, 'where a governing class working for its own exclusive advantage has further promoted the welfare of a subject class' (1963, para. 2249). It follows that the political problem for democratic as for other societies is to create a culture and establish institutions which are likely to produce elites who advance the interests of their nation and its members.

Pareto's view that governmental elites should comprise the most competent and courageous individuals, in fact, is remarkably similar to the young John Stuart Mill's belief that a society, including a democratic society, 'may be said to be in its *natural* [best] state when worldly power, and moral influence, are habitually and undisputedly exercised by the fittest persons whom the existing state of society affords' (Mill, 1973, p. 17). But whereas Pareto was often content with exposure and ridicule, and the hope that the lions might be more assertive, Mill followed Tocqueville in trying to discover the institutions and the type of formal and informal education, for both elites and ordinary citizens, that might mitigate the dangers in democratic government while releasing its potential to improve the lives of citizens. The pertinent objection to Pareto's views on modern democracy suggested by Mill's thinking, therefore, is not that there is anything amiss in Pareto's demands that the power and importance of elites be recognised, and that rhetoric be distinguished from reality, but that this is what the best of democratic theorists do and, in contrast to Pareto, without falling into a misleading and confusing rhetoric.

Mosca's Ruling and Political Classes

Gaetano Mosca (1858-1941), who made a challenging analysis of modern democracy as a part of a proposed universal political philosophy and science, considered Pareto to be a plagiarist of his work which, like Pareto's, emphasised the inevitability of minority rule. But Mosca in the last part of his life, unlike Pareto, was explicit that the minority rule of modern representative government was, at least for the post-1918 world, the foundation for the best of possible political regimes. He argued that modern democracy was the best safeguard for what he called *juridical defence* (the liberties and rights of modern liberalism) and the most likely of possible political systems to promote a diverse and worthwhile civilisation. And in his analysis of democratic regimes he tried to identify the conditions which were most likely to produce (1) competent and responsible ruling classes (the people who exercise governmental power), and (2) a wider political class or social strata (from which these rulers are recruited), the members of which as well as being politically skilful are committed to liberal and civilised values.

Mosca, like Pareto, valued individual liberty and held that its friends should understand the ways of the world and their many threats to liberty. But whereas Pareto was primarily an economic liberal alarmed by the extent to which democratic governments intervened in economic life, Mosca was more of a traditional conservative who, after several decades of doubt, concluded that electoral institutions were compatible with both liberal and conservative values. He was more realistic than Pareto about what could be expected from politics and from economic liberalism. Commenting on the faults of parliamentary democracies, for example, he wrote that they 'seem disastrously grave and of capital importance only to someone who is convinced that it is possible for a country to have a political system that is exempt from the weaknesses inherent in human nature itself' (Mosca, 1939, p. 255).

Mosca, who at various times was a parliamentary official, a parliamentary member, a junior minister, a political journalist who contributed to Italy's leading newspapers, and a university lecturer and professor of politics and law, devoted a large part of his intellectual life to refining and building upon his theory of the ruling class.[4] The theory was wide ranging but organised around a simple idea: that in all societies there is an identifiable (political) class or stratum 'that rules and a class that is ruled' (Mosca, 1939, p. 50). He maintained that whatever the differences between systems of government, be they monarchies, aristocratic republics, democracies or anything else, all societies were governed by small minorities of politicians, advisers and administrators. No monarch, tyrant, despot, hereditary nobility, faction, party or organised citizens could rule without governmental personnel who, in practice, became a directing and ruling minority. In order to understand the politics of any society and why states and civilisations rose or fell, therefore, it was necessary to examine these small ruling classes, their recruitment, traditions, goals, beliefs and everything else of consequence about them.

But a further dimension was given to what might have become a narrow conception of politics by the idea that ruling classes were dependent upon and drew many of their members from a larger class of educated and professional people, who directed economic and cultural life, and who acted as mediators between rulers and the ruled. For Mosca, of even greater importance than the qualities of its rulers, for the welfare and fate of any nation, were the culture and character of the social stratum from which new rulers emerged (1939, pp. 404-6). These concepts of a *ruling class* and a wider *political class* were used by Mosca as an analytical tool for

---

4   Mosca's first thoughts on the theory were as a university student, and various versions of the theory were published from the 1880s to the 1930s. For an English translation of the most comprehensive version, published in Italy in 1923, see Mosca (1939); and for a translation of a revised, concise, 1937 version, see the final chapter of Mosca's *A Short History of Political Philosophy* (1972, p. viii for a note on the Italian publications of the theory). For an earlier translation of the *Short History's* final chapter, see Meisel (1958, pp. 382-91). For basic information on Mosca's life and work, see the 'Chronological Summary' in Albertoni (1982, pp. 5-17).

comparing and evaluating political regimes, and for recommending political standards. The theory's purpose, when applied to modern democratic nations, was not to discredit them but to discover their strengths and weaknesses, and to appraise the ideas which influenced their ruling and political classes. Mosca, particularly in the last decades of his life, wished to help democratic nations to sustain individual liberties and constitutionalism (the fundamental parts of 'juridical defence'), and a civilised culture - his principal criteria for assessing states and societies.

In common with Pareto, he could be highly critical of modern democratic government. He argued that, unless its more dangerous tendencies were checked, it would produce opportunist politicians, mainly concerned with winning elections; inordinate privileges for the wealthy; an excess of legislation, much of it silly; massive, ever expanding public bureaucracies, often staffed by people with little understanding of or devotion to public service; an irresponsible journalism; conformist and manipulated yet volatile electorates, capable of forcing their prejudices and moods on to the ruling class; and political parties which exacerbated democracy's many problems. Moreover, he thought that, as a result of the increasing numbers of professionally trained people who obtained governmental employment, there would cease to be the independent civil societies, middle classes and intelligentsias that were necessary conditions for responsible political and ruling classes.

In 1937, in a statement which foreshadowed Schumpeter's revision of democratic theory, Mosca described parliamentary elections as the instrument of 'diverse organized groups which possess the means to influence the mass of unorganized electors' (1972, p. 253). But he was less sanguine than Schumpeter about the effects of electoral competition. Elections, he wrote, although they enable 'liberal regimes to develop an extraordinary power', compel

> the ruling class to submit to the influence of more numerous elements less aware of the true needs of the society. And it is precisely because of this that the major danger threatening liberal institutions consists in the granting of suffrage to the most uneducated classes of the population (1972, pp. 253-4).

He was disturbed by the spread of what he described as 'Rousseauist' and other egalitarian conceptions of democracy, and naive assumptions about 'the incorruptibility of the majority...once they have been emancipated from every principle of authority that is not rooted in universal consensus' (1939, p. 325). Such thinking, he held, would lead, first, to economically destructive socialist legislation and, eventually, to chaos.

But, though Mosca's original view was that universal and near-universal adult voting were mistakes, he subsequently thought that their abolition would be an even worse blunder (1939, pp. 256-7, 487-8 and 491-2). Restricting the vote would be unlikely to improve the quality of rulers or produce independent, better informed and responsible electors. On the contrary, it would almost certainly be accompanied by an increase in inept autocratic and bureaucratic government, and new forms of absolutism and despotism. Once all adults were granted political rights, the hope for the future lay not in removing these rights but in making democracy a civilising force. This meant furthering democracy's potential to become a mixed society in which the social and political forces of the modern world checked and balanced one another; similarly, political *formulae* (doctrines and their visions of the future) should, by means of public debate, peacefully and productively compete. In these and other ways democracy could give a political education to both rulers and citizens, and become the best of possible regimes. In such a democratic regime

> neither the autocratic nor the liberal system [of power emanating from above or below] prevails and the aristocratic tendency is tempered by a slow but continuous renewal of the ruling class, which thus allows it to absorb those elements of healthy power that are slowly emerging among the ruled classes (Mosca, 1972, pp. 256-7).

Mosca's proposals for remedying the ills of representative democracy, and for encouraging its liberalising and civilising features included reducing the activities of the public bureaucracy; strengthening the middle classes by reducing taxation; and reinforcing civil society by the transfer of governmental responsibilities from centralised, national bureaucracies to local authorities and private associations (1972, pp. 265-70).

Mosca, who lived under Italy's Fascist dictatorship, was not optimistic about the future. But, for all his reservations about parliamentary government and universal adult voting, he preferred to gamble on their producing effective public debate, juridical defence and a satisfactory mixed society rather than turn to autocratic or other alternatives. The task was to ensure that the liberal and democratic principles (for Mosca, basing government on the consent of citizens, and opening political and other positions to all adults) improved the quality of a nation's culture and political rule. Although he was cautious in his support for modern democratic government, unless democracy is interpreted as a libertarian, egalitarian or other utopia, he should be regarded not as an opponent of democracy but as a major twentieth-century democratic theorist.

Both Pareto and Mosca were sceptical about democracy's prospects and they could be brutal in their criticisms of democratic government.

Nevertheless the fundamentals of their work, and their central elite and ruling-class propositions are compatible with the belief that, for modern societies, liberal democracy is the best regime. No great difficulty, therefore, prevents their work from being reconciled with other traditions of non-utopian democratic theory. At issue, however, is the character of the reconciliation. Should a synthesis consist of a democratic theory which performs the public philosophic tasks of promoting the interests of citizens and absorbing the insights of elite theorists, or should the synthesis be more of an elite theory take-over of democratic theory in the interests of elites? Such an elite-theory take-over is the project of the neo-elite theorists to whose work I now turn.

Neo-Elite Theory and Its Attempted Take-Over of Democratic Theory

Neo-elite or neo-elitist theory has been well described by Ettore Albertoni, an Italian political scientist who concluded a (1982) study of Mosca with the advocacy of such a 'neo-elitist' understanding of democracy (pp. 159-64). 'Neo-elitism', for Albertoni, is a branch of elite theory concerned with analysing modern democratic government which, he contends, is superior to all other democratic theory, both empirical and normative. The principal assumptions of this 'neo-elitism' are that (1) 'political power is always exercised by a minority over a majority, even under a system based on freedom and with institutionalized mass participation' (p. 160); (2) political power originates in the complex and constant struggles among minorities; and (3) modern democracies consist, primarily, in the right of minorities and 'the ruled masses [to participate] in institutional life and the circulation of ruling groups' (p. 160). This neo-elitism, Albertoni maintains, reconciles the inevitable 'minority foundation of power with the values of liberal and pluralist democracy in its new mass dimension' (p. 162). The main problem for societies which combine elite rule with democratic objectives, he continues, is the satisfying 'of the need for responsible, efficient, honest, learned and in-sighted leadership' (p. 163). Albertoni, however, is vague about the precise identity and location of the people to whom the elites are 'responsible', and how these people are to ensure that elites are 'efficient, honest, learned and in-sighted'. No information is given on what is to prevent elites from interpreting democratic norms and managing democratic institutions in their own interests, or to stop neo-elite theory from becoming little more than an ideological rationalisation for such elite rule.

A similar neo-elite theory but one to which some populist elements are added is that of Eva Etzioni-Halevy (1993). Whereas Albertoni concentrates on the power of elites over the rest of a population, Etzioni-Halevy emphasises the independence of elites from the state, and maintains that their struggles and conflicts have empowered the public. Elites are not just compatible with democracy, Etzioni-Halevy argues, but necessary conditions for and in practice the creators of modern democracy. Elites are not the 'antithesis of democracy', she writes, and 'may be either democratic or undemocratic' (1993, p. 216). It is crucial, therefore, that a democracy obtains the support of its elites.

Etzioni-Halevy advocates a 'democratic elite or demo-elite perspective...[for understanding modern] democracy' (1989, p. 9). She argues that post-eighteenth-century democratisation has consisted of a succession of elites using their economic, cultural and other resources to assert their autonomy and to force themselves into the power structures of their nations. It is this assertive activity by elites which has created modern democracies and given them their character: for not only are the historical precedents set by one elite followed by others but each elite, in asserting its interests and aspirations, establishes the rights of larger numbers of people. The result is 'that in Western-style democracy today, the governing elite is limited in its power by the countervailing power of other elites, and never has full control over those other elites and over the public' (Etzioni-Halevy, 1989, p. xi).

In the first of her two books on the 'demo-elite' perspective, Etzioni-Halevy summarised her thesis as follows.

> The book's main argument is that democracy emerged out of a struggle over the control of resources - not (as is commonly argued) between classes as such - but between elites, including those of movements representing different social classes and genders, and it evolved through a paradoxical, combined process of the incorporation of successive elites into the establishment on the one hand, and of according more autonomy to elites on the other hand (1989, p. x).

The main contentions of her neo-elite theory are that (1) it is a more effective tool for understanding modern democratic and other societies than are class analysis and pluralist, corporatist and other political-science theories; and that (2) modern democratic regimes are distinguished by (a) the relative autonomy of their elites, from both other elites and the state, and (b), although they may be antagonistic to one another, the willingness of elites to cooperate in sustaining democratic institutions and peacefully resolving their conflicts.

No part of what is at times a perceptive contribution to elite and democratic theory, however, adequately explains why some nations have been successful and others unsuccessful in obtaining autonomous elites sympathetic to democracy. For this purpose it is necessary to cast off the strait-jacket of elite theory, and to turn to wider considerations such as the role of cultural, constitutional, public-philosophic and other traditions, whether economic relations are independent of the state, and whether there is a vigourous civil society. To reduce modern representative democracy to little more than autonomous and integrated elites grossly oversimplifies. It obscures rather than illuminates the character and potential of democratic politics, and it turns democratic theory into a new kind of elite theory, and one that has less of a critical edge than the original elite theories of Pareto and Mosca. Moreover, Etzioni-Halevy's normative recommendations, apart from her basic argument on the need for independent, democratically inclined elites, are only tenuously connected to the empirical parts of her 'demo-elite' perspective. She simply tacks on to her empirical analysis her sympathy for 'lessening inequalities in economic life', 'referenda', 'worker cooperatives' and similar, predominantly leftist recipes (1989, p. 168).

But the most persistent and influential of recent neo-elite theory attempts to take over democratic theory - albeit one which has none of Etzioni-Halevy's egalitarian preferences - has been made by John Higley and his associates (Higley, Deacon, Smart *et al*, 1979; and Field and Higley, 1980). For these neo-elite theorists, a pivotal feature of the history of modern Western nations has been the loss of social and political hegemony by landed and commercial classes to the elites of 'post-industrial' societies. These post-industrial elites are described as

> the persons who occupy strategic positions in public and private bureaucratic organizations (e.g. governments, parties, militaries, productive enterprises, trade union and other occupational organizations, as well as media, religious and educational organizations, various organized protest groups and so on). Where the interest is *national* elites...these organizations are those that are large or otherwise powerful enough to enable the persons who command them to influence the outcomes of national policies individually, regularly and seriously (Field and Higley, p. 20).

The effect of this slow revolution is that, in modern democratic nations, national elites now have the social and political hegemony which Marxists have attributed to slave-owning, feudal and capitalist classes. Birth and wealth, it is said, now give political power to their possessors only if they are used to acquire the education and skills that lead to elite positions.

Higley, his associates and other contemporary neo-elite theorists, however, are not the first authors, subsequent to the original elite theorists, to attribute political and social hegemony to the elites of modern democracies. Three notable predecessors are James Burnham (1945), C. Wright Mills (1956) and Suzanne Keller (1963). For Burnham, political and other managerial elites occupied the dominant positions in what were becoming managerial societies. Wright Mills coined the term 'power elite' to argue that the United States was largely controlled by the holders of the top positions in its political parties, business corporations and military forces. Keller wrote of a 'strategic elite', which she described in an introductory article on elites as 'those elites which claim or are assigned responsibilities for and influence over their societies as a whole, in contrast with segmental elites, which have major responsibilities in subdomains of the society' (1968, p. 26). (See also Keller 1963, pp. 23 and 259-63.)

A new concept in the work of Higley and his associates, however, is that of 'consensual unified elites'. This concept is used in both (1) their empirical studies of power in Australia and other nations, and (2) their normative advice to Western elites that they adopt a more 'self-consciously elitist frame of reference' (Field and Higley, p. 130). More explicitly than Albertoni and Etzioni-Halevy, they acknowledge and indeed commend the oligarchic features of elite rule. Australia is not alone, they write, in having 'national leaders' who

> view existing institutions as providing them with the psychic and social rewards that derive from the possession and exercise of power, and...[seeing] the institutions as facilitating their managerial and non-egalitarian interests with regard to social organization itself (Higley *et al*, p. 264).

Modern nations are said to have one of four possible kinds of elite rule. They will possess either (1) a *disunited elite*, in which a ruthless struggle for power makes stable government impossible; (2) an *ideologically unified elite* such as those of communist, fascist or other totalitarian or semi-totalitarian nations; (3) a *consensual unified elite*, the members of which co-operate in maintaining a political system even though they are divided by ideas, party membership, and economic and other interests; or (4) an *imperfectly unified elite*, in which political parties accept the electoral results which enable another party and its leadership to monopolise governmental power (Field and Higley, pp. 35-43). Consensually unified elites, it is argued, are a necessary condition for successful democratic government.

This emphasis on unified elites leads Higley and his colleagues to try to instil into the elites of democratic nations a consciousness of themselves as elites. Elites should understand the need for a consensus among themselves on how a nation's constitution should be interpreted, the rules for playing the political game, and the boundaries for policies and political and other change (Higley *et al*, pp. 142-5). Whether this advice would prove to be prudent or counter-productive for elites who acted on it is a question which will be returned to at the end of this chapter. Here, it is sufficient to say that it is of limited and dubious value for democratic theory and practice. It is inadequate because it fails to distinguish between a consensus on what aggrandises a nation's elites and what benefits a national community. Indeed, on the central normative issues of what should be the relations between democratic communities and their elites, and the type of elites they require, the work of Higley and his co-authors falls short of Pareto and Mosca's. For Pareto, there were profound differences between a consensus among opportunist foxes on how to survive and prosper, and, by contrast, a consensus among lions and the more farsighted of the foxes on the policies which strengthen a nation. Likewise, for Mosca, rulers and their societies need more than consensuses and cooperation. A political 'formula' or theory is required which, in addition to informing elites about themselves, their society and their civilisation, and which justifies their rule, has the support of the ruled and gives rulers and their society worthy goals. For Mosca, as for Pareto, a consensually unified elite would be a disaster for a nation if its consensus conflicted with the long-term interests of a nation and its people.

In comparison, the neo-elite theories of Higley and his colleagues, like those of Albertoni and Etzioni-Halevy, narrow both practical and theoretical horizons. Substantive normative issues are swamped by such formal concepts as autonomous, integrated and consensually unified elites. Pareto and Mosca would have objected to the formalism of theorists who substitute the urging of agreement among elites for evaluating elite goals and the effects of elite power. Neo-elite theory also compares poorly with the use of elite theory for political and cultural criticism as, for instance, in Christopher Lasch's aptly titled *The Revolt of the Elites and the Betrayal of Democracy* (1995). Lasch uses elite theory to make penetrating criticisms of America's managerial, political, educational and welfare elites, whom he castigates for having abandoned democratic and civilised standards. For Lasch, the United States needs not a stronger elite consensus but the disturbing by 'public intellectuals' of the existing consensus. Such a challenge is necessary, he argues, if a tradition of public debate is to be revived in which citizens are treated as equals rather than as targets for slogans. One does not have to agree with all of Lasch's critique to see that his is a less fawning and more fruitful use of elite theory than that of neo-elite theorists.

More crucially, neo-elite theory compares unfavourably with classical liberal-democratic theory. Neither Tocqueville, John Stuart Mill, T. H. Green, L. T. Hobhouse nor their successors required lectures by neo- or other elite theorists to appreciate the presence of powerful minorities, the importance of political leadership and the need for a consensus on democratic goals and standards. They fully realised the need for normative standards for guiding elites and for regulating the relations between elites and citizens. These were standards, however, not simply for maintaining an elite consensus and unity but for providing good government and helping citizens to acquire prudence and other political virtues. In comparison, the normative advice of neo-elite theorists is either superficial or dangerous. Elite individuals are advised by Higley and his co-thinkers, for example, to avoid the self deception of the democratic rhetoric of equality and popular rule, and to recognise that they are a part of an elite structure to which they have obligations. Instead of seeing themselves as the representatives of citizens, and as the members of privileged groups who have obligations to the members of other groups, they are encouraged to think that it is sufficient to be skilled at managing the non-elite.

Field and Higley contend that, in the second half of the twentieth-century, American and other democracies have been weakened by the intellectual confusion of the dominant liberal ideology. Western elites, they declare, have failed to comprehend issues and threats, and to develop coherent policies because of a fundamental contradiction in their thinking. Although, deep down, they have known that they held privileged and powerful elite positions, they have been incapable of building upon this awareness because of the populist doctrines they embrace (Field and Higley, pp. 48-68).[5] Whether it is appropriate to describe the thinking and behaviour they condemn as *liberal, leftist* or anything else, Field and Higley commendably question individuals and elites who compromise with utopian aspirations to abolish elites, promote an equality of economic condition and political power, and govern nations of tens or hundreds of millions of people as if they were small city states. Unfortunately the objections of Higley and his associates to utopian thinking and to liberals who flirt with it are not accompanied by attention to the need for alternative, realistic, democratic standards for protecting citizens, curbing the power of elites and guiding elite-citizen relations. Thus, along with proposals for mass participation in policy and other governmental decision making, they dispense with the quest for government by consent and what makes it possible: informed and politically educated citizens, and open and serious public debate.

In contrast to populist, participatory democrats who distrust elites but who regard the democratic populace as potentially if not at present incorruptible, Field and Higley distrust voters and depend upon the incorruptibility of consensually unified elites. Thus, in urging elites to dispense with naive forms of altruism and to be guided by an 'enlightened self-interest', they urge that elites place themselves above democratic controls and debate: 'With respect to the functioning of elites it

---

5   Their criticisms of what are in effect the more naive and utopian varieties of post-1940s liberalism were foreshadowed in James Burnham's (1965) onslaught on such liberalism.

[enlightened self-interest] means that there are always matters of dispute that they should not throw open to public argument or democratic decision-making' (p. 129). This prescription for the normal conduct of politics - not an occasional necessity in times of peril - rests on a groundless faith in the competence and good intentions of elites. It relies not on the capacity of democratic societies to sustain institutions and cultures which will promote enlightened elites and impose necessary checks on all elites, but on 'consensual unified elites' being incorruptible. It replaces a utopian faith in the virtue of the masses with an equally groundless faith in the virtue of unified elites.

Conclusions

It is a mistake, it has been argued, to see democratic and elite theory as necessarily antagonistic. Democratic and elite theory collide only when either (1) it is asserted that self-government by a national community is impossible because of the inevitability of elites or when (2) purported democratic theorists propose to eliminate elites. When democratic theorists see the problem as being primarily to ensure that political elites are open, public spirited, and accountable and attentive to citizens, and when elite theorists recognise that the elites and the ordinary citizens of a representative democracy need to co-exist and cooperate to their mutual advantage, then there is only a fine line which separates their theorising.[6] But, although democratic and elite theory may be reconciled, some reconciliations should be avoided by democrats and democratic theorists. Just as government in the interests of elites is oligarchic rather than democratic, so elite theory is incompatible with democratic theory unless it is concerned with the interests of all citizens. Were the neo-elite, formalist understanding of democracy as integrated, consensual elites to prevail, it would further the drift of modern democracies towards rule by and in the interests of what would be a new type of ruling class. Similarly, it would transform democratic theory into a mask for such oligarchic rule.

Neo-elite theory turns its eyes from the danger of an oligarchic subversion of democratic government. It obscures the fact that, if modern

---

6   For the compatibility of elite and democratic theory, see Plamenatz (1973, pp. 52-92); and Sartori (1965, esp. pp. 96-134; and 1987, esp. pp. 131-81). Their more public-philosophic syntheses of elite theory and democratic theory will be discussed in Chapter 8. Also pertinent is the observation of a Marxist critic of elite theory (Bottomore, 1966) that *'the elite theories of Pareto and Mosca were not...opposed to the general idea of democracy.* Their original and main antagonist was...socialism and especially Marxist socialism' (p. 17, emphasis added).

democracy is primarily a system of competitive but integrated elites, held together by a consensus on the limits of inter-elite conflict, then it is compatible with a social reality that is far from government by consent. Despite the divisions within what is in effect a new ruling class, a system of integrated elites means that instead of a political community there are two social classes, two cultures and two languages. Democratic forms would be accompanied by, on the one hand, a rhetorical language of popular government and grandiose future prospects for the masses, fostering illusions of progress and popular power, and, on the other, for communication among elites, a languages of pragmatism, cost-benefit analysis and neo-positivist social science, coded to hide the main beneficiaries - political and other elites. Equality, fun and a pseudo-national interest would increasingly become the language of the media, while the elites, including those of the media, would have a more hidden and private language which gave them a firmer grip on social and political realities.

This picture of a possible future is not far-fetched as few Western democracies possess the strong and independent civil societies and intelligentsias on whom Mosca put so much weight. People with a capacity for independent judgement have increasingly been absorbed into the vast governmental, educational, business-corporation and other bureaucracies of modern societies. Moreover, whereas the trade union, socialist and labour movements were once a means whereby working-class people could make their voices heard and exercise their citizenship rights, these movements are now more firmly controlled and integrated into the elite and corporate structures of their societies. Needless to say, the aristocratic ideals and traditions which Tocqueville, Mosca and Schumpeter believed might survive and encourage responsible government have become even more attenuated. If the elites of democratic nations were to follow the advice of neo-elite theorists, and without necessarily advertising the fact to see democracy as a system of elite government, predominantly in the interests of themselves, then checks and balances to control the ambitions and power of rulers would be of little consequence. Constitutional laws and conventions would be secure only if they benefited governmental, judicial and other politically influential elites.

But concerns about the domination of democratic practice by elites and a neo-elite take-over of democratic theory do not entail the belief that the power of elites will lead to the nightmare world of George Orwell's *Nineteen Eighty-Four* - though Aldous Huxley's *Brave New World* may still be a relevant satire. The dangers are more insidious. They are that electoral and parliamentary forms will persist but will be given an oligarchic content. They are that the absence of public philosophic standards shared by elites and citizens, and the lack of effective dialogues between citizens, mediating groups and political elites will lead to government that, in addition to being manipulative and conceited, will be incompetent. Even from the viewpoint of the elites, who are inescapably a part of and dependent upon a wider society, it may well be counter-productive to put narrowly conceived elite interests before democratic theory and practice, and the recovery of a public philosophy.

The next chapter completes the critical survey of formalist and ideological approaches to democratic theory. It will include critical discussions of positions which have been advertised as defences of democratic theory and practice against elite theory and elitism.

References

Albertoni, Ettore A. (1982), *Mosca and the Theory of Elitism*, Blackwell, Oxford.
Arendt, Hannah (1961), *Between Past and Present*, Faber and Faber, London.
Arendt, Hannah (1972), *Crises of the Republic*, Harcourt Brace, New York.
Bellamy, Richard (1987), *Modern Italian Social Theory*, Polity Pr., Cambridge.
Bottomore, T.B. (1966), *Elites and Society*, 2nd edn, Penguin Books, Harmondsworth.
Burnham, James (1943), *The Machiavellians*, Putnam, London.
Burnham, James (1945), *The Managerial Revolution* [1941], 3rd edn, Penguin Books, Harmondsworth.
Burnham, James (1965), *Suicide of the West*, 2nd edn, Cape, London.
Etzioni-Halevy, Eva (1989), *Fragile Democracy*, Transaction Publishers, New Brunswick.
Etzioni-Halevy, Eva (1993), *The Elite Connection: Problems and Potential of Western Democracy*, Polity Pr., Cambridge.
Field, G. Lowell and John Higley (1980), *Elitism*, Routledge, London.
Higley, John, Desley Deacon and Don Smart et al (1979), *Elites in Australia*, Routledge, London.
Keller, Suzanne (1963), *Beyond the Ruling Class*, Random House, New York.
Keller, Suzanne (1968), 'Elites', *International Encyclopedia of the Social Sciences*, (ed.) David L. Sills, vol. 5.
Lasch, Christopher (1995), *The Revolt of the Elites and the Betrayal of Democracy*, Norton, New York.
Meisel, James H. (1958), *The Myth of the Ruling Class: Gaetano Mosca and the 'Elite'*, Univ. of Michigan Pr., Ann Arbor.
Mill, John Stuart (1973), 'The Spirit of the Age' [1831], in *Essays on Politics and Culture*, (ed.) Gertrude Himmelfarb, Peter Smith, Gloucester, Mass.
Mills, C. Wright (1959), *The Power Elite*, 2nd edn, Oxford Univ. Pr./Galaxy, New York.
Mosca, Gaetano (1939), *The Ruling Class* [1923], first Eng. edn, McGraw Hill, New York.
Mosca, Gaetano (1972), *A Short History of Political Philosophy* [1937], first Eng. edn, Crowell, New York.

Pareto, Vilfredo (1963), *The Mind and Society* [1916], 4 vols in 2, (ed.) A. Livingston, 2nd Eng. edn, Dover, New York.
Pareto, Vilfredo (1966), *Sociological Writings*, (ed.) S.E. Finer, Pall Mall Pr., London.
Parry, Geraint (1969), *Political Elites*, Allen and Unwin, London.
Plamenatz, John (1973), *Democracy and Illusion*, Longman, London.
Powers, Charles H. (1987), *Vilfredo Pareto*, Sage, Newbury Park.
Sartori, Giovanni (1965), *Democratic Theory*, 2nd edn, Praeger, New York.
Sartori, Giovanni (1987), *The Theory of Democracy Revisited*, two vols, Chatham House, New Jersey.
Simon, Yves (1961), *Philosophy of Democratic Government* [1951], Univ. of Chicago Pr., Chicago.
Simon, Yves (1962), *A General Theory of Authority*, Univ. of Notre Dame Pr., Notre Dame.
Spitz, David (1949), *Patterns of Anti-Democratic Thought*, Macmillan, New York.
Tucker, Robert C. (1981), *Politics as Leadership*, Univ. of Missouri Pr., Columbia.
Watt, E.D. (1982), *Authority*, Croom Helm, London.

3 Formalism in Democratic Theory: Robert Dahl and Democracy as Political and Social Pluralism

The idea that political and social pluralism is the dominant feature of modern democracy became, during the Cold War, a central part of the contrasts made by Western intellectuals between democracy and communism. But it is an idea which is a product of the American political tradition more than of any other - a product of America's federalism, constitutional checks and balances, diverse society and the absence of centralised parties. Moreover, by the 1950s, this idea that pluralism was the main feature of modern democracies had become the centrepiece of American, behavioural, political and social science.

America's behavioural political scientists sought empirical rather than normative definitions of democracy as a part of their 'scientific' accounts of democratic government, and as the basis for their advice to America's policy makers. Their empirical work on the behaviour of groups, and their attempt to construct and to participate in a unified social science became known as the behavioural revolution. The participants in the project conceived of representative government as an expression of social pluralism, and as free and open political competition by organised interest groups for government support. Their conception of modern democratic government has been aptly summarised as 'a form of stable and institutionalised political competition' (Hirst, 1989, p. 3). Despite the damaging criticism it has received, this pluralist conception of modern democratic government is still a major assumption in much university teaching and media discussion. Yet there are earlier and in many ways more perceptive and fruitful varieties of pluralist political thought. In order to understand the distinctive features of the pluralism of American postwar behaviourism and that of Robert Dahl, its most influential exponent, it is helpful therefore to recall these earlier versions of pluralist political theory.

Early Pluralist Political Theory

Plural the root word of *pluralism* means more than one, and all societies, even the simplest, are in some ways pluralist. Although it is illuminating to contrast pluralist and totalitarian societies, the fact remains that even totalitarian states, in which one-party dictatorships try to control all aspects of individual and social life, are to some extent pluralist. Stalin's Russia, Hitler's Germany and Mao Zedong's China, like Oceania in George Orwell's *Nineteen Eighty-Four*, had divisions between the members and non-members of the party, between party leaders and the rank-and-file, and among the state officials, military, police, industrial managers and other elites. Indeed, Hitler, Stalin and other totalitarian dictators have kept firm grips on power partly by keeping the possible rivals among their followers divided.

All politics like all societies are pluralist in that there are no political issues unless there are conflicts among the interests, values and goals of the members of a society. Whatever other purposes it serves, politics is the alternative to force for overcoming a society's conflicts. Similarly, for over two thousand years, political philosophers and theorists, among their other concerns, have confronted the problem of how the conflicts and problems generated by social pluralism can be overcome, and social peace and cooperation established. Specific pluralist proposals for solving constitutional and other political problems have been a part of political philosophy from the mixed polity of Aristotle to the individual liberties and rights, toleration and separation of power of modern liberalism. But if social pluralism is inescapable, and if the urging of political-pluralist proposals has a two-millennia history, why should any group of political theorists be known as *pluralists*, and what makes their pluralism so special?

Pluralism was first used to describe a group of political theorists when, in the last quarter of the nineteenth century, it was applied to legal pluralists. These were writers on jurisprudence who challenged the legal positivism of John Austin and other Benthamites, especially Austin's contention that law should be seen as the commands of a sovereign. Against the legal positivists, the legal pluralists maintained that law evolved from the complex relations among the plurality of groups, associations and corporations which comprised a society and brought about its progress. Law was not the creation of whoever exercised sovereign power; legal authority, for the legal pluralists, merely formalised what was a social rather than a governmental product. It was social organisation and change, not governments or states, which were the source of law (Kuang Chuan Hsiao, 1927, Chs 1 and 2).

By the end of the nineteenth century, however, these explicitly pluralist ideas had been extended from law to politics. *Pluralism* came to mean opposition to the bureaucratic states established by the absolute monarchs of Europe, the power, size and ever increasing legislation of which had been furthered by industrialisation. In the first quarter of the twentieth century, *pluralism* was used in the United Kingdom and other European nations to describe the ideas of liberal, socialist and other political thinkers and actors who resisted bureaucratic, centralised government and statist legislation. After 1914, the young Harold Laski and other radicals turned to pluralism as a reaction against the slaughter of the First World War, which they regarded as a product of state worship and the 'Moloch-like demands of the state' (Breitling, 1980, p. 11). This early twentieth-century political pluralism was unashamedly normative and prescriptive. The guild socialists, for example, were influential socialist pluralists, who campaigned for a quasi-syndicalist, industrial democracy in which the British parliament, which was based on geographic representation, had to share governmental power with an industrial parliament based on the functional representation of economically productive groups organised in guilds (Cole, 1920; and Hirst, 1989).

Early-twentieth-century pluralists favoured far-reaching social change, but by strengthening the independent associations of civil society rather than by increasing the power of centralised government and public bureaucracies. At the heart of pluralist thought from the 1880s to the 1920s, which may be called *classical pluralism*, was the conviction and normative principle that there were limits to the sovereignty and power of states which citizens should enforce. For these early pluralists, men and women owed loyalties to associations that were not confined by the frontiers of states - for example world churches, charities and reform movements - and associations that were smaller than and internal to their states. The idea that a state or government expressed anything resembling the will of all its members was rejected. For classical pluralists, unless there was a civil society consisting of independent economic, cultural and other associations which mediated between governments and citizens, and which possessed the strength to resist governments, tyranny and despotism were inevitable.

Classical pluralism, however, was not a united movement. There were divisions between, for example, (1) pluralists who favoured a separation between the state and civil society, and the fortifying of civil society, and (2) those who urged that economic and/or other social groups as well as citizens be more integrated into the institutions of government. This second group thus blurred the distinction between and more closely bound together civil society and the state. The dispute was partly between liberal pluralists, whose pluralism was intended to foster individual economic and other liberties, and socialist and corporatist pluralists who desired to constrain the individual liberties that were a part of market capitalism.

Since the Second World War, however, in university politics and other social science departments in English speaking nations, pluralist political theory has come to mean that of the American, behavioural, political scientists who have given it a different content from classical pluralism. But as I wish to avoid stereotyping and oversimplifying this political-science pluralism by constructing a pluralist model or theory which no actual person may ever have held, my critique of it will be concentrated on its most systematic, sophisticated and influential attempt to take over and transform democratic theory: Robert A. Dahl's *Preface to Democratic Theory* (1956).[1]

Robert Dahl's Political-Science, Pressure-Group Pluralism

The Intellectual Background

Robert Dahl's *Preface to Democratic Theory* (1956) inserted into democratic theory Arthur F. Bentley's project of explaining the politics of a society by means of the behaviour and rivalry of groups (people sharing common, especially economic, interests) and group interrelations (Crick, 1959, Ch. 7; Weinstein, 1962; Bentley, 1967; and Garson, 1974). The ground had been cleared for Dahl, however, when, in 1951, a related part of Bentley's project, to make group interests and interrelations the sociological basis for a universal political and social science, was revived by David B. Truman (1971).

Truman's book, which spearheaded the 'behavioural revolution' in university political study and teaching, rejected what it described as the study of the 'formalities' of government, namely 'constitutions and formal institutions' (p. xviii), for testable, general theories about the behaviour of

---

[1] For a survey of American behavioural, political-science pluralists, which argues that, for all their similarities, they never comprised a cohesive school or movement, see Jordan (1990). See also Smith (1990). For a study of their political science and pluralism, which emphasises intellectual sources, see Crick (1959). For a concise recent critique, Statham Jr (1998, Ch. 4, 'The Self-Refuting American Science of Politics'). And for some revealing reminiscences by participants in the 'behavioural revolution', see Baer, Jewel and Sigelman (1991), especially the interviews with Gabriel Almond, Robert A. Dahl, David Easton and Heinz Eulau. For surveys of pre-1940s, European pluralist political thought, see Kuang Chuan Hsiao (1927); Nicholls (1974); and Ehrlich (1982).

interest groups. His contrast, however, was not between political forms and their normative and sociological content - the basis for my classifying of behavioural-pluralist theories of democracy as formalist - but between *formal* and *informal* politics. *Formal* politics meant those of legislative, executive and judicial institutions; *informal* politics or processes meant, primarily, the power exerted on formal institutions by political, economic and cultural pressure groups. But it was Robert Dahl, more than any other American political scientist, who directed the quest for a new political science towards a pluralist, pressure-group-politics revision of democratic theory.

Dahl's revision of democratic theory, which was more anti-elitist and populist than Schumpeter's, was a product of and a response to the political traditions of the United States. It was also a response to the sheer size of the United States, and to its federalism and decentralised political parties which had generated greater pressure-group activity than that of probably any other nation. The main effect of Dahl's response was to make pressure-group politics the central feature of another formalist and - despite the populism of Dahl's thinking - ideological democratic theory.

Robert Dahl's 'Preface to Democratic Theory'

Although Dahl regarded the *Preface* as having implications for other nations, its framework consisted of the politics and political thought of the United States. It was an attempt at a synthesis between what he called the two main American conceptions of democracy: the 'Madisonian' and the 'populistic'.

Madisonian democracy, which Dahl traced back to Alexander Hamilton, James Madison and John Jay's *Federalist* papers of 1787 and 1788 (1971), was seen as the theoretical root of the conservative part of America's political tradition, and, according to Dahl, it had three principal components. First, it considered the main threat to moderate and acceptable democratic government, described by Madison and his collaborators as *republican* government, to be the tyranny of the majority. For the original Madisonians, unless counter-measures were taken, the prejudices, passions and demands of the masses would drive educated and public-spirited people from public life, replacing them with demagogues who pandered to the masses. A second danger was that the leadership of the nation would fall into the hands of the leaders and organisers of factions - powerful minorities who promoted their private economic and other interests, and who were contemptuous of the rights and interests of anyone else. Third, the main protection offered by Madison and his co-thinkers against these dangers was the checks and balances of what became the American Constitution, a safeguard against any branch of government acquiring the power to subordinate the remaining branches of government to itself. In particular, the original Madisonians favoured a strong president and public bureaucracy which they thought - mistakenly, Dahl noted - would resist mass pressure and protect the educated minority from a legislative assembly which was regarded as more likely to become an instrument of the masses. Madisonian democracy, in Dahl's account of it, protected large property owners and a national leadership drawn from them by restricting the popular sovereignty of the new republic. It was a compromise 'between the political equality of all adult citizens, and the desire to limit their sovereignty' (Dahl, 1956, p. 4).

Against Madisonian democracy, Dahl mounted three objections. First, borrowing from elite theory, he argued that a tyranny of the masses was a myth and a foolish fear because it was never the masses or even majorities who ruled but always minorities. It was a mistake, therefore, to weaken the executive and administrative branches of government by checks and balances. But fortunately for the American people, he observed, since the presidency of Andrew Jackson, United States governments had circumvented the Constitution, and the American people had been blessed with strong rather than weak government (pp. 142-5). Dahl's objections to Madisonian democracy, therefore, amounted to a defence of the powers accumulated by nineteenth- and twentieth-century American presidents. But he appeared to misunderstand the meaning given to the *tyranny of the majority* by the authors of the *Federalist* papers. Their fear was not that the majority or the masses would rule directly but that the pressure of their numbers and their use of the vote would compel ruling minorities to submit to their prejudices.

A second criticism of Madisonian democracy was that, if constitutional checks were imposed on factions, they would also bridle well-meaning and responsible groups. Likewise, if desirable minorities were protected, so too were the undesirable. These are logical and pertinent objections to all theories of limited government; advocates of limited government, however, are at least confronting the problem of excessive governmental power. Third, Dahl objected to the emotive language of Madisonian democrats. He denied that distinctions could be made between factions and parties or between responsible and irresponsible groups. Like most American political scientists of the period, Dahl, who was similarly under the spell of sociological positivism, sought a value-neutral language.

Although, according to Dahl, no one had ever been a consistent advocate of 'populistic democracy' - the non-Madisonian wing of the American political tradition - the thinking of any number of individuals and groups approximated to it. Populistic democracy, he wrote, was a consistent application of the principles of 'political equality, popular sovereignty and rule by majorities' (p. 34). Populistic democrats desired that citizens exercise their sovereignty by means of a more or less continual participation in politics. The main reason, Dahl believed, why there had never been a hundred-per-cent populist democrat was that it was impossible to construct a system of government, for a nation as large as the United States, on the basis of the populistic conception of democracy. In addition, for nearly all people, democracy meant more than political equality, popular sovereignty and majority decisions. In an argument which was reminiscent of Schumpeter's and which anticipated that of Pickles, he observed that most democrats were likely to put other values before those of populistic democracy, for example, the protection of life and property, economic prosperity, individual liberties and minority rights. Another of his reservations about populistic democracy was that, as it was always a minority which governed and ruled, 'Doctrines and constitutional procedures providing for absolute popular sovereignty and majority rule provide the weakest checks of all on the rulers' (p. 54).

Dahl's objections to the two main strands of the American political tradition, however, were preliminary discussions. In addition to synthesising the defensible parts of Madisonian and populistic democracy, he proposed to use the empirical methods and findings of behavioural political science to discover the social and political conditions which made possible a viable system of democratic government. The main problem for a democratic nation, he contended, was how to reconcile populistic demands for equality, popular sovereignty and majority rule with minority rights and limited government. His solution was the politics of pluralism or, to use the term he preferred, of *polyarchal* democracy.

In the *Preface* and his subsequent work Dahl has argued that it is more precise to describe existing American and other representative democracies as *polyarchies*. This is because the literal meaning of *democracy*, the rule of the people, is considered by Dahl to be an unrealised ideal. But a more accurate description of the pluralist or polyarchal democracy, which for Dahl was the best of present options and the closest to the democratic ideal, is *pressure-group politics*. *Pressure-group politics* captures the idea at the heart of Dahl's *Preface*: that modern democratic or polyarchal politics consist, mainly, in citizens trying to direct their governments and societies by means of pressure-group activity.

Although pluralist, polyarchal democracy was the principal characteristic of all presidential and parliamentary representative government, according to Dahl it had achieved its most complete expression in what he called the 'American hybrid', a hybrid which was the most effective means yet discovered for satisfying as many individual and group wants as possible. Dahl summarised his view of polyarchal and pluralist politics with the statement that 'in a rough sense, the essence of all competitive politics is bribery of the electorate by politicians' (p. 68). It was by pressure-group activity, in effect the continual harassing of governments by organised interest groups who did not themselves wish to govern to have their bribes increased, that the maximum satisfaction of wants could be achieved.

The starting point of the *Preface*, therefore, was economic: that the main purpose of government was the satisfaction of wants. But whereas laissez-faire liberals and economists look to an economic market and the curbing of governmental interference as the means to satisfy wants, Dahl asserted the more socialist and welfare-state view that the main means should be pressure groups and strong governments responsive to them. It follows that the pluralism Dahl favours does not consist of the independent private associations of a civil society restricting the power of governments - the goal of many classical pluralists - but of organised groups pursuing their goals by means of extensive, interventionist government.

Pluralist politics were, for the Dahl who wrote the *Preface*, the solution to the problem of how to distribute as well as maximise individual satisfactions. They were the means for deciding whose wants were satisfied and who got what. By concentrating on the question of how the wants of apathetic majorities and intense minorities could be balanced, Dahl produced an ingenious solution to the problem of how people with opposed wants and demands could find satisfactory compromises. His argument was that pressure-group activity was the best measure of the intensity of the feelings and commitment of the members of opposed groups. It followed from this proposition that the compromises which resulted from the clashes of pressure groups provided the maximum possible satisfaction of wants and needs. There was therefore nothing undemocratic about minorities rather than majorities being the victors in pressure-group combats; their victories merely demonstrated that the feelings of their members were stronger than those of the majorities who opposed them. When, therefore, Gallup or other polls disclosed that a majority of electors opposed particular governmental policies, there was no reason for democrats to be alarmed; the polls merely revealed that the feelings of the minority who favoured, say, the abolition of capital punishment were more intense than those of the apathetic majority who supported it.

Although Dahl has always regarded himself as a radical and a man of the left, a supporter of at least moderate egalitarian and participatory reform, it is difficult to imagine a more complacent and ideological argument than this part of the pluralist democratic theory advocated in the *Preface*. It follows from the *Preface's* arguments on the maximising of satisfactions that, provided democratic governments are responsive to pressure groups, all legislation and governmental policy comply with both democratic principles and the grand Benthamite, utilitarian objective of the greatest happiness of the greatest number (pp. 90-123).

Dahl, in the *Preface*, expressed most of the 1950s pluralist views of American, political scientists. He contended, for example, that it was by means of group conflicts and compromises, rather than by allegiance to a constitution, and established political institutions and traditions, that political consensuses and a progressive politics and society were achieved. Elections were of secondary importance. They were not the central feature of democratic politics, as they were for Mayo, Pickles and Schumpeter, but a necessary appendage to pressure-group activity. Elections were a necessary condition for democratic (polyarchal) politics but less important for settling group conflicts and satisfying wants than the activity of pressure groups.

Within this pluralist, pressure-group system of government there were, Dahl maintained, effective political rather than artificial-constitutional checks and balances. Although not all pressure groups or social interests were equal in strength to others - neither Dahl nor any other American pluralist ever held this bizarre view attributed to them by some of their critics - Dahl thought that no such group or coalition of groups was likely to maintain a permanent domination over the remainder (pp. 104-5). One reason was that excluded pressure groups would spur the formation of new coalitions. But despite this belief in an invisible hand which protected the losers, Dahl recognised that some social groups might be so weak that they were unable to properly organise to bargain with governments. When this occurred, government agencies should assist them. Pressure-group pluralism also had the built-in safeguard of the multiple membership of social groups, the fact that most people belonged to different and often opposed groups, and were thus encouraged to develop qualities of restraint and to avoid fanaticism. Most citizens were consumers as well as producers, tax payers as well as the beneficiaries of government expenditure, and the members or sympathisers of militant protest groups as well as the public inconvenienced by them.

Dahl's account of the pluralist, pressure-group character of contemporary democratic politics concluded with a panegyric on its American expression. The political system of the United States, he wrote,

> appears to be a relatively efficient system for reinforcing agreement, encouraging moderation, and maintaining social peace in a restless and immoderate people operating a gigantic, powerful, diversified and incredibly complex society. This is no negligible contribution, then, that Americans have made to the arts of government - and to that branch which of all the arts of politics is the most difficult, the art of democratic government (p. 151).

But does the analysis of Dahl's *Preface*, in which the main characteristic of existing democracies (polyarchies) is held to be pressure-group politics, make a considerable or negligible contribution to democratic theory? Does it reveal or obscure political realities? Does it adequately evaluate them? Does it provide appropriate standards for the political activity of governments and citizens? Can it be anything more than an ideology and apologia for the victors in pressure-group combats?

Objections to Pressure-Group Pluralism

The basic insight in the work of Dahl and other post-1940s American pluralists is their awareness that the pressure-group politics of the United States and other democracies have contributed to rather than prevented the achieving of stable political communities in nations inhabited by tens of millions of people with clashing interests and aspirations. Unfortunately, this insight is lost and causal relations are confused when the main explanation for stable, peaceful politics is said to be competing interest and pressure groups rather than tolerant political cultures, citizen support for democratic government and, it will be argued in later chapters, public philosophic traditions. Another post-1940s pluralist insight is that strong pressure groups may embolden governments to resist media-stimulated demands and the incitement of readers. A further insight is the understanding that competition among pressure groups fills a gap in democratic theory and practice: functional representation. To the extent that functional representation (people being represented in accordance with their economic and other activity rather than where they live) is desirable, pressure-group politics achieves it without the reorganising of systems of government. Without second parliaments for the regulation of economic life and other restructuring as urged by earlier pluralists, pressure-group politics makes possible a moderate functional representation.

But Dahl and his co-thinkers, instead of being content with supplementing democratic theory, have tried to transform and take it over. Among the more questionable features of this more ambitious undertaking are (1) its view that social pluralism and pressure-group politics are the essence of modern democracy; (2) that this pluralism has the desirable effects emphasised by Dahl and his co-thinkers rather than the less desirable highlighted by critics; and (3) that pressure-group activity, apart from being constrained by general laws for the prevention of violence and gross corruption, should be unconstrained and allowed to evade the Madisonian distinction between groups which contribute to and those which work against the public good.

Although the 1950s, American, behavioural pluralism, expressed in Dahl's *Preface* still has its adherents, particularly in university social-science departments, it has been severely damaged by several formidable groups of critics. Broadly speaking, they may be classified as New Right; corporatist, traditionalist and conservative; and New Left and neo-Marxist. American political-science pluralism has attracted criticism from otherwise opposed political thinkers because, as Dahl observed about the American political tradition as a whole, it has both elitist and ultra-democratic strands. Its adherents try to weave together (1) an elitist desire to protect the power of the administrators, policy makers and advisers of public bureaucracies and (2) a populist, participatory conception of politics in which citizens exercise their political sovereignty by means of organised and persistent pressure-group activity.

New Right critics include laissez-faire economic liberals, libertarians, neo-conservatives and public choice theorists, not all of whom appreciate the label *New Right* or share a common position. But their prognoses of the ill-effects of pressure-group politics are similar. They agree, for example, that one of the main causes of the persistent economic, political and cultural problems and difficulties which have afflicted Western nations in the second half of the century has been pressure-group politics. For public choice theorists in particular, it is the pressure groups which further sectional economic interests that are the main cause of the 'overloading' of Western governments, that is to say the inability of governments to finance the military, welfare, educational, environmental-protectionist and other services demanded of them. Indeed, one public-choice critic, Mancur Olson, Jr (1986), has argued that the main reason why, after 1945, West Germany and Japan had such apparently miraculous economic recoveries and fared better economically than several of the Second-World-War victors was their military defeats and enemy occupation. Defeat and occupation enabled their economic and social reorganisation to escape disruption by well organised pressure groups.

The successful courting of politicians and public servants by pressure groups, New Right critics argue, turn modern states into legislative and administrative machines with vast, unmanageable, socially-intrusive bureaucracies. The problem is worsened by the fact that the economists, lawyers and other professionals who are increasingly employed by government departments and agencies become a new pressure group concerned with improving their status, influence and income. One paradoxical result of pressure-group politics is that although governments and government departments continually have their powers increased, and become more socially intrusive, they become unwieldy, and unable to maintain law and order, and perform other essential functions. Law, in fact, as a result of pressure-group activity, becomes so ad-hoc, complex and at times silly that it ceases to perform its primary role of providing clear rules for social behaviour. Samuel Brittan (1988) put his finger on a fundamental fallacy in Dahl's revision of democratic theory and in all pluralist rhapsodies over pressure groups when he wrote that 'Horse trading between interest groups does not produce a healthy compromise. Each party is likely to be given some concession which is spread over the whole community...' (p. 261). Pressure-group pluralism is seen by New Right critics as a force which, if unconstrained, will both distort for the worse the economic relations of the market to which New Right theorists are committed and subvert democratic politics. Pressure-group pluralism will replace economically independent and politically free citizens and private associations, and government based on discussion and reason, with a network of entrenched, arrogant, pressure groups, and with governmental economic and other policies that are incoherent. And it will lead to the domination of society, including the domination of the people whom the leaders of pressure groups claim to represent, by a new type of ruling class: the victorious elites of pressure-group combats.[2]

But if New Right thinkers have drawn attention to the dangers in the prescriptions of pressure-group pluralists, the corporatists of the 1970s, 1980s and 1990s have cast doubt on pluralist empirical work.[3] For the corporatists, post-1945 government in most representative democracies has been characterised not by opposed pressure groups competing more or less equally for government support, with governments and government departments acting as independent arbitrators, but by the incorporation of pressure groups into the state. Corporatist analyses focus on the cooperation, much of it now institutionalised, between governments and privileged pressure groups such as large business corporations, employers' associations and trade unions in economic life, teachers' organisations in education, and medical and welfare bodies in the administration of health and welfare services. The corporatists have documented how, in return for the favours granted to pressure groups and their leaders, their leaders and

---

[2] For an informed and balanced survey of New Right thinking, see Barry (1987). For some earlier, 1960s, objections to pressure-group pluralism which foreshadow New Right thinking, see Lowi (1979) and Olson, Jr (1965). For objections which have a United Kingdom focus, see Brittan (1975; 1977; and 1988).

[3] Like the political-science pluralists, recent corporatists have concentrated on empirical work. They are sometimes called neo-corporatists in order to distinguish them from Catholic and other nineteenth-century and early-twentieth-century corporatists, primarily normative theorists who sought an alternative social and economic organisation to both capitalism and socialism. For an informed survey of recent corporatist (neo-corporatist) work, see Williamson (1989); and, for a survey which also covers nineteenth-century corporatist thought, Williamson (1985).

organisers will restrain their members. Some corporatists have argued that nations with large and well organised labour movements have been dominated by partnerships between governments and the representatives of business and labour, usually with governments as the senior partner (Pahl and Winkler 1974; and Winkler 1976). Whether or not the work and the vocabulary of today's pluralists can take account of the phenomena emphasised by the corporatists, corporatist work has certainly revealed the need for repair.[4]

By *traditionalist* critics of pluralism are meant theorists who are sympathetic to and who wish to build upon the political traditions and normative work neglected and discarded by behavioural political scientists. Several such critics have mounted an offensive against what they see as the essence of the behavioural project: that the solution to the problems of democratic government resides in the detailed study of the behaviour of politicians, public servants, the leaders and organisers of pressure groups, and voters and other political actors; the setting up of expensively equipped research institutions; the acquiring of the necessary public and private financial support; and partnerships between policy makers and behavioural political scientists. Whereas the behaviourists saw their work as vital for overcoming the internal and external threats to democracy, traditionalist critics have seen the behavioural project as an ignorant abandonment of necessary historical, constitutional and political-philosophic critical perspectives. For such critics, the behaviourists of the 1950s were neglecting their responsibilities as citizens and teachers, and offering an ideological cover for a new class of political rulers and their attempt to join the new class. Moreover, for traditionalist critics, Dahl's Benthamite and Bentleyite view of society as constituted by groups with different interests, competing over who will have their opposed wants and demands satisfied, is simple minded. It forgets the many sub-divisions and the multitude of different interests and viewpoints within the so-called interest groups, and the fact that the members of different and opposed interest groups have many shared interests, including what traditionalists regard as a common good.[5]

Pluralism's left-wing critics, despite their different commitments from those of the traditionalists, have also reprimanded the behaviourists for abandoning critical perspectives, and questioned their motives and the

---

4 For corporatist objections to pluralist empirical theory, and examinations of the relations between corporatist and pluralist phenomena, see Cawson (1982; and 1986); Crouch (1983); Harrison (1980); and Williamson (1985, Ch. 9; and 1989).

5 For such traditionalist critiques, mainly by students of Leo Strauss, see Storing (1962). See also, Statham, Jr (1998, Ch. 4).

effects of their work.⁶ In addition, they have accused the pluralists of focusing on superficial conflicts at the expense of the more fundamental but hidden power relations of capitalist societies (Bachrach and Baratz 1962; and Lukes 1974). They have agreed with E. E. Schattschneider - whose study of American democracy urged the importance of parties rather than pressure groups - that pluralist analyses of democracy were biassed in favour of the propertied classes and privileged elites. In a statement, much quoted by left-wing writers, Schattschneider (1960) had written that the

> flaw in the pluralist heaven is that the heavenly chorus sings with a strong upper-class accent. Probably about 90 per cent of the people cannot get into the pressure system. The notion that the pressure system is automatically representative of the whole community is a myth fostered by the universalizing tendency of modern group theories. *Pressure politics is a selective process* ill designed to serve diffuse interests. The system is skewed, loaded and unbalanced in favor of a fraction of a minority (p. 35).⁷

It is not necessary to agree with the theoretical and practical alternatives of the leftist critics of post-1945 pluralism to see the truth in the charge of ideology. Pluralist like other formalist analyses of democratic government, which have few if any independent evaluative criteria for distinguishing between democratic and non-democratic outcomes, have a built-in tendency to legitimate as democratic the institutions and practices that are examined. Post-1945 pluralism has been ideological, however, not, as its Marxist and other socialist critics allege, because it is pro-capitalist - its exponents have usually had a preference for some variety of socialism - but because it is formalist. In practice, it gives democratic credentials to almost anything produced by social pluralism and pressure-group politics. But let us now turn to the some of the offspring of behavioural, political-science pluralism.

Neopluralism and Dahl's Post-Pluralism

Since writing the *Preface to Democratic Theory*, Dahl's views on modern democracy have been modified; many of the book's assumptions and

---

6   See for example the essays in Roszak (1969).
7   For examples of New Left, Marxist, and neo-Marxist criticisms of the American pluralists, see Bachrach (1969); Connolly (1969); Held (1989, pp. 57-76); Kariel (1961); McCoy and Playford (1967); Macpherson (1977, 'Model 3: Equilibrium Democracy'); and Miliband (1969).

conclusions, however, continue to be made and accepted by political scientists and theorists, including Dahl. They survive in some strengthened forms, which will be described as *neopluralist*, and in some more questionable forms, including Dahl's *Democracy and Its Critics* (1989), which will be described as *post-pluralist*.

Neopluralism

Neopluralist theorists try to revitalise political and social pluralist democratic theory by fusing it with ideas taken from its New Left, New Right, neo-elite-theory, corporatist and other critics. Probably the most thorough of such attempts is William Kelso's *American Democratic Theory* (1978).

Kelso identifies three varieties of pluralism: *laissez-faire, polyarchal* and *public*. For Kelso, laissez-faire pluralists, who should not be confused with laissez-faire liberals and economists, postulate a self-regulating mechanism among organised groups which prevents any of them from obtaining permanent privileges at the expense of others. The task of government, for such theorists, is little more than to maintain the rules of fair competition. Polyarchal pluralists, however, whom Kelso sometimes calls *corporatist* or *elitist* pluralists, agree with Schumpeter that a more important consideration than rules of fair competition is the maintenance of a division between elites and non-elites. Polyarchal pluralists desire strong governments and governmental elites with wide-ranging powers, and corporate relations between governments and pressure groups. The third form of pluralism (public pluralism), according to Kelso who champions it, successfully avoids the defects of both laissez-faire and polyarchal pluralism.

Against polyarchal pluralism and in his advocacy of public pluralism, Kelso asserts the psychological and educational benefits of political participation. Ethnic minorities and the poor, in particular, benefit from being reminded of their political rights and encouraged to organise politically. In contrast to his American pluralist predecessors, however, Kelso is more suspicious of the state, and of political and technocratic elites. Bureaucratic interventions in society, he maintains, are often inept, and the only liberties which elites should be relied on to respect are their own. His argument is that a (public-pluralist) pressure-group politics which is suspicious of governments and elites, which recognises the class divisions in democratic societies, and which empowers weak minorities is, for large nations, the most attractive and effective system of democratic government.

He contends that political participation by means of pressure groups is superior to the participation of citizens in politics by means of neighbourhood government and the management of schools, hospitals, local services and suchlike. The reason is that these local forms of popular participation lead either to inefficiency and a lack of resources, particularly in poor neighbourhoods, or to grossly discriminatory policies in areas dominated by racist or other bigots. Participation by means of pressure groups is also superior to federal or state referenda as referenda are more likely to produce inconsistent legislation.

Kelso's main objection to laissez-faire pluralism is that self-regulating mechanisms are a mirage; unless governments oversee pressure groups to prevent some groups from becoming too powerful, and to assist weak groups to organise and to gain access to government, no genuine competition will occur. Governments, therefore, should 'intervene to hinder the development of semi-closed systems of decision making' (p. 28). Laissez-faire pluralists are also accused of being naive about bureaucracy, and failing to appreciate that public administrators further their personal interests and those of their bureaucratic unit. Governments, therefore, have a responsibility to curb both pressure groups and public bureaucracies. They must prevent pressure-group demands and bureaucratic excess from making public policy and legislation incoherent, and budgets unbalanced. Yet for all of Kelso's suspicion of pressure groups, governments and public bureaucracies, his proposed constraints lack bite. His proposals are admirable but pious; they depend upon the good will of the bureaucrats and administrators he distrusts.

The root of the problem is that his public pluralism lacks a conception of a common good that goes beyond some minimal government constraints on pressure-group politics. He seems unaware of the tension between (1) calling for the politicisation of the community by means of pressure-group politics and (2) calling for checks to the effects of pressure groups - privileged private interests, bureaucratic government, ad-hoc legislation and policies, and irresponsible financial management. Kelso's attitude to pressure groups is ambivalent. On the one hand, he is enthusiastic about the popular participation they make possible, and he wants government policy to be the product of their activity, on the other, governments are urged to assert their authority and to control pressure-group activity.

Robert Dahl's Post-Pluralism

To the extent that Kelso separates necessary and desirable from reprehensible forms of pluralism, he contributes to a public-philosophic democratic theory, and his book acts as a bridge from pluralism to public philosophy. By contrast, Dahl's most ambitious post-pluralist reworking of democratic theory, his *Democracy and Its Critics* (1989), though in some respects public philosophic, is more a bridge from the *Preface to Democratic Theory*'s pluralism to populism, and from the *Preface*'s formalism to utopianism.

Whereas the *Preface*'s analysis of democracy was the foundation for an inductive argument about democracy in which Dahl built upon the pluralist, empirical work of American political scientists, his longer, and more comprehensive (1989) study is organised around a deductive argument. The book is an exercise in what Edmund Burke (1969) in his objections to the French Revolution's leaders, theorists and apologists denounced as dangerously abstract, a style of political thought, however, which does not always take extreme, Jacobin or other revolutionary forms. It may, as in much current university political theory, be given various liberal, democratic socialist, quasi-anarchist and other expressions. The theorist who engages in such abstract political theory begins by trying to convert the reader to his or her values before turning, though usually only in theory, to applying them to changing the world.

Dahl, in a similar fashion, devotes the first third of his (1989) book to justifying his three principal values (*equality, freedom*, in the sense of *personal autonomy*, and *self government* or *popular sovereignty*) and his conception of the democratic process, before applying them to a range of theoretical and practical problems. Dahl maintains that, for all the natural and socially acquired differences among people, they possess an inherent equality as persons and citizens which should be respected and made inviolate. He contends that equality is a rational and largely self-evident principle and value, supported by most people in Western democratic nations and by democrats in other parts of the world. Likewise, he contends that there is no rational alternative to recognising the personal autonomy of people, in particular the fact that every mentally sound person is the best judge of his or her interests. Popular sovereignty, which completes Dahl's trio of fundamental democratic values, is considered to be both a condition for and an expression of the intrinsic equality and personal autonomy of people. Only if the members of a community or society govern themselves democratically, directly as in the Athenian polis or indirectly as in representative or - as Dahl continues to call them - *polyarchal* institutions, will their equality and freedom be effectively protected and acquire a political content.

The democratic process, Dahl notes, has taken two historical forms or, to use his vocabulary, has had two *transformations*. The first was that of small republics from Ancient Greece to Renaissance Italy. The second, the polyarchal government of pluralist nations, was born in the seventeenth century and reached maturity in the twentieth with universal adult voting. But Dahl also looks forward to and advocates a third transformation in which the representative government of nation states is supplemented with larger regional units, a devolution of power from national to local government, and the application of telecommunications to informing citizens about public policy, thus narrowing the gap between governments and citizens. In many ways, however, Dahl's proposed third transformation would lead to greater rather than less power over citizens by governments. This is because Dahl wants governmental power to be used to extend the principles of equality, freedom and self government into industrial and economic life. For only if there is greater economic equality, he argues, will political equality become genuine. And only if self-government is introduced into the workplace will people have their personal autonomy fully respected on the basis of equality.

For all Dahl's caution and skill in developing his argument, it is unlikely that his conception of the democratic process and his third transformation would persuade anyone who did not already share his predilection for the varieties of equality, freedom and self government which he fovours. Moreover, in both how he justifies his values and how he applies them to practical issues he is inconsistent. After grounding his conception of the democratic process on a formalist rejection of substantive conceptions of democracy, he then puts considerable normative substance into the 'democratic process'.[8] Although his formalist rejection of a substantive view of democracy and his preference for seeing democracy as a process may at first sight suggest a similarity to the procedural view of democracy of Mayo and Pickles, there are important differences. Dahl's democratic process is not just a procedure for reaching decisions on disputed issues; it is the means whereby citizens express their equality and autonomy, and seek happiness and fulfilment for themselves - but on the basis of their understanding of happiness and the good life rather than someone else's.[9] For the Dahl who wrote *Democracy and Its Critics*, decisions and practices which conflict with these ends do not satisfy the criteria of the democratic process. Decisions and policies must in their

---

8   Dahl's main objections to substantive conceptions of democracy are that they require the authoritarian custodial proposition that *A* knows better than *B* what is in *B*'s interests; they require concepts such as *justice* or the *common good* which are interpreted differently by different groups of people; they lack an objective basis; and they give a 'priority to the justice or rightness of the substantive outcomes of decisions rather than to the process by which the decisions are reached' (1989, p. 116).

9   '*A person's good or interest is whatever that person would choose with the fullest attainable understanding of the experience resulting from that choice and its most relevant alternatives*' (Dahl, 1989, p. 307). Dahl, however, seems unaware of the contradiction between this emphasis on a person being the best judge of his or her best interests and his (Dahl's) view that the collective power of an organised democratic community be mobilised to maximise economic and other social equality.

substance as well as the procedures by which they are reached comply with his conception of the democratic process.

Dahl's *Democracy and Its Critics* (1989), despite its going further than the *Preface to Democratic Theory* (1956) in confronting normative issues, is a less satisfying volume. The *Preface* tried to synthesise the insights of two rival conceptions of democracy, described by Dahl as the *Madisonian* and *populist*, and, whatever the limitations of its argument, made a coherent and stimulating contribution to democratic theory. *Democracy and Its Critics*, however, is less coherent, and the populist components of Dahl's thinking triumph over the Madisonian. The book combines a defence of the institutions and structures of modern Western democracy with the advocacy of a new kind of egalitarian, mass-participatory democracy. In defiance of his value-relativist strictures that substantive conceptions of democracy rest on subjective, unprovable conceptions of the common good and the good life, Dahl attaches such a substantive conception to his otherwise formalist view of democracy as process.

> We need to reject...the familiar contrast between substance and process. For integral to the democratic process are substantive rights, goods, and interests that are often mistakenly thought to be threatened by it. Among these are the right to self-government....Nor is the right to self-government a right to a 'merely formal process', for the democratic process is neither 'merely process' nor 'merely formal.'...[It] is also an important kind of distributive justice. For it helps to determine the distribution of other crucial resources as well. The right to the democratic process....is ...a claim to all the general and specific rights - moral, legal, constitutional - that are necessary to it, from freedom of speech, press, and assembly to the right to form opposition political parties (Dahl, 1989, p. 175).

Dahl's contention that conceptions of the democratic process always contain some normative substance is fully justified. He further contends, however, that the vision of the good life embodied in his conception of the democratic process, in effect a socialist reconstruction of democratic societies by means of a combination of state power and mass participation, is not a personal preference but a higher stage of democracy (a 'third transformation'). This vision of a good life is described as follows.

> The vision of the democratic process that has guided the argument of this book stretches human possibilities to their limits and perhaps beyond. It is a vision of a political system in which the members regard one another as political equals, are collectively sovereign, and possess all the

capacities, resources and institutions they need in order to govern themselves (1989, p. 311).

It is a democratic process in which property rights and a capitalism of freely consenting adults are expected to give way to economic as well as political equality. Dahl writes that if

> income, wealth and economic position are also political resources, and if they are distributed unequally, then how can citizens be political equals? And if citizens cannot be political equals, how is democracy to exist (1989, p. 326)?

Whether Dahl's *Democracy and Its Critics,* and its concluding mix of populist egalitarianism and socialism should be classified as ideological or utopian is a difficult question. On the one hand, as in all of Dahl's work, the formalist framework for his discussions is different from those of Pickles, Mayo, Schumpeter and most of the neo-elitists in having a leftist bias. His conception of a democratic process in which property rights are subordinated to popular sovereignty and a quest for greater economic equality appears to confirm Dahl's claim to be both a radical and a man of the left.[10] On the other hand, the political, economic and cultural elites of present day democratic nations have little difficulty in using such leftist talk as Dahl's for their own ends. Indeed they welcome it. It is frequently how they justify their grip on government and the state. Dahl's preferred values of equality, autonomy and popular sovereignty are rhetorical nourishment for large numbers of politicians and public servants, and the advisers and consultants who surround them. Governments, bureaucrats and technocrats have little difficulty in justifying increases in their power and intrusiveness in terms of promoting liberty and equality, and as an expression of popular sovereignty.

Conclusion

The political and social pluralism espoused in Dahl's *Preface to Democratic Theory,* to a lesser extent in his *Democracy and Its Critics,* and in other

---

10 Dahl, who has always considered himself a socialist and a man of the left, was irritated by 1950s and 1960, New Left student and academic critics who dismissed his work as an apologia for Western capitalism. See, for example, his response to these critics in his *After the Revolution* (1970); the autobiographical discussions in the Introduction to his *Democracy, Liberty and Equality*, (1986); and the interview with him in Baer, Jewel and Sigelman (1991).

work by Dahl and his American political science contemporaries has always been an incomplete theory which attracts other ideas. When used for the empirical study of existing democracies it tends to adopt the values of the institutions and groups being observed, and to function as a legitimating ideology. But as well as serving ideological functions for well established, narrowly conservative, privileged groups, it may be fastened, as in Dahl's *Democracy and Its Critics*, to a more utopian politics and rhetoric.

But for all its populism and utopianism, parts of Dahl's *Democracy and Its Critics* may be regarded as public philosophic. Despite Dahl's dislike of the idea of a common good, the book is at times a thoughtful and challenging exploration of what the common good could and should be for nations committed, as most democracies supposedly are, to the values of political equality, toleration, individual liberty and self government. Similarly, for all Dahl's dislike of the idea of substantive democracy, he gives democracy as process a substance which, until its drift into populism and utopianism, can be, like Kelso's public pluralism, a bridge from the formalism of pluralism to an empirically based, normative, public-philosophic democratic theory.

The ambivalence of Dahl's *Democracy and Its Critics*, its swaying between realism and the public philosophy on the one hand and utopia on the other, therefore, signals the end of the grand, American, behavioural projects for (1) reconstructing political science on the empirical study of group behaviour and relations, and (2) reconstructing democratic theory on the idea of political and social (pressure-group) pluralism. The participants in these projects produced important empirical studies of and stimulated normative thinking about democracy. Indeed a part of their offspring has been the many commendably balanced, critical studies of pressure groups which demonstrate how pressure groups perform necessary functions for while simultaneously undermining current democratic politics - for example, Berry (1989), and Cigler and Loomis (1995). But the behavioural, political-science, pluralist project of the 1950s was flawed from the start, and there is no longer anything resembling a robust and united group of theorists and researchers in this mould.

Nevertheless the idea that political and social pluralism captures the essence of modern democracy survives, though often in new forms. It survives, for example, in movements which promote multiculturalism, ethnic and other group rights, and greater popular participation in politics - some examples of which will be discussed in subsequent chapters, beginning with the next chapter on utopianism in democratic theory.

References

Bachrach, Peter (1969), *The Theory of Democratic Elitism: A Critique*, 2nd edn, Univ. of London Pr., London.

Bachrach, Peter and Morton S. Baratz (1962), 'The Two Faces of Power', *American Political Science Review*, vol. 56, pp. 942-52.

Baer, Michael A., Malcolm E. Jewel and Lee Sigelman (eds) (1991), *Political Science in America: Oral Histories of a Discipline*, Univ. Pr. of Kentucky, Lexington.

Barry, Norman P. (1987), *The New Right*, Croom Helm, London.

Bentley, Arthur F. (1967), *The Process of Government* [1908], (ed.) Peter H. Odegard, Harvard Univ. Pr., Cambridge, Mass.

Berry, Jeffrey M. (1989), *The Interest Group Society*, 2nd edn, Scott, Foresman, Glenview, Ill.

Breitling, Rupert (1980), 'The Concept of Pluralism', in Stanislaw Ehrlich and Graham Wootton (eds), *Three Faces of Pluralism: Political, Economic and Religious*, Gower, London.

Brittan, Samuel (1975), *Participation Without Politics*, Institute of Economic Affairs, London.

Brittan, Samuel (1977), *The Economic Consequences of Democracy*, Temple Smith, London.

Brittan, Samuel (1988), *A Restatement of Economic Liberalism*, Macmillan, Basingstoke.

Burke, Edmund (1968), *Reflections on the Revolution in France* [1790], (ed.) Conor Cruise O'Brien, Penguin Books, Harmondsworth.

Cawson, Alan (1982), *Corporatism and Welfare*, Heinemann, London.

Cawson, Alan (1986), *Corporatism and Political Theory*, Blackwell, Oxford.

Cigler, Allan J. and Burdett A. Loomis (eds) (1995), *Interest Group Politics*, 4th edn, CQ [Congressional Quarterly] Pr., Washington, D.C.

Cole, G.D.H. (1920), *Guild Socialism Re-Stated*, Leonard Parsons, London.

Connolly, William E. (ed.) (1969), *The Bias of Pluralism*, Atherton Pr., New York.

Crick, Bernard (1959), *The American Science of Politics*, Routledge, London.

Crouch, Colin (1983), 'Pluralism and the New Corporatism', *Political Studies*, vol. 31, pp. 452-60.

Dahl, Robert A. (1956), *Preface to Democratic Theory*, Univ. of Chicago Pr., Chicago.

Dahl, Robert A. (1970), *After the Revolution*, Yale Univ. Pr., New Haven.

Dahl, Robert A. (1986), *Democracy, Liberty and Equality*, Norwegian Univ. Pr., Oslo.

Dahl, Robert A. (1989), *Democracy and Its Critics*, Yale Univ. Pr., New Haven.

Ehrlich, Stanislaw (1982), *Pluralism On and Off Course*, Pergamon Pr., Oxford.

Garson, G. David (1974), 'On the Origins of Interest-Group Theory', *American Political Science Review*, vol. 68, pp. 1505-19.

Hamilton, Alexander, James Madison and John Jay (1971), *The Federalist* [1787-88], Dent/Everyman, London.

Harrison, R.J. (1980), *Pluralism and Corporatism: the Evolution of Modern Democracy*, Allen and Unwin, Winchester, Mass.

Held, David (1989), *Political Theory and the Modern State*, Polity Pr., Cambridge.
Hirst, Paul Q. (ed.) (1989), *The Pluralist Theory of the State: Selected Writings of G.D.H. Cole, J.N. Figgis, and H.J. Laski*, Routledge, London.
Jordan, Grant (1990), 'The Pluralism of Pluralism: An Anti-theory', *Political Studies*, vol. 38, pp. 286-301.
Kariel, Henry S. (1961), *The Decline of American Pluralism*, Stanford Univ. Pr., Stanford.
Kelso, William Alton (1978), *American Democratic Theory: Pluralism and Its Critics*, Greenwood Pr., Westport.
Kuang Chuan Hsiao (1927), *Political Pluralism*, Kegan Paul, Trench, Trubner, London.
Lowi, Theodore J. (1979), *The End of Liberalism* [1969], 2nd edn, Norton, New York.
Lukes, Steven (1974), *Power: A Radical View*, Macmillan, London.
Macpherson, C.B. (1977), *The Life and Times of Liberal Democracy*, Oxford Univ. Pr., Oxford.
McCoy, C.A. and John Playford (eds) (1967), *Apolitical Politics*, Crowell, New York.
Miliband, Ralph (1969), *The State in Capitalist Society*, Weidenfeld and Nicolson, London.
Nicholls, D. (1974), *Three Varieties of Pluralism*, Macmillan, London.
Olson Jr, Mancur (1965), *Collective Action: Public Goods and the Theory of Groups*, Harvard Univ. Pr., Cambridge, Mass.
Olson, Mancur (1986), *The Rise and Decline of Nations*, Yale Univ. Pr., New Haven.
Pahl, R.E. and T.J Winkler (1974), 'The Coming Corporatism', *New Society*, Oct. 10.
Roszak, Theodore (ed.) (1969), *The Dissenting Academy*, 3rd edn, Penguin Books, Harmondsworth.
Schattschneider, E.E. (1960), *The Semisovereign People*, Holt, Rinehart and Winston, New York.
Smith, Martin J. (1990), 'Pluralism, Reformed Pluralism and Neopluralism...', *Political Studies*, vol. 38, pp. 302-22.
Statham Jr, E. Robert (1998), *The Constitution of Public Philosophy: Toward a Synthesis of Freedom and Responsibility in Postmodern America*, Univ. Pr. of America, Lanham.
Storing, Herbert J. (ed.) (1962), *Essays on the Scientific Study of Politics*, Holt, Rinehart and Winston, New York.
Truman, David B. (1971), *The Governmental Process* [1951], 2nd edn, Knopf, New York.
Weinstein, Leo (1962), 'The Group Approach: Arthur F. Bentley', in Herbert J. Storing (ed.), *Essays on the Scientific Study of Politics*, Holt, Rinehart and Winston, New York.
Williamson, Peter J. (1985), *Varieties of Corporatism*, Cambridge Univ. Pr., Cambridge.
Williamson, Peter J. (1989), *Corporatism in Perspective*, Sage, London.
Winkler, T.J. (1976), 'Corporatism', *European Journal of Sociology*, vol. 17, pp. 100-36.

4 Utopianism and the Utopian Challenge to Democratic Theory

Although this chapter examines several varieties of utopian thought, it is not a complete survey of utopianism, and many types of utopianism in present day political thought will be ignored. It will concentrate on the work of political theorists who, like Schumpeter and Dahl, tried to redefine and revise democratic theory but who, in several instances, claimed to be building upon rather than rejecting pre-Schumpeter democratic theory. It will be argued however that their work turns *democratic theory* into little more than a code word for a socialist, quasi-anarchist, utopian project. This argument however is not intended to imply that there are no conservative, liberal, market-capitalist and other non-socialist varieties of utopianism. It is simply that such utopian thought is irrelevant to this chapter as it does not masquerade as democratic theory. Neither is the chapter's critique of writing on democracy that is utopian and socialist intended to imply that all socialist thought is utopian. The objection to utopian democratic theory is not that it is socialist or otherwise on the left but that, among its other inadequacies, it is naive and irresponsible. It creates confusion about the meaning and purposes of modern democratic government.

What is Utopianism?

Contrary to the assertions of many utopians, utopianism is not simply moral or political idealism. Being a utopian is not the same as possessing ideals, and idealists and there ideals are not necessarily utopian. Whereas it is possible if not always easy to distinguish between realistic and unrealistic ideals, it makes little sense to distinguish between realistic and unrealistic utopias. Utopian speculation, by its nature, is concerned with perfect societies, fundamentally different from past and present societies. Although, as utopians like to remind us, ideals which now appear to lack realism may sometime in the future become realistic, they are made utopian by the fact that, for the foreseeable future for present generations, they are unlikely to be achievable, and that, because of their lack of realism, acting on them is almost certain to be counter-productive.

Utopia originally meant an imaginary society which, as a result of its harmony and the absence of evil from the intentions and activities of its members, transcended human experience. *Utopia*, the root word for *utopian* and *utopianism*, comes from Greek words for nowhere or no place (*ou* = not, and *topos* = place), and from Latin words which can be roughly translated as a good landscape or place (*eu* = good, and *topia* = ornamental garden) (Georghegan, p. 1; F.E and F.P. Manuel, pp. 1-4). When Thomas More, in 1516, coined the word *Utopia* for the name of an imaginary ideal society and for the title of his novel, a pun may have been intended by him. But whatever the precise origins of the root word, an apt dictionary definition of being *utopian* is the 'proposing or advocating [of] impractically ideal social and political schemes' (*Webster's*, 1977). Less pejoratively, but without anything of substance being changed, another dictionary definition states that a *utopia* is 'any imaginary state of ideal perfection' (*Chambers*, 1973).

Some utopian speculation, of course, does have a place in democratic and other political theory. Most normative political theorists find it necessary or helpful to consider what it would mean for an ideal, institution or proposed reform to achieve its most complete and perfect realisation. Such speculation may reveal both agreeable and disagreeable possibilities. Fruitful forms of utopian thought, therefore, should be distinguished from the naive and willful. As its admirers note, utopian thinking may be characterised by vision, fertile dreaming and playfulness, farsighted and imaginative social criticism and bold proposals for social reform; sceptics, however, point to its dogmatism, lack of common sense and blindness to many of the political and other consequences of the social changes it proposes or intimates.[1]

Contrary to normal uses of the word *utopianism*, to point to a want of realism, at least one academic commentator on utopianism has made *realism* its defining feature. According to J. C. Davis (1984), utopians are only one of five kinds of theorists of ideal societies, and it is their realism which separates them from the remaining four. For Davis, there are four unrealistic types of ideal societies: (1) Lands-of-Cockaygne where there is the instant gratification of the senses, (2) societies in which there is a natural abundance and restrained appetites, (3) perfect moral commonwealths inhabited by fully virtuous members, and (4) the millennium, which 'assumes that nature and man will be transformed by a

---

[1] Contrast, for example, Karl R. Popper's linking of utopianism to violence in his influential essay, 'Utopia and Violence' (1963) and Thomas Molnar's more comprehensive criticism (1972) with Ruth Levitas's (1990) promotion of utopian studies as an academic discipline sympathetic to utopianism and Judith Shklar's lament over the apparent demise of utopianism (1957).

force arising and acting independently of the wills of individual men and women' (p. 8). By contrast, in (5) utopian theory, realistic systems are devised 'whereby men will be able to offset their own continuing wickedness and cope with the deficiencies of nature' (p. 9).

In addition to the oddity of associating utopianism, with realistic programs for moral improvement and political reform, there is at least one other serious flaw in Davis's classifications. His categories exclude one of the most widespread forms of modern utopianism: secular millenarianism. In addition to Christian millenarians, whom Davis appears to have in mind in his accounts of millenarianism, there are secular millenarians who rely not on God or any other supra-human force to produce a millennium in which evil will be purged from the world but on political and other human action. For secular millenarians, it is by human means, sometimes described as *praxis*, that societies will be established in which all the worthy aspirations, and moral and social visions of men and women harmoniously co-exist. One critic of this millenarian utopianism, Isaiah Berlin, has appealed to a pluralist conception of values in order to rebut it. Berlin follows Friedrich Nietzsche and Max Weber in insisting that fundamental values resemble warring deities who refuse to be reconciled; such values cannot be placed in a hierarchy or otherwise harmonised, not even in meta-ethical or other philosophic theory let alone in social life. The harmony and perfection of communities of shared values which millenarian and other utopians seek, therefore, can never be realised, not even as a theoretical undertaking. Ideals and other values are achieved only at the expense of opposed ideals and values; human life, it follows, is inescapably tragic.[2]

It is not necessary, however, to share Berlin's value pluralism to see the strength of his objections to millenarian and other utopianism. Even if conflicts among values were overcome in a philosophic synthesis, the possibility of other philosophers, and the politicians and voters of democratic nations being convinced is so remote that it may be discounted. Apart from small communities of saints who freely accept a common moral code, only in a society totally controlled by philosopher rulers, as in Plato's *Republic*, by genetic engineers, as in Aldous Huxley's *Brave New World*, or by a totalitarian party, as in George Orwell's *Nineteen Eighty-Four*, could conformity to the norms of a utopian - or dystopian - society be achieved.

But the secular millenarian desire to achieve a utopia or heaven on earth by revolutionary or more moderate political and other human activity

---

2   For Isaiah Berlin's objections to utopianism, see his essays on 'The Pursuit of the Ideal' and 'The Decline of Utopian Ideals in the West' (1990). For discussions of his value pluralism, see George Crowder (1994; and 1998); Isaiah Berlin and Bernard Williams (1994); and John Gray (1995).

is by no means uncommon; since the 1950s, both the many branches of Marxism and neo-Marxism, and the work of the utopian democrats have exemplified it.[3] As the Greek word for practice, *praxis*, is now widely used to describe a revolutionary theory and practice of this - usually Marxist or neo-Marxist - utopianism, I shall make use of it in discussing Marx's and subsequent secular millenarianism, including that of the utopian democrats.

Marxist and Other Utopian Praxis

Well before the word *utopia* had been coined, many of its egalitarian and other aspirations for a new kind of world had been expressed in the slave uprisings of the Ancient World, in medieval rebellions of the rural and urban poor, and in the more politically radical of medieval and later Christian heresies.[4] These aspirations and a politics driven by them were given a new, professedly non-utopian, scientific and politically realist foundation by the founders of Marxism.

Karl Marx and Friedrich Engels, beginning in the 1840s, used the adjective *utopian* for propaganda purposes, applying it to the work of rival socialist writers, principally the Comte de Saint-Simon, Charles Fourier and Robert Owen. Marx and Engels claimed that, in contrast to their 'utopian' rivals who had spun social fantasies out of their subjective wishes, Marx's communism was a realistic political project based on the scientific study of modern capitalism, and the revolutionary potential of the proletariat (for Marx, the industrial working class).[5] The proletariat, it was asserted, comprised an exploited class of people who, in order to liberate themselves, had no choice but to establish a radically new (post-historical) society. The

---

3 Significantly, although F.E. and F.P. Manuel (1979) in their magisterial study of utopianism scrupulously refrain from defining their subject, they are emphatic that underlying its many varieties is the desire to create a 'heaven on earth', an aspiration which merges the Greek quest for an ideal city with Judeo-Christian conceptions of a transcendental world (p. 17).

4 For sympathetic discussions of pre-modern utopianism and utopian socialism, see Max Beer (1957); for a more critical examination focussed on Christian millenarianism, Norman Cohn, *The Pursuit of the Millenium*, 2nd edn, Temple Smith, London, 1970; and for a wide-ranging exploration of the relations between utopia and revolution, Melvin J. Lasky (1977).

5 The claim that their communist project was not utopian is a prominent part of their *Communist Manifesto* of 1848, and of Engels's 1880 pamphlet, *Socialism: Utopian and Scientific*, which by the end of the century rivalled the *Manifesto* as the most widely read of Marxist texts. Both pamphlets are in most selections of their writings, including the selection edited by Robert C. Tucker (1972).

proletariat were expected to build upon the industrial and other achievements of modern capitalism to establish a way of life, communism, which previous generations could imagine only in religious symbols and utopian fantasies. This propaganda was successful, inasmuch as many non-Marxist historians and other writers joined Marx's followers in separating the Marxist from other varieties of socialism and regarding only the non-Marxist as utopian.

Yet the Marxist was as utopian if not more utopian than rival socialist projects. Indeed some critics of Marxism spotted that, in several ways, the so-called utopian socialists were more scientific than the Marxists. Ludwig von Mises (1951), for example, noted that whereas Marxists refused to outline their communist alternative to capitalism and the transition to it, on the grounds that the shape of future societies would be decided by the men and women of the post-revolutionary world, the 'utopian' socialists described their proposed societies and the routes to them, thus allowing empirical investigations and comparisons with capitalism.

Marxists, however, for all their notorious vagueness about the eventual communist society, have said enough about it to make it as fanciful as anything dreamed of by 'utopian' socialists. Marxists, in a typically utopian fashion, appear to have believed that, under communism, as a result of the economic productivity of the post-capitalist world, the desires of people for material goods will cease to outstrip resources and economic scarcity will be overcome, labour will be a joy rather than a necessary burden, social and industrial divisions of labour will cease to exist, social classes will disappear, states and their coercive powers will wither away, and there will be no social obstacles to the enjoyment by all human beings of autonomous, creative, cooperative lives.

In recent years, in fact, many Marxists and neo-Marxists have been explicit about Marxism's utopianism. As a result of the disintegration of Russian and other communist regimes, and the loss of plausibility by Marxist conceptions of history and analyses of capitalism, many Marxists and neo-Marxists have been urging that it is the utopian elements in Marxism which should be emphasised. Vincent Georghegan (1987), for instance, begins his espousal of a utopian Marxism by declaring that, 'I wish to defend that "unrealistic", "irrational", "naive", "self-indulgent...elitist", activity known as utopianism'; and that 'I want to argue for a self-consciously utopian Marxism' (pp. 1 and 7). Other attempts to revive Marxism by making its utopianism explicit include those by Ruth Levitas (1990, pp. 35-58) and Steven Lukes (1984). Whatever else this 1980s and 1990s neo-Marxism accomplishes, it demonstrates that, far from having broken from utopianism, Marxism has always been an instrument for injecting doses of utopianianism into political life.

Neo-Marxist and other exponents of a leftist utopian praxis adopt one of two possible attitudes to democracy: either they reject democracy or they assert that they are post-democratic, in other words more democratic than other democrats. Either they rely on a benevolent revolutionary elite to rule a society on the basis of Marxist, ultra-democratic utopian objectives or they have the anarchist goal of replacing government and law with what are said to be non-coercive forms of cooperation and communal life. Only thus, so neo-Marxist and quasi-anarchist utopians tell us, will it be possible to achieve the democratic objectives of individual autonomy, social equality and self-directing communities.[6] Although these two responses to democracy seem incompatible, there has been at least one twentieth-century, secular-millenarian utopian movement which has attempted a fusion: Marxism-Leninism. For Marxist-Leninists, although the eventual communist society is supposed to be largely if not entirely anarchist, the transition to communism requires revolutionary vanguards, organised in centralised, hierarchic communist parties, and political dictatorships.

Marxist and other utopians of praxis temper their ultimate objectives with short-term demands which have the veneer of realism; but the purpose of even their more realistic demands and tactics is an unrealisable social perfection. Because social institutions are always imperfect, and unable to fully express human freedom, equality and other ideals, utopians find major flaws in all past and present political, economic and cultural life. Social imperfections are regarded not as a part of the human condition or the tragic in human life but as removable obstacles to the emancipation of human potential.

Despite the absence of realism in their assumptions and ends, utopians of praxis frequently convince themselves that, because they emphasise the obstacles to human happiness rather than their ultimate utopian ends, they are realistic social critics and practical social reformers. They see their projects as 'inspired by hatred of present obstacles, not by an infatuation with kingdoms of the imagination' (Yack, 1986, p. 27). A related tendency is to regard modern society as a unified structure, cultural epoch or other totality against which political campaigns are parts of a total struggle. Even when utopian praxis is reformist, and relies on educational, literary and other endeavours to 'raise the consciousness' of the uninitiated, the purpose of the political gradualism and patient persuasion is total revolution.

Another characteristic of secular-millenarian utopians is the counterposing of morality to political and social realities. Such utopians

---

6   It follows from the argument of this chapter that anarchism is a species of utopianism. For introductions to mainstream anarchist utopianism, see Emma Goldman (1969); Marshall S. Shatz (1972); and George Crowder (1991).

dislike and polemicise against moral and political realism, for it removes what they regard as the moral imperatives from public life. Whereas for Machiavellian advocates of a *realpolitik*, conventional moral rules are irrelevant to political life, for utopians it is the observable world which, on the basis of their moral code, must be transformed. In common with crude realists, therefore, utopians reject the quest for balanced political theories and practices in which political goals rest on a combination of moral principle, a realistic appreciation of political possibilities, and an awareness of the likely consequences of political activity. Moral theory is transformed by utopians of praxis from a concern with the standards which should guide and restrain the conduct of individuals into a left-Kantian revolutionary quest, gradual or otherwise, for a society in which there are no restrictions on the individual as an autonomous moral agent, the author of his or her moral rules.

An emphasis on education is another part of utopian praxis. But, as with ethics, subtle and some not so subtle changes are made to its meaning. Education is seen not so much as the transmitting of the culture and values of the past from one generation to another but as the liberating of new generations from the dead hand of the past. It becomes the means to create a new kind of person, with a new type of consciousness and behaviour. Similarly, there is hostility to the idea that there are permanent features to human nature and a suspicion of historical study. The idea that there are limits to human potential, which historical knowledge reveals, is regarded by the advocates of a utopian praxis as a conservative ploy to resist social change. History, it is contended, does not reveal human nature as there is no human nature; history is simply a process whereby men and women continually create and recreate themselves anew. Such a denial of natural limits to political and other human power, and the related idea that the democratic process should be a means for sloughing off the past and creating new kinds of politically virtuous citizens are made explicit and conspicuous in Benjamin Barber's *Strong Democracy* (1984) and they pervade the thinking of other utopian democrats.

Utopians of praxis are millenarian in their anticipation of a new type of person and a new age, they exhibit a secular, political messianism in their search for agents who will inaugurate the new age, they are promethean in their revolt against everything which impedes the realisation of their conception of human happiness, and they are romanticist in their desire to transcend the immediate and commonplace. They are possessed by what Bernard Yack (1986), in his study of Rousseauist, left-Kantian, left-Hegelian and Nietzschean thought, has called a longing for total revolution. It was for similar reasons that Karl Mannheim (1936), who regarded utopianism as an obsessive sentiment rather than a rational theory, used it as a synonym for revolutionary ideology. As Giovanni Sartori

(1987) has observed, utopia 'is no longer an intellectual game and an object of contemplation. The twentieth-century utopian has become a man of action' (p. 63).

But the styles of thought which I have described as secular millenarian and a utopianism of praxis, in which utopian ideals are sought by political or other practice, are not always as extreme as descriptions such as *millenarian*, *messianic*, and *promethean* imply. There are degrees of utopianism. And utopianism in some form or other has become a major part of twentieth-century Western culture not because a majority of people or intellectuals are extreme revolutionaries but because so many of them are moderate utopians. And moderate utopians are more sympathetic to extreme utopians than they are to utopianism's conservative, liberal and other critics.[7] Utopian assumptions have become widespread not because of their sociological insights or moral qualities but because of their psychological effects. For many people they give a meaning to their lives and fill the void left by the absence of religious belief. Utopianism, either of an armchair or more active variety, has proved a powerful temptation for academics and other intellectuals. For press, radio and television journalists, it serves another purpose; it enables them to confront politicians with destructive criticisms of all political policies, while giving themselves what appear to be impeccable moral and political credentials.

However, in order to understand more fully the origins and character of the utopian democrats who have tried to redefine democracy in utopian terms, and to make it a revolutionary praxis, albeit a gradualist one, it is necessary to recall a slightly earlier, more activist, leftist praxis, that of the New Left. Utopian democratic theory is, in many ways, an offshoot of the New Left movements of the 1950s and 1960s, and their pursuit of socialist objectives by different, purportedly more democratic routes from those of previous socialists.

The Utopianism of the New Left

The New Left acquired its name and became a radical movement of consequence in 1956, the year of the Anglo-French occupation of the Suez Canal, the Hungarian uprising, and, in the United States, the beginning of the Civil Rights movement led by Martin Luther King. The West European

---

7   For a 1960s criticism of and tirade against Western, principally American liberals for compromising with and succumbing to the thinking I am attributing to leftist utopians, see James Burnham (1965). See also Eric Voegelin (1974); and Reinhold Niebuhr (1941 and 1943). Niebuhr, unlike Burnham and Voegelin, however, writes as a liberal and a sympathetic critic of other liberals.

New Left originally consisted of dissident and former members of its Communist Parties, the more radical of democratic socialists, the members and ex-members of Trotskyist and other left-wing groups, and the participants in unilateral-disarmament and other neutralist movements. In East Europe, it consisted of the East European revisionists, dissident intellectuals who hoped to reform their communist regimes. The theoretical issue with which European, New Left, intellectuals grappled was why socialism had culminated in little more than bureaucratic, authoritarian communist regimes, at one end of Europe, and the absorption of democratic socialist parties into corporate-capitalist institutions at the other. Although left-wing intellectuals in the United States shared these concerns, the driving force of America's New Left soon became the civil-disobedience campaigns which began with the 1956 Montgomery, Alabama, boycott of segregated buses, and the subsequent radicalisation of university students. Later, opposition to the war in Vietnam became its main driving force.

The New Left was at its strongest in the decade prior to 1968, the year of student revolts, the May events in France when New Left students, and working-class and other militants appeared to come close to toppling the Charles de Gaulle regime, and, in August, the Soviet invasion of Czechoslovakia. After 1968, the New Left began to disintegrate, often into increasingly fractious groups, with many former members turning to feminist and environmentalist causes. From 1956 to 1968, their heyday, New Left theorists and activists tried to combine radical socialist ends with quasi-anarchist democratic means. Common to the New Left's bewildering array of individuals and groups, at least until the late 1960s when various Marxist and quasi-Marxist sects competed to collect the remains, was the conviction that the failures of both Marxist and reformist socialism were caused by their reliance on centralised political parties and the pursuit of state power.

The New Left's alternative was quasi-anarchist strategies and tactics, which were intended to make revolutionary struggle more congruent with what were regarded as socialism's ultimate semi-anarchist ends. Movements which sought to abolish capitalism, economic classes, social hierarchy and elite-dominated societies, it was said, had to be characterised by a democracy that was more libertarian, egalitarian and robust than liberal democracy. Political elitism, especially the domination of leaders over followers, was to be prevented by leaving decisions to the rank and file. The movement had to guard against the emergence of a stratum of leaders and organisers separate from the workers, ethnic minorities, women, students and others whom it hoped to mobilise. Participation by the masses in direct action, and in the creation of free, egalitarian self-directed communities became both an end and a means. *Act Now, Participation* and *Spontaneity* became popular rallying cries.[8]

Closely associated with the New Left was a utopian neo-Marxism which built upon the 1840s work of the young Marx, and the post-1918 voluntarist interpretations of Marx by Karl Korsch, Georg Lukacs and Antonio Gramsci rather than on those by Engels or Lenin. New Left and neo-Marxist intellectuals mutually influenced one another, and a major influence on both was *critical theory* - a code term for the reconstructed Marxism of the Frankfurt School and the School's most extreme and explicit utopian, Herbert Marcuse.[9] Marcuse's utopian neo-Marxism, which mingled with a utopian revision of Freudian psychoanalysis, was regarded by Frank and Fritzie Manuel (1979) as of sufficient importance to be made the subject of the concluding chapter to their comprehensive history of utopian thought. The goal of what the Manuels called 'Freudo-Marxism' was to free the creative and loving potential of human beings from internal as well as external repression. This psycho-analytic, politically-utopian neo-Marxism became, in the United States and elsewhere, an entrenched part of university-based, leftist politics.

A basic part of this university-based political radicalism has been the attempt to transform democratic theory and practice. One of its main theoretical results has been utopian democratic theory, a diluted, more or less academically respectable version of New Left politics.

Utopian Democratic Theory

C. B. Macpherson, who was more of a Marxist than a neo-Marxist, was both a participant in and an influence on the New Left. His books and articles on democracy go back to the 1940s, and in nearly half a century of

---

8 A history of the New Left which though more sympathetic and comprehensive than my brief sketch does not depart from its essentials is that of Nigel Young (1977). For collections of New Left writings, see Massimo Teodori (1970); and Carl Oglesby (1969). For two New Left texts which concentrate on Europe, see Gabriel and Daniel Cohn-Bendit (1969); and Richard Gombin (1975). Maurice W. Cranston (1970) edited some critical essays on New Left theorists by their contemporaries; Ayn Rand (1971) has written a more blistering attack; Herman Belz's informed (1974) critical article concentrates on New Left academics; and Michael Walzer's *Radical Principles* (1980) contains some balanced reflections by a cautious participant in the American New Left (Part 2, 'The New Left').

9 Rolf Wiggershaus (1994) has written a detailed study of the Frankfurt School and its critical theory. The utopianism in Marcuse's work is explored by Paul Eidelberg (1969); and Alasdair MacIntyre (1970).

writing he tried both to impart a Marxist content into the idea of democracy and to clothe Marxism in a democratic language. He chastised liberals for performing ideological functions for capitalism, he proposed to extricate democracy from their embrace, and he portrayed democracy as, primarily, the struggle of the poor and the exploited for greater equality - all of which became persistent themes in utopian democratic theory. Marx's ideas were expressed by Macpherson in novel ways, with the labour theory of value becoming the transferral of human powers, and the ultimate communist goals of a classless society and the subordination of the state to society becoming a post-capitalist developmental democracy. But a change to the content rather than the language of Marxism was made when, as the agency for the transition to socialism and communism, Macpherson substituted a coalition of left-wing intellectuals, aggrieved groups and radicalised democratic citizens for Marx's proletariat.[10]

According to Macpherson, a developmental democracy in which men and women fully develop their human powers in cooperative harmony was an objective which Marxists shared with the bolder of liberal thinkers such as John Stuart Mill and T. H. Green; but only the Marxists had understood that its achievement required the abolition of capitalism. In 1976, in one of the more explicit statements about his commitment to Marxism, Macpherson wrote that

> what I have been trying to do all along (and I am still trying to do)...is to work out a revision of liberal-democratic theory, a revision which clearly owes a good deal to Marx in the hope of making that theory more democratic while rescuing the valuable part of the liberal tradition which is submerged when liberalism is identified with capitalist market relations (in Panitch, 1981, p. 144).

A socialist critic, attached to the unfashionable view that Marxists and other socialists should not portray themselves as something else, has commented on Macpherson's undertaking as follows. Macpherson

> often appears to be self-consciously addressing an audience that needs to be persuaded that socialism - a doctrine which, apparently, must parade in sheep's clothing as something called 'participatory democracy' - is the last

---

10 The main text for C.B. Macpherson's revisions of democratic theory is his *Democratic Theory: Essays in Retrieval* (1973). Two popularisations of his work are *The Real World of Democracy* (1966) and *The Life and Times of Liberal Democracy* (1977). His attitude to Marxism and liberal democracy are discussed in his, 'Do We Need a Theory of the State?' (1989). For a critical survey of his political thought, see John Dunn (1974).

and best form of liberal democracy, preserving what is essential and valuable in the liberal tradition and devoid of its evils (Wood, 1981, p. 154).

Another influential exponent of utopian democratic theory is Peter Bachrach. Prior to Bachrach, utopian democratic contributions to academic thinking about democracy had, apart from Macpherson's, largely been confined to journal articles critical of behavioural political-science and other procedural and pluralist conceptions of modern democracy. Bachrach, who formulated a more systematic, utopian, democratic theory, argued that, beginning in the 1950s, American and other Western political scientists and theorists had transformed democratic theory from a set of ideals and norms into a legitimating ideology for the elites of modern industrial capitalism - hence the title of his influential book, *The Theory of Democratic Elitism* (1967). Against this elitism, he emphasised the goal of popular sovereignty, and for its achievement called for an equality of power and economic condition, an end to elites, and the formation of communities which broke down the barriers between politics and economics. His means for accomplishing these tasks was a participatory democracy which encompassed factories and other places of work, as well as neighbourhood and local government. He proposed to radically reduce the power of public bureaucracies and to subject large business corporations to the control of employees and local communities. His book also contained an explicit defence of utopian, 'unrealizable', ideals.

Anticipating that some readers might consider a program which proposed to abolish elites, subject industry to workers and neighbourhood control, and ignore the rights of property owners as provocative rather than practical, Bachrach wrote that ideals do not have to be achievable.

> I see no reason why a principle, serving both as an ideal to strive for and as a standard for judging the progress of a political system toward the achievement of that ideal, must be realizable in practice to perform its function. The doctrine of the 'brotherhood of man' is beyond reach in large or small systems, but is this adequate reason to reject it as a sound principle with which to appraise human relations (p. 86)?

It is true that no political or moral ideal is ever fully realised, and that there are always gaps between moral ideals and human behaviour. But this truism evades the issue of the difference between utopian and realistic ideals. One difference is that even though realistic ideals are never fully achieved, it is realistic to expect that attempting to approximate to them will be beneficial rather than harmful. It is for this reason that the 'brotherhood of man', depending on precisely what is meant by it, may be regarded as a realistic ideal. Even though, for example, it may be unrealistic to expect that all members of a society would always act as if they were close friends or members of a closely knit family, it is reasonable to believe that striving to do so would bring social and personal benefits. But such claims cannot be made for Bachrach's utopia of an equality of power, entailing the abolition of elites, a radical social levelling and the destruction of property rights. Not only is it only people with a dogmatic faith in such an egalitarian socialism who are likely to be persuaded that a large modern industrialised society could ever approximate to this 'ideal' but attempts to approximate to it are likely to be disastrous. They are liable to lead not to the more democratic and cooperative society desired by Bachrach but to the disasters of communist and other command economies or, in industrialised nations with liberal-democratic traditions, severe economic problems and bitter social and political divisions.

Carole Pateman's, *Participation and Democratic Theory* (1970) similarly championed a participatory democracy which extended the political principles of self government into the economic life of modern nations. Pateman, who conflated sensible proposals for greater consultation of workpeople by management with a syndicalist control of industry by workers, made one of the main slogans of the New Left, participation, the chief value and centrepiece of her reconstruction of democratic theory. Her insertion of a syndicalist utopianism into democratic theory, however, was presented as a defence of classical democratic theory against the revisionism of Joseph Schumpeter, Robert Dahl and others. Pateman, in her participatory alternative, conflated three quite different sets of proposals: Rousseau's advocacy of small republics, directly governed by their citizens; John Stuart Mill's proposals to encourage the participation of citizens in the public life of representative democracies by extending the jury system and the functions of local government; and G. D. H. Cole's early twentieth-century, quasi-syndicalist guild-socialist proposals to democratise industry and the economy.

Anthony Arblaster and Steven Lukes have made joint and individual contributions to a similar revision of democratic theory to those of Macpherson, Bachrach and Pateman, and have followed Bachrach in defending its utopian elements. In the Introduction to a jointly edited collection of writings on the good society (1971), they grounded a defence of utopianism on a similar voluntarism to that of the New Left, and on a relativist and subjectivist conception of moral theory. They argued that the politics of realists as much as utopians rest on subjectively chosen values and ideals rather than being responses to objective facts. The two authors emphasised not the ways in which value choices were affected by a person's understanding of the world but the ways in which perceptions and understandings of the world were affected by personal tastes and preferences. People who were charged with being utopian, they wrote, were predominantly radical socialists who had chosen equality as their chief value, while their critics were liberals and conservatives who preferred some combination of inequality, hierarchy and individualism. They wrote that criticisms 'of utopianism were essentially moral and evaluative, implying not an unobtainable moral neutrality, but simply a different moral standpoint or vision' (p. 5). Thus, liberals

> look with instinctive suspicion upon...extensions [of governmental power] and activities because of the great value they attach to the liberty, self-development, privacy and autonomy of the individual....those accused of utopianism see the present condition of human circumstances very differently....Their eyes are fixed upon the grim facts of social and economic inequality and oppression... (p. 9).

For Arblaster and Lukes, at least in these statements of their views, political judgements and decisions are the product of the psychology and emotional condition of the person who makes them rather than attempts to respond to political and other circumstances as honestly and rationally as possible. Their defence of a utopian radical politics, therefore, rested on an appeal to value relativism if not political and moral irrationality. The very distinction between realism and utopianism, they asserted, was nothing but a propaganda device: 'the distinction between realism and utopianism is itself a misleading and value-loaded, indeed polemical distinction, serving to conceal the value premises from which it is made' (p. 10). Depending on what exactly they meant by *realism* and by *utopianism* being evaluative ('value loaded'), their proposition about them are either trivial or false. It is true but trivial to say that the words *realism* and *utopianism* are evaluative; it is not true and it is misleading to suggest that such evaluations simply express arbitrary personal preferences or tastes. Evaluations of political and social phenomena, if they are worth anything, rest on observation, experience and historical, sociological or other empirical evidence. Utopian democrats like everyone else have a responsibility to confront the empirical claims and arguments of critics, not airily dismiss them because their language is affected by values and judgements. To do otherwise is to imply that all judgements and values, no matter how bizarre they may be, are of equal worth.

Steven Lukes subsequently made further moral-relativist defences of leftism and utopianism. For instance, in an essay on relativism (1977), he used for leftist, utopian purposes the argument of David Hume and other moral sceptics who have drawn conservative political conclusions from relativist meta-ethical premises. But, whereas conservative-inclined moral sceptics have argued that, as there are no incontrovertible rational grounds for making political choices, we should uphold familiar institutions and be guided by familiar customs and practices, Lukes drew opposite conclusions. He used moral scepticism to argue that radical and utopian proposals must be granted the same status and consideration as established conditions and practices. More recently, however, he has been more cautious in his socialism, and less the utopian. In an amusing but telling (1993) article, for example, he satirised the (utopian) absolutising of utilitarian, communitarian, Marxist and laissez-faire principles by discussing imaginary societies called *Utilitaria, Communitaria, Proletaria* and *Libertaria.*

Anthony Arblaster, who co-authored with Lukes the (1971) value-relativist defence of leftism and utopianism, later wrote, among other books, an ambitious historical study and critique of modern liberalism (1984). From the perspective of understanding Arblaster's utopianism, its relevance is its condescending attitude to liberals, whom Arblaster, in a typically utopian-democratic fashion, accuses of being hostile to the poor and to the working class, terrified of the popular power implied by democratic theory and practice, and of being the bearers of an anaemic politics. The point is that his objections and his haughty attitude to liberalism rest upon utopian assumptions. He assumes that the capitalism upheld by liberals is a system of exploitation which, once destroyed, will be followed by conditions which approximate to utopia, and that the popular power which replaces liberal democracy requires next to no constitutional or other checks to it.

A subsequent work by Arblaster, *Democracy* (1987), builds upon that of Macpherson, Bachrach and Pateman in its view of democracy as a combination of popular sovereignty, mass participation, economic equality, an equality of power, the democratisation of industry, a revival of civic virtue, radically new kinds of personal development and opposition to elites. But Arblaster regards all these components of democracy as derivatives of one overriding principle: popular power. Popular power incorporates and goes beyond popular sovereignty, a principal which, Arblaster asserts, limits the power of people to voting in periodic elections. But popular sovereignty, he argues, even to the limited extent to which it has been realised, has been imposed on the ruling classes of capitalist democracies by socialist and other popular, mainly working class movements. The British Chartists of the 1830s and 1840s, he writes, typify the forces of democracy as, for the Chartists, democratic reform was 'the key which unlocked the door to a radical or even a revolutionary social and economic change' (1987, p. 100). On the other hand, the contribution to democracy's evolution made by the dominant social classes and their political parties has been to confine the extensions of the franchise to a capitalist social and economic order. For Arblaster, as for other utopian democrats, there is an irreconcilable conflict between the egalitarian logic of democracy and the distribution of power in capitalist nations, a distribution which follows 'the gross inequities of the capitalist market' (1987, p. 102). For Arblaster, democracy and the achieving of popular power entail a long, permanent, socialist revolution.

By the middle of the 1980s, however, most utopian democratic revisions of democratic theory had become anarchist rather than Marxist or even neo-Marxist. In comparison with the works of Macpherson, Bachrach, Pateman, Lukes and Arblaster, which were heavily influenced by that of the young Marx, subsequent utopian democratic work has become more reminiscent of Proudhon, Bakunin and Kropotkin. John Burnheim's (1988) and Philip Green's (1985) books exemplify this revival, in the guise of democratic theory, of an anarcho-communist utopianism.

In Burnheim's *Is Democracy Possible?* (1988), *democracy* means a world not of states but of small, self-governing anarchist communities that have disposed of armies, police forces, bureaucracies and elites. The supporting arguments are often clever, and many of the criticisms of contemporary democracies are warranted, but the title *Is Anarchism Possible?* would have been a better description of the book's argument, which Burnheim summarises as follows.

> Democracy does not exist in practice. At best we have what the ancients would have called elective oligarchies with strong monarchical elements. Most contemporary discussions of democracy assume that the task of democratic theory is to provide either some justification for these regimes or some normative guidance for their improvement. It is assumed that the state is a necessity of social life. The question is whether it can be made more democratic. One of my aims is to disprove this assumption by showing how a polity might function without the centralization of government that constitutes the state (p. 1).

Burnheim accepts a need for representation, but not for representatives with the authority to deliberate and decide. Ballots, he contends, should be replaced by sampling procedures to ensure that representatives are typical of the people they represent and share their attitudes, and all representatives and office holders should occupy their positions for only limited periods. In Burnheim's new democracy, or 'demarchy' as he sometimes calls it, there will be no national states monopolising the use of force; instead, there will be a network of local, regional, national and international organisations, held together by voluntary agreements: 'a community of organizations rather than a community of individuals' (p. 120). He is rather woolly however on how, in this new 'democratic' world, agreements are to be enforced and conflicts settled non-violently.

The renovated democracy urged by Philip Green in his *Retrieving Democracy* (1985) for replacing what he calls pseudodemocracy is similar to Burnheim's 'demarchy'. But whereas Burnheim's main objective is the creation of new kinds of face-to-face associations and communities, Green's principal goal is equality - political, cultural and economic. For Green, political equality, in the sense of everyone obtaining the same amount of power, is the essential meaning of democracy, and it requires a strict economic and social equality. In pursuit of his egalitarian goals, Green proposes to abolish capitalism; to devolve state power to small communities; and to end all social divisions of labour, including the separation of mental from physical labour, and divisions which result from different levels and types of knowledge. He proposes to end the differences between teachers and administrators within educational institutions by making administrators teach and teachers administer. Other differences to go are those between teachers, administrators and students, on the one hand, and support staff, on the other. Television networks, newspaper chains and specialised journalism are to be replaced by everyone having equal access to the means of communication (pp. 3, 5-6, 9-10, 22, 57, 86, 96, 102, 114, 118, 208, 220, 224, 239-40, 255, 259, 266 and 270).

Green is convinced that, once present inequalities are destroyed, the citizens of future socialist and democratic societies will share his devotion to social levelling, and refrain from using their newly acquired powers for behaviour unbecoming to socialist citizens. He also manages to believe that this social levelling will maximise individual freedom and social diversity. Moreover, his confidence that a radically egalitarian democracy is the solution to social problems leads him to brush aside controversies about the respective merits, for the obtaining of a prosperous economic life, of market freedoms and centralised planning. He is sublimely confident that, without either a market economy or planning, democratic equals will establish economic relations in which they undertake the work they choose while obtaining the goods and services they require. The phantasmagoria in Green's book are probably more glaring than in any other utopian revision of democratic theory.

Objections to Utopian Democratic Theory

The utopianism of the above and similar utopian democratic theorists, who have tried to give a perfectionist, fundamentally socialist, quasi-anarchist content to democratic theory, is exhibited primarily, in most instances, by some combination of the following five characteristics. These characteristics are (1) naive assumptions about men and women, and their actual and potential behaviour, (2) a neglect of the consequences of the political activity which is intended to achieve egalitarian, libertarian and populist projects, (3) the basing of political and other objectives on abstract moral and other philosophic analyses rather than on psychological, social and political realities, (4) giving one or more favoured values an absolute status, and (5) assuming that greater participation by voters in government will radically improve their political skills, and their judgement and other political virtues, thus making them incorruptible and impervious to manipulation.

For utopian democrats, it is the dominant economic classes and non-leftist elites of democratic nations, and their political parties who are the source of the political opportunism, incompetence, corruption of democratic institutions and other deficiencies of contemporary representative democracies. The citizens on whose votes and acquiescence democratic political practice depends, by contrast, are considered to be victims rather than actors. They are victims, however, who are regarded as a latent force with the potential, once it is unleashed, to make their societies conform to the values and goals of the utopian democrats. Little attention is paid by the utopian democrats to the inevitability of new elites, and to the likelihood of the opportunities brought about by popular power being seized not only by the most fanatical and power-hungry of egalitarian and populist demagogues but by nationalist, racist and other extreme-right individuals and groups also skilled at operating in the institutions of popular participation. The apparent conviction of the utopian democrats that the social and political transformations they propose can be achieved peacefully and by means of democratic procedures displays, at best, a dangerous naivety. They seem unaware that should their projects go beyond their university rooms and conferences, they would destroy the trust which makes possible agreement on constitutional and other conventions, stable compromises on the limits of policy and a peaceful politics. Indeed, on the issue of the scale of the opposition to their projects and how the opposition should be confronted, the utopian democrats may be less ruthless than the anarcho-communists and Marxists of the past but they are also less plausible. The classical anarchists and Marxists were at least aware of the revolutionary nature and implications of their ideas, and the hostility and resistance they would encounter.

The abstract moral-philosophic character of utopian democracy and its indifference to political realities received one of their clearest statements in the Introduction to Carol C. Gould's utopian democratic text, *Rethinking Democracy* (1988).

> This book proposes a fundamental rethinking of the theory of democracy. It presents the philosophical foundations of a theory that argues that democratic decision-making not only should apply to politics but should be extended to economic and social life as well. I offer a normative argument for the right of participation in decision-making in all these domains....I develop an argument concerning the pre-eminent value of the freedom of individuals and their equal right to the conditions of self-development....On the basis of these various philosophical considerations, I go on to propose concrete forms of social and economic institutions that would serve to realize the philosophical principles (pp. 1-2).

Present day democratic societies, which rest on the electoral support and tacit consent of citizens, are to be reorganised, Gould proposes, not because of the felt political and social needs of their members but in order to make them conform to conclusions drawn from her philosophic analyses of favoured values. Her book provides a classic example of what Anthony Quinton (1993) - in following Edmund Burke's, 1790, denunciation of French Jacobinism - described as 'abstract political theory'.

> Abstract political theory starts from certain propositions about ends, typically about the universal rights of man or the supreme political values, and proposes, usually in a fairly simple-minded way, means to those ends. A utopia is a conception of society in which those ends are fully realized (p. 255).

Such abstract political theory and the drawing of political conclusions from privileged values was found in the work of Bachrach (popular sovereignty and economic equality), Pateman (popular participation), Arblaster (popular power), Burnheim (self government) and Philip Green (social and political equality). In common with Carol Gould, these writers forget that, whereas in philosophic analysis it is appropriate to press sets of ideas to their limits, in political practice, and in political theories intended to guide it, it is necessary to seek compromises and reconciliations. In a democratic theory which is intended to influence political practice, whatever the strength of an author's convictions, he or she is obliged to respect and to seek reconciliations with opposed assumptions and goals. Similarly, movements which express interests and promote causes, if they are to participate in a peaceful politics, must respect and be willing to compromise with opposed movements.

A different version of abstract political theory from that of Gould characterises the branch of utopian democratic theory in which it is praxis, the activity of a class, mass movement or the democratic process itself that is made the solution to political and other human problems. This has been a part of the work of Macpherson, Pateman, Bachrach and Arblaster. An even clearer and more pronounced example of it, however, is Benjamin R. Barber's *Strong Democracy* (1984). Barber, in a typically utopian-democratic fashion, sharply separates democracy from liberalism, and contends that liberalism is the source of the ailments of modern democracies. But, instead of grounding his 'strong' democratic alternative on a few supreme values, as Gould does, he takes a value-relativist stand and follows the young Karl Marx in denying that there are supreme values separable from the social and political 'praxis' by which they are created. In place of Marx's proletarian revolution, however, Barber turns to the participatory democratic process of utopian democracy. This democratic process is made the solution not only to perceived theoretical and practical political problems but to what have hitherto been thought of as epistemological and other philosophic problems. 'Strong democracy', he tells us, substitutes 'the politics of process for prepolitical and preconceptual meaning' (p. 158).

> When politics in the participatory mode becomes the source of political knowledge - when such knowledge is severed from formal philosophy and becomes its own epistemology - then knowledge itself is redefined in terms of the chief virtues of [strong] democratic politics. Where politics describes a sovereign realm, political knowledge is autonomous and independent of abstract grounds. Where politics describes a realm of action, political knowledge is applied or practical and can be portrayed as praxis....[Such] political knowledge is provisional and flexible over time....[And it is] communal and consensual rather than either subjective (the product of private senses or of private reason) or objective (existing independently of individual wills) (p. 167).

Barber does not take the Gould route of making freedom, equality, a right to self development, justice or any other conceptually developed value supreme; supremacy is reserved for the praxis of the democratic process, a praxis which is made immune against reasoning and knowledge that differ from those produced by his proposed democratic process.[11]

---

11 The concrete proposals, mainly for the United States, which constitute Barber's (1984) praxis and his strong democratic process, include 'a national system of neighborhood assemblies of from one to five thousand citizens....a national civic communications cooperative to regulate and oversee the civic use of new telecommunications technology and to supervise debate and discussion of referendum issues....experiments in decriminalization and informal lay justice by an engaged local citizenry....a program of universal citizen service, including a military service option for all citizens....[and the] public support of experiments in workplace democracy, with public institutions as

In their different ways both Gould and Barber demonstrate the utopian-democratic failure to understand the differences between philosophy and politics. They seem unaware that whereas philosophy is a theoretical undertaking concerned primarily with truth, democratic politics is a practical activity which should be concerned with achieving the best possible life for the members of a community. It is true of course that politics and philosophy should assist each other, and that philosophic analysis is necessary for the clarification and criticism of political assumptions and goals. Nevertheless it is a fallacy to think that philosophy can be substituted for politics or politics for philosophy. But whereas Gould and other utopian democrats hope to deduce the solutions to political problems from philosophy, Barber sees politics as the solution to epistemological and other philosophic problems.

Utopian democrats remind us, and rightly so, that democratic government entails ideals, norms, and the right and duty of citizens to contribute to the government of their nations. But they forget that the ideals and norms of one part of the community, including those of left-wing intellectuals and militants, must be reconciled with those of opposed groups. Modern democracy is a project for self government by citizens on the basis of laws, institutions and established conventions and practices to which the consent of all sections of a political community is required; it is not a project for the abolition of capitalism or other revolutionary change by means of mass participation. Where an economy is predominantly capitalist, private or corporate, or a mixture of capitalism, corporatism, socialism or anything else, and there is no consensus on departing from it, then it has to remain as the economic infrastructure for political life. Individuals and groups are of course entitled to advocate revolutionary change; but it is irresponsible and confusing to advertise it as the last word in democratic theory and practice.

A democratic politics which rests on consent rather than on coercion, either that of the state or the power of numbers, requires that, as far as possible, policies, goals and projects be subjected to practical experience and empirical inquiry, and that acceptable and rational compromises be found. Compromises on ends and means are not so much an imperfection for a democratic community as a condition for its existence - which is not to say that all compromises are to be welcomed. In democratic theory as in democratic practice, a place has to be found for all the values and ends of citizens that are compatible with democratic government. This means not only the leftist values of the utopians but such countervailing ones as authority, law, order, constitutionalism,

---

models for economic alternatives' (p. 307). Capital letters have been removed from parts of the quotation.

consideration for minorities, and private-property and other individual rights. The professed commitment of utopian democrats to democracy, therefore, is undermined by their determination to brand as anti-democratic and to use democratic institutions to conduct a relentless struggle against the liberties and rights which obstruct the political realisation of their conceptions of democratic perfection.

Whereas political and public philosophers expect to find gaps between ideals and reality, between theory and practice, and between the standards which should guide politics and the interests which do - which does not mean that they think that the gaps should not be narrowed - utopian democrats propose to close the gaps by turning democratic government into an agency for radical, leftist, social reconstruction. Partly via the writings of the young Karl Marx, the utopian democrats have introduced into democratic theory the left-Hegelian conceptions of philosophy as subversive social criticism and of politics as the realisation of philosophy. The utopian democrats have thus brought to democratic theory the problems which have bedevilled Marxist and other revolutionary movements of the left.[12]

If democratic theorists and other citizens are to understand not only democracy's potential for enabling people to lead fulfilling lives but the dangers that always accompany democratic politics, then they must distinguish between democracy and utopia. Once it is realised that democratic institutions and values do not imply a quest for political and social perfection, or a classless, socialist commonwealth untarnished by elites, then a great deal becomes clear. If democracy is not utopia but closer to Aristotle's mixed regime, or the system of government with the fewest evils (Winston Churchill's frequently quoted view[13]), then democratic theory's primary tasks consist of clarifying and helping to solve the normative and other problems of modern democratic nations, warning against dangers, including the taking of democratic ideas to utopian or other extremes, and providing guiding standards for governments and citizens. Democratic theory thus becomes a public philosophy and ceases to be a monopoly of utopian democrats, behavioural political scientists, neo-elite

---

12 For an inquiry into modern revolutions in which it is argued that, since the American War of Independence and the founding of the United States, revolutionary movements have become increasingly unsuccessful because of their utopianism, that is the determination of revolutionaries to create new, more perfect societies rather than concentrate on establishing improved political institutions, see Hannah Arendt (1973).

13 Churchill's view was given to the House of Commons, and reported in *Hansard*, November 11, 1947: 'No one pretends that democracy is perfect or all wise. Indeed it has been said that democracy is the worst form of government, except all those other forms that have been tried from time to time' (quoted in Linz, 1997, p. 132).

theorists or any other group of thinkers. It becomes partly a contribution to and partly an area of public discourse and debate open to political philosophers, social scientists, political actors and other citizens who wish to participate in clarifying and overcoming the problems and difficulties of modern democratic government.

Such a public-philosophic democratic theory is not an ideological or conservative contrivance for legitimating a status quo and its privileged beneficiaries. Unlike the formalist, ideological branches of democratic theory, it is a political irritant which questions and challenges the possessors of power and privilege. But it avoids the utopian temptation. It censures democracies not for falling short of the communism of the young Marx, Kropotkin's anarchism or the nostrums of other utopians, but for neglecting the principles which make modern constitutional and representative democracy, for all its imperfections, superior to other possible systems of government for modern nations. It is to democratic theorists in this public philosophic tradition, who have sought a middle way between and an alternative to ideological and utopian democratic theory, that the Part II chapters turn.

References

Arblaster, Anthony (1984), *The Rise and Decline of Western Liberalism*, Blackwell, Oxford.
Arblaster, Anthony and Steven Lukes (eds) (1971), *The Good Society: A Book of Readings*, Methuen, London.
Arendt, Hannah (1973), *On Revolution*, 3rd edn, Penguin Books, Harmondsworth.
Bachrach, Peter (1969), *The Theory of Democratic Elitism: A Critique* 2nd edn, Univ. of London Pr., London.
Barber, Benjamin R. (1984), *Strong Democracy: Participatory Politics for a New Age*, Univ. of California Pr., Berkeley.
Beer, Max (1957), *The General History of Socialism and Social Struggles*, Russell and Russell, New York.
Belz, Herman (1974), 'New Left Reverberations in the Academy', *Review of Politics*, vol. 36, 1974, pp. 265-83.
Berlin, Isaiah (1990), *The Crooked Timber of Humanity*, John Murray, London, 1990.
Berlin, Isaiah and Bernard Williams (1994), 'Pluralism and Liberalism: a Reply', *Political Studies*, vol. 42, pp. 306-9.
Burnham, James (1965), *Suicide of the West*, 2nd edn, Cape, London.
Burnheim, John (1985), *Is Democracy Possible?: The Alternative to Electoral Politics*, Polity Pr., Cambridge.
Chambers Twentieth Century Dictionary (1973), (ed.) A.M. Macdonald, 2nd edn, Chambers, Edinburgh.
Cohn, Norman (1970), *The Pursuit of the Millenium*, 2nd edn, Temple Smith, London.

Cohn-Bendit, Gabriel and Daniel (1969), *Obsolete Communism: The Left Wing Alternative*, 2nd edn, Penguin Books, Harmondsworth.
Cranston, Maurice W. (ed.) (1970), *The New Left: Six Critical Essays*, Bodley Head, London.
Crowder, George (1991), *Classical Anarchism: The Political Thought of Godwin, Proudhon, Bakunin and Kropotkin*, Clarendon Pr., Oxford.
Crowder, George (1994), 'Pluralism and Liberalism', *Political Studies*, vol. 42, pp. 293-305.
Crowder, George (1998), 'John Gray's Pluralist Critique of Liberalism', *Journal of Applied Philosophy*, vol. 15, pp. 290-8.
Davis, J.C. (1984), 'The History of Utopia...', in Peter Alexander and Roger Gill (eds), *Utopias*, Duckworth, London.
Dunn, John (1974), 'Review Article: Democracy Unretrieved, or the Political Theory of Professor Macpherson', *British Journal of Political Science*, vol. 4, pp. 489-99.
Eidelberg, Paul (1969), 'The Temptation of Herbert Marcuse', *Review of Politics*, vol. 31, pp. 442-58.
Georghegan, Vincent (1987), *Utopianism and Marxism*, Methuen, London.
Goldman, Emma (1969), *Anarchism and Other Essays* [1919], 3rd edn, reprinted, Dover, New York.
Gombin, Richard (1975), *The Origins of Modern Leftism*, Penguin Books, Harmondsworth.
Gould, Carol C. (1988), *Rethinking Democracy*, Cambridge Univ. Pr., Cambridge.
Gray, John (1995), *Isaiah Berlin*, Harper Collins, London.
Green, Philip (1985), *Retrieving Democracy: In Search of Civic Equality*, Methuen, London.
Lasky, Melvin J. (1977), *Utopia and Revolution*, 2nd edn, Macmillan, London.
Levitas, Ruth (1990), *The Concept of Utopia*, Philip Allan, New York.
Linz, Juan J. (1997), 'Democracy Today: An Agenda for Students of Democracy', *Scandinavian Political Studies*, vol. 20, pp. 115-32.
Lukes, Steven (1977), 'Relativism: Cognitive and Moral', in *Essays in Social Theory*, Macmillan, London.
Lukes, Steven (1984), 'Marxism and Utopianism', in Peter Alexander and Roger Gill (eds), *Utopias*, Duckworth, London.
Lukes, Steven (1993), 'Five Fables about Human Rights', in Stephen Shute and Susan Hurley (eds), *On Human Rights*, Basic Books/Harper Collins, New York.
MacIntyre, Alasdair (1970), *Marcuse*, Collins/Fontana, London.
Macpherson, C.B. (1966), *The Real World of Democracy*, Clarendon Press, Oxford.
Macpherson, C.B. (1973), *Democratic Theory: Essays in Retrieval*, Clarendon Pr., Oxford.
Macpherson, C.B. (1977), *The Life and Times of Liberal Democracy*, Oxford Univ. Pr., Oxford.
Macpherson, C.B. (1989), 'Do We Need a Theory of the State?', in Graeme Duncan (ed.), *Democracy and the Capitalist State*, Cambridge Univ. Pr., Cambridge.
Mannheim, Karl (1936), *Ideology and Utopia*, Routledge, London.
Manuel, Frank E. and Fritzie P. (1979), *Utopian Thought in the Western World*, Harvard Univ. Pr., Cambridge, Mass.

Mises, Ludwig von (1951), *Socialism: An Economic and Sociological Analysis* [1922], 4th Eng. edn, Yale Univ. Pr., New Haven.
Molnar, Thomas (1972), *Utopia: The Perennial Heresy*, Tom Stacey, London.
Niebuhr, Reinhold (1941 and 1943), *The Nature and Destiny of Man*, 2 vols., Scribner, New York.
Niebuhr, Reinhold (1960), *The Children of Light and the Children of Darkness* [1944], 2nd edn, Scribner, New York.
Oglesby, Carl (ed.) (1969), *The New Left Reader*, Grove Press, New York.
Panitch, Leo (1981), 'Liberal Democracy and Socialist Democracy: The Antinomies of C. B. Macpherson', in Ralph Miliband and John Saville (eds), *The Socialist Register 1981*, Merlin Pr., London.
Pateman, Carole (1970), *Participation in Democratic Theory*, Cambridge Univ. Pr., Cambridge.
Popper, Karl R. (1963), 'Utopia and Violence' [1948], in *Conjectures and Refutations*, Routledge, London.
Quinton, Anthony (1993), 'Conservatism', in Robert E. Goodin and Philip Pettit (eds), *A Companion to Contemporary Political Philosophy*, Blackwell, Oxford.
Rand, Ayn (1971), *The New Left: The Anti-Industrial Revolution*, New American Library/Signet, New York.
Sartori, Giovanni (1987), *The Theory of Democracy Revisited*, 2 vols, Chatham House, New Jersey.
Shatz, Marshall S. (ed.) (1972), *The Essential Works of Anarchism*, Quadrangle Books, New York.
Shklar, Judith (1957), *After Utopia: the Decline of Political Faith*, Princeton Univ. Pr., Princeton.
Teodori, Massimo (ed.) (1970), *The New Left: A Documentary History*, Cape, London.
Tucker, Robert C. (1972), *The Marx-Engels Reader*, Norton, New York.
Voegelin, Eric (1974), 'Liberalism and Its History', *Review of Politics*, vol. 36, pp. 504-19.
Walzer, Michael (1980), *Radical Principles*, Basic Books, New York.
Webster's New Collegiate Dictionary (1977), (ed.) Henry Bosley Woolf, 5th edn, Merriam, Springfield, Mass.
Wiggershaus, Rolf (1994), *The Frankfurt School: Its History, Theories and Political Significance* [1986], first Eng. edn, MIT Pr., Cambridge, Mass.
Wood, Ellen Meikins (1981), 'Liberal Democracy and Capitalist Hegemony...', in Ralph Miliband and John Saville (eds), *The Socialist Register 1981*, Merlin Pr., London.
Yack, Bernard (1986), *The Longing for Total Revolution: Philosophic Sources of Social Discontent from Rousseau to Marx and Nietzsche*, Princeton Univ. Pr., Princeton.
Yack, Bernard (1993), *The Problems of a Political Animal: Community, Justice and Conflict in Aristotelean Political Thought*, Univ. of California Pr., Berkeley.
Young, Nigel (1977), *An Infantile Disorder?: The Crisis and Decline of the New Left*, Routledge, London.

PART II
DEMOCRATIC THEORY AS PUBLIC PHILOSOPHY

Behind the sovereign and his protection of legal rights must always stand the might of the people, which can be bound by no law and must be, as Aristotle said, based upon the justice inherent in the people themselves, and upon their recognition and performance of their duties....Such freedom can be permanently secured in no other way than...in the education of the citizens of a state in the ideals and methods and duties of ruling and being ruled in turn like freemen for the sake of the good life of the whole.

C. H. McIlwain,
Constitutionalism and the Changing World, 1939

In those days [1900] we had a real political democracy led by a hierarchy of statesmen and not a fluid mass distracted by newspapers. There was a structure in which statesmen, electors and the press all played their part.

Winston Churchill,
My Early Life, 1930

The political problem of mankind is to combine three things: economic efficiency, social justice, and individual liberty.

John Maynard Keynes,
Essays in Persuasion, 1931

5 Walter Lippmann's Call for and Contribution to a Public Philosophy

This chapter, the first of four on the nineteenth- and twentieth-century public philosophic tradition of democratic theory, introduces the tradition by means of a sympathetic but critical examination of Walter Lippmann's *Essays in the Public Philosophy* (1955), and a review of his other work as an outstanding twentieth-century democratic theorist. Although it is argued that his book provides a first-class account of the character and functions of a public philosophy, I express some major reservations about a central feature of his account, partly by appealing to his own work as a democratic theorist and public philosopher.

Lippmann, who advocated a public philosophy in which citizens and their governments shared common standards, defined the public philosophy in terms of *natural law*, by which he meant objective and discoverable moral rules and political standards. His conception of a public philosophy, therefore, mixed together two different issues, and it separated Lippmann from many potential supporters. This was because the main part of his argument for a public philosophy, that modern democratic government requires both political elites and citizens to understand the necessary conditions and support the fundamental principles for sustaining their political communities, does not entail his other proposition that only the natural law tradition can supply such an understanding and principles. This conflation of different issues was unnecessary as well as confusing as it is possible for both natural law theorists and critics of natural law to cooperate as democratic theorists in clarifying and developing standards, and confronting the challenges to modern democratic government.

One curious result of Lippmann's combining of the call for a public philosophy with the urging of a revival of natural law was that it not only downgraded the work of Alexis de Tocqueville, John Stuart Mill and other seminal writers on democratic government from outside of the natural law tradition but it devalued his own contributions to democratic theory. The implication of his *Essays in the Public Philosophy* (1955) was that, in order to understand the norms which should guide modern democracies, it was necessary to turn not to writers who had systematically examined modern democratic politics but to Plato, St Thomas Aquinas, Edward Coke,

William Blackstone and other pre-nineteenth-century philosophers and jurists, praised by Lippmann, who had no knowledge of industrialised societies with universal adult voting. It was this natural-law feature of his (1955) *Essays* which allowed critics to dismiss them as an exercise in nostalgia. But before examining these essays, as they marked a turning point in Lippmann's thinking about modern democratic government, it is necessary to know something about the man and the evolution of his thought.

Life and Thought

Walter Lippmann was born in 1889, in New York, where he grew up in a cultivated family of German-Jewish origin. His father was a prosperous clothing manufacturer who retired young; his mother was a university graduate. Walter's university education was at Harvard, from 1906 to 1910, where, after graduating, he stayed for a year's postgraduate study and teaching. While at Harvard he formed friendships with three teachers who were among the leading thinkers of the day: William James, George Santayana and Graham Wallas. Lippmann could have embarked on a university career but, as in later life, he preferred journalism and independent scholarship. In 1914, prior to wartime service, he helped to found the *New Republic*, becoming one of its first editors. During the war, after serving as a wartime propagandist with the American army in France, he joined the staff of Edward Mandell (Colonel) House, an adviser and friend of President Woodrow Wilson. As a member of Colonel House's staff, he helped to prepare Wilson's Fourteen Points and, at the end of the war, he attended the Versailles Peace Conference.

Later, Lippmann joined the editorial staff and, from 1921, directed the editorial page of the New York *World*, a popular daily newspaper which combined muck-raking, sensational news reporting with intellectually demanding editorials. From 1931 to 1962 he wrote the New York *Herald Tribune*'s internationally respected 'Today and Tomorrow' columns, more or less signed editorials which were syndicated and published throughout the United States. The *Herald Tribune*, which was conservative and Republican, allowed Lippmann to express contrary views. In the 1960s he wrote for *Newsweek,* and gave several much acclaimed television interviews. From the end of the 1930s to 1967 he lived in Washington, where he mixed with leading politicians. He was personally acquainted with practically every American president from Theodore Roosevelt to Lyndon Johnson, and was consulted by Franklin Roosevelt, John Kennedy and - until Lippmann's opposition to the war against North Vietnam - Lyndon Johnson. Lippmann, however, was always scrupulous about maintaining his independence. From the 1920s to the 1960s he was probably the most respected political writer in the United States, influencing both policy makers and public opinion. He died at the end of 1974.[1]

On leaving Harvard, where he had been an active member and president of its Socialist Club, although he remained a member of the American Socialist Party until about 1915, he became increasingly sceptical about socialism, transferring his determination to promote social improvement to Theodore Roosevelt's Progressive Party. In his first books, *A Preface to Politics*, 1913, and *Drift and Mastery*, 1914, he urged that forceful and imaginative political leaders should be aware of breakthroughs in the natural and social sciences, including the work of Freud, and should utilise the expertise of the new scientific-minded intelligentsia to reconstruct their nations. America's political leaders were urged to look to the future rather than cling to the past; welcome the growth of industry; remedy the grievances of the labouring classes; cooperate with feminist and other progressive movements; and seek a middle way between market capitalism and socialism. Intellectuals should support political leaders with such goals by keeping them informed of scientific discoveries and assisting in the political education of citizens.

But by the 1920s, Lippmann's youthful optimism about social progress had given way to a pessimism about American and Western civilisation, and their democratic and other institutions. He had been shaken by the First World War's destructiveness, wartime propaganda, the confusion and irresponsibility of the negotiators and reporters at Versailles, the vindictiveness of the Versailles peace treaty, Bolshevik power in Russia, and the European post-war crises that preceded and followed Mussolini's 1922 seizure of power. Barbarism, he concluded, was an ever present danger which could take novel forms. His fears gave him new concerns, primarily the immaturity of voters, and the exploitation of their immaturity by irresponsible journalists and unscrupulous politicians.

---

1   Ronald Steel's *Walter Lippmann and the American Century* (1980), the most detailed of the Lippmann biographies, is informative on Lippmann's journalism and methods of work. But as its discussions of Lippmann's more ambitious political books, apart from those on American foreign policy, are far from exhaustive, the earlier biographies are still worth consulting. See, for example, those by Larry L. Adams (1977); John Luskin (1972); E. L. and F. H. Schapsmeier (1969); and Charles Wellborn (1969). For a novel, by a friend of Lippmann's, which was loosely based on his life, see Louis Auchincloss, *The House of the Prophet* (1980). For a collection of essays on Lippmann, see Marquis Childs and James Reston (1959); and for a collection of Lippmann's correspondence, with a substantial Introduction, John Morton Blum (1985).

Lippmann's pessimism and new concerns were expressed in two pioneering studies of the press, public opinion and voting behaviour: *Public Opinion* (1960), first published in 1922, and *The Phantom Public* (1925). Both books articulated his doubts that twentieth century voters possessed the good sense on which Jefferson, Madison and other founders of the American republic had relied, and the qualities to which Lippmann and other pre-1914 progressives had appealed. The root of the problem, he argued, was the complexity of twentieth century politics. Even the best intentioned of journalists and politicians had to oversimplify, substituting stereotypes for careful analyses, while the judgements of even well-educated people preceded rather than followed the evidence. As a consequence, political consent was manufactured rather than genuine.

> In the life of the generation now in control of affairs, persuasion has become a self-conscious art and a regular organ of popular government....the knowledge of how to create consent will alter every political calculation and modify every political premise (1960, p. 248).

John Dewey, who was among the many commentators to praise Lippmann's path-breaking studies, wrote that *Public Opinion* was 'perhaps the most effective indictment of democracy as currently conceived ever penned' (in Steel, p. 183). Lippmann's scepticism about the ability of people to construct reliable pictures of the political world led to different emphases from his earlier calls for inspired leadership. His 1920s recommendations were that policy making be separated from expert advice; that throughout society greater use be made of experts, who should make impartiality their vocation; and that journalists, by raising the standards of their profession, prevent the freedom of the press from corrupting democratic government.

It was not until Franklin Roosevelt's 1932 presidential victory and the early years of the New Deal that Lippmann's optimism about the possibility, in constitutional democracies, of citizen support for firm, decisive leadership was rekindled. By the mid 1930s, however, to the chagrin of many of his friends, Lippmann became hostile to Roosevelt and the New Deal. He thought that not only had Germany and the Soviet Union become militarist, despotic dictatorships, and that another world war was inevitable, but that the United States and other democracies were jeopardising vital principles. Civilised, constitutional, liberal and democratic standards were being abandoned by politicians, business and other practical men, and a majority of the intellectuals as well as most voters. Roosevelt's 1936 threat to pack the Supreme Court was seen by Lippmann not as an aberration on the part of the President and his advisers but as evidence of what he called a 'derangement' in American and Western political life.

Lippmann's mid-1930s thinking was set forth in *The Good Society* (1943), first published in 1936, his most comprehensive study of modern democratic society and politics. By the *good society* was meant a combination of constitutional and other law; the individual freedoms and divisions of labour of modern capitalism; and the liberal and democratic rights which had triumphed in the nineteenth century. Lippmann held that, in addition to being threatened by Communist and National Socialist dictatorships, the good society was being undermined, partly by undisciplined masses and partly by the political elites of Western nations who were repudiating its traditions. The *Good Society* (1943) also contained, in the concept of a *higher law*, a foreshadowing of the view that democracy depended upon Western civilisation's natural law traditions.

For many of Lippmann's admirers he was not only an outstanding political journalist but a leading political philosopher and the century's most probing analyst of democratic politics; for his critics, however, his work did not justify the assurance with which it was written. Several have considered it vague and irrelevant to modern conditions, little more than a cry of despair about modern society and politics. Benjamin F. Wright (1973), for example, has argued that, far from Lippmann's work being consistent let alone profound, it contained at least five distinct public or political philosophies, the only common feature of which was their having the same author.[2] Lippmann's replies to the charge of inconsistency appealed to common sense. His changes of mind, he suggested, were products of his attention to the politics of a turbulent century, and his acquiring of greater understanding. In a 1949 letter, he wrote,

> I might make one suggestion that you may find useful if you undertake to study the work of any...man who lives through a troubled period in history. It is that no one is born with a full and clear knowledge of his times, nor with a doctrine that answers all the problems of his times and that, therefore, every human career can be studied most interestingly not by the criterion of how a man has departed from the ideas he held when he was young, but by the criterion of what he has learned by experience as he grew older. You may even find in your own life work that if you continue to search for truth, you will not end where you began (in Blum, 1984, p. 16).

---

2 Another commentator to find contradictions in Lippmann's thought is Arthur M. Schlesinger, Jr. (1959). Studies which find an underlying consistency in his thought include Adams (1977); and D. Steven Blum (1984). Steel (1980) simply documents many of Lippmann's shifts and changes of mind.

Lippmann was a public philosopher who, in his 'Today and Tomorrow' and other newspaper and magazine articles, wrote in a non-philosophic language for a wide readership, bringing political principles and a philosophically literate mind to clarifying, interpreting and responding to political events and trends. The quality of his work has been well summarised by Steven Blum (1984). Lippmann, Blum has written,

> viewed the arena of practical politics as his 'laboratory' and used the insights gained from his involvement with the news to probe beneath and beyond the headlines. He tackled enduring political and moral controversies in an unaffected idiom, accessible to the general educated reader....Lippmann served the ends of philosophy well, demonstrating ably that serious political speculation need not be the preserve of academic specialists, need not have a hearing in the classroom alone (pp. 10-11).

Lippmann's Analysis of the Public Philosophy

Walter Lippmann's *Essays in the Public Philosophy* (1955) advocated, as a guiding theory for democratic nations, a public philosophy which had four principal features. The first (my order of exposition) was that, as no civilised, democratic society could sustain itself and prosper unless its citizens understood and supported the principles embedded in their political institutions and practices, a public philosophy had the task of sustaining these basic political principles. Beliefs about indispensable principles, Lippmann contended, should not be looked on as private matters. Politicians, journalists, teachers and other intellectuals were obliged to ensure that fundamental principles were upheld, cultivated and passed from one generation to the next.

Second, the public philosophy, which was the product and responsibility of participants in governmental and political life, on the one hand, and scholars, journalists and other intellectuals and concerned citizens on the other, mediated between political theory and political practice, and between the community and its political leaders. Such mediation was a necessary condition for good government which, for Lippmann, meant maintaining law and order; achieving effective political opposition and the peaceful replacement of one government by another; ensuring that legislation, policy making and other governmental activity were rational, consistent and comprehensible; and discouraging unrealistic expectations and demands. From the days of ancient Greece and Rome, he maintained, Western societies, when at their best, had possessed a public philosophy of this kind which encouraged good government, and which rulers and their advisers, and politically powerful groups and individuals, even the more irresponsible and reckless, were compelled to respect and be moderated by - even when they departed from its norms.

Third, the public philosophy affirmed that in constitutional states, as distinct from tyrannies and despotisms, their members had moral and political obligations, as far as their capacities and situation allowed, to uphold and nurture the laws and institutions of their states as well as to improve themselves and their communities. On the basis of this combination of moral principle and political realism, Lippmann distinguished the public philosophy from *Jacobinism*, a term he applied not just to the doctrines of the original Jacobins but to subsequent anarchist, Marxist, technocratic and other revolutionary dogmas. Lippmann, in fact, used the term *Jacobinism* similarly to how *utopianism* is used in this book. Jacobin doctrines, for Lippmann, differed from the public philosophy in their assumption that, by means of some brew of technology, economic growth, political struggle and legislation, it was possible to expel poverty, ignorance, vice and other imperfections from human life. By contrast, the public philosophy did not seek final solutions to human problems by reconstructing politics and society; it sought stable and just standards for going from one temporary solution to another in what would always be imperfect societies. Adherents to the public philosophy fought against hardship and injustice; but they did not delude themselves with notions of complete victories.

Fourth, the public philosophy for Western nations was considered by Lippmann to be dependent on if not synonymous with natural-law traditions of political thought. These were traditions which maintained that humans could discover natural (beneficial) and unnatural (harmful) ways of life for themselves and their communities, a knowledge of which supplied objective standards for the conduct of personal and political life. Lippmann contended that without the natural law belief that evidence, reason, practical experience and/or revelation could yield the political knowledge and objective standards by which to live, neither a public philosophy nor a civilised democratic or other society could be secured.

> The public philosophy is known as *natural law*.... This philosophy is the premise of the institutions of the Western society, and they are, I believe, unworkable in communities that do not adhere to it. Except on the premises of this philosophy, it is impossible to reach intelligible and workable conceptions of popular election, majority rule, representative assemblies, free speech, loyalty, property, corporations and voluntary associations. The founders of these institutions, which the recently enfranchised democracies have inherited, were all of them adherents of some one of the various schools of natural law (1955, pp. 79-80).

Natural law styles of thought, Lippmann argued, had prevailed among the citizens and rulers of ancient Greece and Rome, medieval Europe and, prior to the end of the nineteenth century, modern Europe. But in his account of natural law, Lippmann tended to obscure the differences between (1) natural law theories which rested on Christian or other theist belief, and (2) Stoic, Roman-law, modern natural-right and other conceptions of natural law which appealed to philosophic and other reason, and to political prudence and wisdom. For Lippmann, however, what counted was that both 'naturalists and supernaturalists' agreed 'that there was a valid law which, whether it was the commandment of God or the reason of things, was transcendent....It was there objectively, not subjectively. It can be discovered. It has to be obeyed' (1955, p. 133).

But, Lippmann argued, during the nineteenth century the public philosophy and its natural law foundations had been undermined by cultural and intellectual trends, a major cause of which was the materialism of Western men and women, their unwillingness to believe in anything intangible. In the twentieth century these materialist and sceptical attitudes had been furthered by the positivist dogma that anything that was not reducible to empirically tested hypotheses or deductions from them was merely a personal preference. A culture permeated by such scepticism about values, Lippmann believed, could not sustain a public philosophy. Without a moral and cultural renaissance, and a philosophic counter-attack against crude positivist and other value scepticism, there could be no public philosophy. Lippmann saw his books and much of the journalism of the last decades of his life as contributing to a counter-attack and, ideally, a renaissance.

The purpose of several of his (1955) essays on the problems of American and other democratic politics was to reestablish normative principles that could attract the support of thoughtful and well meaning people and a majority of voters, irrespective of their different religious, political and other affiliations. For example, towards the end of a discussion of private property as a system of rights and duties, considerable weight was put on the work of the eighteenth century jurist, Sir William Blackstone. Lippmann argued that Blackstone offered a superior natural law alternative to the later view that property was an absolute right. He wrote that the principles to which Blackstone appealed

> are the laws of a rational order of human society - in the sense that all men, when they are sincerely and lucidly rational, will regard them as self-evident. The rational order consists of the terms which must be met in order to fulfil men's capacity for the good life in the world. They are the terms of the widest consensus of rational men in a plural society.

They are the propositions to which all men concerned, if they are sincerely and lucidly rational, can be expected to converge. There could never be a consensus that Africa belongs to the descendants of Dutch settlers; a property system founded on that contention cannot be generally acceptable, and will generate disorder. The classical doctrine has a superior validity in that a system of property based upon it may obtain a consensus of support in the community, and would have the prospect of being workable (p. 95).

Lippmann's analyses of property rights, among other specific problems, and his appeal to Blackstone, therefore, led him to an idea which differed from the view that a public philosophy for democratic nations required natural law foundations. This other idea was that a public philosophy rested not so much on a past wisdom, or on objective moral and political rules, as on the fact that it could command the assent of a democratic people to intellectually defensible political norms that promoted the good life. In other words, even in culturally diverse, politically pluralist nations, where the natural law tradition was weak, and where there was a cynicism about the existence of objective values and standards, a rational and general agreement on the political needs of a community was possible.

Since the 1950s, although the problems of democratic government which concerned Lippmann have persisted and, as was noted in this book's Introduction, the idea of a public philosophy occasionally surfaces, Lippmann's *Essays in the Public Philosophy* have received little attention by either politicians or academic and other intellectuals. To the extent that the issues they raised are still debated, the debates are usually conducted under different headings, for example, *political culture*, *consensus*, *constitutionalism* and *justice*. But this neglect of Lippmann's central concept, the *public philosophy*, is unfortunate as it possesses distinctive features missed by other concepts.

But if a public philosophy as advocated by Lippmann is so fruitful an idea and so desperate a need for democratic government, why has there not been a greater positive response to Lippmann's attempt to revive it? A part of the answer is that Lippmann attached to his advocacy of a public philosophy ideas and positions which were more contestable. The main example is his insistence that the public philosophy depends on natural law assumptions. By making the public philosophy, in effect, a monopoly of natural law theorists, he discouraged cooperation with sceptics about natural law and people attached to different schools of thought. Another example was Lippmann's habit, both in the *Public Philosophy* (1955) and other work, to blame the voters of modern democracies for the decay of the public philosophy. He thought that pressure by mass electorates on governments and political elites had prevented Western governments from having consistent and responsible foreign policies, and economic and other internal policies. It was for this reason that, for the United States, he favoured constitutional changes to protect presidents and their administrations from pressure by voters and Congress. His work, therefore, sometimes displayed an elitism that suggested that liberal democracy was not the alternative to but a branch of Jacobinism. Such elitism implied that Lippmann's goal was not the extrication of democracy from Jacobin taints but the rolling back of democracy. If, however, democracy is seen not as a vehicle for Jacobinism but as the alternative to it - which as Lippmann acknowledged was how its American, British and other founders and major theorists perceived it - then a renewal of a public philosophy becomes a more realistic project than one which requires a return to natural law.

Natural law assumptions and theories thrived in pre-modern societies, before beliefs in the Judeo-Christian God and/or an ordered universe were debilitated by modern secularism. Natural-law political theory, particularly its medieval Christian versions, was also weakened by the Protestant Reformation's emphases on God's will rather than the orderliness of creation, and on the conscience of the believer rather than external authority. A practical problem for twentieth century, natural law and other theorists who challenge modernity's atheism, agnosticism, relativism and subjectivism, therefore, is that whatever the intellectual merits of their challenge it is unlikely that, in the foreseeable future, their views will become dominant. To identify the public philosophy with and to urge a return to natural law, it follows, is on a par with the belief that humanity's troubles would end if everyone were converted to the doctrines of a church or to some version of Kantian, utilitarian, communitarian or other secular humanism.

In practice, for a public philosophy for democratic nations to be effective, it has to obtain the support not only of natural law thinkers but of sceptics and critics of natural law. For societies that are culturally diverse and doctrinally pluralist, an effective public philosophy must therefore be philosophically neutral. Philosophical neutrality, however, does not mean that philosophic questions are of no consequence for politics and must be avoided, only that no school of philosophy be accorded a monopoly of wisdom, and that participation in a public philosophy be open to everyone. A public philosophy has political philosophic components; but, if it is to be of practical consequence for intellectually-pluralist democratic nations, it cannot and should not be the monopoly of any one school of political philosophy or other intellectual discipline. It should express standards to which people who have different religious, philosophic, political and other opinions are able to assent. The only possible basis for such a philosophically neutral public philosophy for modern democratic nations, therefore, is one which has the purpose of preserving, strengthening and improving their laws, institutions and associations, and maximising the opportunities of their citizens to achieve worthy and happy lives.

But this substitution of philosophic neutrality and a normative democratic theory for Lippmann's natural law as the theoretical foundation for a public philosophy does not mean that natural-law theory must be regarded as antipathetic to democratic theory and practice. In Chapter Eight, in fact, it will be argued that twentieth-century natural-law political philosophers have made important contributions to democratic theory as a public philosophy. The objection is not to natural law as such but to Lippmann's unnecessary and self-defeating attempt to make it the public philosophy for modern democratic nations. The remainder of this chapter will develop this conception of a philosophically neutral public philosophy for democratic nations by building upon Lippmann's own public philosophic contributions to democratic theory and practice. Many of these contributions were made in work in which natural law was less prominent than in his (1955) *Essays in the Public Philosophy*.

Lippmann as Democratic Theorist and Public Philosopher

Human Nature

Lippmann combined flexibility on immediate issues with a consistency in his concerns and the principles he applied to them. Among his permanent interests were human nature, the psychological and moral questions of how people, in their private and public lives, could achieve happiness and fulfilment - the ultimate purpose of political association - and the relevance of his findings to politics. For Lippmann, without an understanding of human instincts and passions, and of how they should be controlled and directed, it was impossible to understand modern or any other politics. His responses to these issues, however, were changeable. Whereas, in his pre-1914 books he emphasised the capacity of men and women to make and remake themselves and their world, the message of *A Preface to Morals* (1929), one of his most popular books, was more stoic. It was that under inevitably difficult circumstances people should seek maturity by disciplining and sublimating their instincts and desires, and confronting the complexities of modern life calmly and courageously. A quarter of a century later, in the *Public Philosophy* (1955), he advised that happiness could be achieved by supplementing material goals with the life of the mind. A part of the explanation for these different viewpoints was a tension in his thought: his sharing with George Santayana of a philosophic-idealist reverence for the life of the mind, and with William James a delight in personal relations and public concerns. Similarly, he always tried to balance the aristocratic inclinations he shared with Santayana with the democratic instincts he shared with James.

Despite, as he grew older, becoming increasingly sympathetic to the thought of pre-modern philosophers, Lippmann never forgot the insight in his first books that good government, and satisfactory individual and social lives required not only sound principles but an understanding of the distinctive features of twentieth century life. Serious thought and successful living required a knowledge of what had been unleashed in the modern world: science, technology and industrialisation; individual liberties; social and industrial divisions of labour; and social mobility, urbanisation, and population growth. For Lippmann, who constantly looked for new ideas, and was excited rather than repelled by technological and other innovation, the question was how the revolutionary forces of the modern world could be mastered. How were they to be made to serve human interests, and to enhance rather than cripple the lives of people, and their communities and associations? And a related question which was always prominent in his work was 'whether liberal democracy - the open society which rests on constitutional procedures - is or can ever again be a viable way of life' (Rossiter and Lare, p. xvi). None of these questions however, Lippmann thought, could be answered without an understanding of human potential and its limits.

Lippmann considered it a mistake to conceive of individual men and women solely in physical terms, maintaining that their mental lives, and their decisions and actions eluded theories of physical causation. The life of the individual was unique, and characterised by a freedom which made political liberties and rights indispensable for happiness and fulfilment. These ideas were at the heart of his political thought. 'How could you affirm', he asked,

> that freedom is better than tyranny if you are not able to affirm that it is the destiny of man's nature that he should be free? No one can prove the value of liberty by drawing up a balance sheet of profits and losses. If men do not understand that the origin of their liberties is in the nature of man, they will not really understand their liberties, nor learn to value their liberties until they have let them be destroyed ([1939] in Rossiter and Lare, p. 133).

The emphasis on freedom was accompanied by a similar stress on the need for self restraint. Lippmann became increasingly convinced that the rational restraint which made possible the all-round development of the citizen - the ideal of the ancient Greeks and Romans - was the proper end for modern Western civilisation, not quantitative conceptions of individual pleasure and social progress. Most modern notions of progress, he wrote, encouraged the belief that happiness was achieved by increasing and satisfying desires and wants. But, he objected,

> a philosophy which fails to insist upon the limitation of desire must make men forever unhappy - forever incapable of being satisfied....The true principle of action, long known but in our century not remembered, is that man is so constituted that his greatest need is not the satisfaction of his desires but that his reason shall impose law and order upon his desires....To pursue the good life, as described, for example, by Aristotle, is to cultivate not some but all the human dispositions by limiting each to a Golden Mean... ([1942] in Rossiter and Lare, pp. 165-6).

Capitalism Versus Socialism

A search for a mean also characterises Lippmann's writing on economic issues, especially those of capitalism versus socialism, and the market versus government control. The apparent differences in his opinions were the result, primarily, of different empirical assessments of the condition of the United States and other nations rather than unstable principles. Once Lippmann abandoned his youthful socialism, from the 1920s to the 1960s the fundamentals of his thinking on economic problems were consistent: he sought a synthesis of the best features of capitalism (its market freedoms) and of socialism (its recognition of the need for checks to the market in the interests of citizens and their communities and associations). A capitalist market and the freedom to make contracts on which it rested, along with its divisions of labour in factories, industries and nations, and its creation of a global economy were regarded as economically superior to socialist and other command economies. In addition, a capitalist market provided the economic underpinning for individual freedoms, for liberal democratic government and for modern civilisation (the good society). But, in contrast to many laissez-faire economists and liberals, Lippmann saw modern capitalism as dependent on constitutional and liberal-political foundations rather than vice versa. Not only was a market-capitalist economy impossible without a legal and constitutional system which guaranteed its freedoms and contracts, but, Lippmann argued, law and politics were crucial in shaping the type of culture on which a successful capitalist economy depended. It was, he contended, the failure by so many nineteenth-century liberal advocates of laissez-faire principles to realise the dependence of a capitalist economy on law and constitutionalism, and their transforming of laissez-faire principles from a practical guide to inviolable rights which provoked hostile reactions.

The search for a middle way between an unchecked market capitalism and a government dominated economy underlay Lippmann's mid-1930s opposition to Roosevelt's New Deal. Lippmann did not object to Roosevelt's strengthening of farmers, workers and other groups with weak bargaining positions, and to the administration's social insurance and other welfare policies; his worry was the New Deal's challenge to law - an indispensable condition for the rights of individuals, a prosperous economy and good government. Roosevelt's administrations, instead of respecting the Constitution and what it stood for, acted, Lippmann believed, as if they were establishing a collectivist dictatorship. The right and the duty of governments to intervene in the economy when necessary was being abused and its abuse was sapping the constitutional roots of the good society.

Linked to Lippmann's criticisms of the New Deal was the fact that, from the 1930s to the 1960s, he applied to economic issues a version of Keynesian economic theory to which he gave a colouring of his own. In 1934, in a lecture to a Harvard University audience, shortly after a visit to London when he met Keynes, he argued, a little simplistically, that the democratic state, by means of its taxation and spending policies, and control of interest rates, should

> counteract the mass errors of the individualist crowd by doing the opposite of what the crowd is doing; it saves when the crowd is spending too much; it economizes when the crowd is extravagant, and spends when the crowd is afraid to spend...it becomes an employer when there is no private employment, and it shuts down when there is work for all (in Steel, p. 308).

His was a Keynesianism, however, that was sensitive to the tension between economically interventionist government, on the one hand, and the legal and constitutional foundations of a liberal democratic civilisation on the other. The purposes of Keynesian and other interventions in the economy, for Lippmann, should not be a government controlled economy, electoral popularity or the appeasement of pressure groups but the strengthening of the market and the freedoms on which it rested, and the protection of people who, for no fault of their own, were the victims of economic change. Interventions by governments in economic life were both desirable and inevitable, but they had to be constrained by constitutional checks, responsible as well as expert advisers, and an effective public philosophy.

Political Culture

It followed from Lippmann's conviction that the good society, and its market and other freedoms depended on law and on a respect for law that democratic nations needed political and other cultural support. Indeed, practically everything he wrote could be discussed under the headings of *leadership, education* - in the widest sense of the word - and *citizenship*. Journalism and the press, not surprisingly, were considered a central and crucial part of modern politics and culture. Unless they met their responsibilities, social and political leadership and the education of the public would be dangerously inadequate. In 1960, he perceptively described the vocation of a serious and responsible political journalist as being 'what every sovereign citizen is supposed to do but has not the time or the interest to do for himself' (in Rossiter and Lare, p. 534). When discussing citizens and their duties, however, he was modest in his expectations. He thought it inevitable that in the post-1918 world most citizens would be ill-informed about political issues, ill-equipped to decide on matters of detail, and primarily concerned with their private lives; nevertheless citizens should at least be aware of broad political choices, possess a sense of justice, be restrained in their expectations, and support leaders who promoted the interests of their nations. Such modest political virtues are essential because, although the citizens of representative and constitutional democracies do not govern, they are the final political court of appeal, the source from which rulers are drawn, and, ultimately, the bearers of a political culture that either safeguards or threatens individual liberties and the good society.

But for voters to acquire citizenship qualities, crucial roles had to be performed by politicians, university and other educators, journalists and other intellectuals and members of the professions. When Lippmann despaired about democratic government, it was usually because of the self-centredness, incompetence and ever increasing disposition of political elites to flatter rather than educate voters. The temptations to which educators were drawn were to submit to the pressures of politicians, powerful local and national groups, and their students, and to fail to build upon and transmit the achievements of past generations. Likewise, public servants, lawyers and other professionals were easily tempted into putting personal advancement, easy options and monetary rewards before their obligations to their office and vocation. The temptation for journalists, press proprietors and managers was to amuse their readers rather than to encourage them to go beyond scandal and knee-jerk reactions to events.

The preference of voters and the political class in most democratic nations for soft options produced incompetent governments with no sense of state craft, while inept government pushed democratic societies on to a downward spiral. Governments, Lippmann wrote, 'are unable to cope with reality when elected assemblies and mass opinions become decisive in the state, when there are no statesmen to resist the inclination of the voters and there are only politicians to excite and exploit them' (1955, p. 42). Earlier, in *A Preface to Morals* (1929), the point was made in a comparison between politicians and statesmen: a

> capacity to act upon the hidden realities of a situation in spite of appearances is the essence of statesmanship. It consists of giving the people not what they want but what they will learn to want. It requires the courage which is possible only in a mind that is detached from the agitations of the moment (p. 283).

In 1931 he wrote that the

> enduring popularity of public men does not come from trying to guess what the people will applaud but from conveying to them the feeling that they can rely on the superior judgment of that man when they need him. It is no comfort whatever to know that he is a good judge of public opinion; they will really trust him only if they have some evidence that he is a good judge of the public interest (in Rossiter and Lare, p. 476).

Educators, as much as politicians, Lippmann thought, were evading their responsibilities. In 1941, nearly half a century before the 1980s and 1990s university-curicula controversies over the great books of the Western canon, he castigated university and other educational staff for 'progressively...[removing] from the curriculum of students the Western culture which produced the modern democratic state....and [for] sending out into the world men who no longer understand the creative principle of the society in which they must live' (in Rossiter and Lare, p. 418). Such an education was disastrous, for it was in

> the creative cultural tradition of Europe and the Americas....[that] our world was made. By this tradition it must live. Without this tradition our world, like a tree cut off from its roots in the soil, must die and be replaced by alien and barbarous things ([1941] in Rossiter and Lare, p. 420).

Lippmann's worries about the drift of politics and education cannot be explained away as a distaste for or fear of change. Indeed, with regard to his own profession, journalism, he applauded the many improvements in its technology and standards - its capacity to provide reliable news in a popular and coherent manner. Whereas in his *Public Opinion* and *Phantom Public* of the 1920s he had condemned the press for, among other offences, turning gossip into an industry, inducing the public to think in stereotyped terms, trivialising and sensationalising both the news and public issues, and making little effort to raise journalism's standards 'to the level say of medicine, engineering or the law' (1960, p. 335), by 1931 he was congratulating schools of journalism and the profession itself for having raised their standards (Rossiter and Lare, pp. 405-6). In the 1950s, however, Lippmann became alarmed by television's debasing of journalism by its gross commercialism and its indulging in the cruder of popular tastes. Unlike the press which, whatever the extent of its oligopolist ownership, had to face the competition of independent magazines, journals and other printed matter, television companies monopolised television viewing. As a remedy for the United States, Lippmann proposed a non-commercial company and increased regulation (Rossiter and Lare, pp. 413-16).

Modern democratic government, Lippmann believed, derived not so much from the thinking of philosophers as from the achievements of practical men. Prominent among Lippmann's heroes in both the *Good Society* (1943) and the *Public Philosophy* (1955) were the English lawyers of the seventeenth and eighteenth centuries, principally Sir Edward Coke, John Selden and Sir William Blackstone, who had defended and furthered, for the first two at great personal risk, the individual and political liberties embedded in the common law. In 1934, Lippmann observed, democracy 'is not the creation of abstract theorists. It is the creation of men who step by step through centuries of disorder established a regime of order' (in Rossiter and Lare, p. 230).

Democracies achieved maturity when constitutional rights and duties were augmented with universal adult voting. But universal voting, Lippmann contended, should not be interpreted as majoritarianism. Majorities should decide elections, and the majority principle was necessary to terminate parliamentary and other debates - but only within a framework of rules and consent to the rules. Modern democracy meant respect for the laws and conventions which, by setting limits to the power of majorities, preserved minority and other rights. The purpose of democratic institutions should be the obtaining of competent government in the interests of and accountable to the community, not the means whereby majorities, genuine or manufactured, asserted and tried to enforce the same claims as those of the absolute monarchs of the past or of modern dictators. Like sovereign princes and other rulers, Lippmann wrote, the people 'are illserved by flattery and adulation. And they are betrayed by the servile hypocrisy which tells them that what is true and what is false, what is right and what is wrong, can be determined by their votes' (1955, p. 19). Democratic leaders therefore should not exult over the majority principle but, to use one of Lippmann's favourite Freudian concepts, *sublimate* the majority principle, thus ensuring that it leads to good government and a worthwhile civilisation.

Majoritarianism and the flattery of voters generated and were perpetuated by a cynical, relativist, populist culture in which one opinion is considered as good as another, truth an illusion, and one person as equally deserving of respect as another, irrespective of his or her conduct or achievement. Such crudities become particularly prevalent, Lippmann wrote, when democratic government and the economic market fail to function effectively, and millions of people are condemned to lead meaningless lives. The

> disbelief in the existence of a central tradition of human wisdom is the philosophy of the spiritual proletariat. This feeling which pervades the great urban centres, that all things are relative and impermanent and of no real importance, is merely the reflection of their own separation from the elementary experiences of humanity ([1938] in Rossiter and Lare, p. 176.)

For Lippmann, majoritarianism, relativism and egalitarianism were closely linked and basic parts of Jacobinism.

Jacobinism, the Higher Law and the Quest for the Mean

Jacobinism, a politics and style of thought similar to what I have called a 'utopianism of praxis', was discussed by Lippmann in the *Public Philosophy* (1955), where it was explained in terms of two realms of human existence. Lippmann argued that human life oscillated between a material and a spiritual realm. The material realm was that of bodily needs, the physical senses and observable behaviour. The spiritual realm was that which was explored by contemplation, by mystics, Platonic and other idealist philosophers, and by Christian and other religious thinkers. In both individual and social life, the two realms mingled yet remained discrete. Whereas a person's goal in the material realm should be the maximising of material happiness, in spiritual life he or she should seek serenity, an immunity from the cares of material existence. By contrast, Jacobinism, a politicisation of Christian heresies, assumed that the transcending of evil and the limitations of material existence, which was possible only in the spiritual realm, could be achieved in the material realm - by political means. The goal of Jacobinism was not good government, and greater opportunities for individual and social development but a new world in which men and women were no longer subject to pain, suffering, and the frustrations of material life. The radical error of the Jacobin gospel, Lippmann wrote (1955), is its confusing 'of these two realms...an ultimate disorder. It inhibits the good life in this world. It falsifies the life of the spirit' (pp. 109-10).

Shortly after the 1955 publication of the *Public Philosophy*, Lippmann, in a rejoinder to criticisms of its account of Jacobinism, added another dimension to his thesis. It was an error, he argued, to confuse the realm of philosophic and other reflection (the theoretical life), in which there are no limits to a person's freedom, with political and other practical life where one person's freedom is constrained by and must co-exist with other people's.

> The mortal disease of free societies is to confuse the two realms, and to practice in the public world not a constitutional liberty but that boundless liberty which belongs to the inward country of the individual human spirit. That inward country may be the consciousness of genius and of a benefactor of mankind. It may also be the inward country of a Hitler or McCarthy (in Blum, 1984, p. 160).

Lippmann's alternative to Jacobin perfectionism was democratic governments which respected what in the *Good Society* (1943) he called the higher law and later (1955) natural law. Far from being a mask for vested interests, this higher law provided rational grounds for challenging vested interests. In the *Good Society* Lippmann argued that it was because nineteenth-century British and other liberals had confused the higher law and its post-medieval expression, natural rights, with the interests of the privileged classes of their nations that both liberalism and a belief in a discoverable higher law had been discredited. Far too many liberals had retained the language but corrupted the meaning of a higher law and natural rights. For Lippmann, however, the higher law unmasked vested interests, and legitimated the laws enforced by governments and courts. It demanded rational rather than wilful, arbitrary authority.

> The denial that men may be arbitrary in human transactions *is* the higher law. That is the substance of the higher law....without which the letter of the law is nothing but the formal trappings of vested rights or the ceremonial disguise of caprice and wilfulness....Among a people which does not try to obey this higher law, no constitution is worth the paper it is written on: though they have all the forms of liberty, they will not enjoy its substance....By this higher law all formal laws and all political behavior are judged in civilized societies....If the sovereign himself may not act willfully, arbitrarily, by personal prerogative, then no one may. His ministers may not. The legislature may not. Majorities may not. Individuals may not. Crowds may not. The national state may not....To those who ask where this higher law is to be found, the answer is that it is a progressive discovery of men striving to civilize themselves, and that its scope and implications are a gradual revelation that is by no means completed (1943, pp. 346-7).

The higher law is not a millenarian-utopian search for perfection in human affairs or intended for communities of saints; it is for associations of men and women who will always be imperfect. It is a quest for an Aristotelean mean - a middle way, but one which locates the best conduct or compromise rather than a mathematically middle point. It avoids excess and deficiency, and it tries to synthesise what is defensible in opposed political and related views. Several examples are to be found in Lippmann's work. Democratic governments, for Lippmann, must be accountable to their citizens but, between elections, they must be allowed to govern. Popular sovereignty, in which ultimate power is in the hands of the people, like the power of other sovereign rulers, must be exercised with restraint and bound by constitutional laws and conventions. Majority decisions are required, but within an agreed framework of rules and ends in which the interests and rights of all are respected. A balance has to be found between the power of citizens and that of political, educational and other authorities.

Lippmann cannot be labelled simply as a liberal, conservative or socialist; his thinking on democracy combined all three elements. His work contains the liberal commitments to individual liberties and rights, market capitalism and private enterprise; a conservative respect for tradition and law, including a higher or natural law; and a socialist insistence on the duty of governments to intervene in the economy and society when no one else responds to problems of injustice and hardship. Lippmann would have found little that was odd or puzzling in the title and content of Leszek Kolakowski's (1990) affirmation of the possibility of being a 'conservative-liberal-socialist'.

On international relations, and the principles which should guide the foreign policy of the United States, Lippmann similarly avoided excess. He had no reservations about the need to defend the United States against totalitarian challenges; but American foreign policy had to be conducted without the rhetoric and hysteria of a moral crusade, and without ignoring the legitimate national interests of itself, its allies and its enemies. Military strength was necessary but, as far as possible, confrontations and armed interventions were to be avoided. Lippmann also found a mean between what are usually regarded as opposed political-philosophic positions: pragmatism and natural law. In all his work there is a pragmatist streak in which the test for philosophic, political-philosophic or other thought was its practical effects, whether it generated worthwhile and effective action. But this pragmatism was moderated, by the end of the 1930s, by the belief that natural law thinking, which asserted that human activity should be guided by permanent truths about human life and a higher law, satisfied pragmatist criteria.

At times Lippmann was pessimistic about human beings and the survival of the good society; he was alarmed by the successes of the totalitarian regimes of Hitler, Stalin and other dictatorships, the ineptitude of democratic governments, and the deficiencies of their elites and electorates. He was also unhappy about the extent to which democracies had become permeated by Jacobin styles of thought. But he never doubted that Jacobinism, and fascist and other twentieth century dictatorships were in conflict with human nature, and the human capacity and desire for freedom. Neither did he doubt that, for all the weaknesses and follies of twentieth century democracies, representative democracy had grown out of and was the best of possible regimes for satisfying the needs and aspirations of the men and women of the modern world.

Lippmann's Achievement

If democratic theory as a public philosophy is the mean between ideological and utopian thinking, and a remedy for their distortions, then Lippmann is probably its foremost twentieth-century exponent. His *Essays in the Public Philosophy* (1955) is the classic statement of the need for and the purposes of a public philosophy, and his half a century of commentaries on American and other democratic government are an outstanding attempt to elucidate the standards which should guide democratic states and their citizens. But, as I have tried to show, there was towards the end of his career a tension in his political thought between his identifying of the public philosophy with natural law theory and his actual writing as a public philosopher - when he was more of a democratic than a natural law theorist. The contributions of his books and journalism to both explaining the need for and demonstrating the character of a public philosophy for democratic nations cannot be praised too highly; but, by too closely associating the public philosophy with natural law theory, he discouraged a revival and wider appreciation of it.

His writings on democratic politics are also open to other objections. There was for example the excessive optimism, shared with most of his contemporaries, about the ability of democratic governments to successfully engage in Keynesian economic management - the main defects and abuse of which became clear only in the last years of his life. Another weakness was that, owing to his work being focussed on the United States, where centralised political parties have been slow to develop, he devoted little attention to the consequences, for democratic government, of centralised parties acquiring an ascendancy over parliaments. His neglect of the dangers in tightly controlled political parties is one reason why his thinking on the relations between the executive and legislative branches of government has dated. For Lippmann, the problem was nearly always legislators exerting excessive pressure on the executive rather than, as a result of centralised parties, party leaders, ministers and government departments subjugating parliaments. Yet, even regarding the United States, his view of legislative-executive relations was one-sided. Despite his reservations about Roosevelt's New Deal, far less than many of his contemporaries, he failed to appreciate the extent to which the power of American presidents and their administrations had expanded.[3]

Lippmann's interpretation of the Western political tradition in the *Good Society* (1943), *Public Philosophy* (1955) and elsewhere also has at least one serious deficiency. It suggests that, from the early decades of the nineteenth century to Lippmann's 1930s discovery of the importance of a higher law, there was no liberal-democratic or other normative-political tradition of writing with serious public philosophic claims. This is the view expressed in what was probably his most influential book, *The Good Society*. After praising early nineteenth-century liberals for promoting individual liberties, he alleged that they and their successors failed to appreciate the importance of government and law, and confused the freedom of individuals with the privileges of the upper classes. Although some liberals may have been guilty, it is not at all evident that the alleged mistakes were made by, for example, John Stuart Mill, T. H. Green, and Green's New Liberal followers. In any case, Lippmann - like so many subsequent critics of liberalism - made little attempt to substantiate his charges. In the following three chapters I shall make a different interpretation of modern liberal-democratic thought, one which implies that Lippmann underestimated the variety in the liberal tradition, its contributions to a sound public philosophy and what he shared with it.

References

Adams, Larry L. (1977), *Walter Lippmann*, Twayne, Boston, 1977.

Auchincloss, Louis (1980), *The House of the Prophet*, Houghton Mifflin, Boston.

Blum, D. Steven (1984), *Walter Lippmann: Cosmopolitanism in the Century of Total War*, Cornell Univ. Pr., Ithaca.

Blum, John Morton (ed.) (1985), *Public Philosopher: Selected Letters of Walter Lippmann*, Ticknor and Fields, New York.

Burnham, James (1959), *Congress and the American Tradition*, Henry Regnery, Chicago.

Childs, Marquis and James Reston (eds) (1959), *Walter Lippmann and His Times*, Harcourt Brace, New York.

---

[3] For detailed studies, by contemporaries of Lippmann, of the growth of American presidential power, see James Burnham (1959); and Arthur M. Schlesinger, Jr (1973).

Kolakowski, Leszek (1990), 'How to Be a Conservative-Liberal-Socialist: a Credo', in *Modernity on Endless Trial*, Univ. of Chicago Pr., Chicago.

Lippmann, Walter (1925), *The Phantom Public*, Harcourt Brace, New York.

Lippmann, Walter (1929), *A Preface to Morals*, Macmillan, New York.

Lippmann, Walter (1943), *The Good Society* [1936], 3rd edn, Grosset and Dunlap, New York.

Lippmann, Walter (1955), *Essays in the Public Philosophy*, New American Library/Mentor, New York, a paperback edn of a Little Brown, 1955, hardcover edn.

Lippmann, Walter (1960), *Public Opinion* [1922], 2nd edn, Macmillan, New York.

Luskin, John (1972), *Lippmann, Liberty and the Press*, Univ. of Alabama Pr., Alabama.

Rossiter, Clinton and James Lare (eds) (1963), *The Essential Lippmann: A Political Philosophy for Liberal Democracy*, Random House, New York.

Schapsmeier, E. L. and F. H. (1969), *Walter Lippmann: Philosopher-Journalist*, Public Affairs Pr., Washington, D.C.

Schlesinger Jr, Arthur M. (1959), 'Walter Lippmann: The Intellectual v. Politics', in Childs and Reston.

Schlesinger Jr, Arthur M. (1973), *The Imperial Presidency*, Houghton Mifflin, Boston.

Steel, Ronald (1980), *Walter Lippmann and the American Century*, Little, Brown, Boston.

Wellborn, Charles (1969), *Twentieth Century Pilgrimage: Walter Lippmann and the Public Philosophy*, Louisiana State Univ Pr., Baton Rouge.

Wright, Benjamin F. (1973), *Five Public Philosophies of Walter Lippmann*, Univ. of Texas Pr., Austin.

6 Democratic Theory as Public Philosophy: Its Nineteenth-Century Foundations

Alexis de Tocqueville, John Stuart Mill and the late-nineteenth-century New Liberals, on whom this chapter concentrates, made major contributions to establishing a public philosophy for modern democracies. They developed politically realist, normative standards for the governments, elites and citizens of democratic nations, and they avoided both the complacency of formalism and ideology, and the naivety and perils of utopianism. They did not deduce standards from the abstract analysis of ideals but grounded them on what it was realistic to expect from democratic governments and citizens. They brought a range of historical and philosophic perspectives to the understanding of modern democracy and, as in any tradition of political theory and practice, they gave the values and goals they shared different emphases and priorities. But they were all determined to resist the dangers which accompany democratic government, to further the potential of democratic politics and culture to improve human life, and to discover the steps which had to be taken if democracy's potential was to be realised and its dangers averted. Although their political thinking derived from ideas which had been developed in earlier societies and they did not make sharp breaks from earlier thought, it is nevertheless appropriate to date democratic theory as a public philosophy not from earlier natural-law, social-contract or other traditions but from Alexis de Tocqueville - the first major political thinker to write comprehensively on the democratic politics of post-French-Revolution industrialising societies. Tocqueville considered the democratisation of European and other industrialised nations to be inevitable, he wished to understand the ramifications of democratisation, he desired to curb its worse and promote its better features, and for these reasons he desired to understand the institutions and culture of the United States, the first large nation to undertake a democratic revolution.

Alexis de Tocqueville and His Understanding of Democracy

Life and Work

Alexis de Tocqueville was born in Paris in 1805, the eldest son of a French aristocratic family with whom, after the 1830 revolution which brought Louis Philippe to the French throne, he quarrelled. The family were outraged when Alexis took an oath of allegiance to the new king and served him as a provincial magistrate. In 1830 and 1831, with a lifelong friend, Gustave de Beaumont, Tocqueville spent several months touring the United States. The ostensible reason for the visit was to study the American prison system; Tocqueville's main purpose, however, was to better understand American democracy. He recorded the details of interviews with both unknown and prominent Americans, including America's political leaders, and used these notes during the ten years he spent writing the two volumes of *Democracy in America* (1968). The book was published in France in two parts, in 1835 and 1840, and the English and other translations of the first volume made Tocqueville an internationally renowned political thinker.

Democracy in America, a superb account of the United States in the early years of Andrew Jackson's presidency, has become a major primary source for the early history of the United States. Tocqueville described the United States when it was still in its infancy - a frontier nation, relentlessly expanding and industrialising, and with confident citizens seizing, among their other opportunities, cheap land. Tocqueville, however, saw his subject not as the United States but as democracy. In a letter to John Stuart Mill, he wrote that 'America was only my framework; democracy was my subject' (Tocqueville, 1968, p. iii). European readers were told that he had written on the United States because it was the first large nation to complete a democratic revolution, and that by understanding American society they would better understand their own political options. Although Europe's future was not predetermined, and its history, institutions and culture differed from those of the United States, the American experience revealed to Europeans, Tocqueville firmly believed, democracy's possibilities for both good and ill.

In 1838, between the publication of the two volumes of *Democracy in America*, Tocqueville was elected to the French parliament, when he acquired a reputation as an authority on foreign policy, and was associated with prison reform, abolishing slavery from the French colonies and promoting French settlements in Algeria. At the end of 1847, after warning his fellow parliamentarians about the imminence of revolution, he supported the overthrow of the Louis Philippe regime. He was elected to the National Assembly, and in the June of 1849 he became the foreign minister in Odilon Barrot's liberal government. Earlier, alarmed by the activities of radical republicans and socialists, he participated in the suppression of the June, 1848, Paris uprising. He subsequently opposed the 1851 coup of Louis Napoleon and, after a brief imprisonment, retired from public life. His retirement was used for historical research and for writing on the causes and aftermath of the 1789 French Revolution - *The Ancien Regime and the French Revolution* (1966) and *The European Revolution* (1959). Tocqueville died in 1859.[1]

There are several reasons why Tocqueville should be considered the founder of a public philosophic tradition of writing on modern democratic politics. He was more thorough and judicious, and less concerned with advocating or opposing immediate causes or reforms than his contemporaries who wrote on democracy, and he brought a historical perspective to his task rather than seek to promote a particular political or other doctrine. In the Preface to the second volume of *Democracy in America* (1968), he declared that he wrote as a friend rather than as a flatterer of democracy. But unlike the many people who 'advertise the new benefits which democracy promises to mankind', he would 'point out the distant perils with which it threatens them' (p. 546). This writing was undertaken from a privileged historical position. For the same reason that Plato and Aristotle were able to write so strikingly and profoundly on Greek city-state democracy, Tocqueville was able to write the classic study of modern democracy. Just as, in the fourth century BCE, the direct, citizenship democracy of Athens and other city states was still a novelty, and Plato and Aristotle were able to contrast it with older forms of government that still survived, so Tocqueville could compare a regime in which government was subordinated to popular sovereignty with the older, more autocratic and aristocratic political systems it challenged. America's aristocratic observer, therefore, could see with clarity and with a friendly but critical and balanced mind the political innovations and the new way of life which Americans were already taking for granted.

'Democracy in America'

Modern democracy, the project that was born with the late-eighteenth-century American and French revolutions, was seen by Tocqueville as driven by the desire for the political sovereignty and equality of all men, yet

---

[1] For Tocqueville's account of French politics in the revolutionary years from 1848 to 1851, and his participation in events, see Tocqueville (1970). For biographies, Jardin (1988); and Mayer (1960). For interpretations of Tocqueville's thinking on modern democracy, see Drescher (1968); Goldstein (1975); Hereth (1986); Lively (1962); Manent (1996); and Zetterbaum (1967).

moderated by caution, and the constitutional and other liberal principles it inherited. Modern democracy's distinctive governmental features were regarded as legislative assemblies and, for American and other republics, presidents accountable to voters at elections; a movement towards universal adult suffrage; the abolition of hereditary, class and other political privileges; personal liberties and legal rights on the basis of equality; and the political freedoms of speech, assembly and association which made possible a free press, mass political parties, diverse private associations and other instruments of self government. American democracy, for Tocqueville, had at its core a set of political institutions - but it was also a culture and a society. It was a society in which there were no insurmountable obstacles, at least for the white population of European descent, to social mobility, and to participation in the associations, institutions and life of the community. Although equality in America, Tocqueville was pleased to find, was tempered by the desire for political and individual liberty, and equality in the sense of identical incomes and ways of life was not regarded as a necessary or desirable part of democracy, he thought it inevitable that democratic politics would stimulate a passion for social levelling. For Tocqueville, equality was paradoxically both the great danger and the force which could save democracy. No contradiction was involved, however, as he distinguished between two kinds of equality.

> There is indeed a manly and legitimate passion for equality which rouses in all men a desire to be strong and respected. This passion tends to elevate the little man to the rank of the great. But the human heart also nourishes a debased taste for equality, which leads the weak to want to drag the strong down to their level and which induces men to prefer equality in servitude to inequality in freedom (p. 66).

As the direction taken by democratic civilisation in particular nations would depend upon whether citizens moderated the desire for equality with a love of liberty, and how they responded to the problems which were always a part of democratic politics and government, Tocqueville tried to understand, on the basis of the American experience, the culture of democratic people, the challenges and problems they would have to confront, the possible responses to them and the effects of the responses.

One political problem which he emphasised was the difficulties democratic nations would have in finding competent and public spirited leaders able to communicate with and to further the political education of citizens. The problem was that well meaning and sensitive people would have to compete for votes against demagogic and opportunist rivals who could be malicious towards opponents. The tendency in democracies, therefore, would be for decent people - apart from heroic exceptions - to stay out of politics. For Tocqueville, a paradox in democratic government was that, though it was vitally important that democracies possess able and morally sensitive leaders and politicians, the very nature of democratic politics worked against the emergence of such leaders and politicians. A related political problem and paradox was that, though democracies depended upon citizens being politically informed, prudent participants in political life, citizens were likely to have opposite qualities. The vastness and complexity of their societies, and the character of industrialised urban life were likely to produce politically apathetic, socially alienated individuals, immersed in their narrow, private preoccupations. A citizenship ethos was necessary, but the fears of people for themselves and their families could prevent them from understanding and working for the community's good. Isolated and frightened individuals would be helpless before and increasingly dependent upon governments and officials.

But despite and in some ways because of their deficiencies, the people who comprised the majorities of democratic populations, as a consequence of their numbers, would become the dominant social and political power. Their anxieties would animate public opinion, and public opinion could become untamable. The 'tyranny of the majority', therefore, was for democracies an ever present danger. This was a tyranny which few could escape as, in addition to exerting a direct pressure on individuals, it used the powers of the state. Revolutionary, egalitarian and despotic instincts, Tocqueville wrote, may 'gradually be transformed into mores of government and administrative habits' (p. 908). No monarch or other autocrat possessed the power of majorities when popular sovereignty became the supreme political principle, and increases in the size of a country and its population aggravated the problem: 'All passions fatal to a [democratic] republic', Tocqueville warned, 'grow with the increase of its territory, but the virtues which should support it do not grow at the same rate' (p. 196).

The character of politicians and voters would, among its other effects, make it difficult for democratic governments to have prudent and consistent foreign policies. Because of the desire of voters for material comfort, democracies were likely to be excessively conciliatory, and unwilling to devote the necessary resources to military defence. Yet, Tocqueville thought, once a democracy engaged in a war, its people were likely to become aggressively nationalist and, if victorious, vindictive. Long-lasting peace settlements therefore would be rare. At the root of such problems was greed. Whereas in aristocratic societies everyone knew their place, and there were limits to how far the members of social classes could rise or fall, democracies broke down the barriers. Far more than in earlier societies, therefore, the members of the labouring and middle classes would become excessively ambitious, while the members of the upper classes would be fearful of losing their wealth and position, and more willing to turn to political conspiracy and rebellion.

Their greed and anxieties would prompt majorities to demand that their states intervene to further social equality, while the increased powers of centralised, potentially despotic states would generate fierce political conflicts as sectional groups fought to harness the powers of the state to advance their interests. Such despotic government, Tocqueville wrote, would generate another danger - anarchy.

> The government of the American republic seems to me as centralised and more energetic than the absolute monarchies of Europe. So I do not think that it will collapse from weakness. If ever freedom is lost in America, that will be due to the omnipotence of the majority driving the minorities to desperation and forcing them to appeal to physical force. We may then see anarchy, but it will have come as a result of despotism (p. 321).

But, fortunately for democracies, their political culture nurtured at least some checks to greed and excessive ambition. Democracy's egalitarian ethos encouraged both a sympathy for the victims and counter measures against groups which exploited their wealth, power and position.

Another of Tocqueville's concerns was the secularism of democratic societies. He thought that, as a result of the weakening of religious belief, men and women were likely to become ever more sceptical about divine judgement, and about an afterlife or any other kind of spiritual life. The problem would worsen because, when material goods ceased to satisfy, scepticism would be transferred from the spiritual to the material world. The people of democratic nations would become cynical about everything and attached to nothing. The result would be an exhausted, hedonistic culture, with men and women leading lives without purpose and living for the moment. Tocqueville held that one of the main reasons why a politically stable and flourishing democratic community had been established in the United States, and the hazards of democratisation largely overcome, was that religious belief was more prevalent than in Europe. He was convinced that, for Western democracies, unless there were Christian religious foundations, including a belief in an afterlife, for moral teachings and conduct, a destructive materialism and egalitarianism would be inescapable. Religious belief and political moderation had been sustained in the United States because of the strong puritan-religious element in its culture, and because the American churches, unlike the European, had allied themselves with democracy. Tocqueville was disturbed by the possibilities that in France and other European nations where the Roman Catholic Church supported royalist and aristocratic causes, and in Britain where the Anglican Church supported the Tory Party, democracy would be accompanied by atheism, and the discredited churches would be unable to sustain moral codes and check democratic excess.

Tocqueville was certain that the days of monarchic and aristocratic government in Europe were numbered. Political democracy and greater social equality were inevitable, and for many reasons to be welcomed - mainly because of the better lives they offered the labouring classes. But what remained in doubt was whether democracy's egalitarian ethos would be accompanied by a respect for individual liberty, property and other rights, and the necessary constitutional, moral and other checks to governmental power, or whether it would be an unrestrained equality which prevented democracy from becoming a stable and worthy civilisation. But what exactly, according to Tocqueville in his *Democracy in America* (1968), had to be done to ensure that democracy took a satisfactory direction?

First (my enumeration), Tocqueville favoured institutional checks and balances along American lines. He urged bicameral parliaments; independent judiciaries; and local-government authorities with wide-ranging powers and responsibilities. Second, he urged that political parties should be attached to constitutional principles and politically realistic ideals, rather than the extreme goals of French radicals or, as in the United States, the opportunist promoting of economic interests and searching for popular causes. Third, as the frequent elections of the United States caused endless 'feverish agitation', while 'rare' elections 'expose the state to violent crises' (p. 248), European nations should seek a more balanced middle way. Fourth, Tocqueville praised the willingness of American citizens to participate in private associations, a habit which he hoped Europeans would copy. Associations were 'great free schools' (p. 673) that drew people out of their private lives, making them confident, and giving them social and political skills. But, it was private associations to which Tocqueville was attracted, associations which performed economic, charitable and other functions, and which acted as a check to governments - not pressure groups demanding greater governmental activity.

> An association, be it political, industrial, commercial, or even literary or scientific, is an educated and powerful body of citizens which cannot be twisted to any man's will or quietly trodden down, and by defending its private interests against the encroachments of power, it saves the common liberties (p. 905).

Fifth, despite his concern over the many abuses of the press in both the United States and Europe, Tocqueville maintained that a free press was a necessary condition for democracy. He favoured, however, a large number of competing local and regional newspapers, as in the United States, rather than, as in France, a small number of giant, semi-monopoly national papers located in the nation's capital.

Sixth, he believed that an efficient economy compatible with democracy necessitated the private ownership of economic resources and market relations. He was aware, however, that private property and the market would encourage economic inequalities, and that economic inequalities would be perceived as conflicting with political equality and other democratic norms. For these reasons he proposed taxes which would benefit poorer citizens. Subsequently, after 1848 for France, he became bolder in his proposals for public charity (the welfare-state principle).[2] Despite his aristocratic disdain for commerce, and his sympathy for the losers, Tocqueville wished to strengthen capitalist economic relations, which he thought were indispensable for the maintenance of individual liberty. He had spotted that, though the very rich in modern capitalist societies could become arrogant, hostile to and a threat to democracy, for most people commerce had a civilising effect. It encouraged thrift, prudence, initiative, honesty, trust and other qualities that were basic for citizenship. In addition, private property and market relations gave many sections of the community the independence and strength to resist governments and public bureaucracies. Although, as Tocqueville recognised, the industrial conditions of the capitalism of his day were often demanding and harmful, he realised that they had the capacity to make possible, for all people, greater leisure and the life of independent citizens. In addition, industrial capitalism demonstrated that it was society and not governments which produced material and other goods.

Seventh, it was important that religious belief be maintained. 'How could society escape destruction', Tocqueville asked, 'if, when political ties are relaxed, moral ties are not tightened? And what can be done with a people master of itself if it is not subject to God?' (p. 364). In order to preserve and widen the influence of the churches, Tocqueville advocated the separation of church and state. Independent churches, he urged, should support liberal and democratic aspirations, and emphasise Christian moral teachings - for Tocqueville, the original source of the idea of the equality of all men and women - rather than theological or metaphysical doctrines. Eighth, although aristocratic rule could not survive, he hoped that the best of aristocratic virtues and values, especially honour and a sense of duty, would continue to influence public and private life (pp. 201-2).

Tocqueville was often ambivalent in his attitude to democracy. Unlike many advocates of democracy, he refrained from comparing the virtues of democracy with the vices of non-democratic societies, just as he did not follow its enemies in comparing its vices with the virtues of more

---

2   For Tocqueville on social reform, see Drescher (1968b).

aristocratic societies. The richness of his insights into democracy's politics and culture, and democracy's strengths and weaknesses stemmed from his comparing of like with like: both the virtues and vices of democracy with those of aristocracy. 'One must be careful', he wrote, 'not to judge nascent societies on the basis of ideas derived from those which no longer exist' (p. 915). Democracy should be supported and furthered, Tocqueville contended, not because there were no grounds for scepticism or resistance but because, for Western nations, it provided the only realistic option for maintaining and advancing civilised life. Self-government, by means of constitutional and representative principles, and greater social and political equality was irresistible. Only ruthless and brutal tyrannies and despotisms could repel it. But human thought and action still had the power to decide the type and to mould the character of democracy and equality. This was the essence of his argument, summarised in the final paragraph of his classic study of modern democracy.

> The task is no longer to preserve the particular advantages which inequality of conditions had procured for men, but to secure those new benefits which equality may supply....The nations of our day cannot prevent conditions of equality from spreading in their midst. But it depends upon themselves whether equality is to lead to servitude or freedom, knowledge or barbarism, prosperity or wretchedness (p. 916).

John Stuart Mill's Utilitarian Public Philosophy and Democratic Theory

The principal political writings of John Stuart Mill, the second major founder of a public philosophic tradition of writing for democratic nations, were grounded on and permeated by a philosophy of history and a related conception of democracy. For Mill, the history of the civilised world consisted of countless practical experiments and struggles by men and women to master nature, achieve stable communities and systems of law, live under fair and efficient systems of government, and discover the best ways to live. As a result, progress occurred in history. Individuals, their families, and wider groups and communities acquired a knowledge of improved ways to organise themselves and to live. Despite wasted efforts, set-backs and false directions, national and other communities gradually became more civilised, and created greater opportunities for the achievement of individual happiness. And happiness, for Mill, was more than sensory pleasure; it was the enjoyment of the 'higher pleasures' of a fulfilled, flourishing life - the exercise of intelligence and energy, creative cooperation with others in worthy causes, and a love of truth and beauty.

Modern representative democracy, for all its faults, Mill never doubted, was the highest stage yet reached in the human quest for the best possible life. It was the creation of civilised peoples who tried to learn from the mistakes and to further the achievements of their predecessors and contemporaries.[3]

But, Mill warned, democracy guaranteed neither further progress nor the individual liberty that made it possible. As in all societies, deterioration was a permanent possibility, prevented only by the efforts of minorities. Moreover, democracy created new threats to liberty and progress. Majority decisions, at the national or any other level, did not ensure that decisions were rational and in the interests of voters. They might be the products of ignorance and prejudice; an unruly community bitterly divided into religious, ethnic and other factions; a dominant, unenlightened, economic class; or a servile populace dependent on an intrusive public bureaucracy. For individuals and minorities to be subject to the political power and social pressure of the majorities of such nations - Tocqueville's 'tyranny of the majority' or what Mill in *On Liberty* called the 'collective mediocrity' of the masses (1993, p. 134) - was likely to be worse than subjection to a despotic dictator or oligarchy. It was essential for democratic nations, therefore, that their citizens and leaders understand not only the potential of their societies to improve human life but its seamier possibilities. The public philosophy which Mill grounded on his view of history and conception of democracy, therefore, may be described in terms of how democracy's achievements and capacity to improve human life are to be advanced and its dangers overcome. It was a public philosophy which grew out of and became a part of his life and vocation.

He was born in a north-east suburb of London in 1806, the eldest child of James Mill, himself a leading British economist, historian (of British India) and political writer. The son's intense, private education was conducted personally by his father, who, at the time, was Jeremy Bentham's principal assistant in propagating utilitarian philosophy and organising the work of the utilitarian reformers or Philosophic Radicals as Bentham and his supporters were then known. John Stuart Mill, who was successfully groomed by his father to become a leading utilitarian thinker, eventually constructed a more open and flexible utilitarian political philosophy than that which Bentham and his father had centred on a pleasure-and-pain view of human behaviour. He published work on logic, economics, political philosophy and political reform which made him a leading philosopher, political economist and political thinker, and a moulder of mid-nineteenth-

---

3   These conceptions of history and democracy are fundamental to and expressed in Mill's *Essay on Liberty* of 1859 (1991; and 1993). They were first developed in 'The Spirit of the Age', 1831, and 'Civilization', 1836 (1973). See also *Considerations on Representative Government*, 1861 (1991; and 1993).

century British public opinion. He was a major influence on both the New Liberals and the Fabian socialists. He wrote for eminent radical and other journals, sometimes in articles that were subsequently published as books. His regularly reprinted *System of Logic*, 1843, and *Principles of Political Economy*, 1848 (1987), served as textbooks for generations of readers, while his *Utilitarianism* of 1861 (1993) made utilitarian moral and political philosophy, for most people, a more appealing and persuasive doctrine than those of Bentham and James Mill. From 1865 to 1868 he was the M.P. for Westminster.[4]

Mill saw himself as the same kind of democratic theorist as Tocqueville, a position which he considered compatible with the insights of Benthamite utilitarianism, the conservative thinking of Samuel Taylor Coleridge and, at one time, the positivist sociology of Auguste Comte. In a review of the second volume of *Democracy in America* he transferred to Britain Tocqueville's response to American democracy: the British government and public, he wrote, should encourage 'those [tendencies] in democracy which are salutary, and...[work] out the means by which such as are hurtful may be counteracted' (1973, p. 257). But whereas Tocqueville contrasted democratic with aristocratic government, Mill thought that the only alternative for economically developed nations was bureaucratic government. Democracy was preferred because even the most benevolent of bureaucratic regimes retarded the self development of men and women. And Mill was convinced that, without energetic, morally sensitive human beings, nothing of worth could be accomplished. He followed Tocqueville in trying to understand the cultural and economic as well as the political causes and effects and necessary conditions for modern democracy; but whereas Tocqueville's focus was the United States, Mill's was Britain.

Culture and Political Culture

Culture, which Mill often used interchangeable with *civilisation*, meant the beliefs, habits, and styles of thought and activity which expressed and shaped the lives of individuals and communities. It was, for Mill, a nation's

---

4   John Stuart Mill's other major writings, relevant to his democratic theory and public philosophy, include his substantial reviews, 1835 and 1840 (1973), of Tocqueville's *Democracy in America; The Subjection of Women*, 1869 (1991); and *Chapters on Socialism*, 1879 (1967). For his life, see one of the several editions of his *Autobiography*, 1873 (1964); August (1975); Mazlish (1975); Packe (1954); and Skorupski (1989). For the utilitarian movement, see Halevy (1928); and Hamburger (1965). For Mill's political thought, see Berger (1984); Burns (1969); Cowling (1963); Garforth (1980); Himmelfarb (1974); Jacobs (1993); Robson (1968); Ryan (1974); Semmel (1984); and Thomas (1985).

culture, in particular the capacity of its people for and their commitment to liberty and the responsibilities it entailed which enabled them to successfully govern themselves by means of representative institutions. Without such a culture, which he thought was achievable by all peoples but in his day was largely confined to the predominantly protestant nations of Europe and America, the successful establishing of representative democracy was impossible. Moreover, it was the effects of self government on a nation's culture, whether it enhanced or debased it, which made democracy deserving of praise or condemnation. It was their culture which, for Mill, explained why some nations creatively confronted crises while others, stagnated, withered, or consumed their energies in an unproductive nationalism and militarism. But the tolerant and public spirited culture on which self government depended was fragile. In comparison with technological progress, which could persist under despotic systems of government, cultures and their moral standards were more susceptible to decay or destruction. Of vital importance for a democratic nation, therefore, were the moral qualities and political skills of its leaders. A democratic like any other nation, Mill thought, possessed a 'natural' order whereby leadership and authority were in the hands of its most virtuous and competent members. In 'The Spirit of the Age' he wrote that a society 'may be said to be in its *natural* state, when worldly power, and moral influence, are habitually and undisputedly exercised by the fittest persons whom the existing state of society affords' (1973, p. 17).

Mill was committed to the liberty and self government of democracy because they challenged government by or for 'sinister interests'. What had to be prevented, however, was a challenge to all power and authority, and to a political community's natural leaders. As power and authority in democracies rested on reason and persuasion rather than force or deception, finding people with the requisite qualities and skills was a difficult but necessary task. Cultural and political leaders had to treat people with respect and as equals rather than as inferiors to be commanded or administered. In turn, citizens had to accept the guidance of those who were better informed and wiser than themselves. In his review of the first volume of Tocqueville's *Democracy in America*, Mill wrote,

> Provided good intentions can be secured [by regular elections and an extensive franchise], the best government...must be the government of the wisest, and these must always be a few. The people ought to be the masters, but they are masters who must employ servants more skilful than themselves: like a ministry when they employ a military commander, or the military commander when he employs an army-surgeon (1973, p. 195).

Modern representative democracy, by its parliamentary deliberation and public discussion, was a means for mediating between citizens and their governments, and between not only freedom and equality but between freedom and equality, on the one hand, and power and authority on the other. Similarly, by parliamentary and public discussion, representative government sought to balance other principles and goals which pulled in different directions, including progress and order, majority decisions and wise leadership, and tradition and reform. Representative democracy, for Mill, was therefore the solution to what is sometimes regarded as the problem of value relativism. He saw democracy as an open society in which opposed values, conceptions of truth and ways of life co-existed and peacefully competed to their mutual advantage. Their competition, Mill thought, would lead not to chaos or to one doctrine or way of life completely triumphing over rivals but to their partial truths being better understood and reconciled.

Mill's love of individual liberty and social diversity, foundations for the quest for truth and the good life, infused his classic *On Liberty* essay (1991; and 1993). His emphasis on the need for orderly societies with 'natural' leaders, along with his awareness of the importance of cultural issues are to be found in his essays on culture.[5] Both these sides of his thought found expression in his desire to promote and protect an informed intelligentsia which was bold in its advocacy of change and reform while being responsible and restrained, which appreciated tradition yet encouraged people to think for themselves, and which consisted of men and women who, in their own lives, were energetic and imaginative. For Mill, such qualities were for democratic as for all societies the only forces which could overcome ignorance, inertia and sinister interests. In *Representative Government*, he wrote, 'It is what men think that determines how they act' (1993, p. 198), and 'One person with a belief is a social power equal to ninety-nine who have only interests' (1993, p. 197).

Although Mill welcomed social diversity and the clash of opposed goals and norms, there was one normative principle to which he gave a priority, and held to be the final appeal court for value conflicts: utility. Utility, for Mill, was not a Benthamite or other cost-benefit tool for enabling administrators to make choices for and to manage the rest of a population; it was more of a means for sustaining the independence of a society against governments and bureaucracies. Indeed, individual liberty was a necessary part of Mill's utility principle. His utility principle did not possess a precise content, and neither specific reforms nor radical programs

---

5 Especially 'The Spirit of the Age', 1831, 'Civilization', 1836, 'Bentham', 1838, 'Coleridge', 1840, and 'Tocqueville on Democracy in America', I and II, 1835 and 1840 (all included in Mill, 1973).

for change could be deduced from it. It was an aid to rather than a substitute for individual reflection and public debate on how to reconcile and achieve the rich variety of goals and aspirations that were compatible with democratic life. The *utility* principle, for Mill, performed similar functions to those performed by the *common good, public interest* and *justice* for other democratic theorists and public philosophers. It meant the promotion of human happiness in the sense of maximising the opportunities of people to develop themselves and achieve fulfilling lives. This conception of utility explains Mill's dedication to modern democracy; it also gave him criteria for comparing and assessing different democracies and their institutions.[6]

Parliamentary Government

For political parties in Britain, which in Mill's day consisted of little more than loosely organised groups of parliamentarians, supported by small constituency parties and a few national officials, he urged a rivalry between a conservative party and one which pushed for radical and other reforms. The opposed parties should take their principles seriously and be combative. Only then would their merits be appreciated and their deficiencies rectified. Internal democracy and debate within the parties was said to be necessary for the political education of both members of parliament and their extra-parliamentary supporters, while political education, for Mill, meant that they put national interests before their party's. It was to promote public interests that he urged that political parties be based on political principles rather than economic interests. If they were not, parliamentary and other politics would degenerate into socially destructive battles between opposed economic classes and their allies. Instead of legislation in the nation's interest, there would be class or other sectional laws and policies. It was mainly for this reason that he lamented what he regarded as the Liberal Party's abandoning of liberal principles and the forsaking of conservative principles by the Tories, subsequently the Conservative Party, the supposed conservative guardians of tradition. Unless political conflicts were over principles, and sensible compromises were sought, party politics would become nothing more than battles between rival groups of demagogues.

As preventive measures, in addition to urging that political actors adhere to rationally defensible principles, he proposed further checks and balances to parliament, particularly its strongest parts, the House of

---

6   For Mill's revision of Bentham's conception of utility, see *Utilitarianism*, 1861, (1991; and 1993). See also his 'Bentham' (1973); and *Principles of Political Economy*, 1848, (1987), for Book 5, 'On the Influence of Government'.

Commons and the cabinet. Such constraints were necessary if effective opposition was to be sustained. Like Gaetano Mosca, Mill thought that democratic societies were more dependent on the strength and character of their oppositions, both in their parliaments and the nation at large, than on their governments and dominant political elites. In a 1838 essay on Bentham, for example, he wrote that a

> society should make provision for keeping up...as a corrective to partial views, and a shelter for freedom of thought and individuality of character, a perpetual and standing Opposition to the will of the majority. All countries which have long continued progressive, or been durably great, have been so because there has been an organized opposition to the ruling power...plebeians to patricians, clergy to kings, freethinkers to clergy, kings to barons, commons to king and aristocracy. Almost all the greatest men who ever lived have formed part of such an Opposition Wherever such quarrel has not been going on - wherever it has been terminated by the complete victory of one of the contending principles, and no new contest has taken the place of the old - society has either been hardened into Chinese stationariness, or fallen into dissolution (1973, p. 111).

It was Mill's commitment to effective opposition, and to strengthening the people of intelligence, energy and virtue against the people of property and numbers that explains his advocacy, in *Representative Government* (1991; and 1993), of extra votes for educated and professional people of proven ability, and their representation in a reformed House of Lords.

For the British parliament to provide strong oppositions as well as effective governments, Mill argued that its principal legislative body, the House of Commons, should concentrate on the functions for which it was suited and allow other functions to be given to a new part of parliament. Mill proposed that in addition to the Commons and the Lords there should be an independent chamber of lawyers and civil servants responsible for the drafting and revision of legislation. This was partly to prevent the incoherence in the law which resulted from an assembly of over six hundred members voting on legislation clause by clause. The Commons, he thought, should concentrate on selecting and replacing prime ministers, cabinets and individual ministers; questioning, checking and censuring governments; ensuring that the general principles of policies and laws were thoroughly debated and considered; and making electors aware of the difficulties and complexities of government, and governments of the concerns of voters. The Commons should be 'the nation's Committee of Grievances, and its Congress of Opinions' (1993, p. 258). But for the members of the Commons to properly perform these functions, it was essential that they preserve their independence, and not allow themselves to become voting fodder for their parties or self-interested groups of electors.

Mill also challenged what was already becoming the dominant conception of voting in general elections, arguing that voting was a citizen's duty rather than a right. A vote for a member of parliament, he contended, was analogous to a juror's vote on whether an accused person was guilty or not guilty. Just as jurors were obliged to vote on the basis of evidence, relevant laws, court proceedings and jury-room discussions, rather than their personal preferences or what might benefit or please the juror, so members of parliament and their parties should be judged by voters on their record and whether their future actions were likely to be in the public interest - to benefit the nation and as far as possible all its citizens. Mill, in fact, in *Representative Government*, in order to encourage voting to be undertaken publicly and thus seen as a public responsibility rather than a piece of personal property intended to benefit the individual voter, was a lonely voice among the radicals and democrats of his day in opposing the secret ballot. It was, he believed, as reprehensible for voters to vote on the basis of their private interests as it was for jurors, and even more reprehensible for political leaders and other politicians to encourage them.

Mill also swam against the tide of radical and democratic opinion when, again in *Representative Government*, he opposed the payment of salaries to members of the House of Commons. Such payment, he wrote, would create a class of professional demagogues.

> It amounts to offering 658 prizes for the most successful flatterer, the most adroit misleader, of a body of his fellow-countrymen. Under no despotism has there been such an organised system of tillage for raising a rich crop of vicious courtiership (1993, p. 338).

Mill maintained that genuine dialogues, in which participants in a debate listened to one another and were willing to be persuaded by evidence and argument, were fundamental to both parliamentary and wider public discourse. Apart from anything else, as he astutely observed in *Representative Government*, 'those whose opinion is overruled [must] feel satisfied that it is heard, and set aside not by a mere act of will, but for what are thought superior reasons' (1993, p. 239). This is advice which is pertinent to all democratic organisations from large nations to small committees. A person or group of people will tolerate being overruled, and may indeed feel properly recognised or even flattered if they believe that their arguments have been seriously considered. But they will resent and react against being ignored because they command fewer votes. When majorities abuse democracy's deliberative processes and their votes in this way, democracy no longer exists; force has taken the place of consent.

These were among the main parts of Mill's public philosophic response to the cultural and political problems of the democracies of his day. For his response to their economic problems and, in particular, to the capitalism-versus-socialism issue, it is necessary to turn to his *Principles of Political Economy* (1987) and *Chapters on Socialism* (1967).

Capitalism or Socialism

The overall argument of the *Principles* (1987), summarised in its final chapter, 'Of the Grounds and Limits of the Laisser-faire or Non-Interference Principle', clarifies and defuses the capitalism-versus-socialism issue. The essence of Mill's argument is that, although there is no absolute or inviolable principle which in all circumstances prohibits governments from intervening in an economy, as laissez-faire market principles are for most purposes the most effective for the production and distribution of goods, and for maintaining individual liberty, unless there are strong reasons for departing from them, they should be followed. The simple question with which he began was 'what are the advantages, and what the evils or inconveniences, of government interference' (p. 942.)? By thus dispensing with inflexible laissez-faire and socialist dogmas, Mill opened disputes about capitalism and socialism to empirical evidence and made them subject to pragmatic criteria. He also made these disputes, for all but the most fanatical of partisans, subject to shared values.

Despite some of the details of Mill's argument having dated, its premises and logic are as compelling as ever, and have become a part of standard defences of a mixed economy, in the sense of a modified market capitalism. He supported his premise that non-interference was for most purposes the economic principle for governments to follow partly by arguing that individual liberties were the means for achieving satisfaction in economic activity just as they were in other parts of life. A related reason was that 'people understand their own business and their own interests better, and care for them more than the government does' (1987, p. 947). In addition, interventionist governments tend to become the tools of irresponsible majorities and powerful sectional interests, and the greater the powers claimed by governments, the more inefficient governments will be in performing essential law-enforcing and other tasks. Finally, the more dependent a people are on the state, the less innovative and energetic they will be.

But laissez-faire principles, for all their merits, Mill argued, were not infallible guides; at times they should be departed from. One example was that, as neither poorly educated parents nor their uneducated children could be competent judges of schools, governments - without restricting the variety of schools or controlling the education they offered - should ensure that schools maintained adequate standards. Education thus supported the general principle that, because competition between buyers and sellers did not benefit buyers when they lacked relevant knowledge, whenever goods and services were excessively complex and/or buyers insufficiently knowledgeable, government-backed public authorities should ensure that basic standards were maintained. Governments were also obliged to act when, in economic production, there were substantial hidden costs such as river or other pollution. Governmental action to strengthen the bargaining power of people who were too weak to freely negotiate employment or other contracts was also justified. In addition, Mill, who after the limited-liability legislation of 1855, was suspicious of the joint-stock companies which were displacing those controlled by entrepreneurs (owner-managers), saw this change as calling for governmental action. Because managers were no longer restrained by owners, greater public surveillance was required. State intervention was also necessary, he thought, when services such as roads, canals and railways were natural monopolies. A government's toleration of such a monopoly 'does much the same thing as if it allowed a private individual or an association to levy any tax they chose' (1987, pp. 962-3).

Mill's conception of the economic responsibilities of governments, it follows, may be appealed to by partisans of both democratic socialism and market capitalism. Its adaptability, however, does not mean that it is incoherent or trivial. It is a means for countering both laissez-faire and socialist excesses, and for preventing the issue of capitalism or socialism from bitterly dividing a nation. It is not the final word but a tool for turning doctrinal disputes into specific problems, thus opening them to informed inquiry and public debate.

If Tocqueville was the founder of a public philosophy for modern democratic nations, then Mill was its first great systematiser. Whereas Tocqueville was an aristocrat and a conservative who saw the inevitability of and the justice in democratic demands, Mill was a democrat and a radical who respected the insights in conservative thought. Mill, of course, has frequently been accused of being an eclectic who unsuccessfully tried to combine the pleasure-and-pain principle of his father and Bentham with what he regarded as superior criteria (giving 'higher' pleasures a priority over cruder or 'lower' pleasures). It is more accurate, however, to see him as constructing a public philosophy for democratic nations by incorporating into a flexible utilitarian political philosophy the insights of other political philosophies and projects, including those of Socratic political philosophy, Coleridge's conservatism, feminism, science and technology, positivist sociology, laissez-faire economics and socialist alternatives to market capitalism.

Among Mill's achievements was that of charting the course that the New Liberals were to take. The New Liberals, though critical of Mill's empiricism and what remained of his original Benthamite utilitarian philosophy - with many New Liberals substituting for them idealist philosophies derived from Kant and Hegel - saw themselves as developing the insights of Mill's liberal-democratic, public-philosophic thought.

The New Liberalism as Public Philosophy

New Liberalism was a term which was used from about the 1880s to the First World War to describe a broad, mainly British movement of liberal writers, politicians and activists who were a major influence on the 1905-1916 Liberal governments of Henry Campbell-Bannerman and Herbert Asquith. Because this movement along with its expectation of further Liberal governments disintegrated, during and after the First World War, many historians and analysts have concluded that the New Liberalism was little more than a bridge by which intellectuals and voters crossed from liberalism and the Liberal Party to socialism and the Labour Party. Although this interpretation accounts for some of the historical effects of the New Liberalism, it obscures the content of its politics. Like John Stuart Mill, the New Liberals had political principles and objectives which challenged not only laissez-faire liberalism but much Labour Party and other socialism.

The New Liberals grounded their political philosophy on a richer conception of human life than the Benthamite view of men and women as pain avoiders and pleasure seekers. They contended that, for the achievement of a satisfactory and fulfilling human life, a person had to combine personal independence and moral character with citizenship virtues, including a commitment to the common good. In order to make such a life possible for everyone, they held that states - by which they meant citizens and their associations and communities as well as governments and governmental structures - were obliged to help the poor to overcome their poverty, lack of education and other hindrances to a satisfying human life. They were, at least until the end of the nineteenth century, confident about the future; but their optimism was always tempered by a realisation of the problems and difficulties in further liberalising, democratising and morally improving social and political life.

John Stuart Mill foreshadowed the New Liberalism, but the person with a much stronger claim to be its founder was the idealist philosopher and Oxford University lecturer, T. H. Green (1836-1882). Bernard Bosanquet (1848-1923) and several other idealist philosophers were New Liberals, and among the New Liberal journalists was C. P. Scott (1846-

1932), for over half a century the editor of the *Manchester Guardian*, Britain's leading liberal and radical newspaper. Other prominent New Liberal writers included Arnold Toynbee (1852-1883), whose *Industrial Revolution* (1884) with its concern over the social effects of industrialisation was a landmark publication; Leonard Trelawny Hobhouse (1864-1929), a distinguished sociologist and political theorist, and a leading *Manchester Guardian* journalist; and his friend John Atkinson Hobson (1858-1940), a maverick economist and critic of imperialism. Among the leading Liberal Party politicians who contributed to or were significantly influenced by the New Liberalism were James (later Viscount) Bryce (1838-1922); Richard Burdon (later Viscount) Haldane (1856-1928); Herbert (later Viscount) Samuel (1870-1963); and, to a lesser extent David Lloyd George (1863-1945) and, in his early Liberal Party days, Winston Churchill (1874-1967).[7]

A striking feature of New Liberal writing was its high moral tone. Readers were exhorted to view themselves as citizens with duties to others and to the democratic community. Many New Liberals were motivated by classical Greek ideals, and saw modern liberalism as again making possible the life of a *liber* (free person). In 1902, Herbert Asquith, the future Liberal prime minister, expressed New Liberal sentiments when, in his Introduction to Herbert Samuel's *Liberalism*, he wrote that to

> be really free...people must be able to make the best use of [every] faculty, opportunity, energy, life. It is in this fuller view of the true significance of liberty that we find the governing impulse in later developments in Liberalism, in the direction of education, temperance, better dwellings, an

---

7   For an introduction to the New Liberal thought of T.H. Green, L.T. Hobhouse and J.A. Hobson, see Wintrop (1983). For more extensive discussions of New Liberal thinkers and thinking, Freeden (1978); and Wieler (1982). For the politics of the philosophic idealists associated with the New Liberals, Gordon and White (1979); Milne (1962); and Vincent and Plant (1984). For a history of liberalism which contains discussions of the New Liberals and is written from a New Liberal standpoint, see Ruggiero (1961). For subsequent reflections on the movement by participants, see Haldane (1928); Hobson (1976); and Samuel (1945). For substantial, critical biographies of Green and Hobhouse, see Richter (1964); and Collini (1979). See also Bellamy (1992), esp. pp. 9-57. For a more sympathetic study of Hobhouse than Collini's, see Owen (1974). Major New Liberal writings on democracy and its problems include Bosanquet (1923); Bryce (1909); Fisher (1924); Green (1986; and 1964); Hobhouse (1904; and 1964); Hobson (1902); and Herbert Samuel's contemporary but now neglected summary of New Liberal thinking (1902). Also of interest is a (1909) collection of Churchill's speeches.

improved social and industrial environment, everything in short, that tends to national, communal and personal efficiency (p. x).

Freedom, a necessary condition for and a goal of democratic government, was associated with reciprocal obligations, and a virtuous life in which people had a duty both to develop themselves and to assist other citizens in their development. Free and moral persons were social beings obliged to continually improve themselves, and to struggle to help others to free themselves from poverty and other obstacles to a similar freedom. As Herbert Fisher wrote, 'man is a social animal...it is his duty to perfect his being as a member of a commonwealth so constituted and organised as to maintain conditions under which it is possible to lead a moral life' (1924, pp. 19-20). Central to the public philosophy of New Liberal thinkers, therefore, were the duties which they regarded as basic for the citizens, politicians and social leaders of democratic nations. At least five kinds of duties were emphasised.[8]

First, although most New Liberals supported the compulsory national insurance and other welfare legislation of the pre-1914 Liberal governments, many of the welfare functions which governments have since acquired were regarded as social rather than state responsibilities. Charity, therefore, was considered a duty. Citizens were not only responsible for the health, education and livelihood of themselves and their immediate family, and for assisting their wider families, friends, fellow workers or business associates, but for assisting other members of their society. Philanthropy, either by voluntary work or at least donations to private charities, was, until the end of the nineteenth century, considered the main weapon in the struggle against poverty. It was not until the apparent failure of private charity to deal with the persistent poverty of the industrial towns and cities, the conditions which led to the Royal Commission on the Poor Law of 1905, that most New Liberals gave their support to compulsory national insurance.[9] But the widening of state functions which came with early-twentieth-century welfare legislation made it imperative, New Liberals believed, that private charities and their more flexible approaches survive, and that the provision of libraries, museums, local and national parks, and other public amenities remain with society rather than the state, and with local rather than national government. A second and related duty was that citizens in their villages, towns, cities and regions establish and sustain

---

8   For New Liberal discussions of the duties of citizens, in addition to those by Bosanquet; Bryce; Fisher; and Green; see Jones (1905); and Maccunn (1894).

9   For the controversies among New Liberals on the issue of private charity versus public welfare, see the study of the Charity Organisation Society, the principal private charity of the period, and one with which Bernard Bosanquet was associated (Mowat, 1961).

schools and other educational institutions. Indeed, New Liberal theorists and politicians were instrumental in establishing, for Britain, a national system of school and university education (Gordon and White, 1979). Tertiary education was seen by New Liberals not as a right but as a privilege which imposed duties. People were obliged to use their education to help others, rather than treat it as a means to increase their wealth and that of their families.

A third category of citizenship duties, for most New Liberals, were religious. Citizens should share in family and public worship, engage in church activities, and respect the religious opinions of others. Religious duties were seen as complementary to the basic liberal-democratic demand - never fully achieved in the United Kingdom - that church and state be separate. If religion and the churches helped to sustain democracy, as most New Liberals believed, then citizens should ensure the survival and development of religion, the churches and the basic moral rules which they helped to uphold. Fourth, for the New Liberals, the public duties of citizens did not end at the frontiers of their nation. Citizens should inform themselves about foreign affairs, and insist that their nation have a moral as well as prudent foreign policy. The early nineteenth-century cooperation among nations in suppressing the slave trade was frequently cited as an example of a moral foreign policy. But on empire issues the New Liberals were divided. For some, a moral policy meant improving the conditions in the British and other European empires; others, however, opposed imperialism, demanding that the overseas territories be quickly prepared for independence. Fifth, the New Liberals agreed with Mill that voting was a duty rather than a right. Voters, in common with office holders, should use political power justly, to benefit their political community and its members. In turn, if an informed, just and prudent electorate was to be created, then public debates had to be orderly and restrained as well as spirited. During and between elections, politicians should avoid abusive and hysterical campaigns, and they and their supporters should not confuse shared prejudices with rational decisions. A 'large and victorious majority...[should not mistake] the volume of its own agreement for a public verdict in its favour' (Maccunn, 1894, p. 125). Voters were urged to inform themselves about current issues of importance, and to try to understand at least the rudiments of the history, constitution, and traditions of their nations.

A century later, it is tempting to dismiss as unrealistic and naive the duties which the New Liberals urged upon the citizens and politicians of modern, industrialised nations. Such judgements, however, should not be made too hastily. The New Liberals were well aware that a citizenship ethos would be difficult to achieve and maintain. It was because, in common with Tocqueville and Mill, that they appreciated the extent of the forces which worked against a citizenship ethos that they gave so much prominence to it. By the beginning of the twentieth century, however, the emphases in New Liberal writing had changed. Increasingly, the appeal was to prudence and an enlightened self interest rather than to more demanding moral and citizenship codes. When, after the Boer War of 1899-1902 and the jingoism which it brought to the surface, it became evident that a major task was the defence of past liberal-democratic gains, the heady abstractions of Green and other philosophic idealists gave ground to more empirical and cautious approaches to politics. On this change of emphasis, it is illuminating to contrast the content and style of Green's political writing, at the beginning of the 1880s, with that of Hobhouse two decades later.

Green had a similar conception of history to that of Mill, as progressing towards greater freedom, and having culminated in modern democracy, a democracy that was far more than electoral procedures and governmental institutions. Democracy, for Green, was the activity of citizens, organised by means of a legal system and state, who expressed their freedom by creating new and better ways of life. Democracy was a project for advancing the common good by the exercise of freedom, the extension of rights and a greater understanding of responsibilities. Green's conceptions of democracy and citizenship were the bases for his challenge to the laissez-faire belief in minimal government, and his call for liberal-democratic governments to be more socially interventionist in a struggle to overcome poverty, drunkenness, ignorance and the other hindrances to free lives and political virtue.

By contrast, Hobhouse, who held similar conceptions of democracy and citizenship to those of Green, combined them with a far greater emphasis on social and political difficulties. Large parts of his neglected *Democracy and Reaction* (1904), for example, resembled a catalogue of the ways in which democratic politics and a citizenship culture were being disabled. In a previous discussion of the New Liberals, I itemised his concerns as follows:

> (1) a hardening of the moral arteries of politicians and civil servants, which in Africa had led even to a revival and toleration of slavery; (2) the emergence of 'mob man' who, always in a hurry and unable to think independently, was easily manipulated by the popular press and the political demagogue who saw no further than the next election; (3) middle classes who used the privileges of education not to educate themselves morally and as citizens but to acquire further privileges; (4) a decline in religious belief which had led not to a secular humanitarian ethic but, at best, to a 'good-natured scepticism, not only about the other world, but also about the deeper problems and higher interests of this

world': (5) a form of Hegelianism in which intellectuals, following Bismarck's example, thought that a superior synthesis to that of classical individualist liberalism was embodied in the national state; (6) biological theories of evolution which encouraged a hardness toward the weak and the defeated, whose principal moral criterion was newness, and which fatalistically considered reason and thought as merely the products of physical and social processes and thus unable to provide grounds for liberties and rights; (7) a politics of narrow and selfish class interests, encouraged by crude varieties of socialism; (8) a bureaucratic mentality, in government and among intellectuals, whereby the government of the people was seen as a technique producing organisation and efficiency at home, conquest and mastery abroad; (9) the success of the imperialist party in masking a lust for empire in an idealist rhetoric of taking British conceptions of law and freedom to less-privileged peoples; and (10) the failure of working class voters to resist nationalist demagogy (Wintrop, 1983, pp. 107-8).

In brief, the New Liberal attitude to citizenship and its relation to the democratic project may be summarised as follows. Either democratic nations progressed to become communities of citizens endeavouring to advance their common good, or democracy would decay and lead to either a masked or more unadorned despotism. Unless democratic elites and voters acted as citizens who cared about their common good, there would be a crippling rather than an enriching of the lives of men and women.

The idea of a common good, which the New Liberals tried to instil into governments and citizens, was an aspiration and a means for reconciling the values, goals, rights and duties of a healthy liberal democracy. As such, the common good performed a similar role to John Stuart Mill's highest value, utility. It was a tool for harmonising a wide range of political, economic and cultural goods. It was also an ideal which generated duties, and which made the 'essential doctrine' of liberalism the idea that it was 'the duty of the state [citizens and government] to secure to its members, and all others whom it can influence, the fullest possible opportunity to lead the best life' (Samuel, 1902, p. 4). A faith in the potential of a public philosophy and public debate to clarify the common good, and in the ability of citizens and governments to advance it might be difficult to sustain, but, for the New Liberals, if democratic government was to be more than a sham the maintenance of that faith and the determination to act on it were indispensable conditions.

The next two chapters will turn to the work of twentieth century writers who made major contributions to the public philosophic tradition of democratic theory established by Tocqueville, John Stuart Mill, the New Liberals and kindred nineteenth-century thinkers.

References

August, Eugene (1975), *John Stuart Mill: A Mind at Large*, Scribner, New York.
Bellamy, Richard (1992), *Liberalism and Modern Society*, Polity Pr., Cambridge.
Berger, Fred R. (1984), *Happiness, Justice and Freedom: The Moral and Political Philosophy of John Stuart Mill*, Univ. of California Pr., Berkeley.
Bosanquet, Bernard (1923), *The Philosophical Theory of the State* [1899], 4th edn, Macmillan, London.
Bryce, James (1909), *The Hindrances to Good Citizenship*, Yale Univ. Pr., New Haven.
Burns, J.H. (1969), 'J. S. Mill and Democracy, 1829-61', in J. B. Schneewind (ed.), *Mill: A Collection of Critical Essays*, 2nd edn, Macmillan, London.
Churchill, Winston Spencer (1973), *Liberalism and the Social Problem*, Haskell House, New York, a reprint of the 1909 edn.
Collini, Stefan (1979), *Liberalism and Sociology: L. T. Hobhouse and Political Argument in England, 1880-1914*, Cambridge Univ. Pr., Cambridge.
Cowling, Maurice (1963), *Mill and Liberalism*, Cambridge Univ. Pr., Cambridge.
Drescher, Seymour (1968a), *Dilemmas of Democracy: Tocqueville and Modernization*, Univ. of Pittsburgh Pr., Pittsburgh.
Drescher, Seymour (ed.) (1968b), *Tocqueville and Beaumont on Social Reform*, Harper and Row, New York.
Fisher, Herbert (1924), *The Common Weal*, Clarendon Pr., Oxford.
Freeden, Michael (1978), *The New Liberalism: An Ideology of Social Reform*, Oxford Univ. Pr., Oxford.
Garforth, F.W. (1980), *Educative Democracy*, Oxford Univ. Pr., Oxford.
Goldstein, Doris S. (1975), *Trial of Faith: Religion and Politics in Tocqueville's Thought*, Elsevier, New York.
Gordon, Peter and John White (1979), *Philosophers as Educational Reformers*, Routledge, London.
Green, T.H. (1964), *The Political Theory of T. H. Green*, (ed.) J. R. Rodman, Appleton-Century-Crofts, New York.
Green, T.H. (1986), *Lectures on the Principles of Political Obligation* [1882] *and Other Writings*, (eds) Paul Harris and John Morrow, Cambridge Univ. Pr., Cambridge.
Haldane, Richard Burdon (1928), *An Autobiography*, Hodder and Stoughton, London.
Halevy, Elie (1928), *The Growth of Philosophic Radicalism*, Faber and Faber, London.
Hamburger, Joseph (1965), *Intellectuals in Politics: John Stuart Mill and the Philosophic Radicals*, Yale Univ. Pr., New Haven.
Hereth, Michael (1986), *Alexis de Tocqueville: Threats to Freedom in Democracy*, Duke Univ. Pr., Durham.
Himmelfarb, Gertrude (1974), *On Liberty and Liberalism: The Case of John Stuart Mill*, Knopf, New York.
Hobhouse, L.T. (1904), *Democracy and Reaction*, Fisher Unwin, London.

Hobhouse, L.T. (1964), *Liberalism* [1911], 2nd edn, Oxford Univ. Pr., Oxford.
Hobson. J.A. (1902), *Imperialism*. Fisher Allen. London.
Hobson. J.A. (1976). *Confessions of an Economic Heretic*. 2nd edn, Harvester Pr., Brighton.
Jacobs. Struan (1993). 'John Stuart Mill and the Tyranny of the Majority', *Australian Journal of Political Science*, vol. 28, 1993, pp. 306-21.
Jardin. Andre (1988), *Tocqueville: A Biography*, Peter Halban, London.
Jones. Henry (1905), *Social Responsibilities*, James Maclehose, Glasgow.
Lively. Jack (1962), *The Social and Political Thought of Alexis de Tocqueville*, Clarendon Pr., Oxford.
Maccunn, John (1894), *Ethics of Citizenship*, James Maclehose, Glasgow.
Manent. Pierre (1996), *Tocqueville and the Nature of Democracy*, Rowman and Littlefield, Lanham, Md.
Mayer. J.P. (1960), *Alexis de Tocqueville: A Biographical Study in Political Science*, 2nd edn, Harper, New York.
Mazlish. Bruce (1975), *James and John Stuart Mill*, Hutchinson, London.
Mill, John Stuart (1964), *Autobiography* [1873], Foreword Asa Briggs, New American Library/Signet, New York.
Mill. John Stuart (1967), *Chapters on Socialism* [1879], in the *Collected Works of John Stuart Mill*, (ed.) J.M. Robson, vol 5, Univ. of Toronto, Toronto.
Mill. John Stuart (1973), *Essays on Politics and Culture*, (ed.) Gertrude Himmelfarb, 3rd edn. Peter Smith, Gloucester, Mass.
Mill. John Stuart (1987), *Principles of Political Economy* [1848], new edn, (ed.) Sir William Ashley, Longmans, Green, London, 1909, reprinted Augustus M. Kelley, Fairfield, N.J.
Mill. John Stuart (1991), *On Liberty and Other Essays*, (ed.) John Gray, Oxford Univ. Pr., Oxford.
Mill. John Stuart (1993), *Utilitarianism, On Liberty, Considerations on Representative Government, Remarks on Bentham's Philosophy*, (ed.) Geraint Williams, Dent/Everyman, London.
Milne. A.J. (1962), *The Social Philosophy of English Idealism*, Allen and Unwin, London.
Mowat, Charles Lock (1961). *The Charity Organisation Society, 1869-1913*, Methuen, London.
Owen, John E. (1974), *L. T. Hobhouse: Sociologist*, Nelson, London.
Packe, Michael St. John (1954), *The Life of John Stuart Mill*, Secker and Warburg, London.
Richter. Melvin (1964), *The Politics of Conscience: T. H. Green and His Age*, Weidenfeld and Nicolson, London.
Robson, J.M. (1968), *The Improvement of Mankind: The Social and Political Thought of John Stuart Mill*, Univ. of Toronto Pr., London.
Ruggiero. Guido de (1959), *The History of European Liberalism* [1927], 2nd edn, Beacon Pr., Boston.
Ryan, Alan (1974), *John Stuart Mill*, Routledge, London.
Samuel. Herbert (1902), *Liberalism; An Attempt to State the Principles and Proposals of Contemporary Liberalism in England*, Grant Richards, London.
Samuel. Viscount (1945), *Memoirs*, Cresset Pr., London.

Semmel, Bernard (1984), *John Stuart Mill and the Pursuit of Virtue*, Yale Univ. Pr., New Haven.

Skorupski, John (1989), *John Stuart Mill*, Routledge, London.

Thomas, William (1985), *Mill*, Oxford Univ. Pr., New York.

Tocqueville, Alexis de (1959), *'The European Revolution' and Correspondence with Gobineau*, Doubleday/Anchor, Garden City, N.Y.

Tocqueville, Alexis de (1966), *The Ancien Regime and the French Revolution* [1856], Collins/Fontana, n.p.

Tocqueville, Alexis de (1968), *Democracy in America* [1835, 1840], 2 vols, J.P Mayer and Max Lerner (eds), 2nd edn, Collins/Fontana, n.p..

Tocqueville, Alexis de (1970), *Recollections* [1893], Macdonald, London.

Vincent, Andrew and Raymond Plant (1984), *Philosophy, Politics and Citizenship: The Life and Thought of the British Idealists*, Blackwell, Oxford.

Wieler, Peter (1982), *The New Liberalism*, Garland, New York.

Wintrop, Norman (1983), 'Liberal-Democratic Theory: the New Liberals', in Norman Wintrop (ed.), *Liberal Democratic Theory and Its Critics*, Croom Helm, London.

Zetterbaum, Marvin (1967), *Tocqueville and the Problem of Democracy*, Stanford Univ. Pr., Stanford, Ca.

7 The Last of the New Liberals, and Analytic-Philosophic Public Philosophers

Tocqueville, John Stuart Mill and many New Liberal and other nineteenth-century public philosophers combined political writing with being either members of their parliaments or otherwise engaged in national or, as with T. H. Green, local politics. Public philosophic journalists and academics, less personally involved in practical politics, also saw themselves as political participants in that their work was intended to sway politicians and the public. This public philosophic tradition of theorists being political actors and vice versa has survived but has been less conspicuous in the twentieth century. Lippmann and a few other writers with public philosophic claims have had the ear of politicians, while several leaders of democratic nations have been influential political writers. They include America's Woodrow Wilson, Britain's Winston Churchill, Czechoslovakia's Thomas Masaryk and Vaclav Havel, and India's Jawaharlal Nehru. In addition, most democratic nations have had at least some politicians and political activists whose books, journalism and speeches have risen above self promotion and party-political and pressure-group rhetoric to achieve a public philosophic status.

Nevertheless a significant difference between the politics of nineteenth- and twentieth-century democratic politics has been the extent to which political theory has become dominated by academics - Lippmann being one of the few exceptions. Whereas neither Tocqueville nor Mill, the two public philosophers who received most attention in the previous chapter, held university posts, all the twentieth century writers whose work is reviewed in this and the following chapter have. It is partly as a consequence of political theorists being less involved in mainstream politics that public philosophic writing has persisted but, particularly since the Second World War, has had less political impact. In this and other ways normative political theory has been separated from governmental practice, and the separation goes a long way in explaining the prevalence in democratic theory of formalism and utopianism. Formalism expresses the attitude of the spectator; utopianism that of the politically marginalised intellectual.

These two chapters on twentieth-century public philosophers, however, will review the work of major democratic theorists who have resisted both formalism and utopianism, and who, from various philosophic and political perspectives, have developed the tradition's understanding of democratic government and the standards which should guide it. This chapter will concentrate on writers who have brought historical and philosophic perspectives to these tasks; the following will turn to theorists whose perspectives have been more psychological and sociological.

The last of the New Liberals: A. D. Lindsay and Ernest Barker

A. D. (Alexander Dunlop) Lindsay (1879-1952), who became Baron Lindsay of Birker in 1945, and Ernest Barker (1874-1960), who was knighted in 1944, were in many ways the last of the New Liberals. Lindsay was educated at and held major teaching and administrative posts at Glascow and Oxford, the two university strongholds of philosophic idealism and the New Liberalism. From 1924 to 1949 he was the Master of Balliol College, Oxford, which from the days of Benjamin Jowett and T. H. Green had been at the centre of the university's philosophical idealism and New Liberalism. He was the Vice-Chancellor of Oxford University from 1935 to 1938 and, after the Second World War, the first head of the University College of North Staffordshire, subsequently Keele University. From 1907 to 1914, before his post-1918 concentration on political theory, he published studies of the philosophies of Bergson and Kant, and translated, edited or introduced texts by Plato, Hobbes, Berkeley and an edition of George Grote's *History of Greece*. He also published work on Christian belief.

Ernest Barker acquired his university education at Balliol College, from 1893, and then taught at three other Oxford colleges. From 1920 to 1928 he was the Principal at King's College, London, and from 1928 to 1939 the first holder of the Chair of Political Science at Cambridge University. After his retirement, he was an honorary fellow at Peterhouse College, Cambridge, the city where he lived, and at Oxford's Merton College. The best known of his many books are on ancient Greek political thought, mainly that of Socrates, Plato and Aristotle (1918; and 1959). But he also wrote on the political thought and culture of the last centuries of the ancient world, and those of medieval and modern Britain and Europe, as well as translating from the German the studies of natural law and related topics by Otto von Gierke and Ernst Troeltsch. A selection of his essays which embraced all these interests, *Traditions of Civility* (1948b), stimulated Walter Lippmann's interest in civility, natural law and the public philosophy. Both Lindsay and Barker wrote important but neglected public philosophic studies of modern democratic politics. I shall begin with Lindsay's.[1]

A. D. Lindsay

A. D. Lindsay was one of many twentieth-century British intellectuals who, influenced by New Liberal thought, became a democratic socialist and a member of Britain's Labour Party. He advised the Labour Party on educational policy, and, in 1938, unsuccessfully contested a by-election in Oxford on an anti-Munich, anti-appeasement platform. His *Essentials of Democracy* (1935), first published in 1929, which contains less than eighty pages, is probably the best short book on democracy in the English language. His more ambitious *The Modern Democratic State* (1962), first published in 1943, assessed the condition of British and other democracies, and what Lindsay called their 'operative ideals'. A promised further volume on 'the problem of democratic control', and how a democratic government could make a democratic 'community more truly a community' (1962, p. 286) never appeared. His two published books on democracy, however, contain detailed examinations of the origins, evolution and character of modern democracy, and the many challenges to it.

In common with most New Liberals, Lindsay agreed with Aristotle that the proper end for a political community was the good life of its citizens. But Lindsay added the modern historicist idea that the good life was not timeless but subject to evolution; it was 'in the minds of the members of the state as to what kind of common life should be encouraged' (1962, p. 3). Lindsay maintained that although science and the improvements to human life which it promised had been a driving force behind modern democratic revolutions, more powerful causes had been the Reformation and, in Britain, the nonconformist churches. It was the nonconformist churches which, in the seventeenth and eighteenth centuries, seeking religious toleration, generated the ideas that all people were essentially equal and worthy of respect, and should possess political rights. In addition, the nonconformist churches provided an education in self government for large numbers of the activists and leaders of eighteenth-century democratic reform movements and nineteenth-century trade unions. Further influences on modern democracy, he thought, were Aristotelean political philosophy, Greek city-state politics, Roman law,

---

[1] For information and comment on Lindsay, see Richter (1968); and Maddox (1986). For Barker, see Barker (1953); and Stapleton (1989; and 1994). See also the articles on them in *The Dictionary of National Biography* (1971).

medieval constitutionalism, and Renaissance and Enlightenment individualism and rationalism.

Democratic theory and practice, he argued, had found a middle way between a Hobbesian pessimism about the nature of human beings and a naive faith in their perfectibility. Democracy's founders had held realistic conceptions of human potential, similar to the Christian view of men and women as sinners, but as sinners who were made in the image of God and who were capable of repentance and good works. Democratic government, unlike absolute government or anarchism, rested on the commonsense view that 'in all societies, some men go beyond what is expected of them, some do what custom requires and no more, and some are known to be bad men' (1962. p. 96). The leaders and citizens of democratic nations therefore should be as wise as serpents and as harmless as doves, a proposition to which Lindsay added the rider, 'Whether in a world where we need to be as wise as serpents and as harmless as doves it is worse to be as wise and harmful as serpents or as harmless and stupid as doves it is difficult to say' (1962, p. 99).

Democratic government was preceded or accompanied by the construction of nation states, and it was strengthened, Lindsay argued, by feelings of loyalty to those states and damaged by extreme forms of nationalism. Nation states were established by Europe's absolute monarchs at the end of the Middle Ages and subsequently democratised; but, Lindsay observed, whereas in most West European nations early forms of democracy preceded feelings of national loyalty, in Eastern Europe nationalism came first. Nationalism in East Europe expressed a hatred of foreign oppressors rather than loyalty to an established national community; it became, therefore, an obstacle to democracy. Moderate nationalism of the British variety, however, was a necessary condition for a democratisation in which people transformed themselves from subjects to citizens.

> A state becomes a nation when instead of its members being primarily divided between sovereign and subjects, government and citizenship become a common task, demanding not passive citizenship but active co-operation from all....the effect of this sense of nationality is normally democratic. If on the other hand, for the division between sovereign and subjects, is substituted the division between ruling and subject races, something very different may happen. Nationality becomes nationalism, democracy's bitter enemy (1962, p. 151).

Lindsay, like most liberals, distinguished between the state and society, a separation which he described as being between the community and its government and state. The community was the source of a nation's energy and achievement, an energy which came from its individual members forming associations and cooperating in pursuit of their individual and collective well-being. Although democratic like other states possessed laws backed by sanctions, their strength resided in their popular support, not their coercive power. Governmental coercion was consented to because, by enforcing necessary and beneficial laws, it served the interests of citizens. Echoing T. H. Green's dictum that states rested on will and not force, Lindsay wrote that we

> are sometimes told that the state rests on force. That is not true....the state possesses and uses organized force because most people in the state are determined that the rule of law shall prevail, are prepared to insist on a peaceful and constitutional settlement of differences....It is also clear that the state can only enforce obedience to law if the laws are such that most people do not want to break them (1935, pp. 55-6).

Moreover, in a democratic nation, neither a branch of government, the state nor the electorate as a whole possessed absolute sovereignty. It was not primarily popular or legal sovereignty which constituted democratic government but the rule of law and a population's consent to it. Lindsay did not mean that every person agreed with every law, or that constitutional or other laws should never be modified; his point was that neither political leaders and elites, majorities nor anyone else was above the law. Such constitutionalism, which he traced back to the Levellers and the Putney Debates of the seventeenth century, was considered fundamental to modern democratic theory and practice. A parliamentary or electoral sovereignty was tolerable only so long as it was exercised responsibly and respected the interests and rights of all citizens. What was incompatible with constitutionalism, democracy and justice, he wrote in 1943, was arbitrary government and unpredictable courts.

> When German courts are instructed that the welfare of the Reich is to outweigh in their decisions all other principles, we rightly denounce that as a travesty of justice. The reason for that is simple. No one can know with any assurance at all what a judge is going to say is for the welfare of the Reich and therefore no one can regulate his conduct accordingly (1962, p. 221).

Lindsay's emphasis on the rule of law in his analyses of democracy, however, was combined with an emphasis on culture. He did this with the concept of an *operative ideal*, and by insisting that political institutions rested on ideals. Although ideals, in common with institutions, could be corrupted by national leaders, office holders, and/or powerful classes, it was democracy's ideals, not their abuse, which defined a democratic community. To understand a democratic or other society, therefore, one must know its operative ideals. It followed that a major task for political theorists was public philosophic - to reveal, clarify, further and, when necessary, try to change the ideals of a political community. The political theorist, Lindsay wrote, should understand

> the state as it is, and [he or she] is therefore, concerned with the ideals which are actually operative - operative enough in men's minds to make them go on obeying a particular form of government or, at times, to make them break up the form of government they are accustomed to and try to construct a new one (1962, p. 37).[2]

West European and North American nations became democratic in the nineteenth century when, as an operative ideal, it was recognised 'that all members of society ought equally to count' (1962, p. 136). For all the natural differences and inequalities among men and women, all people became equally entitled to the protection of their rights and, as far as it was compatible with the rights of others, their extension. It was Lindsay's affirmation of this fundamental equality of status and the 'fellowship' which ought to accompany it which underlay his commitment to socialism.

His was a socialism, however, which rejected social levelling, and which derived from the New Liberal principle that modern democratic states were obliged to combat the hindrances to the moral and other development of their members. Lindsay's socialism rested on the belief that major twentieth-century obstacles to human development included (1) gigantic financial and business companies which ignored their responsibilities to society, and (2) the division between the people who managed and controlled industry and those who were managed and controlled. Although both hindrances were associated by Lindsay with modern capitalism, he acknowledged that oligarchically organised factories and industries, and enmity between managers and the managed could occur under socialism.

The socialist measures which he thought followed from democratic ideals and empirical realities consisted of typical mid-twentieth-century democratic-socialist demands: legislation to reintroduce competition in industries dominated by monopolies or oligopolies; the nationalisation of

---

2   This conception of political theory bridged the gap between facts and values. As Melvin Richter has written, it 'rejected the distinction between the state as studied by political theorists (in the form it ideally should have) and the state as studied by political scientists (in its actual form). Lindsay argued that these two views of the state are analytically and empirically inseparable' (1968, p. 308).

industries which were grossly exploitative or necessary to national life but inefficient; and a general governmental responsibility for the economy. To overcome what he regarded as the oligarchic character of industrial relations in Britain, he favoured strengthening and extending the industrial rights of workers and their opportunities to participate in and be consulted by management. Trade unions and workshop democracy were considered the main means for this empowering of factory and other workers. Trade unions, he urged, should check industrial managers, while workshop democracy, shop-steward and other trade-union rank-and-file movements should check trade-union officials. Lindsay, therefore, was more perceptive than most intellectual sympathisers of trade unions in recognising the problems of internal autocracy and authoritarianism.

Although modern capitalism had other features which disturbed Lindsay, such as the profit motive's encouragement of greed, and the inevitable injustices of market relations as some people suffered for no fault of their own, he realised that modern capitalism was a system of contractual relations and cooperation as well as competition. For all its defects, and the problems it caused democratic societies, capitalism was a product of the freedom, individualism and cooperation of the modern democratic world rather than of coercion or deception. Lindsay's socialism, therefore, was far from dogmatic, and it was subordinate to his commitments to democracy and fellowship. It subjected the issue of capitalism or socialism to empirical inquiry, and it combined a commitment to the fundamental equality of all people with an acceptance of the need for hierarchy and authority in industrial and economic as well as political life. A modern democratic state, Lindsay wrote, 'is only possible if it can combine appreciation of skill, knowledge and expertness with a reverence for the common humanity of everyday people' (1962, p. 261).

A similar balance, accompanied by an important but neglected distinction, was brought to Lindsay's encounter with the problem of technology. He urged democrats to distinguish between science and technology, and to support the freedom of scientific inquiry; on the other hand he denied that the freedom to which science was entitled should automatically be extended to technology. When necessary, when for example 'technical inventions' had 'far-reaching effects on social habits...for ill' (1962, p. 169), restrictions were justified. Technical progress, Lindsay contended, 'inherited undeservedly the prestige of its father, free scientific inquiry, and it was almost regarded as improper to suggest that the child of such a father could be bad or even wanted watching' (1962, p. 170). But Lindsay, who was no lover of restrictions on freedom or of governmental and bureaucratic power, urged that governmental constraints on technological and industrial development be subject, in addition to parliamentary checks, to public scrutiny and discussion.

Elsewhere, in an outstanding analysis of the purposes of public discussion, he argued that its function was not to legitimate policy by the obtaining of a consensus but to discover the best policy. When 'we take discussion seriously', he wrote, 'we are committed to the view that we are concerned not primarily to obtain or register consent, but to find something out' (1935, p. 34). For all its imperfections, 'modern representative government...does make possible an immense deal of real and effective discussion' (1935, p. 36). Public debate was a source of social energy and wisdom, and much of its strength came from the participation of private associations. But, as such political participation could be sectional, public discussion was necessary not only as a check to governments, parliaments, courts and public bureaucracies but to the voluntary associations themselves. Even private associations with the most morally motivated and benevolent of professed purposes, including the churches, Lindsay observed, could develop interests opposed to those of the rest of the community.

Public discussion was both an essential complement and a justification for universal adult voting. Universal adult voting was necessary if all sections of a political community were to be heard and properly considered; but, to avoid disasters, there had to be effective public debate. Public debate, not John Stuart Mill's proposed preferential voting (extra votes for educated and professional people), was for Lindsay the democratic means for preventing democracy from being perverted into the tyranny of majorities and/or political parties.

> The democratic opponents of such [preferential voting] devices would say that they do not deny the difference between men's political capacities, but would maintain that wealth or wisdom or leadership will have their natural effect in the discussion that precedes the voting, and no doubt therefore on the voting (1929, p. 41).

Lindsay had a conception of democratic politics as a unity of theory and practice in which the institutions and day-to-day politics of democratic states both expressed and acted as a constraint on their operative ideals - ideals which, in this book, are a primary concern of democratic theory as a public philosophy. The business of democratic politics, Lindsay wrote,

> is to take this elaborate complex of individuals and institutions [of a modern state] for granted, try to understand the principles and fundamental ideas which inspire it, diagnose the evils from which it is suffering: and then by state action seek to remove the disharmonies which are threatening its life and checking its vitality (1962, p. 244).

Ernest Barker

Ernest Barker's contributions to democratic theory as a public philosophy supplement rather than replicate Lindsay's. Whereas Lindsay's studies give prominence to the origins and historical context of modern democracy and its operative ideals, Barker's main text is more consistently philosophic. His *Principles of Social and Political Theory* (1961) examines democratic government's ends and guiding standards, and contends that *justice* is democracy's main normative principle. But, despite his procedure for examining *justice* and other democratic norms being mainly analytic, in common with Lindsay his starting point is the history and character of modern democratic nations and their civilisation rather than abstract, universal moral principles. Although Barker's study now receives little attention, I shall argue that its analysis of justice is superior to those of later, more acclaimed studies.

For Barker, it is the subordination of governments to their societies that is the great political achievement and hallmark of modern liberal democracies. The achieving of citizenship rights by all the adult members of these national communities has enabled them to become states (law making, interpreting and enforcing authorities), and transformed what had formerly been states that depended on force rather than consent into governments that are accountable to their societies.

> The state is now the whole community: the whole legal association; the whole of the juridical organization. This is democracy, or the result of democracy: we must henceforth think of the State as ourselves (or as the juridical organization which we have given to ourselves, or the legal association into which we have formed ourselves); and we must henceforth give the name of 'Government' to the authority - before called 'State' - which is now seen as exercising on our behalf the powers which it had hitherto claimed as its own (1961, p. 91).

Strong national communities which guaranteed the liberties and rights of their members were, Barker agreed with Lindsay, the foundation for modern democracy. The British nation and its many sub-communities, which had their roots in ancient Greek and Judeo-Christian traditions, had, from the seventeenth to the nineteenth century, established democratic institutions on such a foundation. Democracy in Britain was the product of the struggles of the common lawyers, independent parliamentarians, nonconformist churches and the economically productive classes.

Governments contributed to and formalised democratic change, but the initiative came from the national community.[3]

Barker thus held a legal pluralist conception of law in which law was not a sovereign's commands, as asserted by legal positivists, but a set of socially beneficial, liberty enhancing rules enforced by the courts. It followed from this legal pluralism that the great political problem was not a conflict between law and liberty, for law was an expression and consolidation of liberty; it was that one legally recognised liberty could clash against another. 'But if liberty and law do not quarrel, liberty may quarrel with itself' (1961, p. 146). As a consequence, an overriding, arbitrating principle was required for governments and citizens. For this purpose, Barker turned not to Mill's *utility* or the *common good* of the original New Liberals but to *justice*. Although justice - the supreme normative principle for the guidance of citizens and governments - was a part of ethics, for Barker its primary location was not the moral life of individuals but their social and political activities and relations. Just acts were usually the product of just intentions, but justice's main concern was not internal mental processes but external behaviour. Justice meant that when there were conflicts between interests, liberties or principles, the criterion for arbitration was how best to maximise the rights, freedom and opportunities for the personal development and happiness of citizens without reducing the opportunities of others. In a different approach from that of utopian and other theorists of justice who use the concept of justice as a synonym for one or more favoured ideals such as freedom, equality or property rights, Barker held to a more open, Aristotelean and pluralist conception of justice.

> We [modern democrats] recognize a number of different values as necessary to an organized system of human relations. There is the value of liberty: there is the value of equality: there is the value of fraternity, or (as it may also be called, and is perhaps better called) co-operation. All these values are present in any system of law; but they are present in different degrees in different periods of time, and there is a constant process of adjustment and readjustment between their claims....From this point of view the function of justice may be said to be that of adjusting, joining, or fitting the different political values. Justice is the reconciler and the synthesis of political values: it is their union in an adjusted and integrated whole... (1961, p. 102).

---

3   For Barker's views on the origins and sources of modern democracy, see 'Book I, State and Society: An Historical View...' in the *Principles* (1961); and *National Character* (1948a). See also *Church, State and Education* (1957); and the pertinent essays in *Traditions of Civility* (1948b); and *Essays on Government* (1951).

For many analytical philosophers and proponents of less Aristotelean conceptions of justice, Barker's is lacking in precision. But unless *justice* is to be made synonymous with a small number of privileged values which, contrary to the assertions made for them, divide rather than unite a democratic nation, it is difficult to see how justice can be made more precise without abandoning it for something else.[4] Barker's main academic target however was not theorists who gave an absolute status to what were only parts of justice but moral relativists. He argued that if, as a result of moral relativism, the idea of justice were abandoned, there would no longer be any rational criterion by which opposed interests could be assessed and compromises reached. 'All wants would appear...to be equal: equally final; equally absolute' (1961, p. 172). Such relativism, which refused to appeal to justice or similar criteria, or which reduced 'justice to a mere *de facto* balance of different social wants, controlled by no criterion', would inevitably generate an opportunist conception of law as a tool for the control of societies by governments, experts and powerful sectional interests:

> pragmatic justice necessarily has for its fellow an equally pragmatic system of law. Law, which is the visible expression of justice, becomes accordingly a simple activity of 'social engineering', which drives the best-graded road that it can through the intricate hills of social wants (1961, p. 172).

It was essential that the citizens who comprised a democratic state understood that it was justice and not their will which should inspire their laws. If we make an unrestrained will final, Barker warned 'we really make force final, for the will which prevails just because it is a will, without regard to the object it wills, or the standard by which it wills, is a force' (1961, p. 216).

It was only when law, and the coercive and other powers of a state were just that political obligation, a necessary condition for stable democratic government, would be accepted by citizens as an essential duty. Their obligation, however, was always to law as such not to specific laws which, though the products of parliament and enforceable in the courts, could be incompatible with the spirit of the law - justice. When citizens thought they had good reasons for regarding a law or governmental policy as fundamentally unjust, they had to choose between evils, or *mischiefs* as Barker called them. These were the mischief of allowing a pernicious law to entrench itself, and thus contaminate a community, and the mischief of

---

4 Comparisons with later theories of justice and the argument in favour of Barker's will be returned to in Chapter 9's section on 'Promoting Justice'.

resistance to the law. Resisting the law, though sometimes warranted, was always mischievous, for even when resistance came from the purest of motives, it encouraged disaffection by the less morally scrupulous.

> The resister who defies a law is also disturbing (and incidentally encouraging others - less scrupulous than himself and more intent on private ends - to disturb) the *general* scheme of law and order and the *general* validity of obligation (1961, p. 224).

Barker, in his analyses of liberty, equality, justice, obligation and other democratic norms, was a typical public philosopher in his quest for a mean between extremes, and syntheses of the insights in different positions. Julie Stapleton (1989; and 1994), however, has argued that Barker failed to reconcile two of the basic parts of his political thought: English idealist philosophy's extension of universal moral principles to society, and the Whig view of politics as the expression of national traditions. But far from this attempted reconciliation being a failure, it is in many ways one of the strengths of Barker's democratic theory and public philosophy. His understanding of democratic politics as a project for expressing both the moral principles appropriate for political life and those parts of a nation's culture which embody and are compatible with moral principles contains, as Stapleton insists, a tension. But it is a necessary and sustainable tension that is superior to the extremes which it avoids: a politically utopian moral perfectionism and a politics of national or group aggrandisement. The reconciling of moral principles with the interests and traditions of a nation is an essential part of a public philosophy, as it is for a moral as well as prudent statecraft - or what Barker called 'statesmanship'.[5]

Formalist accounts of democracy as little more than free elections, competing parties, integrated elites and social pluralism were rejected by Barker. Democracy was substantive. It was the product of two thousand years of struggle by Western communities to civilise themselves, and to achieve self government and lives of dignity for their members. Such a substantive democracy was accessible to non-western peoples with different histories and traditions, but, if it was to take root, more was required than the transplanting of democracy's formal institutions. A successful democracy required, in addition to leaders and elites who possessed practical political skills, a political culture that was imbued with

---

5   For Barker's reflections on statesmanship, see his Second World War discussion, 'British Statesmen', included in his *Essays on Government* (1951). See also, for his understanding of academic and other political theory as a fusion of moral, historical, juridical and other thought, 'The Study of Political Science', in *Church, State and Education* (1957), reprinted in King (1977).

a restrained and responsible freedom, the recognition of an underlying human equality, religious and other toleration, and the willingness of people to deliberate and compromise. Reflecting on the history of democracy in the first half of the twentieth century, Barker wrote that

> by 1914 there were forms of parliament established from London to St. Petersburg, and from Stockholm to Rome and Athens. But a form of parliament is not the whole of the system of parliamentary democracy. Organized parties with some historical roots, and a temper which combines the spirit of party zeal with a sense of national responsibility; an electorate with some education in the use of the franchise and some capacity of discussing the issues on which it casts its vote; above all, a cabinet at once responsible to parliament and capable of guiding its deliberations and its decisions - all these are also elements (1942, p. 266).

In his *Reflections on Government* (1942), Barker confronted the question of whether modern democracies were capable of withstanding the threats from German National Socialism, Italian Fascism and Russian Communism. For Barker, for all the variations in the totalitarianism of these regimes and movements, there was in the twentieth-century world a fundamental conflict between two radically different mental states or tempers, the democratic and the despotic. And neither in his (1942) wartime book nor earlier, during the international crises of the inter-war years, did Barker lose faith in democracy. The grounds for his confidence were concisely stated in a 1933 lecture to a Liberal Party summer school on 'The Breakdown of Democracy', a lecture in which he denied its title. To say that democracy had broken down, he declared, was to admit 'that the free spirit of man has broken down and ceased to be free' (1937, p. 22). He built upon this idea and, later in the lecture, described democracy as being

> two things. It is the principle of the action of the human spirit - the principle that free spirits, in the area of social and political as well as of individual life, should freely guide themselves to freely determined issues. It is also a system of institutions, operative in a political community, which enables this principle to be realised and serves as the means of its realisation (1937, p. 25).

Analytical Philosophy and Democratic Theory: S. I. Benn and R. S. Peters

Eight years after the original publication of Barker's *Principles* (1961), his main study of the democratic state, two English analytical philosophers, S. I Benn and R. S. Peters, one of whom (Peters) was subsequently to become an internationally respected educational theorist, published their *Social Principles and the Democratic State* (1959). Although the authors had similar intentions to those of Barker - to understand and clarify democracy's normative principles - they wrote a different kind of book with a different style, thus illustrating some of the differences between pre- and post-1940s writing on democracy. Barker may not have published his main study of democratic norms until 1951, but he was very much a man of the first decades of the century, whose thinking was excited by his knowledge of ancient, medieval and early modern history and political philosophy, and who saw one of his tasks as being to defend British and Western traditions against intellectual fashions. Benn and Peters, by contrast, were political theorists trained in analytic, linguistic philosophy and influenced by the empirical political and social science of the 1940s and 1950s. They were also more concerned about protecting their book against the then fashionable charge that normative political theory, by its nature, was woolly in both content and expression. Like Lindsay and Barker, however, they were heavily indebted to previous normative writing on politics, particularly that of Hobbes, Locke, Bentham and John Stuart Mill, and their conclusions were not all that different from Lindsay and Barker's.

For about a decade and a half, Benn and Peters's (1959) study of democracy was probably the main text for the teaching of democratic theory in British universities and those of several Commonwealth countries. One reason for its success was that it was infused with the confidence, widespread in the 1950s, that Keynesian economic management enabled governments to concentrate on extending liberty and furthering equality of opportunity rather than being continually diverted by intractable economic crises. But the main reason for the book's success was its positive response to the concern, widespread among 1950s political scientists and theorists, that normative political theory and philosophy had no answers to the positivist inspired objections that they were nothing more than subjective preferences. The strategy of Benn and Peters, in their response and challenge to the apparent value relativist undermining of normative political theory, was to reveal, clarify and argue for democratic government's underlying moral and other norms, to appeal to common sense, to carefully define their terms, and to write in a precise and neutral rather than a more morally elevated or emotive and rhetorical language.

They argued that states were a particular type of human association, and modern democracies a particular type of state. By an *association* was meant a group of people held together by their consent to a system of normative rules and authorities (the arbiters of the rules, and the policy makers for the association). Democratic states were distinctive because, first, their constitutions and laws had, as a result of free elections, the consent of their members, and, second, universal adult voting and free elections made governments responsive to citizens. In addition, democratic states institutionalised tacitly-agreed conceptions of justice, equality, liberty and authority which, once they were made explicit, could withstand the objections of both moral sceptics and anti-democrats.

Democratic rules and principles were moral and universal in that they were applicable to all human beings in similar circumstances, and that their supporting reasons could withstand objections. The 'characteristic of a moral rule' Benn and Peter wrote, was 'that it should be regarded as universally applicable and rationally acceptable to the individual' (p. 27). Moral rules were self evidently reasonable, and morality itself was a species of reason. The citizens of modern democracies were law abiding and supported their systems of government, Benn and Peters argued, because they were confident that their states expressed conceptions of freedom, equality and justice which could be sustained by moral arguments. Although only a small minority of citizens could clearly articulate such arguments, most were satisfied that their institutions were backed by practical experience and moral principles, and expressed something more than the power of privileged groups. Freedom of speech, the foundation for this confidence in democratic institutions, was thus a necessary condition for democratic governmental and other authority. A democracy did not provide unlimited freedom, and certainly not a freedom from rules, but for rules to be authoritative all citizens had to possess the freedom to challenge them, a freedom which like all freedom had to be exercised responsibly.

Justice was the main moral principle applicable to democratic politics and, like liberty, it was closely associated with equality, with both justice and equality requiring that people in authority act impartially. 'To act justly', Benn and Peters wrote, 'is to treat all men alike except where there are relevant differences between them' (p. 111). Similarly, on equality, they declared that what advocates of equality mean when they 'say that all men are equal, is that *none shall be held to have a claim to better treatment than another, in advance of good grounds being produced*' (p. 110). These conceptions of justice and equality were interpreted and applied along New Liberal and democratic socialist lines, similar to those of Lindsay, with the two authors favouring redistributions of social resources when remediable ignorance and poverty prevented people from living the lives of independent moral agents and citizens.

In addition to impartiality being fundamental to both justice and equality, it was asserted that impartiality was the only serviceable part of the concept of the *common good*. The term *common good* was avoided because, it was said, in addition to its alleged imprecision it hid the fact that when there were political conflicts there were always losers. The common good, it was concluded, made sense only to the extent that it meant impartiality. These reasons for rejecting the *common good*, however, are far from compelling, for, although there are losers in most political settlements, as John Stuart Mill noted the pertinent issue is whether people lost because they lacked the numbers or because there were better arguments, and fairer and more sensible policies than theirs.

The attention paid to liberty, justice and equality constituted the politically radical parts of the Benn and Peters analysis; the conservative parts were the emphases on responsibility and authority, and on law as the means for securing life, property, and stable and predictable political outcomes. Democratic government was held to be moral and reasonable partly because of the balance between its radical and conservative sides, and partly because, more than any other system of government, it expressed the principle of impartiality. Democracy implied that, although not all persons, groups or associations were likely to obtain the same standard of life, they and their interests would be given a similar hearing and respect. As far as possible, compromises would be sought, and the losers in political conflicts compensated. It was only when they governed impartially that democratic governments were entitled to claim that they governed in the interests of all; without such impartiality, democracy degenerated into government on behalf of irresponsible majorities or minorities. Similarly, it was their impartiality which, ensured that members of parliament, cabinet and other ministers, judges, public servants, influential political journalists and others were authorities rather than privileged wielders of power. In the final chapter, democracy was described in normative and substantive terms as follows. Democracy is

> not merely a set of political institutions like universal suffrage, parliamentary government, and decisions by majority procedure, but also a set of principles which such institutions tend to realize....These are intimately connected...with the...principles of impartiality and respect for persons as sources of claims and arguments...which underlie all the central political ideals, like justice, liberty and equality....democracy is a way of coming to terms with the need for authority without accepting a duty to submit to whatever abuse it might bring in its train....Democracy provides a peaceful way of getting rid of governments which fail to convince a majority of their adult subjects that they have a lively concern for the interests of the governed (p. 355).

The term *public philosophy* played no part in their analysis but, by means of a different vocabulary, Benn and Peters recognised the need for a public philosophy. They argued that unless political actors consented to fundamental principles and rules - of the type described in this book as public philosophic - so-called democratic states would lack the trust, toleration and public examination of issues that democracy required.

> Freedom of discussion is...a condition for democracy....Discussion presupposes...a consensus on fundamentals, for where this is lacking, men will treat one another as scoundrels, and differences of opinion will be undiscussible....Where men start from different assumptions, there are no adjustments and no compromises generally felt to be fair and reasonable. In such conditions, politics is a cynical grasping for whatever advantages temporary power combinations can secure (pp. 352-3).

Public discussion and wise leadership, it followed, were necessary conditions for a flourishing democracy. Indeed, on the topic of leadership, they cited Lippmann's *Public Philosophy* as a source for the observation that if 'leaders will not lead, but prefer to play for easy popularity, democratic government degenerates into mob-rule' (p. 342).

Benn and Peters's attempt to make a normative, substantive, conception of democracy palatable for readers who were cynical about arbitrating between values and the utility of normative political philosophy produced an innovative book. They brought to normative, public-philosophic democratic theory the precision and careful arguments of the best of analytical philosophers. Unfortunately, however, although their analytical style and techniques became widely adopted in Western universities, their political realism and common sense were too often displaced by what I have called 'abstract political theory' and 'utopianism'. Their book made a major contribution to clarifying the democratic norms on which they concentrated, but their coverage of many political as well as cultural and economic issues was more limited than that of other mid-century public philosophers and democratic theorists. It is to some of this work by writers who brought to their tasks the insights of other traditions of thought to that of analytic philosophy that the next chapter turns.

References

Barker, Ernest (1918), *Greek Political Theory: Plato and His Predecessors*, Methuen, London.
Barker, Ernest (1937), *The Citizen's Choice*, Cambridge Univ. Pr., Cambridge.
Barker, Ernest (1942), *Reflections on Government*, Oxford Univ. Pr., London.

Barker, Ernest (1948a), *National Character* [1927], 4th edn, Methuen, London.
Barker, Ernest (1948b), *Traditions of Civility*, Cambridge Univ. Pr., Cambridge.
Barker, Ernest (1951), *Essays on Government* [1945], 2nd edn, Clarendon Pr., Oxford.
Barker, Ernest (1953), *Age and Youth*, Oxford Univ. Pr., London.
Barker, Ernest (1957), *Church, State and Education* [1930], 2nd edn, Univ. of Michigan Pr., Ann Arbor.
Barker, Ernest (1959), *The Political Thought of Plato and Aristotle* [1906], Russell and Russell, New York.
Barker, Ernest (1961), *Principles of Social and Political Theory* [1951], 2nd edn, Oxford Univ. Pr., Oxford.
Benn, S.I. and R.S. Peters (1959), *Social Principles and the Democratic State*, Allen and Unwin, London.
The Dictionary of National Biography 1951-1960 (1971), (eds) E.T. Williams and Helen M. Palmer, Oxford Univ. Pr., Oxford.
King, Preston (ed.) (1977), *The Study of Politics: A Collection of Inaugural Lectures*, Frank Cass, London.
Lindsay, A.D. (1935), *The Essentials of Democracy* [1929], 2nd edn, Clarendon Pr., Oxford.
Lindsay, A.D. (1962), *The Modern Democratic State* [1943], 2nd edn, Oxford Univ. Pr.
Maddox, Graham (1986), 'The Christian Democracy of A. D. Lindsay', *Political Studies*, vol. 34, pp. 441-55.
Richter, Melvin (1968), 'Lindsay, A. D.', *International Encyclopedia of the Social Sciences*, (ed.) David L. Sills, vol. 9.
Stapleton, Julia (1989), 'The National Character of Ernest Barker's Political Science', *Political Studies*, vol. 37, pp. 171-87.
Stapleton, Julia (1994), *Englishness and the Study of Politics: The Social and Political Thought of Ernest Barker*, Cambridge Univ. Pr., Cambridge.

8 Twentieth Century Natural-Law, Augustinian-Realist and Democratic-Elite-Theory Public Philosophers

In comparison with the historical and philosophic perspectives on modern democracy of Lindsay, Barker, and Benn and Peters, those of the five theorists examined in this chapter are more psychological and sociological. Jacques Maritain and Yves Simon brought Christian natural-law and Reinhold Niebuhr brought Augustinian-Christian conceptions of human nature to their analyses, while those of John Plamenatz and Giovanni Sartori have been largely based on what they have considered a fundamental sociological fact: the inevitability of political and other elites.

Twentieth-century natural-law theorists, two of whom are the first of this chapter's topics, have built upon central parts of Western natural-law thought, a tradition which has a history of more than two-thousand years. The most assertive of the century's natural law theorists have been the Thomists, sometimes called neo-Thomists, mainly Roman Catholic writers who have worked in the tradition founded by the thirteenth-century scholastic and natural-law philosopher, St Thomas Aquinas. The Thomists have swum against the century's intellectual tides in resisting the views that moral and other normative judgements necessarily rest on subjective preferences, and that the members of one society and culture should not and cannot judge the values of another. They maintain that there are objective moral and normative-political laws - principles as well as rules - that are discoverable by the human intellect, and which provide standards for social and political life. These laws are objective in that they are independent of any person or group's preferences. Natural, unlike civil, laws are not made by the decrees of rulers, parliamentary statutes or the decisions of judges, and it is the compatibility of civil with natural law which makes the laws of a nation just. The natural laws of natural law theory, therefore, are not the empirical laws which are hypothesised and tested by physicists and other natural scientists. The word *natural* refers not to what is observable in the physical world or to the more complex subject matter of natural scientists but to the ancient Greek distinction between the conventional (the rules of human associations established by force or agreement) and the natural (what is independent of the human will). The natural laws of natural law theorists, therefore, include the permanent features of social life. They are laws which all living beings must follow if they are to lead secure and satisfactory lives. But whereas other animals follow them by instinct, humans must supplement and control their instincts with reason.

For Thomist and other natural law theorists, the natural laws of human life are universal in their scope; if individuals, groups or societies transgress them, disaster is likely. But they are laws which have to be acted on flexibly, on the basis of circumstances and a society's customs. By being *natural* to all men and women is meant that they promote security, virtue and happiness, thus enabling people to actualise the best of their human potential; but they are not instinctive or habitual - for instinctive and habitual behaviour may be vicious and/or self-destructive.

Although natural-law moral and political thought has its roots in both pre-Christian and Christian theist conceptions of the world, and the Thomists uphold Christian conceptions, they and other natural law theorists insist that natural law is not dependent on theist belief, and that all moral and other normative thinking which seeks to free itself from self interest and the prejudices of a time and place will approximate to it. And, in practice, premises, arguments and conclusions similar to those of Thomist natural-law theory are found in social-contract, Kantian, utilitarian and other normative theory. A part of the explanation is that the Thomists try to absorb the teachings and findings of other traditions into their own, which they call the *perennial philosophy*.

This chapter's first two section, however, will examine not Thomist or other natural law theory in general but the political thought of two outstanding Thomist natural-law political theorists who have written extensively on modern democracy: Jacques Maritain and Yves Simon.[1]

Natural-Law Democratic Theory: Jacques Maritain

The Man

Probably the century's most respected natural-law political philosopher has been Jacques Maritain (1882-1973), a Thomist philosopher and one of France's most controversial Catholic writers. He was influential, however, not only in France but the United States, where he lived during the German

---

1   For introductions to the main branches of Western natural-law political thought, from the ancient Greeks to the present century, see Passerin d'Entreves (1951) and Sigmund (1971). For a systematic and comprehensive restatement of a predominantly Thomist natural-law ethics and jurisprudence, see Finnis (1980). See also Simon (1965).

occupation of France, and from 1948 to 1960, from when he resigned from being the French ambassador to the Vatican to his return to France. At various times he taught at the universities of Chicago, Columbia, Notre Dame and Princeton.[2]

For most of his life he represented a minority view in the Catholic Church and, probably more than any other of its intellectuals, he was instrumental in making the Church more sympathetic to liberalism and democracy. The many controversies he sparked continued practically until his death, with the final controversies being provoked by the publication, in France in 1966, of *The Peasant of the Garonne* (1968). In this book, written after Maritain had been hailed as the liberal Catholic who more than any other had provided the intellectual foundations for the 1962 Second Vatican Council's liberalisation of the Church's teachings, he made major criticisms of the Council. He objected to the encouragement which it and the Church hierarchy gave to people he described as irresponsible neo-modernist theologians and clerics. By their *irresponsibility* he meant a love of novelty for its own sake, a failure to resist intellectual fashions, a delight in abandoning tradition, and a kneeling before the material world. By *neo-modernism* he meant a revival of the modernist doctrines condemned by Pope Pius X in 1907, that the Bible and Church tradition be interpreted in accordance with the latest scientific and philosophic views, and the predilections of people whom the Church hoped to attract.

Maritain was a prolific writer on theology, philosophy and politics, and although he frequently wrote hurriedly, as a response to rapidly changing events and fluid controversies, or to meet publishers' deadlines, his writing was thoughtful, generous to the views of opponents, informed and characterised by a profound philosophic intelligence. His main contribution to democratic theory was his *Man and the State* (1956), substantial parts of which were foreshadowed and, on some topics, more fully developed in *The Rights of Man and Natural Law*, 1944, *Christianity and Democracy* (1945), and *The Person and the Common Good* (1946).[3] In *Man and the State* (1956), Maritain argued for a set of standards or norms for modern democratic nations, largely derived from what it was to

---

2   For Maritain's life and work, see Doering (1983); Schall (1998); and Smith (1976). See also Evans (ed.) (1963), esp. Charles O'Donnell, 'Jacques Maritain - Political Philosopher'.

3   For an introduction to the range of Maritain's political thought, see the selections from his political writings edited by Evans and Ward (Maritain, 1955); and for its philosophic foundations, the selections edited by Evans and Ward (Maritain, 1966). See also Maritain's *The Range of Reason* (1953); and, for a substantial statement of his thinking on epistemology, metaphysics and theology, *The Degrees of Knowledge* (1959).

have human needs and to be a person. Both here and in his other writings, however, there is a typically Thomist ambivalence. On the one hand he contended that, without Christian or similar conceptions of God and God's relation to the world, it was impossible to understand human life. On the other hand he argued that human reason, even when unassisted by religious faith - provided that the reason was not contaminated by a dogmatic atheism or entrenched self-centredness - could achieve a similar understanding of human life to that of Christian natural-law thought. Maritain's view was that his work was inspired by the Christian gospels, but directed to the reason and common sense of secular readers. This was possible because, as Aquinas contended, faith and reason were allies. On this issue, Maritain wrote,

> supernatural faith does not provide us with any particular social or political system. In such matters supernatural faith must be complemented by sound practical philosophy, historical information, and social and political experience. (1953, pp. 170-1.) [The] light of Christian philosophy [Thomism] is not the light of faith using reason in order to get at some understanding of revealed mysteries, but the light of reason assisted by faith so that it may better perform its own work of intellectual inquiry (1968, p. 164).

Maritain, who shared Walter Lippmann's views on both natural law and the political need for a consensus on fundamental values, was, however, more aware than Lippmann of the differences between them. More than Lippmann, he concerned himself with the relations between natural law and other political philosophies, and the need for all political theorists, sympathetic to democratic aspirations, to learn from one another in clarifying and helping to resolve the normative and other disputes which divided the citizens of their nations. He tried to construct bridges between secular and religious theorists of and participants in democratic politics, and for this purpose he emphasised the functions of rights.

Maritain's Political Thought

Maritain's political-philosophic starting point was that men and women have material and spiritual needs which, in order to be satisfied, demand political and other rights and the recognition of corresponding duties. Human needs entitle men and women to rights; but as rights do not always easily co-exist, guiding principles and a (public philosophic) tradition of prudential judgement for reconciling rights are required. Rights, Maritain believed, were both a practical necessity, and a means for understanding and civilising politics. Their clarification and reconciliation made it necessary for people who held different political, philosophic, religious or other views to seek agreement on political and social principles. But, in addition to their mutual rights and duties, the state and its citizens, families and associations received rights from and had duties towards associations which went beyond the confines of a nation state. The Christian churches were a prime example as, though they were within the jurisdiction of states, they were also parts of an international church or federation of churches.

Citizens comprised the body politic, and the purpose of the state, which was an instrument of the body politic, was to sustain and promote rights. But not even the body politic, the whole of a national community, possessed absolute sovereignty. Maritain thus challenged the post-medieval, Hobbesian idea that national states were sovereign entities. The state might monopolise coercive and legal power on a territory, but neither it nor the body politic itself should be deified; they were human associations which had to co-exist with other human associations. Maritain realised that in all systems of government a branch or branches of it possessed legal supremacy; his objection was to the view that this sovereign part of a state, be it a president, parliament and cabinet, the electorate or any combination of them, possessed unlimited authority.

The view that the sovereignty of states was unlimited, he argued, was not a democratic notion, but a mistaken theory, a part of the rhetoric of early-modern absolute monarchies. Rousseau was the main culprit in bringing about its association with democratic theory, as, by means of his concept of the *general will*, he had transferred the absolutism desired by extreme monarchists to an intoxicating conception of democracy (Maritain, 1956, pp. 44-6). For Maritain, however, states, be they large or small, were not autonomous and absolute but heteronomous; they were subject to natural (moral) law. Because people and their communities had a right to self government, democratic government was morally justified, and inherently superior to other government. But democratic governments were subject to the moral principles which legitimated them, and they had no right to inflict harm on their own or other people. Anything which harmed or destroyed human life was an evil, and states and citizens were obliged to promote life and eschew evil. Evil was always self-destructive - but not always during the lifetimes of the guilty. When evil was perpetrated by governments, states or societies, the victims could be subsequent generations.[4]

An awareness of political evil and the need to combat it was imperative, Maritain believed, if democracies were to survive and prosper. He argued that, since the sixteenth century, monarchic, democratic and

---

4   For systematic discussions by Maritain of rights and duties, and of political sovereignty and its limits, see *Man and the State* (1956), esp. Chapters 2 and 4.

other states had been tempted into a Machiavellian, immoral and self-destructive politics. The Machiavellian temptation consisted of ignoring justice, the common good and other moral principles, and trying to 'gain success and power by means of evil' (1953, p. 145). Machiavelli, to his credit, Maritain acknowledged, was aware of the differences between good and evil, and never called immoral acts anything else but evil. Machiavelli was an artist who encouraged an immoral but, at times, creative politics. But the diffusion of his ideas led to cruder forms of Machiavellianism displacing artistic and nobler forms; behaviour which Machiavelli would have recognised as politically dangerous as well as evil became acceptable parts of politics. Although rulers and politicians had always acted in immoral ways, until Machiavellian thinking legitimated injustice, most of them were troubled by guilty consciences, and felt a need for excuses and justifications. By the twentieth century, however, abuses of parliamentary government which previously had been regarded as reprehensible were taken for granted; all that was required was that the perpetrators appeared to be committed to worthy causes. But, whatever the short-term benefits for individual Machiavellians, or even for their nations, unless democratic communities cast off Machiavellian doctrines, so Maritain argued, the democratic experiment would fail. The choice before modern democracies was 'either to perish by continuing to accept...the principle of Machiavellianism, or to regenerate by consciously and decidedly rejecting this principle' (1953, p. 164). Maritain's alternative to Machiavellianism was a politics which, for its means and ends, was guided by natural-law principles of justice, the common good, and the freedom and responsibility of the person. It entailed

> a transvaluation of cultural principles....of quality over quantity, of work over money, of the human over the technological, of wisdom over science, of the common service of human persons over the individual covetousness of unlimited enrichment, and...over the State's covetousness of unlimited power (Maritain, 1955, p. 309).

Maritain's rejection of Machiavellianism was grounded on his Christian faith; however the essential condition, if democratic nations were to cast off Machiavellianism, was not that citizens, political elites and governments be converted to Christianity, or adopt Thomist or other natural law philosophy, but that they respect the dignity, status and freedom of the person. Cooperation between Christian and secular intellectuals and political actors on this and other central political issues was possible, Maritain maintained, because modern democracy, in its essentials, was a secularised expression of Christian teachings. He followed Tocqueville, his French Catholic predecessor, in seeing democracy as a product of the

Christian emphasis on the fundamental equality of all people. He did not claim that Christianity was incompatible with monarchic and aristocratic societies, or that all Christians were democrats; his proposition was that democracy, more than any other system of government, expressed Christian teachings. It was Christianity which taught

> the unity of the human race, the natural equality of all men...the inalienable dignity of every soul fashioned in the image of God, the dignity of labour and the dignity of the poor...the inviolability of consciences...[and] the obligation of those who govern and on those who have possessions to govern in justice (Maritain, 1945, p. 29).

Democracy was affected by folly and other vices, as were all forms of government and society, but it had its roots in the teachings of Western Judeo-Christian traditions.

Moreover, in the modern world, democrats confronted the same enemies as Christians, and were in need of the cultural nourishment of Christian ideals, and the Christian awareness of human deficiencies.

> Not only does the democratic state of mind proceed from the inspiration of the Gospel, but it cannot exist without it....[Consider] the immense burden of animality, of egoism, and of latent barbarism that men bear within themselves and which keeps social life still terribly far from achieving its truest and most elevated aims (Maritain, 1945, pp. 39-40).

The tragedy of modern democracy was that, although it was inspired by 'the Gospel and cannot subsist without it', democrats had repudiated Christianity while Christians and the Christian churches had often fought against 'democratic aspirations in the name of religion' (Maritain, 1945, p. 18.)

Maritain, however, was more circumspect about modern capitalism than he was about modern democracy, and he was saddened by its excesses. While sharing Aquinas's view that the private ownership of economic resources was necessary and desirable, for most of his life he thought that large property owners had become arrogantly and dangerously selfish, and had abandoned their responsibilities to other human beings and to nature. He frequently described such selfishness as 'bourgeois' and 'bourgeois liberal'. Bourgeois liberalism, which tried to 'ground everything in the unchecked initiative of the individual, conceived as a little God, and the absolute liberty of property, business and pleasure', he declared, 'inevitably ends in statism' (1972, pp. 91-2). But, in 1956, in a series of University of Chicago seminar papers, Maritain modified his hostility to industrial capitalism, which he argued was becoming less bourgeois.[5] His years in the United States, he said, had convinced him that the social scientists who contended that the United States was creating a post-capitalist, superior economy and society were right. Far from being extravagantly individualist, American economic life was increasingly characterised by cooperation and community spirit. There were new styles of sensitive and imaginative management that respected the dignity and encouraged the creativity of employees, and a cooperation between companies and their employees that included the trade union representatives of labour.

At least one commentator, Michael Novak (1981), has considered Maritain's admiration for American mid-century industrial and economic change as an important addition to his thinking on democracy. Novak has found in Maritain's *Reflections on America* (1975) the view that, for Christians and non-Christians, the best modern society is one which maintains a division while encouraging a partnership between a democratic politics, a capitalist economy, and a morality and culture inspired by Judeo-Christian values. For Novak, this is the only society which, for the foreseeable future, is able to secure individual freedom, self government, buoyant economic conditions, opportunities for individual and cooperative initiatives, and meaningful communities. Novak, on the direction which democracies should take, is probably right; but whether Maritain would be persuaded that, at the end of the twentieth century, such a society had been achieved or was being approximated to is a different question.

Although, for Maritain, the natural laws which should guide human affairs were unchangeable, he thought that our knowledge of them was always limited. Societies became more civilised, and moral progress occurred when their members acquired a greater knowledge of and attachment to natural laws, and realised that they embraced people of different cultures. The natural law principles which he commended to governments and citizens were not rigid dogmas but a mean between (1) an absolute ethics, or what he sometimes called a *hypermoralism*, in which a person followed moral principles and rules, and left the consequences to God or to fate, and (2) an ethics of responsibility in which the likely consequences of an act were given a primacy over general principles.[6] For

---

5   The seminar papers were revised and published as *Reflections on America* (Maritain, 1975).

6   The distinction between an absolute and a responsible ethics has been popularised in the English speaking world, since the 1940s, by Max Weber's 1918 essay, 'Politics as a Vocation', in Gerth and Wright Mills's (1970) selections from his work, first published in 1948. But whereas Maritain sought a synthesis which embodied the truths in both conceptions of ethics, Weber argued that it was the ethics of responsibility, not that of 'ultimate ends', that should be followed in politics.

Maritain, political judgement had to find a middle way in which permanent moral principles were applied intelligently, flexibly and in accordance with knowledge and circumstances. Actions based on natural law avoided both moral fanaticism, as occurs when an absolute ethic is followed unswervingly, and the relativism which leads to irrationality when permanent principles are abandoned.

Maritain rarely if ever used the term *public philosophy*, but the recognition of a need for such a guiding and restraining theory was implicit in his thinking about democracy, and his conceptions of prudence and political judgement. In *Man and the State* (1956, pp. 108-46), for example, considerable emphasis was put on the need for a democratic faith, centred on a 'democratic charter', which all well meaning people, including religious believers and secular rationalists, could share. A *democratic charter* meant, primarily, the rights to which people who otherwise disagreed in their political and other values could give their assent, even though their justifications for them might differ. Religious honesty and philosophic truth required that what were considered errors in opposed views be challenged, and that philosophers, in particular, confront objections to their own views; at the same time democratic life required that intellectual opponents cooperate in clarifying and defending the (public philosophic) principles which sustained a tolerant society where different doctrines and ways of life peacefully competed. In Maritain's last major book, he wrote that cooperation for the common good of mankind requires

> an intellectual agreement on the basis of common practical principles in spite of...irreducible divisions on the level of speculative convictions...[But the] more we fraternize on the level of practical principles and common action, the more we should strengthen the edges of the opposite convictions which divide us in the speculative order and on the level of truth... (1968, pp. 69-70).

Maritain, whose natural inclination was for a life of contemplation, prayer and philosophic speculation, led an intensely public life as a public philosopher, theologian, philosopher and Catholic layman. He participated in controversies about the internal politics of democratic nations, and how they should resist both Communism and, the century's ultimate political evil, National Socialism; he engaged in bitter disputes over the Spanish civil war, when he resisted the Catholic hierarchy's support for General Franco; and he was shaken by the military defeat and humiliation of France in 1940, which led to his support for General de Gaulle and the Free French. Throughout his political life he was subjected to the calumnies of the political left and right, from both inside and outside the Catholic

Church. Yet practically everything he wrote was distinguished by its serenity as, according to his many friends, was his personality.

A part of the explanation for his serenity was his conception of history in which, in strange and unpredictable ways, this gigantic battleground for the conflicts between good and evil - sometimes described by Maritain as encounters between God, the Devil and man - was ultimately subject to God's purposes. A similar view was taken of modern democracy and its ideal of self government by free persons, persons whose ultimate end, Maritain believed, was supernatural. Conflicts between democracies and dictatorships, and conflicts over the goals and nature of democracy - both public and in the hearts and minds of men and women - were all, for Maritain, a part of the great battle between good and evil. Democracy was also the means by which imperfect, suffering and sometimes despairing men and women, at all levels of society, by their struggles, conflicts and cooperation, brought reason, hope and justice to the world, thus civilising it.

> With democracy mankind has entered the road to the only genuine, that is *moral* rationalization, of political life: in other terms, to the highest terrestrial achievement of which the rational animal is capable here below. Democracy carries in a fragile vessel the terrestrial hope, I would say the biological hope, of humanity. Of course the vessel is fragile. Of course we are still at the very first steps of the process. Of course we have paid and we are paying heavily for grave errors and moral failures. Democracy can be awkward, clumsy, defective, open to the risk of betraying itself by yielding to instincts of cowardice, or of oppressive violence....Yet democracy is the only way through which the progressive energies in human history do pass (Maritain, 1956, pp. 59-60).

Natural-Law Democratic Theory: Yves Simon

Another outstanding natural law discussion of democracy, but with different emphases from Maritain's, was that of another French Thomist political philosopher, Yves R. Simon (1903-1961). Simon's main work on democracy, his *Philosophy of Democratic Government* (1961), concentrated on the meaning and limits of democracy's most emphasised norms, *freedom* and *equality*, and on what he argued was an equally important but neglected norm: *authority*. The book's subject matter therefore resembled that of Benn and Peters's study; but the priorities and the more extensive meaning which it gave to *authority* were different. Simon's starting point was what he regarded as a puzzle: that despite the fact that without authority there could be no self-governing society of free and equal citizens, and no achieving of worthy goals by citizens and their associations, the character and role of authority had been neglected by most liberal and democratic theorists.[7]

Simon argued that democratic government depended upon political, economic and cultural leaders, their ability to understand the needs and aspirations of citizens, their commitment to the common good, and the acceptance of their authority by citizens. Such leaders were necessary for coordinating the activities of people, and for making the multiplicity of decisions which are a part of modern life, decisions which have to be taken without waiting for majority verdicts. Effective cooperation for the achievement of goals by groups, private associations, public bodies and governments depends upon authoritative persons whose expertise and practical judgement entitle them to respect. Authority, therefore, is a source of social and political energy and knowledge. For the acquiring of both theoretical knowledge and practical skills, Simon observed, at some point the questioning of a teacher by a learner had to stop, and some knowledge taken on trust. It was also 'expedient that those who are less gifted - less intelligent, less experienced, less strong-willed, less virtuous - be guided by those who possess a more eminent degree of reason, will power and virtue' (1968, p. 51).

But authority, Simon observed, had acquired a bad name, by becoming associated with forms of power that were unconstrained by conceptions of a common good. The leaders and elites of democratic nations had forgotten Aquinas's injunction that 'dominion over free men is exercised either for the sake of the governed - as in the case of children - or for the sake of the common good' (1962, p. 160). It was a person's commitment to the common good, the welfare of a political community and its members, that made him or her a leader or other authority rather than merely a successful adventurer or member of a privileged group. Simon, in fact, could be scathing about irresponsible intellectuals, elites and dominant economic classes, whom he blamed for the ill repute of the authority with which their power was confused. On intellectuals, he was aware of the utopian temptation, and wrote that whereas workers 'are possessed of occupational guaranties of loyalty to the real; for intellectuals, on the other hand, corruption by the ideal is an occupational risk' (1961, p. 92). He was also aware of the faults of traditional rulers. On the myth of a 'propertied class as an elite dedicated to lofty pursuits', he observed that

---

7   Simon's examinations of authority are to be found in his study of modern democracy, the *Philosophy of Democratic Government* (1961), in his *General Theory of Authority* (1962); and the relevant parts of *Freedom and Community* (1968). For his underlying natural law theory, see *The Tradition of Natural Law* (1965).

the catastrophes of the twentieth century have proved instructive. They have taught us a great deal about the weak points of the upper class: the lack of realism, the hedonistic isolation from common suffering and common anxiety, the lack of a sense of history and the meaning of the present, frivolity and conceit, a readiness to make alliances with the worst elements of the rabble. Germany was delivered to Hitler by Franz von Papen - this will not be effaced from the pages of history (1961, p. 93).[8]

To further explain democracy's need for authority, Simon distinguished between partnerships and communities, and noted that it was only the latter which possessed a common good and required authorities. In a partnership, for example between a merchant and a banker, there were common interests but no common action, and no common good, only the sum of private interests. But unlike 'mere partners, the members of a community - family, factory, football team, army, state, church - are engaged in a common action whose object is qualitatively different from a sum of interdependent goods' (1962, p. 30). For partnerships, contracts were sufficient. For a purely individualistic, contractual society, nothing more was required for enforcing contracts than properly trained lawyers and police. Democratic nations, and their institutions and communities, however, needed a more traditional type of authority: educated people with the relevant training who possessed judgement and wisdom, and who had earned respect. With arguments that foreshadowed the objections to individualist liberalism made by the communitarians of the 1980s and 1990s, Simon urged democrats to abandon contractual for community-based understandings of democracy. Unlike the hedonistic, individualist view that democracy meant a life of ease, fun or cultivated private pleasures, democracy was seen by Simon as an arduous, shared undertaking. Unless the citizens of democratic nations found satisfaction in cooperating in worthwhile activities which furthered their development as civilised beings, democracies would become inhuman places.

> Communions in immanent actions make up the most profound part of social reality; theirs is a world of peace where ennui is impossible and where death itself can be sweet - there alone the individual is freed from solitude and anxiety. Mere partnership, on the other hand, does not do

---

8   As even seemingly virtuous elites were not to be trusted, it followed that constitutional and electoral constraints were necessary. Experience shows, Simon wrote, 'that the operation of elites is not reassuring for those who happen not to be included in any recognized elite. Even if it were possible to designate infallibly...men perfectly qualified for government, it would still be a good precaution to erect in front of such a chosen few, as a check and a complement, the power of numbers' (1961, p. 98.).

anything to put an end to the solitude of the partners. They may be better off as a result of their contract, but their contract will not relieve their lonesomeness (Simon, 1961, p. 65).

It followed from the importance of community that a proper understanding of authority meant not that governmental power and responsibility should be centralised and increased but decentralised and reduced. For Simon, as for Aristotle and Aquinas, states and governments were positive goods rather than necessary evils, and as much a product of human sociability as of human deficiencies. His concern was that in the twentieth century world of bureaucratic organisation, and complex communication and other technology, states and their personnel had acquired an insatiable appetite for growth. States 'have a tendency to take over, whenever they can, functions that used to belong to smaller units of public administration, such as provinces or counties, or to private organizations, such as business enterprises, or to families or to the church' (1961, p. 132).

Simon's disquiet about the growth of governmental power made him more pessimistic than Maritain about the prospects for democratic nations. In theory, he agreed with Aquinas and Maritain that government was natural and good; in practice, he was disturbed by how twentieth century governments regularly departed from their professed humane, liberal and democratic objectives. Significantly, in the midst of an account of the naturalness and goodness of government, he added that, in

> truth, the ratio of failures is extremely high in all domains of activity which require virtue as an intrinsic condition of success. In civil government difficulties are more serious than elsewhere, and failures often entail dreadful consequences....[It] may take some fortitude to realize the excellent goodness, the reverence inspiring sublimity, of this institution, civil government, in spite of the overwhelming weight of its failures and abuses (1961, p. 68).

The democratic problem was to ensure that governments were constrained, and made responsive to the needs and aspirations of citizens and their communities, while allowed the necessary power and discretion to govern. Political authority, once granted, Simon maintained, must be accepted and obeyed, and only in circumstances of gross injustice and extreme urgency resisted. This was the essence of political obligation, for persons were entitled to the state's protection and other benefits only if they accepted its authority. Governments should not be subjected to continual harassment, a vice to which democracies were prone, as were the desires for complete and unlimited freedom (always to be able to do as one wanted), and for an equality of social condition.

More than anything else, Simon's contribution to a public philosophy for democratic nations was his examination of authority, and the insights his examination yielded on the meaning of *community* and the *common good*. Many other democratic theorists have separated the types of freedom and equality which are necessary for or compatible with democracy from those which are not; Simon's achievement has been to carefully separate the authority which is necessary for or compatible with democracy from authoritarian abuses and corruptions. His work points to the fact that freedom and authority are interdependent rather than antagonistic.

It is now appropriate, however, to discuss a theorist who challenged many of the natural law premises of Maritain and Simon, and who built upon a different tradition of Christian political thought, but whose work on democracy, along with theirs, is a major contribution to a public philosophy for democratic nations.

Augustinian Realism: Reinhold Niebuhr

Reinhold Niebuhr (1892-1971) was a distinguished American Protestant theologian and moral philosopher, and as prolific a writer on politics as Lippmann and Maritain. In the 1920s, his political commitments went from liberalism to a quasi-Marxist socialism, before, about a decade later, returning to liberalism. In the 1950s and 1960s, until incapacitated by illness, he was both an influential political commentator and a member of or an adviser to governmental and semi-governmental agencies and committees. Although two of his last books were on democratic politics, *Man's Nature and His Communities* (1966) and *The Democratic Experience* (1969), which was jointly authored with Paul E. Sigmund, his thinking on democracy was most thoroughly explained over twenty years earlier in *The Children of Light and the Children of Darkness* (1960), first published in 1944. Here, he applied to politics the ideas developed in his two volumes on theology, the philosophy of history and ethics: *The Nature and Destiny of Man* (1941 and 1943).[9]

Niebuhr contended that Catholic natural-law theorists, liberal Christians of all denominations, Deweyite pragmatists, secular rationalists and most other liberals and socialists had an excessive faith in human reason. They were all unwilling to confront the existence of evil. Niebuhr

---

9   For Niebuhr's life and the evolution of his political and other thought, see Bingham (1972); Fachre (1970); Fox (1987); and Merkley (1975).

did not deny that men and women possessed immense potential, including a capacity to love, to reason, to respect justice, and thus to resist evil and improve the world; his point was that these qualities were always corrupted by sin. He sometimes expressed himself in more secular terms, insisting that we were all inclined to be selfish, unjust, foolish, and subject to uncritical tribal loyalties to our nation, political party, economic class, church or other social group. All people, therefore, could endanger themselves and others. Niebuhr like his mentor, St Augustine (354-430), maintained that this sinfulness had its source in the reason and the will as much as in bodily wants. Democrats, it followed, had to be as concerned with restraining the intellect and the will as they were with releasing the best in human potential. The snag was that most democrats had a typically modern, easy going attitude to life, and evaded the problem of evil. History, Niebuhr wrote,

> is filled with manifestations of man's hysterias and furies, with evidences of his daemonic capacity and inclination to break the harmonies of nature and defy the prudent canons of rational restraint. Yet no cumulation of contradictory evidence seems to disturb modern man's good opinion of himself. He considers himself the victim of corrupting institutions which he is about to destroy or reconstruct, or of the confusions of ignorance which an adequate education is about to overcome. Yet he continues to regard himself as essentially harmless and virtuous (1941, pp. 100-1).[10]

Modern thought's neglect of sin and evil, Niebuhr argued, was the result of its being permeated by two flawed views of human nature: naturalism and idealism. Naturalism, which conceived of human beings as entirely subject to physical and biological causation, failed to account for the human ability to comprehend and make changes to the natural world; idealism went to the opposite extreme and, in emphasising reason and the

---

[10] Niebuhr held that, for understanding human psychology and evil, the Bible, especially the Old Testament, was the antidote to the lack of realism in modern secular thought. His political realism has been described as *biblical, prophetic, Christian, Gospel-inspired, Reformation* and *Protestant*. I have called it *Augustinian* because, despite Niebuhr's reservations about Augustine's theology, he acknowledged his debts to Augustine's political thought. 'Whatever the defects of the Augustine approach may be,' he wrote, 'we must acknowledge his immense superiority both over those who preceded him and who came after him....Augustine...proves himself a more reliable guide than any known thinker. A generation which finds its communities imperiled and in decay...might well take counsel of Augustine in solving its perplexities' (1986, pp. 140-1). See also the rest of the essay from which the quotation has been taken, 'Augustine's Political Realism' [1986].

will, forgot both the animal nature of men and women, and their propensity to misuse reason and the will. Few of the people who believed in science and progress understood how men and women could stand outside of scientific inquiries and logical demonstrations, and use them to forward selfish and sectional ambitions. Thus, in a response to John Dewey's calls for impartial, social investigation, Niebuhr, in 1939, remarked,

> When will our modern rationalists learn that men are not logical, not because they do not know logic, but because they are capable of standing outside rather than inside a system of logic, and thus making it the servant of their interests (in Bingham, p. 227).

Modern thinkers failed to comprehend the tragic dimensions to human life, at the root of which was the tension between our awareness of eternity, truth and perfection, and our inability, by human efforts, to transcend a temporal, limited and imperfect condition. For Niebuhr, there was a 'mixture of creativity and corruption which characterises all historic striving' (1943, p. 150). But his Augustinian realism was more of an attempt to advance beyond tragedy than a Stoic acceptance of it. He tried to combine a recognition of the tragic with a quest for justice.[11]

In their failure to understand evil, socialists and other radicals were charged with being as culpable as liberals. Marxists, for instance, expected 'men to be as tame and social on the other side of the revolution as Adam Smith and Jeremy Bentham thought them to be tame and prudential on this side of the revolution' (1960, p. 60). In contrast to liberal democrats who desired a peaceful perfecting of democracy, and Marxists who sought social perfection by means of revolution, Niebuhr's view was that democratic government was the best of the political choices available to inevitably imperfect and unstable societies. 'Unstable democracy is the normal case because the democratic idea still has great appeal, and when the authoritarians fail, as they so often do, the only legitimate alternative is to be found in democratic institutions' (Niebuhr and Sigmund, p. 183).

By the 'children of light', for whom Niebuhr's studies of democracy were written, he meant men and women of good will who were committed to democracy and its values. The 'children of darkness', their adversaries, were selfish if not malevolent. Niebuhr was convinced that, if democratic

---

[11] This combination is well described in the Epilogue to Fox's (1987) biography. Niebuhr's 'prime intellectual contribution was to weld together the tragic sense of life and the quest for justice....The tragic character of human existence placed firm limits on the quest for justice: human community could never be perfected, never attain the level of harmonious fellowship. But the quest for justice undermined any premature appeal to tragic limits, any self serving celebration of the social status quo.' (p. 297.)

nations were to survive and prosper, the children of light had to abandon naive beliefs about the goodness of human beings, and adopt some of the more realistic, Machiavellian and other assumptions of the children of darkness - without themselves becoming children of darkness.

> The children of light must be armed with the wisdom of the children of darkness but remain free from their malice. They must know the power of self-interest in human society without giving it moral justification. They must have this wisdom in order that they may beguile, deflect, harness and restrain self-interest, individual and collective, for the sake of the community (1960, p. 41).

For Niebuhr, modern constitutional democracy had a universal validity inasmuch as no other system of government was likely to be as stable and just; nevertheless democracy was difficult to achieve and sustain, and for some nations could be out of reach. Making a perceptive distinction between validity and attainability, Niebuhr wrote that

> democratic ideals may be universally valid but not universally attainable, since their realisation requires skills and competence which are not easily universalised either within the separate nations or among the nations of the world (1966, p. 61).

Niebuhr's objections to natural law theory, which were more to its dangers than to its intentions and objectives, were similar to those he made to modern liberalism in general. He thought that, in practice, Catholic and other churches, along with secular states and other associations which purported to act in accordance with natural or other moral law, would use the vocabulary of universal moral principles and objective truth as covers for self-aggrandisement and injustice. Niebuhr, however, never asserted that the human intellect and will were so tainted that the quest for natural-law, liberal-democratic, public-philosophic or other standards was inevitably doomed to fail; his intention was to warn natural-law and other liberals and democrats against ingenuousness, self deception, self righteousness and an exaggerated view of the power of reason.

> Men do have to make important decisions in history upon the basis of certain norms, even though they must recognize that all historic norms are touched with both finiteness and sin, and that their sinfulness consists precisely in the bogus claim of finality which is made for them. The perennial mistake of rationalists, whether Stoic, Catholic or modern, is to exempt reason from either finiteness or sin or both and to derive universal rational norms from this confidence in reason (1941, p. 301).

Niebuhr's emphasis on sinfulness - which from about the end of the 1950s he preferred to put in a more secular language as the self-centredness of individuals and the tribalism of social groups[12] - is an important corrective to the inordinately optimistic hopes which continue to tempt democrats. His is a realism about human beings which is expressed incisively in one of his best known aphorisms: man's 'capacity for justice makes democracy possible; but man's inclination to injustice makes democracy necessary' (1960, p. xiii). His realism contrasts with the manic-depressive tendency of so many liberal democrats to swing to and fro between, on the one side, euphoria about human nature and democratic possibilities, and, on the other, anxiety and despair.

A similar, politically realist public philosophy to that which Niebuhr grounded on Augustinian, Christian premises, but reached by a different route and expressed differently, is to be found in the work of two secular democratic theorists, John Plamenatz and Giovanni Sartori, whom I shall describe as democratic-elite theorists. Their studies of democracy will be the final topic of this two-chapter survey of major twentieth-century contributors to democratic theory as a public philosophy.

Democratic-Elite Theory: John Plamenatz

The term *democratic elitism*, as noted in Chapter 4's discussion of utopian democratic theory, has been used pejoratively by Peter Bachrach and other left-wing advocates of participatory democracy to describe the view that elites are a necessary part of democratic politics. However, in examining the work of Plamenatz and Sartori on democracy, which includes an affirmation of the inevitability of elites, I shall use a similar term, *democratic-elite theory*, as a non-pejorative description of their thinking. The contention of Plamenatz (1977) and Sartori (1965; and 1987) is that the democratic problem is not to eradicate elites but to ensure that the people who comprise a political elite treat other citizens as equals, rather than as inferiors, and respect the rights, opinions and interests of citizens.

---

12   Niebuhr gave the following reason for changing the language with which he discussed sin: '"realists", including many, if not most, political philosophers who were in substantial agreement with positions taken in my Gifford Lectures [*Nature and Destiny of Man*], were careful to state that their agreement did not extend to my "theological presuppositions". This present volume, dealing with the same human nature, will understandably use more sober symbols of describing well-known facts. I still think the London *Times Literary Supplement* was substantially correct when it wrote some years ago: "The doctrine of original sin is the only empirically verifiable doctrine of the Christian faith".' (1966, p. 68.)

John Plamenatz was a respected British political philosopher and historian of ideas, whose reputation rested on his careful, critical studies of classical political-philosophic texts. He was a fellow of Oxford University's All Souls and Nuffield Colleges from the 1930s, and the university's Professor of Social and Political Theory from 1967. His best known book is his two-volume *Man and Society: A Critical Examination of Some Important Social and Political Theories from Machiavelli to Marx* (1963), posthumously published (1993) in a longer three-volume edition based on the original text. He did not see himself as a major democratic theorist and, in his main study of democracy, *Democracy and Illusion* (1977), he modestly declared that his intentions were simply to 'scrutinise' some influential twentieth century texts on democratic theory. But, in this scrutiny, damaging criticisms were directed against the texts of Joseph Schumpeter, Robert Dahl and other 'revisionists' who wished to discard previous, normative, democratic theory because of its alleged naivety. Plamenatz's study of modern democracy also contained cogent rejoinders to the academic theorists of the New Left who opposed the revisionists but who substituted their own conceptions of democratic theory and practice for those of both classical writers and the revisionists.

The 'revisionists', Plamenatz wrote, were trying to 'reconstruct democratic theory on new foundations' (1977, p. ix), foundations which he argued were unsound. Despite having different values and goals from those of Jean-Jacques Rousseau, Schumpeter and other revisionists agreed with Rousseau's proposition that representative government was always in the hands of privileged minorities. Rousseau's view of representative democracy, Plamenatz further observed, had been taken up by anarchists and Marxists for the propagation of their revolutionary challenge to modern democracy, and by the elite theorists (Mosca, Pareto and Michels) - whom Plamenatz described as the 'academic critics of democracy' - for their more conservative purposes. The revisionists shared the anarchist, Marxist and elite-theory view of Western parliamentary democracy but drew new and distinctive conclusions. They redefined democracy, and changed the criteria for determining whether or not a society was democratic. Plamenatz conceded that they had made a contribution to democratic theory by the questions they raised, but he argued that their answers were flawed, and he denied that the work of their liberal democratic predecessors was as inept as they alleged. The revisionists, in fact, did not appear to understand the democratic theory they rejected.

Most of the ideas that the revisionists attributed to Jeremy Bentham, James and John Stuart Mill and other nineteenth-century democratic theorists, Plamenatz wrote, were concocted by the revisionists. Few liberal democratic theorists had supposed that representative democracy required a general will, and none had doubted that divisions between leaders and followers would survive democratic change, or that governmental power and authority would be in the hands of a small minority of citizens. No major democratic theorist had denied that democracy would require a leadership stratum and a professional administration. At the most, the ideas attributed to classical democratic theorists were those to be found in the loose talk of populistic journalists and politicians. The view that democracy requires a common or general will, Plamenatz wrote, is

> much better called *popular* than *classical*; it is to be found much more in the speeches of radical politicians, in newspapers and journals with a wide circulation, and in ordinary talk about politics than in the works of serious students of government, not to speak of books that are recognized classics....What political scientists, especially in America but not only there call 'the classical theory of democracy' is, I suggest, an invention, or rather construction out of bits and pieces, of the writers who attack it (1977, p. 39).

In order to demonstrate the boundaries as well as the necessity and importance of elite functions for small as well as large democratic societies, Plamenatz asked his readers to imagine a community with no more than about a hundred members, in which only about ten members put proposals to and spoke at the community's decision-making meetings (1977, pp. 57-8). He argued that, provided this leadership was the product of the majority preferring to be listeners and arbitrators, and provided the listeners had the right to ask questions, intervene and vote, there was nothing undemocratic or undesirable about the division between actors and spectators. The greater prominence of the ten leaders did not give them greater influence, as the advice of an industrious speaker might be rarely taken, while people who appeared to be apathetic and of little consequence might regularly be members of victorious majorities. Far from the ten leaders controlling the community, they depended upon the willingness of the remaining ninety to act on their advice.

Similar conclusions about the indispensability of leaders and political elites for a democracy, Plamenatz wrote, followed from considering, in addition to fictitious small societies, the actual experience of modern nations.

> The demand for democracy, when it first arises, comes from persons who believe (or affect to believe) that rulers are neglecting the needs and aspirations of their subjects, and that this neglect will continue for as long as they are not responsible to their subjects. These champions of democracy, sincere or otherwise, either want to be leaders themselves or

want the people to have leaders. For unless there are leaders whom the people, or some considerable part of them, follow, it is unlikely that the demand for democracy will be conceded....Wherever there is democracy there is plenty of leadership of this kind (1977, p. 89).

For Plamenatz, it was nonsense to believe that, until the middle of the twentieth century, major writers on democracy failed to notice the presence of administrators, political leaders, party organisers and persuasive journalists. It was foolish therefore to disparage and discard the work of previous democratic theorists. Trenchant criticisms were also directed against what Plamenatz regarded as the vague, procedural definitions of democracy and the economic determinism of much revisionist theory, and against the utopianism and social levelling of quasi-anarchists and neo-Marxists. In challenging the leftist view that representative institutions should be strengthened or replaced by smaller units of direct, participatory democracy, Plamenatz observed that ordinary citizens might find it even more difficult to check and control small decision-making units than the large representative institutions of modern nations.

The arguments of *Democracy and Illusion* (1977) add up to a public philosophic call for an improved understanding of the principles of liberal democracy and, for this purpose, a return to the work of classical theorists. It was also a call for political and other elites to be guided by such principles. Should they fail to do so, modern democracies would become shams, and the 'more a regime that calls itself democratic is a sham democracy (the less it lives up to its own principles), the more people inside it are confused about these principles' (Plamenatz, 1977, p. 205).

Democratic-Elite Theory: Giovanni Sartori

Giovanni Sartori is an Italian political scientist and theorist, a native of Florence, who for half a century has held teaching, research and professorial posts at leading Italian and American universities and research institutions. His main contributions to normative democratic theory are his *Democratic Theory* (1965), which was first published in Italian in 1958 and in English in 1962, and *The Theory of Democracy Revisited* (1987), a two-volume substantial revision of the earlier book. His recognition of the importance of the character of their elites for any society makes him an elite theorist; his thinking on what should be the relations between elites and the other citizens of democratic nations makes him a democratic theorist and public philosopher.

Despite the overall unity of his two studies of democracy, there are significant differences in their emphases and the attention paid to topics. In the 1987 book, the many academic disputes about democracy of the preceding three decades receive considerable space, and the main threats to democratic theory and practice are seen in a new light. In the 1950s, Sartori considered the main threat to democratic theory to be the then fashionable positivism of much behavioural political science and analytical philosophy, and the hostility it generated to previous political philosophy and democratic theory. At the end of the 1980s, however, he was more worried by the utopian and perfectionist prescriptive theory which academic radicals had substituted for analytical philosophy and positivist social science, along with classical democratic theory. Common to both books is a concern about the abandonment of traditional, Western, political philosophy and democratic theory.

For Sartori, it is a perfectionist error to conceive of democracy not as a project for achieving a sound system of government and competent, responsible leaders but for mass participation and an equality of power. In common with Plamenatz he shares the premises of the original elite theorists that societies and systems of government require elites, and that the crucial issues are the character of these elites and their relations with the rest of the population. Sartori, in fact, included the idea of an elite, in its original approbatory sense, in what he offered as a 'normative definition' of modern democracy: 'Democracy should be a *polyarchy of merit*' (1987, p. 169). He argues that, for democrats, the goal should be the obtaining of elites who are both competent and loyal to democratic values. Although he considers democracy to be a society and civilisation as well as a system of government, he is emphatic that, unless democracies establish efficient systems of government, they will fail: for 'if a democracy does not succeed in being a system of government, it does not succeed - and that is that' (1965, p. 110). The problem for democrats is 'how we are to be ruled, not to avoid being ruled' (1965, p. 120).

Democracy, for Sartori, is the product of Western civilisation including its political philosophy; unlike communism, however, its directing principles cannot be traced back to a small number of thinkers and actors. Because democracy consists of actual social and political realities, as well as ideals and values, democratic theory is both empirical and normative, and it always contains tensions. At one extreme it falls into the 'misplaced realism' of describing and excusing a status quo; at the other, it falls into a perfectionism that scorns existing institutions and practices. Although democracy is always more than a governmental or political system, and it is possible to speak of industrial, economic, social and other types of democracy, Sartori is emphatic that democracy is primarily political. Unless a nation's system of government is democratic, any other democratic structures will depend upon the interests and whims of whoever possesses governmental power, as was the fate of the self-management experiments in industrial democracy of Tito's Yugoslavia.

The greatest of the achievements of modern democracy, for Sartori, is the liberal tradition of constitutionalism and the rule of law, a *sine qua non* for the protection of individual liberties and rights against governments. But for maintaining or, what is even more difficult, developing a constitutional tradition, there must be strong civil societies with a variety of independent associations able to stand up to governments and to mediate between governments and citizens. Firmly rejected is the view that there could be a communist, socialist, third-world or other non-liberal democracy. Any so-called democracy that rejects liberal principles, Sartori asserts, must become autocratic, and it is an abuse of language to describe an autocratic government as democratic. At best, such a regime would be an autocracy which used non-democratic means to establish some democratic goals. But as it is actual institutions and methods, and observable practices, rather than promises and professed ideals, which entitle a nation to be described as democratic, nations with autocratic systems of government should not be classified as democratic. To define democracy in non-liberal terms is to operate with arbitrary and confusing, stipulative, definitions rather than definitions based on historical experience. Indeed, for Sartori, it is because arbitrary, stipulative definitions have become prevalent in political theory that political theorists have difficulty communicating with each other, and, in universities as much as the media, there is confusion about the meaning of such terms as *democracy, constitutional government, freedom, equality* and *justice*. Although, for analytical purposes, it is sometimes useful to separate the liberal from the democratic components of liberal democracy, if *democracy* is to mean government that rests on a genuine rather than a manufactured consent by citizens, then liberal principles are an indispensable part of it.

In Sartori's discussions of liberal principles, however, he distinguishes between liberalism as a political project for protecting people from their rulers, and liberalism as the liberties which make possible a market economy. He sometimes calls this latter (economic) liberalism *liberism*. Of the two liberalisms, it is the political which Sartori emphasises. Economic liberalism or liberism, however, is an additional achievement which has given democratic nations an efficient economy, and which provides the economic foundation for political liberalism. The theory and practice of modern liberalism, Sartori notes, go back to and were developed in the seventeenth- and eighteenth-century political challenges to autocratic monarchies. It is a mistake, therefore, to define classical liberalism in terms of narrow, atomistic conceptions of society, rampant individualism, laissez-faire economic policies or an unrestrained accumulation of wealth. Assuming that such extreme forms of individualism were ever a part of modern liberalism, they were not attached to it until the end of the eighteenth century.

With the extension of the franchise, however, the distinctively democratic part of liberal democracy, the majority principle, comes into its own. Democracies, Sartori argues, use and are dependent on the majority principle; but the majority principle, properly understood, means not all power to majorities - which would make a stable democracy impossible - but a combination of majority decisions and minority rights.

> Democracy, I have argued...is not pure and simple popular power. I shall now insist that democracy is not pure and simple majority rule either. Indeed, 'majority rule' is only a shorthand formula for *limited* majority rule, for a restrained majority rule that respects minority rights. Until a few decades ago this was well understood, I doubt that this is still the case today (1987, p. 31).

Sartori sees the justifying of democracy as an issue; but justifying democratic government, for Sartori as for Churchill, does not require a demonstration that it is morally and politically beyond criticism. It is sufficient that democratic governments and societies be superior to possible alternatives. Such a superiority resides in democracy's constitutional and other checks to governmental power, and in free elections and the political rights which make governments accountable to citizens. These democratic institutions do not guarantee the good life or even good government, but they are far more likely to promote them than are any alternative. Sartori's reply to the value-relativist objection that justifications of democracy in terms of life, security and freedom rest on a personal preference or Eurocentric bias is cutting: 'I am at a loss' he writes, 'in finding any rational way of sustaining that a person may prefer death, torture, prison, and arbitrary dispossession of home or harvest to their avoidance' (1987, p. 273).

On economic organisation, he follows other public philosophers in opting for a mean between capitalism and socialism. Sartori's view is that although liberal democracies are incompatible with the large-scale economic planning of command economies, they are compatible with limited planning, public welfare, and cooperation between governments, trade unions and private companies. But despite this support for a limited governmental overseeing of and for interventions in the market, Sartori maintains that the terms *mixed economy* and *mixed society* are confusing and should be avoided. They hide the fact that a choice must be made: 'at stake...is not the extent of state intervention or regulation but whether our economic systems should remain, at base, market systems. Market or nonmarket - that is the question' (1987, p. 399). But, in many of the ways in which the idea of a mixed economy or society is used, Sartori appears to favour a similar mix. No objections are made, for example, to governmental support for those public goods that 'are truly indivisible and thus permit free riding,' or to government interventions when there are 'accumulations of "externalities," such as pollution, degradation and even destruction of the environment' (1987, p. 406). State welfare schemes are an unobjectionable supplement to a market economy because, although an economic market is efficient and benefits a national community, left to itself it can be 'cruel'. The main reason why it is cruel, Sartori writes, is that 'the irremediably unfit are expelled from the market society; they are left to perish or survive on some other arrangement' (1987, p. 411). And even fit people may suffer as a result of unpredictable market fluctuations rather than their personal failings. This is because the

> market is *individual-blind*: it is a ruthless *society-serving* machinery. How this crucial point [that the market benefits societies unevenly and at the expense of particular individuals and groups] can be missed...is a most interesting matter (Sartori, 1987, p. 411).

In common with other public philosophers, therefore, Sartori resists the laissez-faire utopian idea that the solution to the problems of modern democracies is to leave practically everything to the free choice of individuals, and the laws of supply and demand. Nevertheless, he has less reservations about the market than many other twentieth-century public philosophers, and he is less disturbed by the problems of monopoly and oligopoly. His view, which is similar to that of Friedrich Hayek and many other economists, is that, provided there is no legal protection for a monopoly or oligopoly, the possibility of future competition is sufficient to compel the beneficiaries to be efficient and not to abuse their position. A market 'structure is operative', he writes, even

> when 'sufficient competitiveness' is absent, even when competitors are dormant, for a false step of the monopolist will wake them up. A market may in fact be a poor market; even so, the consumers are still defended by a *competition-structured system* (1987, p. 416).

On the character and role of law, Sartori's thinking also resembles Hayek's.[13] He distinguishes between law and legislation, and warns that

---

13 Friedrich A. Hayek's political and economic liberalism, and his distinction between law and legislation are dealt with at length in his *The Constitution of Liberty* (1960); and *Law, Legislation and Liberty* (1973, 1976 and 1979). For studies of his extensive

excessive legislation corrupts and destroys the authority of law, and its capacity to strengthen civil society and check governments. Significantly, he begins a chapter on 'Liberty and Law' with a quotation from Tacitus: 'The more corrupt the Republic, the more the laws' (1987, p. 298). He then argues that the ever increasing mass of legislation in most present-day democracies undermines both liberty and law. We (the citizens of modern democracies) are not politically free because we have 'wanted the laws enacted by our representatives' he writes, 'we are free because we limit and control their power to enact them' (1987, p. 321). The rule of law, it follows, is an indispensable condition for a representative democracy - but the rule of legislators is not the rule of law. If the rule of legislators, irrespective of whether they have majority support, replaces a constitutional tradition, independent courts and a respect for minority rights, then democracy is transformed into an elective autocracy.

Sartori's thinking on democracy is similar to Tocqueville's, a major influence on it, in having as one of its main purposes the identifying of the dangers to democratic civilisation. In common with Tocqueville he sees leadership and the role of civil society and its voluntary associations as crucial, and he identifies two new threats to them. They are, first, the overloading of governments which results from their concessions to powerful lobbies, and the reluctance of party leaders and other politicians to resist electoral pressures, and, second, partly as an effect and partly as a cause of this overloading, governments becoming technocratic as more and more reliance is placed on managerial and other 'experts'. Increasingly therefore, Sartori argues, instead of competent and principled political leadership and government, there is large-scale, incompetent government by demagogues and so-called experts, with democratic societies pulled in different directions by pressure groups and the electoral opportunism of government and opposition parties.

In contrast to many commentators who make similar criticisms of contemporary democratic politics, Sartori is sceptical about mass education being the antidote. Even to the extent that mass education produces a more literate population, he sees it as being compatible with opportunist, manipulative government and undisciplined but essentially conformist voters. Indeed a technological or other non-liberal literacy may work against the self-development and self-expression of individuals, and facilitate an acceptance of covert if not overt autocratic government. The problems which bedevil contemporary democracies cannot be solved by an increase in schooling, higher education or any other easy solution. At their root is the fact that

---

economic and political writings, see Barry (1979); Butler (1984); and Kukathas (1989).

Natural Law, Augustinian Realism, and Democratic-Elite Theory 193

> we [the citizens of democratic nations] are...in the process of creating - at a minimum - a wholly unmanageable and ominous overload....we are living above our means. But we are equally, and even more grievously, *living above and beyond our intelligence*, above our grasp of what we are doing. The more we engage in remaking the body politic, the more I am struck by the uneasy feeling that we are apprentice sorcerers who are turning politics into a gigantic negative-sum, or minus-sum game - a game in which we are all bound to lose (Sartori, 1987, p. 247).

In common with all democratic theorists in the public philosophic tradition, Sartori understands that, perhaps more than anything else, their task and responsibility is to warn.

The Challenge of Democratic Theory as Public Philosophy

The four-chapter review of democratic theorists who have maintained a public philosophic tradition of writing has documented their similar understandings of democratic institutions, ideals and problems while also revealing their different emphases and their disagreements. The review suggests that the public philosophic tradition is a broad rather than a narrow church, and that the texts of its participants are like a battery of searchlights. The searchlights vary in their intensity and coloration, and they come from different directions - but they all illuminate the character and problems of democratic theory and practice. The four chapters reveal that, since the beginning of the nineteenth century and accompanying the democratisation of Western and other nations, there has been a public philosophic tradition of writing which, despite losing ground since the 1940s to formalist-ideological and utopian democratic theory, remains as a well established alternative. It has been created and furthered by a wide range of political writers, including, religious and secular thinkers, empiricist, idealist and other philosophers, democratic socialists and advocates of market capitalism, historians, political and other social scientists, and journalists. In addition, in the governmental, as distinct from the wider life of democratic nations, it has been sustained by those political leaders, politicians and other political participants who have acted on its standards.

Needless to say, the upholders of a realistic democratic theory and practice, for all their achievement, have not solved and overcome all the theoretical and practical problems and difficulties of democratic government. This should not be disturbing or discouraging, for, as public philosophers have always realised, as long as there are nations struggling to democratise and/or to hold on to past gains, there will be theoretical tensions and obscurities, and practical difficulties and dangers to confront. What I have tried to show is that there is an identifiable public philosophic tradition of democratic theory, to which the writers who have been discussed have made preeminent contributions, and a tradition which it is essential to maintain and strengthen if democratic civilisation, nations and citizens are to survive and prosper. In the next chapter, further conclusions about democratic theory as a public philosophy will be drawn by examining its principal functions. In the process, many of its features and implications which so far have only been touched on will receive greater attention.

References

Barry, N.P. (1979), *Hayek's Social and Economic Philosophy*, Macmillan, London.
Bingham, June (1972), *Courage to Change: An Introduction to the Life and Thought of Reinhold Niebuhr*, 2nd edn, Scribner, New York.
Butler, Eamonn (1984), *Hayek's Contribution to the Political and Economic Thought of Our Time*, Temple Smith, London.
Doering, Bernard E. (1983), *Jacques Maritain and the French Catholic Intellectuals*, Univ. of Notre Dame Pr., Notre Dame.
Evans, Joseph W. (ed.) (1963), *Jacques Maritain: The Man and His Achievement*, Sheed and Ward, New York.
Fachre, G. (1970), *The Promise of Reinhold Niebuhr*, Lippincott, Philadelphia.
Finnis, John (1980), *Natural Law and Natural Rights*, Clarendon Pr., Oxford.
Fox, Richard Wightman (1987), *Reinhold Niebuhr: A Biography*, 2nd edn, Harper and Row, San Francisco.
Gerth, H.H. and C. Wright Mills (eds) (1970), *From Max Weber: Essays in Sociology* [1948], 2nd edn, Routledge, London.
Hayek, Friedrich A. (1960), *The Constitution of Liberty*, Routledge, London.
Hayek, Friedrich A. (1973, 1976 and 1979), *Law, Legislation and Liberty*, 3 vols, Routledge, London.
Kukathas, Chandran (1989), *Hayek and Modern Liberalism*, Oxford Univ. Pr., Oxford.
Maritain, Jacques (1945), *Christianity and Democracy*, Bles, London.
Maritain, Jacques (1953), *The Range of Reason*, Bles, London.
Maritain, Jacques (1955), *The Social and Political Philosophy of Jacques Maritain: Selected Writings*, (eds) Joseph W. Evans and Leo R. Ward, Sheed and Ward, New York.
Maritain, Jacques (1956), *Man and the State* [1951], 2nd edn, Univ. of Chicago Pr./Phoenix Books, Chicago.
Maritain, Jacques (1959), *The Degrees of Knowledge*, 2nd Eng. edn, Bles, London.
Maritain, Jacques (1966), *Challenges and Renewals*, (eds) Joseph W. Evans and Leo R. Ward, Univ. of Notre Dame Pr., Notre Dame.

Maritain, Jacques (1968), *The Peasant of the Garonne: An Old Layman Questions Himself about the Present Time*, Holt Rinehart and Winston, New York.
Maritain, Jacques (1972), *The Person and the Common Good* [1946], 3rd edn, Univ. of Notre Dame Pr., Notre Dame.
Maritain, Jacques (1975), *Reflections on America*, Scribner, New York.
Merkley, Paul (1975), *Reinhold Niebuhr: A Political Account*, McGill-Queens Univ., Pr., Montreal.
Niebuhr, Reinhold (1941 and 1943), *The Nature and Destiny of Man: A Christian Interpretation*, 2 vols, Nisbet, London.
Niebuhr, Reinhold (1960), *The Children of Light and the Children of Darkness* [1944], 2nd edn, Scribner, New York.
Niebuhr, Reinhold (1966), *Man's Nature and His Communities*, Bles, London.
Niebuhr, Reinhold (1986), *The Essential Reinhold Niebuhr*, (ed.) Robert McAfee Brown, Yale Univ. Pr., New Haven.
Niebuhr, Reinhold and Paul E. Sigmund (1969), *The Democratic Experience*, Pall Mall Pr., London.
Novak, Michael (1981), 'The Economic System: the Evangelical Basis of a Social Market Economy', *Review of Politics*, vol. 43, pp. 355-80.
Passerin d'Entreves, A. (1951), *Natural Law*, Hutchinson, London.
Plamenatz, John (1963), *Man and Society: A Critical Examination of Some Important Social and Political Theories from Machiavelli to Marx*, 2 vols, Longman, London.
Plamenatz, John (1977), *Democracy and Illusion* [1973], 2nd edn, Longman, London.
Plamenatz, John (1993), *Man and Society: Political and Social Theories from Machiavelli to Marx*, 3 vols, Longman, London.
Sartori, Giovanni (1965), *Democratic Theory* [1958], 2nd Eng. edn, Praeger, New York.
Sartori, Giovanni (1987), *The Theory of Democracy Revisited*, 2 vols, Chatham House, Chatham, N.J.
Schall, James V. (1998), *Jacques Maritain: The Philosopher in Society*, Rowman and Littlefield, Lanham.
Sigmund, P.E. (ed.) (1971), *Natural Law in Political Thought*, Winthrop, Cambridge, Mass.
Simon, Yves R. (1961), *Philosophy of Democratic Government* [1951], 2nd edn, Univ. of Chicago Pr./Phoenix Books, Chicago.
Simon, Yves R. (1962), *A General Theory of Authority*, Univ. of Notre Dame Pr., Notre Dame.
Simon, Yves R. (1965), *The Tradition of Natural Law*, (ed.) Vukan Kuic, Fordham Univ. Pr., New York.
Simon, Yves R. (1968), *Freedom and Community*, (ed.) Charles P. O'Donnell, Fordham Univ. Pr., New York.
Smith, Brooke Williams (1976), *Jacques Maritain: Antimodern or Ultramodern?*, Elsevier, New York.

PART III
CONCLUSIONS

I [have] argued that liberal democracy may constitute the "end point in mankind's ideological evolution" and the "final form of human government," and as such constituted the "end of history." That is, while earlier forms of government were characterized by grave defects and irrationalities that led to their eventual collapse, liberal democracy was arguably free from such fundamental internal contradictions....While some present-day countries might fail to achieve stable liberal democracy, and others might lapse back into other, more primitive forms of rule like theocracy or military dictatorship, the ideal of liberal democracy could not be improved on.

Francis Fukuyama,
The End of History and the Last Man, 1992

The decline of manufacturing and the consequent shortage of jobs; the shrinkage of the middle class; the growing number of the poor; the rising crime rate; the flourishing traffic in drugs; the decay of the cities - the bad news goes on and on. No one has a plausible solution to the intractable problems, and most of what passes for political discussion doesn't even address them. Fierce ideological battles are fought over peripheral issues. Elites, who define the issues, have lost touch with the people.

Christopher Lasch,
The Revolt of the Elites and the Betrayal of Democracy, 1995

9 Functions of Democratic Theory as Public Philosophy

Walter Lippmann's (1955) classic on the necessity of a public philosophy for democratic nations is a helpful starting point for trying to understand the principal functions of democratic theory as a public philosophy. Lippmann gave prominence to eight functions or tasks, the first and primary of which is the maintenance and development of the guiding standards for governmental personnel, political elites and the general public. Such public philosophic norms, however, had to be based not on conceptions of a perfect democracy but on social and political realities, and the principles that are basic to a civilised society and political community. Second, a public philosophy had to mediate between political theory and practice, between intellectuals and political actors, and between leaders and other major political participants on the one hand and citizens on the other. These mediations are to ensure that the standards for political life are known, followed and capable of withstanding objections, and that law and governmental policy are coherent, comprehensible and reasonable. Third, the public philosophy should help to tame the financial and industrial, technological, cultural and other forces of the modern world. For Lippmann, in fact, it was the scale and rapidity of change in modern life that made it imperative that a public philosophy be retrieved. A fourth function is to uphold moral and political responsibility: to teach that, although democratic like other societies will always be far from perfect, they nonetheless oblige their members to be law abiding and, as best they are able, to preserve past achievements, to improve social and political life, and to struggle against poverty, ignorance and other social evils. The performing of these educational responsibilities is partly that of schools, colleges and universities, partly that of politicians, journalists and other moulders of public and elite opinion - and ultimately of individual citizens themselves.

A fifth public philosophic function is to demand and exemplify clarity in political speech and writing. Obfuscation, euphemism, jargon and double talk, particularly when they entrench themselves in government, and in electoral and other politics, are enemies not only of language but of democratic life. A sixth function is to combat scepticism and despair about democratic ideals, partly by giving substance to and thus justifying the use of such fundamental and comprehensive concepts as the *public* and *national* interest, the *common good* and *justice*, concepts which will be returned to and examined later in this chapter. A seventh function for contributors to a public philosophy is, as it was for Lippmann, to be ever alert to both the internal and external threats to democratic government and life and to warn, a task which at the end of the twentieth century is more pressing than ever. But, in contrast to the prominence given to natural law in Lippmann's (1955) essays, I have argued that effective public philosophies for modern, secular, cultural-pluralist democratic nations must rest not on universal natural-law or similar moral presuppositions but on what the citizens of democratic nations are able to perceive as the requirements of a democratic community - a view which is also found in Lippmann's (1955) essays and his journalism. Natural law theorists, I have contended, are only one of several groups of political thinkers and actors who have sustained a public philosophy for democratic nations.

The review of public philosophic writing which followed the Lippmann chapter revealed that one of the most persistent issues the tradition has confronted is that of socialism versus capitalism. Public philosophers, however, even when they appeared to be in opposed camps, have sought a mean - a middle way between market capitalism and socialism which synthesised the economic and other insights of both. Again and again this search for what John Stuart Mill called the 'partial truths' in most opposed political positions typified the response of public philosophers not only to the question of socialism or capitalism but to most political, economic and cultural disputes and divisions. This quest for a mean will be further explored later in the chapter.

A rejection of majoritarian and other populist excesses emerged as another major part of the public philosophic tradition. Public philosophers put individual liberties, minority rights, toleration and responsible, farsighted and when necessary bold and courageous leadership before the pleasing of majorities. Modern democracy, for them, means not all power to majorities or whoever succeeds in mobilising or speaking for majorities but a tolerant culture, and the sharing of the benefits of democratic government by all the members of the political community. More specifically, the public philosophic alternative to majoritarianism has emerged as constitutionalism (the maintenance and refinement of constitutional rules and conventions), and a representative system in which representatives and the represented respect and are mutually responsive to each other, and seek shared objectives. Constitutionalism and representation, among their other purposes, ensure that government is in accordance with known rules and constraints, that public servants, judges and other public officials subordinate their private interests to the requirements of their office, that governments are accountable as well as responsive to citizens, and that political practice leads not to the favouring of some sectional interests over others but to the benefiting of the whole of a national community.

When democratic practice departs from constitutional, representative and other principles of good government, the public-philosophic task is not to adjust democratic theory to the departures, as occurs in formalist theories of democracy, but to resist the practices which corrupt public life. Although it is difficult to locate the precise points where government in the public interest is departed from, where constitutionalism becomes legalism, and where representation - the attempt to achieve self government by the members of large modern states - becomes misrepresentation, democratic theories and would-be public philosophies which fail to make such distinctions further the corruption of democratic government.

It follows from the emphasis by public philosophers on the need for a strong civil society consisting of independent and public spirited citizens and associations - the social foundation for constitutionalism and a genuinely representative politics - that democratic theory as a public philosophy has to sustain and develop individual rights, along with the recognition of corresponding duties, the essence of citizenship. Such an understanding of rights, duties and citizenship was basic to the thinking of T. H. Green and his New Liberal followers, Benn and Peters, Maritain, Sartori and other public philosophers. But, for societies in which rights are confused with wants - a temptation and tendency which become pronounced in long-established, apparently secure democracies - public philosophers try to clarify the grounds for rights, and the criteria for separating rights from unjustifiable demands. They also seek criteria such as *justice* for arbitrating between rights. Clarifying and arbitrating between rights, it should be added, has become, since the United Nations' 1948 Universal Declaration of Human Rights substituted *human* for *natural* rights, an increasingly important public philosophic function.

Natural rights, in both the Medieval-Christian natural-law tradition and the later, more secular, social-contract tradition of Hobbes, Locke and their successors were rights which, because they were necessary for civilised individual and social lives, should be granted by states to all citizens and subjects. The effect of democratisation on states which recognised such natural rights was that natural rights were supplemented by political rights, first for men and then for women, thus enabling subjects to become citizens. By contrast, human rights incorporate public welfare, a minimum standard of life and other economic and social goods which are changeable and expansive. They easily become socially divisive, and they are attainable only in prosperous, economically developed nations. The move from natural to human rights, therefore, has led to a conflict between long-established natural rights, which assert religious, economic and political claims against the state, and more recent economic and social, human rights of entitlement which require powerful redistributionist states.

It was because of the tendency for rights to be confused with wants that most New Liberals preferred to speak of obligations and duties rather than rights. An emphasis on duties is more likely to puncture windy rhetoric and to reveal that rights, if they are to be secured, depend upon all sections of a community regarding them as just and necessary. For similar reasons, Benn and Peters, and Yves Simon urged that liberal democracy's encouragement of the rights which promote liberty and equality be moderated by a respect for authority. For these and other public philosophers, keeping a balance between rights and the freedoms they protect, on the one hand, and responsibilities and obligations on the other are necessary conditions for stable and flourishing democracies.

In practice, if rights are to be maintained and extended, then a public-philosophic political culture, which effectively restrains governments, and both irresponsible majorities and minorities, is vital. As one writer on modern constitutions and constitutionalism has observed,

> for people who are likely to respect rights...a hard and fast declaration of rights in a Constitution is hardly necessary....on the other hand...for people who are not likely to respect rights, will the enunciation of rights in the Constitution go far towards ensuring their effective exercise (Wheare, 1964, p. 70)?

But if the rights and duties of citizens and governments are a part of wider considerations, and if the problem of arbitration when there are disputes among them call for a higher normative principle, then it is appropriate to turn to the idea of *justice* and the public philosophic function of promoting justice. In this discussion justice will be seen as incorporating principles such as the *public interest*, the *common good* and *utility* which, for some democrats, political theorists and public philosophers, take the place of *justice* as the highest normative court of appeal for modern democratic government.

Promoting Justice

From the beginnings of Western history justice has been a paramount concern. In the Old and New Testaments it is largely synonymous with righteousness, a righteousness which human beings should strive for individually and collectively, while for the Ancient Greeks it was a cardinal virtue, pertinent to all human relations. In both the biblical and Hellenist conceptions of justice, as in subsequent Roman and other natural law theory, justice safeguarded rights and reminded people of their duties.[1] It was not an accident, therefore, that the first two classics of Western political philosophy, Plato's *The Republic* (1992) and Aristotle's *The Politics* (1992), were centred on the meaning and status of justice. In both texts, justice was the foundation for personal behaviour, social relations and the organising of political communities and their government. Principles of justice were more than social conventions or compromises; they had an objective status and were accessible to all people who disciplined their thinking, and freed themselves from self-interested and other prejudices. Plato may have thought that the justice of this world was a pale reflection of an ideal justice, while Aristotle tried to discover a more tangible justice in actual social and political relations, but both philosophers firmly rejected the view that justice was simply the product of the subjective preferences of individuals, economic classes or even whole societies.

But as sceptics have insisted, from Callicles and Thrasymachus, the adversaries of Socrates in Plato's *Gorgias* (1959) and *The Republic* (1992), to today's postmodernists, there is no agreement about the precise meaning of justice. For all the disagreement about its content and implications, however, justice has acquired some basic and far from trivial meanings, expressed for example in the precepts of natural justice that are expected to be found in the jurisprudence and government of all civilised societies. Such precepts include the ideas that no person can be a judge of his or her own case; that both parties to a dispute be heard; that judges, legislators and administrators be impartial and reasonable; that persons in need should be assisted, a precept which leads to both private charity and public welfare; and that everyone should be treated equally unless there are relevant reasons for doing otherwise. Precepts of natural justice, unlike many 'social-justice' programs for the redistribution of someone's wealth, are intuitively obvious rather than, at least for many people, counter-intuitive.

Most current conceptions and theories of justice include and build upon several principles, the most usual of which are *impartiality, fairness, need, desert, individual liberties, property and other rights, obligations* and *equality*, principles to which different theorists give different nuances and priorities. Just as the Socrates of Plato's *Republic* maintained that justice was a comprehensive idea which embodied all the virtues, personal and social, so Ernest Barker (1961) reasserted in the more modern idiom of *values* this Socratic idea when, for example, he wrote that justice 'is the reconciler and the synthesis of political values; it is their union in an

---

1   For the similarities between early Greek and biblical views of justice, and an argument that they reinforced one another in giving the West its respect for rights, duties and the impartial administration of law, see Whelan (1982).

adjusted and integrated whole' (p. 102). The fact that, until recent decades, philosophers and political thinkers have considered justice to be a compound of several principles, a pluralist rather than a monist concept, helps to explain why, even among well-intentioned and disinterested inquirers, it has generated innumerable theoretical and practical controversies. Today, depending upon which of its components are given a priority, justice can be given traditional, modern, postmodern, conservative, liberal, socialist and other interpretations. In order for actions to be just, and for *justice* to be used as an arbitration principle, therefore, a balance has to be found not only among the contending claims to which it is applied but within the principle of justice itself. But why is justice fundamental or at least relevant to democratic politics, how should it be integrated into democratic theory as a public philosophy, and which of today's contending theories of justice are the most helpful for explaining its character and answering these questions?

John Rawls's and Other Recent Theories of Justice

If justice is to serve as an effective guiding standard for modern democracies, and as an arbitration principle for both theoretical and practical political conflicts, then it is justice as such not merely one or a small number of its parts to which appeals must be made. It is because John Rawls's *A Theory of Justice* (1973), which for nearly three decades has dominated discussions of justice, lacks this wholeness that it falls short of the claims made for it. Despite the theory's many insights, its attempt at completeness, its author's assiduity in continually reworking it and the enthusiasm of its admirers, for several reasons it fails to provide an adequate conception of justice for democratic nations. Rawls's theory of justice as fairness, in both its original (1973) and revised (1993) versions,[2] reduces justice to a particular mixture of liberty, equality and need in which, it will be argued, equality is made the primary principle, and *justice* becomes the name for what is an unrealistic, egalitarian, social and political project. Principles that are usually regarded as essential to justice but which obstruct Rawls's project are either discarded or given only minor roles.

Rawls grounds his conception of justice on two rules or principles, the second of which is sub-divided. These much discussed rules are that (1) individual liberties should be maximised on the basis of equality ('Each person is to have an equal right to the most extensive total system of equal basic liberties compatible with a similar system of liberty for all'); that, (2a)

---

2 John Rawls, *Political Liberalism* (1993) consists, mainly, of reworked versions of the ideas and arguments of his *Theory of Justice* (1973), first published in 1972.

social and economic inequalities should be 'to the greatest benefit of the least advantaged' and that (2b) these inequalities should be 'attached to offices and positions open to all under conditions of fair equality of opportunity' (1973, p. 302).³ The dominant idea of the two principles, as Rawls has acknowledged, is equality. The

> two principles...are a special case of a more general conception of justice that can be expressed as follows.
> All social values - liberty and opportunity, income and wealth, and the bases of self-respect - are to be distributed equally unless an unequal distribution of any, or all, of these values is to everyone's advantage.
> Injustice, then, is simply inequalities that are not to the benefit of all (1973, p. 62).

Rawls's theory of justice is intended for societies whose members have diverse personal values, goals and ways of life, 'when the belief in a fixed natural order sanctioning a hierarchical society is abandoned' (1973, p. 548), and when there are 'times of social doubt and loss of faith in long established values' (1973, p. 519). Rawls contends, however, that irrespective of their different values and beliefs, it is possible for the citizens of modern nations to agree to the two basic rules of his theory of justice. If, he argues, they first imagine themselves behind a 'veil of ignorance' in which they are rational and possess a knowledge of human societies, history and social options ('the general facts about society' - 1973, p. 547) and, second, if they have the task of deciding on the rules of justice for societies in which they will be members but, third, they do not know the type of person they will be (neither their sex, social position, style of life nor life plans), then they will choose Rawls's two rules. Rational people in this 'original position', Rawls maintains, will agree that his principles are the fairest, most prudent and the most conducive to enabling them to pursue whatever may be their aspirations.

A relativist view of life plans and other personal goals, in which, provided one person's do not infringe on another's, their choices are equally

---

3   In the later (1993) book, Rawls's two principles reappear as follows. 'a. Each person has an equal claim to a fully adequate scheme of equal basic rights and liberties, which scheme is compatible with the same scheme for all; and in this scheme the equal political liberties, and only those liberties, are to be guaranteed their fair value. b. Social and economic inequalities are to satisfy two conditions: first, they are to be attached to positions and offices open to all under conditions of fair equality of opportunity; and second, they are to be to the greatest benefit of the least advantaged members of society.' (Pp. 5-6.)

worthy of respect and protection, is thus made the foundation for agreement by the citizens of democratic nations on rules of justice. These are rules which, if followed, entail a long-term but relentless program for legislative and other major egalitarian changes to democratic societies. By means of a relativist view of values, Rawls thus privileges his preferred value - equality.

In many ways Rawls *Theory of Justice* (1973) justifies the acclaim of its enthusiasts. His arguments are novel and innovative, and he explains and carefully brings together not only the two rules of justice and the procedures for establishing them (the 'original position' and 'veil of ignorance') but what he means by *rational behaviour*, relations between the *right* (justice and other moral principles) and the *good* (the best life), and how people with different conceptions of the good are able to agree to basic moral and political principles. For many of the book's devotees Rawls had achieved what seemed to be no longer possible: the writing of a political philosophic classic comparable to those of the Western tradition from Plato to Hegel, John Stuart Mill and T. H. Green. A more plausible explanation for the book's impact on contemporary thought, however, is that it does not challenge but gives an apparently strong theoretical expression to widespread assumptions and opinions, especially those of egalitarian minded intellectuals and the promoters of redistributionist causes.[4]

Rawls's conception of justice and its justifying theory are ingenious and skilfully argued, but they contain serious flaws, and are marked by both ideological and utopian features. They are ideological in their legitimating of the assumptions and projects of today's leftist elites, and they are utopian in several ways. One utopian assumption is that existing societies should be transformed on the basis of an abstract 'original position' in which the 'rational' beings who choose principles of social justice do not need to know anything of the specific histories, traditions, culture and institutions of the hypothetical societies they will join, or the beliefs, interests and aspirations of their members. A second utopian assumption is the belief that, in present day societies, nearly everyone, including the individuals and groups who rightly or wrongly consider themselves socially meritorious and superior to others, will agree that social rewards are to be decided by what the people who consider themselves deprived, or whoever speaks for them, will regard as beneficial to the deprived. And, third, there is the proposal to eradicate, by legislative and other means, the effects of both natural and social

---

4   As this is not the place to examine all the ramifications of Rawls's theory, my discussion and critical comments are confined to, what are for democratic politics, the more relevant of its basics. For some early responses to Rawls's *Theory of Justice* (1973), see Daniels (1975); for a formidable critique, Bloom (1990); and for a more sympathetic response Kukathas and Pettit (1990).

inequalities, and to achieve a level of social equality to which no human society has or could reach. At the heart of Rawls's writings on justice, therefore, is an egalitarian utopianism that has been described as follows.

> Men [For Rawls] must have equal rights not only to 'life, liberty and the pursuit of happiness,' but to the achievement of happiness. Inequalities, whether they stem from birth, fortune or nature, should be offensive to us. Thus to the familiar principle of liberal democracy that each person is to have an equal right to the most extensive basic liberty compatible with a similar liberty for others, Rawls adds a second principle that all goods are to be equally distributed or, if unequally distributed, this unequal distribution must be agreed to be the advantage of all as measured by the desires of the least advantaged member of society....Rawls's innovation is to incorporate the maxims of contemporary social welfare into the fundamental principles of political justice. Not only must material goods be provided to each citizen, but also an equal sense of his own worth, recognized by others; for, after all, man does not live by bread alone (Bloom, 1990. p. 319).

The main political effect of Rawls's theory of justice has been the encouragement of state enforced schemes for the redistribution of wealth and social resources, and, more recently, the legitimating of affirmative action and other forms of 'reverse' discrimination. Far from leading to the social consensus predicted and desired by Rawls, attempts to act on his and similar social-justice principles have been divisive, with the attitudes and policies they have encouraged provoking neo-conservative, New Right economic-liberal and other opposition to the increased governmental power, expenditure and intrusions they entail. On Rawls's terms, the explanation for the strength and extent of these reactions is that he underestimated the numbers of unjust people. But this explanation follows only if *justice* is the appropriate name for making equality the paramount social value. If, however, the equality favoured by Rawls and theorists with similar conceptions of and attachment to it (for example Dworkin, 1977; and Kymlicka, 1990) is only one part of justice then opposition to it is not against justice but its abuse.

One theoretical reaction to Rawls's egalitarian conception of justice has been Robert Nozick's (1974) theory of justice which went to an opposite extreme. In his 1974 text Nozick reduced justice to individual liberty and desert, and made inherited and acquired property and other entitlements a fundamental part of desert. In contrast to Rawls's emboldening of bureaucratic, interventionist states and their personnel, Nozick posited a *minimal* state as the embodiment of justice. He resisted not only proposals for radical redistributions of wealth, and for social and economic levelling, but even moderate forms of progressive taxation and public welfare. Property and other legal entitlements were made inviolable. Provided that people refrained from criminal acts, they could use their freedom and property as they pleased, irrespective of the political, economic and cultural outcomes. The implication of Nozick's (1974) arguments for modern democracies was that, instead of aiming at becoming free and just societies, they become simply free societies, and societies which made few distinctions between freedom and license. As Aristotle might put it, one partial theory of justice (Nozick's) confronted another (Rawls's).

But at least some post-Rawls, post-Nozick theorists of justice follow Ernest Barker in seeking more balanced theories. J. R. Lucas (1980), for instance, has revived the ancient Greek view that justice is the cardinal virtue. He fuses it with the modern liberal emphasis on individual liberty, and, on this basis, seeks balanced solutions to political and other problems. His discussions reveal the complex and dynamic character of justice, and the impossibility of reducing it to a few simple rules. Michael Walzer (1983), who in many ways shares Rawls's commitment to a more equal society, objects to Rawls's abstract moralism. In his alternative to Rawls's theory of justice, he distinguishes between social 'spheres', such as education, public welfare, industry and political power, and he argues that, as the different spheres have different ends, they require different criteria for deciding just outcomes. It follows from the argument that the various components of justice such as need, desert, liberty and equality have different nuances and priorities in different social spheres. Walzer's contextualism thus provides an antidote to the abstract universalism of Rawls's theory. He reminds us that struggles against injustice require not deductions from a hierarchy of abstract, universal rules but an awareness of different social contexts and circumstances.

William Galston's (1980) challenge to Rawls's theory takes a different path. Galston contends that, far from the right being prior to the good, agreement on principles of justice requires a prior agreement about the good life. This is a public philosophic argument in its urging that democratic communities require a conception of the common good - a proposition which Rawls resists. But Galston makes few distinctions between the *common good* for communities of democratic citizens who disagree about ultimate values and the *summum bonum*, the highest good for the individual and the species. The nature of the *summum bonum* is a fundamental moral and political-philosophic question, and one which is relevant to public life; but, to say the least, it is a question that is unlikely to be answered in the foreseeable future by philosophic inquiry or by social and political practice. A public philosophic conception of justice, therefore, has to be more modest than Galston's.

The outstanding public philosophic analysis of justice for modern representative democracies remains that of Ernest Barker. For Barker, justice mediates between the moral principles which are a necessary condition for civilised societies and the legislative and other laws enforced by their courts. Justice's political purpose is to ensure that the laws, institutions and practices of a state and its citizens comply with universal moral principles without being reducible to or deductions from them. Justice is democracy's highest normative principle, and the standard for settling disputes. Unless a political community and state are guided by the idea of justice, they have inadequate grounds for expecting their members to feel loyal or obligated to them. For Barker, as in the classical Greek and biblical view, justice is an objective principle, universal in its scope. But the knowledge of justice is mainly acquired in practice. Principles of justice are embedded - if they are not lost - by successive generations of people in their institutions and their political and other culture. Justice, Barker wrote,

> is not abstract; nor does it reside merely in the speculative mind of the thinker....The idea of justice resides in *all* minds, and it has been created and developed through the ages by a process of historical social thought, which has made it a common inheritance....[Justice has] a content progressively greater and clearer as those minds think out more fully and consciously the problems of a general right ordering of human relations (1961, p. 167).

Although the idea of justice, like those of constitutionalism and the public philosophy, stands above immediate issues, at the same time it is the product of and never immune from political activity. It is therefore always subject to modification. A shared understanding of basic principles of justice - irrespective of whether they are described in the vocabulary of *justice*, the *common good*, the *public interest*, *utility* or similar comprehensive norms - is a necessary condition for democratic politics. But as such an understanding is an achievement of democratic politics, which is always subject to challenge and decay, the struggle to maintain and further this understanding is unending. With this observation it is appropriate to turn to what is a central function of both justice and democratic theory as a public philosophy: the search for and the finding of a mean.

Finding the Democratic Mean

If a central feature of democratic theory as a public philosophy is finding a mean for the resolution of conflicts and disputes, what exactly distinguishes a public philosophic mean from a compromise at any price or from a middle-of-the-road policy, the only purpose of which is to appease the parties to a dispute and a majority of voters? And how is a public philosophic mean to be defended against the charge that the very idea of a *mean* is empty and useless, and that the word is suitable only for rhetorical purposes. One objection to the idea of a 'golden' mean, as it is sometimes called, is that, as there are no actions which do not avoid behaviour that is even more extreme or foolish, anything can be dressed up as a *mean*. This objection, however, need not delay the discussion as it simply exploits the facts that a mean is not an unquestionable proof but a considered judgement, and that like all judgements it can be contested. A political mean, as its advocates acknowledge, depends upon the intelligence, experience, moral sensitivity, common sense, prudence and wisdom of the person making the judgement, and his or her appreciation of the circumstances and likely effects of an act. Such a mean is not a substitute for investigating an issue and assessing the relevant facts, but the judgement which follows. On urgent issues which call for immediate decisions it is the best of available choices; on long-lasting, persistent issues it identifies the relevant principles. It provides guide-lines which enable governments and citizens to find principled courses of action and compromises which, as far as it is possible, will benefit rather than harm the parties to a dispute and the community as a whole.

The idea or what is sometimes called the *doctrine* of the *mean* has come to Western nations from classical Greece, receiving its most influential statement in Aristotle's *Nicomachean Ethics* (1955). For Aristotle, a mean was the most virtuous of human acts and ways of living, in political and other activity, and it was like hitting a bullseye. All departures from it were either deficient in falling short of the target (virtuous or excellent behaviour) or excessive in going beyond it. But the target was moving rather than stationary, and when it was missed the distance from it varied. Thus, generous acts which hit the target were a mean between those of a miser and a spendthrift, but usually closer to those of the spendthrift; courageous acts were a mean between cowardice and rashness but closer to the latter. A political mean, it followed, was never a mathematical middle point but one to which a prudent, just and informed ruler or citizen aimed. The doctrine of the mean, for Aristotle, was a part of a teleological and theist philosophy in which everything had its natural *telos* (end or purpose), either that of itself or a higher part of an ordered universe. For men and women to seek the mean, therefore, was to act in accordance with and to perfect their nature. But the idea of a mean may be removed from its original, teleological and theist framework without serious political injury. For the politics of post-Aristotelean, secular nations, it can be described as the best of possible choices when decisions are made on the courses of action for the citizens, associations and governments of democratic communities. Often, it will be a lesser evil rather than a positive good.

The foundation on which the idea of the *mean* rests, that rational and defensible judgements can be made in deciding between values and courses of action, challenges the irrationalism of dogmatic forms of value relativism.[5] The idea of the *mean* also challenges the value-absolutist view that there is an ultimate political value or set of values from which the solution to political problems can be deduced. Another challenge is to the view that, on issues in which fundamental values are opposed, only commitment and the will enable choices to be made by governments and other political actors. Also challenged is the idea that liberal democratic theory is an incoherent bundle of dichotomies between, among others, liberty and equality, the rule of law and rule by persons, popular sovereignty and authoritative governmental institutions, political flexibility and constitutional checks, and a global-capitalist market and national interests. It follows from the idea of a public philosophic mean that these dualisms are not contradictions but the principles between which middle ways which most benefit a political community and its members must be found.

In the review of public philosophers from Tocqueville to Plamenatz and Sartori, it was found that again and again, when there are major disputes in democratic societies, public philosophers seek a mean which synthesises what is valid and justified in opposed positions. One such persistent dispute, as has been noted, is the capitalism-versus-socialism issue, a dispute on which the sympathies of public philosophers have varied. A. D. Lindsay and Reinhold Niebuhr, for example, were socialists; John Stuart Mill sometimes called himself a socialist but used the word loosely; Tocqueville and Sartori have opposed socialism, while Maritain was more of the honest broker and Lippmann prone to change his mind. But in all instances their commitment to democracy has been stronger than their commitment to capitalism or socialism. The main

---

5   *Value relativism* is intended to include both the view that fundamental values are subjective preferences, and the view, now often called *value pluralism*, that they are objective but incommensurable. *Value relativism* is intended to cover both its extreme forms that lead to irrationalism and more moderate forms. On the meta-ethical issues of whether moral and other values are ultimately relative or absolute, monist or pluralist, the public philosophy is neutral.

purpose of their analyses of capitalism and socialism has been to help democrats to merge the defensible and better features of both capitalism and socialism. A similar quest for a mean is required for more recent conflicts which, in their intensity, rival those on capitalism-versus-socialism issues.

Like the advocates of unconstrained, laissez-faire capitalist and revolutionary socialist principles so, today, more recent political groups and movements try to give their values and goals a priority over those of liberal democracy. They include radical environmentalists, especially those known as *Deep Green* theorists, radical feminists, the more extreme advocates of affirmative action and government assistance to benefit ethnic and other minorities, the more stubborn of the opponents of these causes, and both dogmatic advocates and critics of global markets and/or supra-national regional government. But, like the extreme parties in the controversies over capitalism and socialism, they too have their public philosophic critics, including other environmentalists, feminists, members of ethnic minorities and the participants in the controversies on the appropriate limits to national sovereignty. The public philosophic task in these disputes is to find the mean which will separate the insights in the opposed positions from emotionalism and rhetoric, and from what is sometimes a sheer hatred of the existing order or, at the other extreme, a refusal to accept any change. The task is to sift what is likely to sustain and improve democratic government and the lives of citizens from what will injure them. Such middle ways are difficult to define and achieve, and even among the most just and knowledgeable of democrats and participants in the public philosophy there will be disagreements about their precise location. But on these and other issues democratic government depends upon the standards of the mean being sought, found and maintained.

The importance of such public philosophic standards points to questions which so far in this book have received little attention. What are the relations between the public philosophy and those philosophic, scientific and other disciplines that share an interest in understanding and improving democratic government and life? What contributions do and should they make to a public philosophy, and what does democratic theory as a public philosophy offer them?

Cooperating with Political Philosophy and the Social and Other Sciences

Political Philosophy

The public philosophy, as the name implies, is closely related to political philosophy. Among the functions they share are clarifying political language and concepts; revealing the issues at the root of linguistic and conceptual disputes; sifting and synthesising the results of empirical work on politics; understanding the appropriate rights and duties of and the relations between citizens and governments; and sustaining a continuity of political judgement.[6] To the extent that Western political philosophy has maintained the objectives of the political science and practical philosophy of Aristotle's *The Politics* (1992) of the fourth century BCE, it has public philosophic qualities. A major purpose of Aristotle's text was to enable Greek citizens to better understand both the potential of their city-state politics to improve their lives and the dangers and corruptions to which it exposed them. Aristotle's political classic did not have knowledge for its own sake as its main end but practical knowledge, how to promote stable and just city states, and flourishing lives for their citizens.

Beginning with Aristotle and his predecessors, Socrates and Plato, Western political philosophy has been both truth-seeking and practical, and has had the problem of combining the search for truth with persuasion. Western political philosophers, in addition to trying to understand the nature and permanent problems of politics, have tried to clarify specific issues and to assist in overcoming the more disturbing political conflicts of their states. They have sought both universal truths and practical benefits. This means that the public philosophy is similar to that part of political philosophy which is more concerned with practical knowledge than with knowledge for its own sake, and that it has amicable relations with other parts of political philosophy. The public philosophy and political philosophy, it follows, are complementary disciplines, with their main differences being that the public philosophy is open to the contributions of political actors who have little interest in political or other philosophy for its own sake, and that, unlike much political philosophy, it is not tied to any one school of philosophy.

---

6   By *political philosophy* is meant both the main Western traditions of the past two and a half millenia and post-1940s analytical political theory.

The Social Sciences

The relations of the public philosophy to economics, sociology and most other social sciences resemble those it has with political philosophy. The public philosophy shares many of the objectives of the social sciences without being reducible to any or all of them. Public philosophers like many social scientists seek explanations as to why, for example, some democracies have less crime and less corruption, superior schools, welfare systems and economies, and a greater respect for authority, minority rights and common interests than others. As an effective public philosophy has to understand the messier and other realities of actual democratic government as well as its long-term positive potential, it needs the procedures and findings of the empirical social sciences - just as it needs those of responsible journalism. In turn, the public philosophy encourages social scientists in disciplines which have different objectives, methods of inquiry and vocabularies to cooperate with and learn from one another in clarifying and suggesting solutions to the problems of democratic nations - thus combining scholarship and public service. Using and urging the use of the findings of the empirical social sciences to improve the theory and practice of democratic government have been a part of the work of John Stuart Mill, Lippmann, Benn and Peters, Plamenatz, Sartori and other public philosophers. Similarly, several studies of the social sciences have concluded that the social sciences should pay greater attention to testing and contributing to normative theories as well as empirical hypotheses on democratic government.[7]

History Some social sciences, of which history is one, are closer to the public philosophy than are others. History shares several concerns with the public philosophy, a principal one being that citizens should be aware of the history of their nations. If a people has little knowledge of or interest in its history, it is pointless for public philosophers to turn to history for evidence and support; they are restricted to current affairs and the offerings of other social sciences. As for historians, if there is little public interest in their work, it is likely to degenerate into antiquarianism, become a branch of popular entertainment and/or fragment into specialist sub-disciplines. Democracy is damaged because history 'may offer no solution for... problems, but it is safe to say that no solution which ignores history is ever likely to be lasting or satisfactory' (McIlwain, 1939, p. vii).[8]

---

[7] For example, Arnold Brecht's wide-ranging and outstanding (1959) study; Runciman (1963); and Thompson (1970). See also Ceaser (1990).

[8] A historian's concern about the decline of interest in history among both political elites and the general public is expressed by J. H. Plumb (1973).

Public choice A rather different social science from history, and one which is a rival to as well as helpful to the public philosophy is public choice. Public choice theorists, sometimes called *rational choice* or *social choice* theorists, build elaborate theoretical structures on a small number of economic and psychological axioms, a strategy which they consider more scientific and superior not only to normative political theory but to behavioural and other empirical political science. Peter Ordeshook (1986, p. ix), for example, has asserted that there was no 'modern political theory' which complied with strict scientific criteria, which he maintains all serious political theory must do, until the pioneering public choice studies of the early 1960s. This purportedly superior science attributes a particular type of rational goal-seeking behaviour to all political actors from prime ministers and presidents to apathetic voters.

Groups and institutions are analysed by public choice theorists in terms of the private, mainly economic interests of the individuals who comprise them. Such norms as the *public* or *national interest* and the *common good* are either dispensed with or reinterpreted as a sum of individual interests. Although, in theory, public choice theorists concede that political activity may at least occasionally be inspired by altruism, and worthy principles and causes, in practice in most public choice work, people are seen as rational egotists. Public choice theorists habitually slide from regarding social phenomena as the product of individual choices to regarding choices as narrowly selfish. They thus oversimplify human conduct and social relations, and play down the affect of history and culture on social and political life.[9]

For at least two related reasons, public choice theory is frequently conflated with economic (laissez-faire) liberalism, and regarded (for example, by three of public choice theory's socialist critics, Self, 1993; and Stretton and Orchard, 1994) as opposed to socialism, the welfare state, and most governmental economic interventions and controls. First, many public choice analyses systematically demonstrate and illustrate the inefficiency of governmental activity. Second, James M. Buchanan and Gordon Tullock, the two most active publicists of public choice theory, are also vigorous advocates of market-economy principles, and of constitutional and other proposals to reduce the power and expenditure of governments. They and many of their students have influenced the New

---

9   For introductions to public choice theory, see McLean (1987); and Mueller (1989). For examples of influential public choice analyses, Downs (1957); Niskanen, Jr (1971); and Olson, Jr (1965).

Right, and the anti-welfare-state wing of the American Republican Party.[10] Nevertheless there is no necessary connection between public choice theory on the one hand and economic liberalism and a minimal state on the other. Iain McLean (1987) is one public choice theorist who contends that public choice is primarily for clarification, to enable everyone, whether their politics are left, right or centre, to make informed choices. Furthermore, he uses public choice techniques to suggest that, for many purposes, anarchism, altruism or governmental initiatives are more effective than profit incentives and the market. For McLean, a capitalist market is simply one method among several for obtaining private and public goods (1987, esp. pp. 177-83).

But whatever the motives and politics of its practitioners, public choice theory has political effects which concern public philosophers. First, its findings, many of which border on the cynical, tempt contemporary politicians the way Machiavelli tempted Renaissance and subsequent princes and rulers. Like Machiavelli's *The Prince*, public choice theory tries to reduce politics to self-interested struggles for power and, implicitly if not intentionally and explicitly, to instruct political actors on what they must do to achieve the position, fame, money and other perks of present-day politics. In the United States where public choice has its roots, and now in most democratic nations, there are multitudes of political consultants, advisers and public-opinion specialists whose chief skill is the ability to apply public-choice-type analyses of current politics to winning elections or otherwise furthering the interests of the leaders, parliamentarians and organisers of political parties and pressure groups. The main political effect of public choice theory and the related 'professionalising' of politics on voters, therefore, has probably been the worsening of their disenchantment with democratic politics.

But, more positively, public choice theorists expose and warn. In the same way that Machiavelli's *The Prince*, whatever the intentions of its author, may be read as an exposure of princely and other government, so public choice analyses may be seen as revealing the effects of egotism and instrumental rationality (the use of reason to achieve goals which are not themselves rationally justified) on democratic politics. Just as Niebuhr urged that the children of light learn from those of darkness, without joining them, so public philosophers and other democrats should learn from public choice analyses without acquiring the attitudes which they suggest are rampant in current democratic politics. Political realism and prudence require that public choice insights into recent political behaviour be

---

10 For their jointly authored, seminal text which argues for a minimal state, see Buchanan and Tullock (1962). For further samples of their work, see Buchanan's essays in Buchanan and Tollison (1984); and Tullock and Perlman (1976).

recognised; but they also suggest that democratic theory and practice be guided by different - public philosophic - standards from those which predominate in current practice. The public philosophy is concerned, primarily, not with whether Machiavellian, public choice or other analyses explain how political actors achieve their preferred goals, but the character of the goals, their effects and repercussions, and whether they benefit or harm democratic politics.

Public policy Policy making by the many departments and other branches of present day democratic government produces a continual need for the advice of social and other scientists, and other trained and experienced professional people. A by-product of this need has been the emergence of public policy as the study of governmental policy making, and as a conduit between a nation's government and its universities and other centres of research and intellectual life. But whereas the public philosophy entails dialogues between governments and citizens to which university and other specialists are encouraged to contribute, public policy may simply mean assisting in the manufacture and selling of the policies of narrowly-focussed, self-seeking politicians and bureaucrats. In brief, public policy is compatible with technocratic government, social engineering by self-styled experts and the oligarchic manipulation of democratic politics, to all of which democratic theory as a public philosophy is opposed.[11]

Public policy, therefore, is not a satisfactory substitute for a public philosophy. Democratic theory as public philosophy resists technocracy, and it enables scientists, social scientists, and other professionals and intellectuals to engage in public life without becoming the tools of politicians, public bureaucracies, political parties and pressure groups. This is not to say that the public philosophy and public policy are necessarily antagonistic, or that all government advisers are rogues; only that in order to deserve the adjective *public*, public policy is another activity which depends upon the survival and inspiration of a public philosophy. Although a public philosophy may not offer the same financial rewards as government posts and contracts, it is better able to provide opportunities for independent, public spirited, creative work, for participation in public debate, and for obtaining the respect of citizens and a person's peers.

---

11 The public philosophy also resists *pedlars of prosperity*, namely university, 'think-tank' and other 'consultants' who simplify complex economic and other issues, and obtain the ear of politicians with proposals for what misleadingly appear to be the quick fixing of problems and easy rides to prosperity. For a description and critique of such peddling, see Krugman (1994).

Warning, Encouraging and Cultivating Prudence

Democratic theory as a public philosophy is not able to provide instant, guarantied cures for the ills of democratic nations. It does not offer political or other salvation, and it is not a substitute for religion, philosophy, art, family life, personal relations or for coping with life's day-to-day troubles. It appreciates the difficulties in finding policies that will produce desired outcomes and, needless to say, it bestows no *charisma*, however that protean and abused word is defined.

But although it calls for more modest attributes than charisma, they are among those which characterise leaders with the ability to inspire democratic nations in times of peril. Winston Churchill and Charles de Gaulle are outstanding twentieth-century examples. Moreover, public philosophic qualities and the endeavour to give public philosophic standards to the new nations they help to found, whatever the precise weighting of their motives and intentions, have characterised the founders of democratic nations from Thomas Jefferson and James Madison to Vaclav Havel, F. W. De Klerk and Nelson Mandela. A nation is fortunate when public philosophic virtues and a commitment to democracy in its leaders are supplemented with great courage, imagination, energy and endurance. But the public philosophic virtues themselves are less demanding.

Public philosophic virtues are grounded on prudence. It is a prudence however which is very different from a self-interested, narrowly conceived pragmatism let alone a crass opportunism. It is sensitive to both moral principles and the related need to understand the likely consequences of political acts. It tries to ensure that means and ends are connected, and that both are morally defensible and politically realistic.

> Prudence...is practical wisdom or that sound judgement which requires conscious and rational adaptation of means to ends. The ends must be proper [rationally and morally justifiable] ends, or else the judgement is not prudent but simply clever, narrowly expedient, or basely pragmatic (Riemer, 1962, p. 60).

The prudence of the public philosophy is that which, for the ancient Greeks, was one of the cardinal virtues; without it, other virtues could become vices. Justice could degenerate into an irrelevant moralism, wisdom into mere cleverness and/or pedantry, and courage into foolhardiness. Prudence or practical judgement (*phronesis*), which encompassed moderation and temperance (*sophrosyne*), meant that Greek citizens, in their private and public lives, disciplined themselves to act firmly as well as cautiously on the basis of knowledge and reason. Prudent voting in the assembly, which of course did not always occur, meant an awareness of different circumstances, considering the consequences of decisions and actions, confronting rather than hiding from dangers, and seeking not perfection but the best possible results.

However difficult it may be to achieve such a prudence, a crucial function for public philosophers, responsible political actors and concerned citizens is to encourage the millions of less concerned citizens, and the elites and government personnel of modern democracies to acquire it. More than anything else, this means - as it did for the citizens of Ancient Greece - the moderating of expectations and demands. The point has been put well by John Dunn in a conclusion to a 1980s essay.

> To see prudence as the central political value, central for citizens just as much as for rulers, yields a permanent reminder that all human beings may judge badly...and perceive the world, greedily and intemperately....To propose the democratization of prudence is to insist that we now understand political, social and economic life well enough to be confident of just one conclusion: that it is irretrievably problematic, and that its problems are ours to cope with for the rest of human time....the democratization of prudence will be a precondition for anything at all resembling a good life....Politics, at least, must learn to cope effectively with the preconditions for a good life before it busies itself too self-importantly with the content of such a life (Dunn, 1990, pp. 214-5).

The prudence which a democratic public philosophy promotes is flexible and adaptable. In complacent societies, instead of indulging in self congratulation, it perceives the risk of ossification, and the need for reform; in societies intoxicated by change, it will see the worth in what is under siege and the disadvantages of innovation. But, at all times, be they complacent or turbulent, its intention is to sustain the political, economic and cultural conditions which nourish democratic government and goals.

It follows from the prudence and realism of the public philosophy, and indeed the very imperatives of democratic politics that two of the public philosophy's main functions are to warn and to encourage. For two centuries, public philosophers have warned their societies about not only the internal and external enemies of democracy but the ever present dangers in democracy itself. These dangers include both the complacency and excessive fondness for present arrangements of ideological thinking and the utopianism of taking parts of the democratic undertaking to unrealistic extremes. If it was Tocqueville who first gave a comprehensive expression to democratic theory as a public philosophy, then it began as warning to democratic peoples to avoid both complacency and excess. Perhaps more than anything else this is the main function of democratic theory as a public philosophy: to warn about complacency, excess and other roads to ruin.

Admonitions, warnings of peril and the urging of remedial action typify the public philosophy, giving it Cassandra-like features. Yet public philosophers do not wish to have the gift of prophecy without being believed. They make suggestions for overcoming difficulties, and they wish to influence governments, political elites and ordinary citizens. When cynicism about democracy is rife, they try to reactivate hopes, find agents and avenues for reform, encourage the faint-hearted and awaken others. At times, they are like doctors who, when there are no known cures, continue to seek cures for their patients while keeping hopes alive. But, if public philosophic warnings and encouragement are to be heard, and to stand a chance of being effective, it is essential that a liberal-democratic tradition of restrained but thorough dialogue and public debate be retrieved, and that citizens and their representatives listen to one another.

The final two chapters will turn from surveying the functions of democratic theory as a public philosophy to assessing its prospects and those for modern democracy.

References

Aristotle (1955), *The Ethics of Aristotle*, (ed.) J.A.K. Thomson, Book II, esp. pp. 64-75, 2nd edn, Penguin Books, Harmondsworth.

Aristotle (1992), *The Politics*, (ed.) Trevor J. Saunders, 3rd edn, Penguin Books, London.

Barker, Ernest (1961), *Principles of Social and Political Theory* [1951], 2nd edn, Oxford Univ. Pr., Oxford.

Bloom, Allan (1990), 'Justice: John Rawls versus the Tradition of Political Philosophy' [1975], in *Giants and Dwarfs: Essays 1960-1990*, Simon and Schuster, New York.

Brecht, Arnold (1959) *Political Theory: the Foundations of Twentieth Century Political Thought*, Princeton Univ. Pr., Princeton, New Jersey.

Buchanan, James M. and Gordon Tullock (1962), *The Calculus of Consent: Logical Foundations of Constitutional Democracy*, Univ. of Michigan Pr., Ann Arbor.

Buchanan, James M. and Robert D. Tollison (eds) (1984), *The Theory of Public Choice - II*, Univ. of Michigan Pr., Ann Arbor.

Ceaser, James W. (1990), *Liberal Democracy and Political Science*, John Hopkins Univ. Pr., Baltimore.

Daniels, Norman (ed.) (1975), *Reading Rawls*, Blackwell, Oxford.

Downs, Anthony (1957), *An Economic Theory of Democracy*, Harper and Row, New York.

Dunn, John (1990), *Interpreting Political Responsibility: Essays 1981-1989*, Polity Pr., Cambridge.

Dworkin, Ronald (1977), *Taking Rights Seriously*, Duckworth, London.

Galston, William A. (1980), *Justice and the Human Good*, Univ. of Chicago Pr., Chicago.

Krugman, Paul (1994), *Peddling Prosperity*, Norton, New York.

Kukathas, Chandran and Philip Pettit (1990), *Rawls: A 'Theory of Justice'*, Stanford Univ. Pr., Stanford, Ca.
Kymlicka, Will (1990), *Contemporary Political Philosophy: An Introduction*, Clarendon Pr., Oxford.
Lippmann, Walter (1955), *Essays in the Public Philosophy*, New American Library/Mentor, New York, a paperback edn of a Little Brown, 1955, hardback edn.
Lucas, J.R. (1980) *On Justice*, Clarendon Pr., Oxford.
McIlwain, C.H. (1939), *Constitutionalism and the Changing World: Collected Papers*, Cambridge Univ. Pr., Cambridge.
McLean, Iain (1987), *Public Choice: an Introduction*, Blackwell, Oxford.
Mueller, Dennis C. (1989), *Public Choice II*, Cambridge Univ. Pr., Cambridge.
Niskanen Jr, William A. (1971), *Bureaucracy and Representative Government*, Aldine/Atherton, Chicago.
Nozick, Robert (1974), *Anarchy, State, and Utopia*, Basic Books, New York.
Olson, Jr, Mancur (1965), *The Logic of Collective Actions: Public Goods and the Theory of Groups*, Harvard Univ. Pr., Cambridge, Mass.
Ordeshook, Peter C. (1986), *Game Theory and Political Theory*, Cambridge Univ. Pr., Cambridge.
Plato, (1959), *Gorgias: A Revised Text with Introduction and Commentary*, (ed.) E.R. Dodds, Oxford Univ. Pr., Oxford.
Plato, *The Republic* (1992), (ed.) Terence Irwin, 2nd edn, Dent/Everyman, London.
Plumb, J.H. (1973), *The Death of the Past*, 2nd edn, Penguin Books, Harmondsworth.
Rawls, John (1973), *A Theory of Justice* [1972], 2nd edn, Oxford Univ. Pr., Oxford.
Rawls, John (1993), *Political Liberalism*, Columbia Univ. Pr., New York.
Riemer, Neal (1962), *The Revival of Democratic Theory*, Appleton-Century-Crofts/Meredith, New York.
Runciman, W.G. (1963), *Social Science and Political Theory*, Cambridge Univ. Pr., Cambridge.
Self, Peter (1993), *Government by the Market?: The Politics of Public Choice*, Macmillan, Basingstoke.
Stretton, Hugh and Lionel Orchard (1994), *Public Goods, Public Enterprise, Public Choice: Theoretical Foundations for the Contemporary Attack on Government*, St. Martin's Pr./Macmillan, Basingstoke.
Thompson, Dennis F. (1970), *The Democratic Citizen: Social Science and Democratic Theory in the Twentieth Century*, Cambridge Univ. Pr., Cambridge.
Tullock, Gordon and Morris Perlman (1976), *The Vote Motive: An Essay in the Economics of Politics*, Institute of Economic Affairs, London.
Walzer, Michael (1983), *Spheres of Justice: A Defense of Pluralism and Equality*, Basic Books, New York.
Wheare, K.C. (1964), *Modern Constitutions*, 3rd edn, Oxford Univ. Pr., London.
Whelan, Frederick G. (1982), 'Justice: Classical and Christian', *Political Theory*, vol. 10, pp. 435-60.

10 Does History End With Liberal Democracy and, If So, What Type?

Although there are firm grounds for being optimistic about the survival of nation states with parliaments, competitive parties, elections and the other formal institutions of modern democracy, and these institutions being adopted by other nations, what is less certain is the fate of substantive democracy (government which is accountable to, has the informed support of and is in the interests of citizens). This chapter in its response to this issue, therefore, will examine the main routes by which nations that are liberal democratic in form may acquire an oligarchic content (rule by minorities in the interests of minorities). The possibility will be also be raised that societies which are liberal democratic in form may even acquire a quasi-totalitarian content.

Although public philosophers like most intelligent democrats have always expected to find gaps between democratic theory and practice, at the end of the twentieth century the issue has become whether the gaps have so widened that the democratic project of establishing self-governing national communities dedicated to maximising the liberties and opportunities of their members has become another variety of utopianism. The prospects for the parliamentary, electoral and other institutions of formal democracy, by contrast, are promising, though not as startlingly so as in the halcyon days at the end of the 1980s when communist and other former autocracies were frantically turning to them. But, even in post-euphoria days, barring unprecedented economic, environmental or other disasters, the prospects for formal democracies are encouraging. Long-established democratic institutions are the rule in most parts of Europe, North America and Australasia; the South-East Asian democracies have demonstrated an ability to survive economic setbacks; and the hope that democratic institutions will spread to more African and South American countries has not altogether been doused. China and most Middle Eastern nations, however, resist democratisation, and Russia and other former communist nations hover between democracy and autocracy, while being beset by criminal gangs, outright corruption and ethnic hatreds on a scale that far exceeds that of the recent past of the long-established democracies.

The steps towards democracy by former military regimes and communist nations, during the last quarter of the twentieth century, and the establishing of a multi-racial democracy in South Africa suggest that present-day elites, and the wealthier and more privileged groups of people, as much as and in some instances more than the rest of the populations of nations with autocratic and authoritarian governments, can be drawn to democratic institutions. The explanation is that democratic institutions are less risky than tribal and semi-feudal rule, army generals, and religious, nationalist or other would-be charismatic saviours. Democratic forms are more likely to serve the interests of dominant groups, and to legitimate their systems of government. But when the question becomes not whether government based on mass voting, reasonably free elections, parliamentary assemblies and tolerably competitive parties will survive and spread but whether it will produce democracies of substance with independent citizens and robust civil societies with which to sustain it, then the prospects for democracy are less rosy. It is in fact democracy's success in attracting the support of privileged and dominant social groups which increases the danger of an oligarchic corruption. So-called 'new democracies' may simply be nations whose oligarchic rulers have discovered new techniques for the management of their societies. A book which has raised most of these issues in a unique and vivid though at times confusing way is Francis Fukuyama's *The End of History and the Last Man* (1992), an expanded version of a controversial and much discussed (1989) article.

Does Political History End With Liberal Democracy?

Francis Fukuyama's understanding of the current state of the democratic project rests on a Hegelian conception of history in which history progressively satisfies by means of social and political change the desires and aspirations of men and women. History is seen as a quest by a succession of civilisations to discover the political and social organisations, and the principles for regulating them that are best able to provide the opportunities for satisfying human needs and aspirations.

> 'History'...can be understood in the narrower sense of the 'history of ideology', or the history of thought about first principles, including those governing political and social organization. The end of history then means not the end of worldly events but the end of the evolution of human thought about such first principles (Fukuyama, 1990, p. 9).[1]

---

1 For similar statements and a further clarification of what Fukuyama means by the 'end of history', see his (1992) book (pp. xi-xxiii).

It follows from such a view of history that, when no further political progress is possible, history ends. This is a condition which, according to Fukuyama, is now being reached, and which was made evident by the Cold War victory of democratic nations.

Fukuyama's thesis is that it is no longer possible to conceive of an achievable alternative to liberal democracy which, on the basis of the needs and aspirations of modern men and women, is superior to it. Liberal democracy thus becomes a hegemonic set of principles and way of life. No other type of society has the capacity to better satisfy human desires for material well being (liberal democracy's market-capitalist component), and, by its individual and political rights, to treat men and women as persons entitled to recognition and respect (liberal democracy's democratic component). For Fukuyama, modern capitalism and modern democracy are basic parts of a long, several-centuries liberal revolution, the individual freedoms of which are the main cause of both the modern world's dynamism and tensions. But these tensions, mainly between modern liberalism's capitalist and democratic components, Fukuyama maintains, are not internal contradictions which will inevitably destroy liberal democratic societies; they may be a constant source of danger but they are also the source of liberal democracy's strength.

Fukuyama contends that with the military defeats of the Fascist and National Socialist powers in 1945, and the collapse of the USSR and other communist regimes at the end of the 1980s, there are no longer any political movements capable of challenging liberal democracy for doctrinal supremacy. Radical Islamic movements may appear to be such a force, but their appeal is limited to the Moslem world. Elsewhere, although liberal democracy may acquire Asian and other regional rather than Western features, and thus become more diverse, for the foreseeable future it will be the world's dominant political doctrine and system of government. Even if some liberal democratic societies fail to adequately respond to difficulties and collapse, the new rulers will be unable to extinguish the desire of people from all classes for the liberties and rights of liberal democracy.

This idea that modern democracy is bringing history, as it has previously been understood, to an end articulates some major parts of what in this book is being called democratic theory as a public philosophy. Fukuyama's thesis affirms that liberal democracy is the most effective political means for expressing current and foreseeable values. It asserts that conservative, socialist, market-capitalist, feminist, environmentalist and other movements with distinct goals, if they are to obtain the support of and to benefit their communities, must accept and adapt to liberal-democratic institutions and values. It implies that the fundamental problem for most nations will be not the search for an alternative to liberal democracy but the character of their liberal democratic institutions and culture. And it challenges leftist and other critics of liberal democracy to cease their endless complaints about liberal democracy's imperfections and to explain the precise character of their alternative. The *end of history*, therefore, does not mean that liberal democracy has solved and overcome all the problems and difficulties of the human condition or even of modern life; it means that liberal democracy is better able to confront them than any possible political alternative.

Contrary to the view of critics who dismiss Fukuyama's (1989) article and (1992) book as exercises in liberal triumphalism, and an impressionistic gloating over the fall of communism, Fukuyama, particularly in his (1992) discussion of the *last man*, raises unsettling and challenging questions. He warns that the desire for mutual recognition and respect, the psychological basis for modern democracy, may fail to be satisfied. It may degenerate into (1), resentment and envy of the success of others, and demands for social levelling, and (2), within the elites, power-hungry individuals seeking not recognition and respect but domination over others. It follows that if the citizens who are caught between these two forces are apathetic, and fail to appreciate and preserve a democratic culture based on the respect and recognition which one free and responsible person gives another, then the result will be a world resembling that described by Nietzsche as the *last man*. Such a world, Fukuyama suggests, would be only superficially democratic; the masses would put their security and amusement before all else, while power was exercised by the most cunning and ruthless of individuals and elites. Societies of 'last men', whether outwardly democratic or not, inevitably fall back into pre-democratic master-slave relations.

But Fukuyama, in expressing his thinking on modern democracy in terms of the end of history, has in some ways hindered an adequate understanding of his arguments and conclusions about modern democracy. This is because Fukuyama neither demonstrates nor indeed asserts that history, in the way in which most historians and other people use the word *history*, comes to a static close with liberal democracy. On the contrary, he leaves his readers with a great deal of what is usually considered to be history. He is emphatic that the fortunes of liberal democratic nations vary, and that democratic institutions are subject to decay, revival and novel developments. Even when nations have completed their journeys to capitalism, liberalism and democracy, they may still, to use his vocabulary, slide or be plunged back into history and have to find new routes out of it. If expressed in a different language, the implication and profound insight in Fukuyama's end-of-history thesis is that the serious discussion of politics must begin with the premise that, for the foreseeable future, liberal democracy will be, for the people of most parts of the world, including their elites, the most persuasive political theory and practice. A question which follows, therefore, is what are the main obstacles to liberal democracy achieving a sustainable worthwhile civilisation which does not simply totter along but which benefits and enriches the lives of citizens? A related question, to use Fukuyama's vocabulary, is who or what will have the power to push nations with liberal democratic institutions back into history?

Corporate-Capitalist Democracy

One possible future for democratic nations is that their theory and practice become little more than legitimating devices for a corporate capitalism, the dominant feature of which would be a partnership between governments and giant financial, industrial information-technology and other companies. The make-up of such a partnership would vary from nation to nation, with in some nations trade unions, and/or privileged rural and other groups participating. But in all instances, primarily in the interests of the partners, there would be extensive government intrusions in and controls over economic, educational and other areas of social life, with few parts of civil society possessing the independence and strength to resist. Corporate capitalism means that nation states function as if they were gigantic business corporations. These states are capitalist in that economic resources are privately owned, and profit remains the incentive for investors and company managers; but, in contrast to market-capitalist societies, it is governments and their partners more than market considerations which determine investment, production and how their nations will compete in what is now called the 'global economy'.

Corporate-capitalist characteristics were prominent in most democratic nations from the 1930s to the 1970s but, since then, have been hidden by the economic changes and the rhetoric associated with monetarism, privatisation, global markets and the success of the 1980s Thatcher and Reagan governments in discrediting - without dismantling - extensive government and corporate relations between governments and the private sector. A further growth of corporate-capitalist institutions and practices, therefore, remains as one of the possible futures for democratic and capitalist nations, particularly in periods of economic crisis.

Although *corporate capitalism* describes many of the features of most present day democracies, it is a term which tends to be used only by its Marxist and other critics. Since the 1970s, in university and other writing on the state and society, its features have usually been described as *corporatist* or *neo-corporatist*.[2] But whether it is called *corporatism*, *neo-*

---

2   Andrew Shonfield (1969), who examined the corporate capitalist trends of the 1950s and early 1960s in European and North American nations, described the capitalism of

corporatism or *corporate capitalism*, it is not new; it is a continuation of rather than a break from nineteenth- and twentieth-century capitalism. Provided that major economic and other crises are averted, the historical record suggests that corporate capitalism is able to maintain, at least for several decades, economic growth, technological progress and social stability. Many nations which have achieved noteworthy economic growth, from Bismarck's Germany to Singapore, Taiwan and the other South-East Asian 'Tigers' of recent decades, have had pronounced corporate-capitalist features. In Austria, West Germany, the Scandinavian and several other countries, since the 1940s, corporate capitalism has brought about a consensual, bipartisan political-party politics and extensive public welfare, and obtained the widespread support of voters.

Strong economic, political and other arguments can be made for a corporate capitalism with a human face and its compatibility with liberal democracy. But, in addition to its endangering of those liberal democratic institutions, constitutional checks, political conventions and individual rights which are inconvenient and impede it, there is at least one other major problem which even the most benevolent of corporate capitalist policies and partnerships create for the democratic project: the fact that they breed and are linked to technocracy - rule by purported economic, managerial and other experts. Although there can be no objection in principle to experts being influential in areas of their proven expertise, it is difficult even for informed and well intentioned government ministers and other politicians, let alone voters and ill-informed and less responsible politicians, to know when it is experts rather than charlatans who offer advice - and when economic charlatans become influential the results can be disastrous.[3] In a phrase, corporate capitalism and the technocratic social management with which it is allied mean a governmental system which may be democratic in form but which is potentially if not actually oligarchic and authoritarian.

---

    the period as *modern*. R.E. Pahl and J.T. Winkler (1974) and J. T. Winkler (1976) have described similar trends simply as *corporate*.

3   On the political effects of charlatanism, Paul Krugman's (1994) survey of the economic policies of American Republican and Democratic presidents from Reagan to Clinton is instructive. Krugman argues that presidents, their immediate advisers and most members of Congress are obsessed with electoral considerations, and have a built-in tendency to prefer the advice of charlatans who tell them what they want to hear to that of knowledgeable and responsible economists who give them sound economic advice.

Technocratic and Managerial Democracy

Technocracy, the root word of which is *techne*, the Greek for knowledge, means rule by people with knowledge or technical skill. But as the question of who possesses relevant knowledge can rarely be answered with certainly, technocracy in practice means rule by people who for good or bad reasons have persuaded others that they possess the necessary expertise. The word *technocracy*, in the second half of the twentieth century, has had three principal uses. First, in Jean Meynaud's *Technocracy* (1968), for example, it refers to post-1945, economists, scientists and other specialists who are recruited into government departments and who displace officials with a more traditional public-service training and ethos. Second, it may mean not that the possessors of technical knowledge are replacing other public servants but that three governmental groups, politicians, public servants and the specialists they employ, are merging to form a new ruling class or dominant political elite. The word may also be used more broadly to describe, third, the domination of democratic societies by more diffuse groups whose power derives primarily from their real or purported knowledge and skills. This third, wider conception of technocratic tendencies in twentieth century democracies, despite the word *technocracy* not always being used, permeates a large and diverse literature, a once influential example of which is John Kenneth Galbraith's *The New Industrial State* (1972), first published in 1967.

According to Galbraith, from the 1930s to the 1960s, the internal organisation of the large business corporations of the United States and other industrialised nations, and the relations which these corporations had with governments and the rest of their societies were transformed. Managers and technicians wrested the control of their corporations from entrepreneurs and shareholders, and closely cooperated with government departments in the management of their industries and, in effect, the economies of their nations. The result was a mixed and semi-planned rather than a market economy. Galbraith, who from the 1950s to the 1980s was a major influence on American welfare-state, post-New-Deal liberal and European democratic-socialist thought, regarded this 'new industrial state' as a progressive product of modern capitalism and democracy. His view was that, depending on the extent of popular pressure, and the strength of American liberal and European democratic-socialist movements, the new industrial states would take one of two possible directions. They would either become increasingly illiberal and oligarchic or foster a more socially concerned, liberal-democratic future - the direction favoured by Galbraith.

For Galbraith, the new industrial state was not a new type of capitalism; it was a technocracy in which the rulers possessed genuine and relevant knowledge, and a preference for exercising their power in a democratic and public spirited manner. The empirical part of his work was similar to that of C. Wright Mills (1959); but, in contrast to Galbraith's stress on the virtues of the new rulers, Wright Mills had described the American branch as a 'power elite' - groups of people who dominated government, business and the military, who cooperated to advance their own interests, and who were antipathetic to democracy. Whereas Wright Mills's work was to inspire the radicals of the New Left, Galbraith's rosier conclusions were closer to those of British and European democratic-socialist politicians and intellectuals, including John Strachey (1956) and Anthony Crosland (1964).

For Strachey, Crosland and other democratic socialists, who from the 1940s to the 1960s saw democratic socialism as the necessary and desirable outcome of Keynesian-economic and welfare-state policies, the task for democratic socialists was to civilise the managers and experts of the post-war world. These technocrats should be taught to appreciate the ideals of liberty and equality, and to be responsive to parliaments, voters, trade unions, and labour and social democratic parties. A similar optimistic view about the relations between the new elites and democratic government is held by writers who are more excited by managerial and technological possibilities than socialist dreams. A recent example is Peter Drucker, an internationally known writer on management, and an advocate of non-authoritarian, experimental and imaginative styles of management. In *The New Realities* (1989), however, he turned his attention to political and sociological issues, and he discussed the class character and power relations of modern democracies. On these questions, two noteworthy arguments are to be found.

The first is that, during the past few decades, the dominant class in industrialised nations has become a new type of middle class, a class of 'knowledge workers' whose employment and social position derive from their education, qualifications and skills. The second is that, contrary to outdated beliefs, 'knowledge workers' are neither conformist, deferential nor authoritarian. In their work and other parts of their lives they behave in liberal and democratic ways. They are a class therefore that encourages and strengthens democratic attitudes. Furthermore, their skills enable democracies to sustain economic growth, and creatively confront environmental, cultural and other challenges. For Drucker, it is a mistake to associate large organisations and their managers with hierarchy and authoritarianism; successful business and other organisations, he asserts, require the dispersal of both knowledge and power. They rely not on externally imposed discipline but on the initiative of their managers and specialists. The authority of their knowledge workers derives from technology, a technology which is nothing more than the knowledge and skills of the new class. Drucker, who dislikes the term *middle class* and prefers to call the knowledge workers a *uniclass*, describes their qualities in glowing terms. The 'knowledge worker', he writes,

> does not fit any interest-group definition. Knowledge workers are neither farmers nor labor nor business: they are employees of organizations. Yet they are not 'proletarians' and do not feel 'exploited' as a class....Many of them are themselves bosses and have 'subordinates.' Yet they also have a boss themselves....It makes absolutely no difference to their economic or social position whether they work for a business, a hospital, or a university (p. 25).

And even

> when knowledge workers are not a majority in their organization, they increasingly set the norms and standards....As knowledge becomes the central resource of the economy, society is bound to evolve into a post-business knowledge society (p. 186).

Unlike writers who see science and technology, and the rapidity of the changes they generate as causing major problems for democratic government, Drucker is an optimist for whom there are few conflicts between technology and democracy which the technocrats, the 'knowledge workers', are unable to overcome.

A questionable assumption in Drucker's perception of knowledge workers, however, is his belief that cleverness and vocational knowledge and expertise are naturally accompanied by moral and political virtues. Drucker and similar optimists forget that mafia and other criminal gangs, totalitarian and comic-opera-style dictatorships, stagnant government departments, unwieldy, bureaucratised tertiary institutions and suchlike organisations have found few difficulties in recruiting 'knowledge workers' to serve their purposes.

Drucker's view that knowledge workers have the potential to become a liberal and democratic force is a timely antidote to the technological determinist view that science and technology inevitably generate a hierarchic technocracy. His work like that of Galbraith, Strachey and Crosland suggests that it is not and idle fancy to think that a substantive, normative democratic theory could become the public philosophy for the managerial elites of parliamentary democracies. But realism also suggests that these authors are unduly sanguine about technocrats and technocratic trends. Certainly, since the 1960s, most democratic nations have departed from the directions Galbraith, Strachey and Crosland urged them to take. For a different response to technocratic trends, and in order to reach a more balanced assessment, therefore, it is pertinent to consider the mid-century writings of James Burnham.

Burnham's first political book, *The Managerial Revolution* (1945), first published in 1941, popularised the concepts of a *managerial revolution* and a *managerial society*, and a constant theme in his later books and journalism was the various forms that managerial and technocratic tendencies could take.[4] His original (1945) argument was that, despite capitalism being in its death throes, it would not be succeeded by a socialism that represented the interests of the working class, ordinary citizens or oppressed groups. A century of socialist struggles, he argued, had demonstrated that neither the industrial workers, on whom Marxist and other socialists had pinned their hopes, nor other poor and exploited classes had the capacity to create the necessary political movements and institutions for acquiring and maintaining social power.

The Russian Revolution of October 1917, he observed, had excited the libertarian and egalitarian radicals of the world for it appeared to suggest otherwise. But Russia's subsequent history had crushed these hopes. The nation-wide soviets or committees of workers, peasants and soldiers which had been hailed as an expression of popular power - economically superior to capitalism, and more democratic and politically effective than 'bourgeois democracy' - had been easily contained and then replaced by a new type of managerial elite, organised in and around the Communist Party. The communist revolution in Russia, the failed socialist revolutions in Germany, Hungary and China of the post-1917 years, and the inter-war history of parliamentary nations all demonstrated that, in the dominant nations of the world, the class which acquired economic, political and cultural power consisted, predominantly, of managers whose power rested not on their property or wealth but their position in and control of the main social and political institutions of industrialised nations (1945, esp. pp. 35-52). Burnham, at the beginning of the Second World War, thought that the dominance and rule of this new class was exemplified most clearly in Mussolini's Italy, Hitler's Germany, Stalin's Russia, and Roosevelt's New Deal. His conclusion was that the future was likely to be neither capitalist nor socialist but managerial. Power would reside with some combination of the managers of industry, mass communications, political parties, government departments, the military and, where they survived, parliaments.

These days, Burnham's thesis of a managerial revolution is often dismissed on the grounds that he saw the totalitarian regimes of Hitler and

---

4   For an introduction to Burnham's writings, and his curious political evolution from being the editor of the American Trotskyist theoretical journal, *The New International*, to one of the editors of the conservative *National Review*, see Frances (1984).

Stalin as the shape of the future, and that history has therefore refuted him. But Burnham's thesis is not so easily dismissed. Burnham was explicit that the regimes of Mussolini, Hitler and Stalin might be as distant from the managerial societies of the future as pre-industrial capitalism was from its post-industrial forms. Furthermore, he argued that Roosevelt's New Deal, which he thought was a movement of America's emerging managerial class, demonstrated the possibility of a managerial oligarchy utilising rather than abolishing democratic institutions. Although, in the decades which followed the Second World War, Burnham rarely used the word *managerial*, the idea of a new, managerial type of elite rule remained a part of his political thought. In *The Struggle for the World* (1947), for example, he argued that the Cold War was a struggle for international hegemony between the elites who dominated the United States and those of the Soviet Union. Because he regarded America's elites as more liberal and civilised, he thought it imperative that international communism be defeated, and he urged the United States and its allies to be more forceful. In the 1960s, however, Burnham's thought took a new turn. In *The Suicide of the West* (1965) he denounced America's elites, arguing that their 'liberal' beliefs in the natural equality and goodness of all human beings were naive, and that the liberal ideologies which rested on them functioned as a justification for a spineless response to communist, third-world-nationalist and other anti-American, anti-Western forces. This view of the elites of the United States and other Western nations as spineless and incompetent was far from the 1941, *Managerial Revolution*, view of them as determined and ruthless.

Unlike Galbraith, Strachey, Crosland and Drucker, Burnham rarely found anything to praise in the new technocratic, ruling class. His final views on it appear to be as follows. First, managers, bureaucrats, intellectuals and other technocrats control industry, government, political parties, trade unions and labour movements, and culture (education, journalism and the entertainment industry). Second, for all their differences and quarrels, these elites have sufficient common interests and goals for them to constitute a socially and politically dominant class, and in that sense a *ruling* class. Third, they may number millions of people but they are an oligarchy in that they are a minority who use their power in their own interests. But, fourth, they are politically incompetent and short-sighted. They deceive themselves and others with naive assumptions about home and international politics. And fifth, although it is impossible to prevent modern, industrialised nations from being dominated by the new technocratic class, this domination is not complete; it can be checked by dissenting intellectuals and other groups, and by popular support for maintaining the independence of (a) parliaments, (b) law and the courts, (c) a culture which respects traditional liberal freedoms and democratic procedures, and (d) an economy which is driven primarily by market forces.⁵

This agreement among writers from the left, right and centre on the emergence of a new class or dominant elite, along with the disputes about its character and social effects bring the following question to the fore. To the extent that, in economically-developed democratic nations, political and social power is grasped by or falls to a class of managers, experts, intellectuals and other technocrats, who is right about how they will affect or change democratic government? Is it optimists like Galbraith, Strachey, Crosland and Drucker, or is it Wright Mills, Burnham and other pessimists? For the optimists, the technocrats have a liberal and democratic potential; for the pessimists they are either oligarchic, inept or both. The question is crucial because it is the character of the dominant elites of democratic nations, and whether they are likely to be influenced by liberal-democratic public-philosophic standards that will determine the future of democratic government.

Totalitarian Democracy

At first sight the idea of a totalitarian democracy seems a contradiction in terms. Modern democracies appear to be one thing, and the totalitarian regimes of national-socialist and communist nations another. But, depending on what is meant by *totalitarianism*, some recent trends in democratic nations suggest that democracies or at least formal democracies can and do acquire pronounced totalitarian features. How, then, should *totalitarianism* be interpreted?

From the 1930s to the 1960s, the word's main function was to stress the novelty of and the similarities between fascist, national-socialist and communist regimes, a function for which pre-twentieth-century political categories appeared inadequate. *Totalitarianism* signalled the fact that the brutality, terrorism, fanaticism and social controls of these regimes went beyond dictatorship (special, originally temporary, powers for a political and\or military leader), tyranny (rule in the interests of a ruler or rulers), despotism (the ruthless use of sovereign power), and absolutism (the absence of constitutional and other legal constraints on a ruler or rulers). The word *totalitarianism* highlighted the fact that the attempts of national-socialist and communist dictatorships to totally control and mobilise their

---

5   For this fifth and little known part of James Burnham's work, see his *Congress and the American Tradition* (1959). Here, Burnham was disturbed, mainly, by the amassing of power by American presidents, and their advisers and backers at the expense of Congress, and he called for a revival of Congressional power.

societies, on the basis of systematic doctrines to which no dissent was tolerated, were unprecedented. The powers of their dictators, and the tyranny, despotism and absolutism of their rule were supported by disciplined parties which suppressed opposition and infiltrated all areas of society; their control of the military, police and secret police; the intimidation if not destruction of the churches; and the subordinating of industry, science, schools, universities, the press and electronic media to the dictator, party and state. The rulers of medieval European and other theocratic and semi-theocratic states may have harboured totalitarian ambitions, but, as pre-modern regimes lacked the military, police, propaganda and other resources of modern states, their methods for indoctrinating and controlling the members of their societies were, in comparison with the regimes of Hitler, Stalin and Mao Zedong, rudimentary.

Clearly, totalitarian attempts to control and intimidate subjects by force are not to be found where parliamentary, political-party, pressure-group and electoral politics survive. What this chapter's discussions of corporate capitalist and technocratic trends in contemporary democracies reveal, however, is the possibility of societies in which there is no effective opposition or dissent to governments not because of the coercive powers of states but because of the support given to the state and the groups which dominate it by a population of conformists. If *totalitarianism* is used to mean not the terror of Hitler, Stalin and Mao Zedong but societies in which the state tries to totally control the whole of human life then modern democracies could approach the level of conformity sought by totalitarian dictatorships. Phenomena which indicate how modern democracies could drift or be pushed towards a totalitarian conformity include the increasing powers of governments and their bureaucracies over economic and other life; the collaboration of and the ties among the members of economic, political and cultural elites; the use of schools for instilling into children the views of the pressure groups favoured by governments; and the concentration of ownership in and cooperation with governments by the dominant groups in the newspaper, television and other communication and entertainment industries. Political parties when in opposition may deplore these trends but, when in office, accentuate or do little to resist them. Moreover, political parties are themselves subject to similar trends, for example their use and widespread employment of marketing and similar specialists, the disappearance of rank-and-file influence, leader-cults, and the subjecting of everything to capturing and retaining power.

It is not my argument that democratic nations are or are likely to become fully totalitarian. Indeed, not even the one-party dictatorships of Hitler, Stalin and Mao Zedong ever achieved the total control and conformity they sought. Totalitarian government, by its nature, its attempt to control all aspects of life, causes social chaos rather than the desired uniformity. My argument is that a formal as distinct from a substantive democracy is vulnerable to concentrations of state and other power, and to the pressures to conform that push modern societies in a totalitarian direction. A totalitarian democracy that is democratic in form but quasi-totalitarian in substance, therefore, is conceivable theoretically and a serious possibility in practice. Three examples of how a totalitarian democracy becomes possible will be given. They are based on Ortega y Gasset's (1961) conception of mass power, Roland Huntford's (1971) view of Sweden in the 1960s, and the demands for political and cultural conformity by American and other movements, in the 1980s and 1990s, which their opponents succeeded in branding as *political correctness*.

Routes to a Totalitarian Democracy

Ortega y Gasset's 1930 classic, *The Revolt of the Masses* (1961), suggests that the main source of conformist trends in modern democracies is the pressure which comes from the *masses*, the atomised and fearful individuals who take the place of the citizens of vibrant civil societies. By the *masses*, Ortega did not mean industrial workers, the poor or an underclass; the masses were drawn from all sections of society, including its wealthiest and most privileged. They were undisciplined people, many of whom might be expensively educated and have highly prized technical skills. People with mass minds who made no effort to think coherently and act rationally, Ortega wrote, had always existed; but, unlike the masses of pre-modern societies, those of twentieth century nations were unwilling to defer to the people who did respect civilised standards.

Because people with mass minds respected neither independent and creative thought nor traditional authorities, and followed no consistent code of conduct, they were subject to moods, anxieties and fears. Their only refuge was their numbers. Their revolt consisted not of fighting at barricades but of using their votes and day-to-day social power to compel governments to give them the security they craved, and everyone else to conform to their prejudices and ways of life. Ortega's book warns that not only could democracies produce conformist and unruly masses but that political power could fall to politicians who shared or preyed on the prejudices and anxieties of people with mass minds. His *revolt* of the masses, therefore, has similar meanings to the *tyranny* of the majority of Madison, Tocqueville and John Stuart Mill.

At the end of the twentieth century, these dangers about which Ortega warned over six decades ago remain, and in many ways have become more serious. Whereas, for example, Ortega (1946) thought that an extension of university education would keep mass styles of thought at bay, extending it has led to demands, under the guise of relevance, that tertiary education conform to the attitudes and expectations of the students and/or the paymasters of the universities. Among the main consequences of increased numbers of students has been the hounding of Western universities for their alleged ivory-tower elitism by politicians, business leaders and student activists.

Another worsening of the dangers to which Ortega pointed is the subject of Christopher Lasch's *The Revolt of the Elites* (1995) - an intended paraphrase of Ortega's *The Revolt of the Masses*. Lasch's argument, which is centred on the United States, is that it is now the elites rather than the rest of the population whose contempt for civilised values is the main threat to democratic government and politics. Writing from a maverick left-wing rather than a conservative or Republican Party standpoint, Lasch's argument is that it is not the general population that recklessly revolts against and discards inherited standards, substituting for them prejudices and poorly-thought-out goals, but a curious mix of America's yuppie, financial whizz kids; the Democratic Party's liberal intelligentsia; and the nation's academically tenured leftists and the university administrators who, possessing no principles of their own, compromise with them.

My second example of a possible totalitarian democracy and the route to it is drawn from what Roland Huntford (1971) contended was the character of social-democratic Sweden at the end of the 1960s, a controversial account which is introduced here for its suggestiveness rather than its historical accuracy. Huntford's argument is that although Sweden possessed the institutional forms of a modern democracy (parliament, constitution, universal voting and free elections), it was a totalitarian society, with its people even more subject to governmental tutelage than those of the Soviet Union. Sweden's economic decisions and policies were made by a corporate partnership comprising government, business and the trade unions, in which business and trade union leaders were more the agents of the partnership than the representatives of their members. Moreover, semi-government organisations, ostensibly for the representation of farmers, householders, tenants, students and other groups, often with mass memberships, acted mainly as government agencies, while, school, university and adult education were closely supervised by governments, with university professors appointed by governments.

The staffs of the vast government and semi-government bureaucracies had an ethos in which they acted as managers, organisers and indoctrinaters rather than as officials and administrators subject to parliament and to the rules and style of a traditional public service. In addition, laws were regarded by governments, lawyers and the public as administrative rather than impartial rules, and judges as the agents of the state rather than protectors of citizens. The state assumed a general responsibility for the parenting as well as the education of children, which meant that welfare officers were unconstrained by the courts when investigating home conditions and removing children from their parents. Governments controlled the radio and television, and worked with a compliant press, while journalists saw their work as forming public opinion rather than informing the public and generating debate. Social welfare was considered a privilege for which a price was paid - loyalty to the community, and to the state and its bureaucracies. Swedish culture, Huntford argued, was permeated by the beliefs that the welfare of the community had precedence over individual rights and personal fulfilment, and that economic prosperity and material security were the highest goals for the individual, society and state. People who rejected these beliefs and behaved unconventionally were ostracised. Socialism, which meant little more than consensus, social harmony and working together for material benefits, was never questioned, and the adjectives *liberal* and *conservative* were words of rebuke. In sexual relations, however, permissiveness prevailed. Promiscuity, contraception and abortion were not so much tolerated as welcomed by both the state and the community. Sex was the outlet for frustrated feelings and lives, and, because their sexual lives were largely unhindered, the Swedes were convinced that they were a free, progressive people. As in Aldous Huxley's *Brave New World*, sex was the safety valve for a totalitarian society.

Swedish totalitarianism, in Huntford's account of it, was not the product of one part of society imposing its will on another by state, revolutionary or other force. It was grounded on cooperation between governments and people. To the extent that it was the product of social engineering, it was a social engineering which had widespread support. It was the outcome of half a century of rule by Sweden's Social Democratic Party which, unlike Russian and other ruling Communist parties, had mass support and could successfully contest free elections. Party members were active in most areas of life, often operating in groups which resembled communist cells, and the party was professional and efficient in its agitation and propaganda. During the half century of Social Democratic rule, Huntford wrote, the bureaucracies of the party, the wider labour movement and the state had overlapped and merged; ambitious people who sought a successful political, administrative or educational career usually joined the party. The executive branch of government dominated and had nothing to fear from the parliament; its *apparatus men*, as Huntford called them, were largely unconstrained. Members of parliament possessed little power as Sweden had a political culture in which people relied on an extra-parliamentary consensus, and governmental and administrative expertise rather than independently minded parliamentarians, political debate and adversary party politics.

Sweden, at the end of the 1960s, for all its parliamentary and other democratic trimmings, in Huntford's portrayal of it, exhibited a more complete and efficient totalitarianism than those of the communist nations. To illustrate his view and the reason for his book's title, *The New Totalitarians*, Huntford quoted from Aldous Huxley's foreword to an edition of *Brave New World*.

> There is...no reason why the new totalitarianism should resemble the old. Government by firing squads...is not merely inhumane...it is demonstrably inefficient, and in an age of advanced technology inefficiency is a sin against the Holy Ghost. A really efficient totalitarian state would be one in which the all-powerful executive of political bosses and their army of managers control a population of slaves who do not have to be coerced because they love their servitude (Huntford, 1971, p. 8).

My third example of a totalitarian democracy and a route to it is what would result if the pressure for political and cultural including linguistic change, in the United States and elsewhere, by the advocates of what has become known as *political correctness*, was successful. *Political correctness* may be described as a more doctrinaire version of the politics of the 1960s American New Left.[6] Its devotees, however, are more entrenched in the structures of the universities and other institutions they challenge. Their demands are more systematic, and their view of the enemy has changed. Whereas for the 1960s New Left the main enemy was American and Western capitalism and imperialism, for their successors another target has come to the fore, privileged white males and their Eurocentric culture. *Political correctness* summarises the doctrines and goals of a movement which, in the 1980s, became a central part of post-Marxist leftism. It is a movement which has tried to transform American and other Western societies but which has had its main successes in the schools and universities.[7] In the preface to a dialogue on political

---

6 But some former, 1960s, New Left, American radicals are critical of political correctness, drawing a line between what they consider the highly militant but genuinely libertarian civil-rights radicals of the 1960s and the later, often well-paid, prim, so-called radicals who push for political correctness. See, for example, Richard Bernstein (1994); and Camille Paglia (1993; and 1994, esp. pp. 97-100 and 117-121).

7 For critical surveys of the demands, campaigns and movements associated with political correctness, see Bernstein (1994); Bloom (1988); D'Souza (1991); Kimball (1990); and Miller (1993). For a concise, critical article, Morrise (1993). For a more sympathetic discussion, Loeb (1994); and for a range of views by mainly British left-wing intellectuals, for and against, Dunant (1994).

correctness, a United States and a Canadian philosopher have itemised the issues it raises as follows:

> new fields of study such as women's studies and African American studies, new disciplinary approaches, such as multiculturalism and feminism, new campus practices, such as speech codes, and new cultural critiques, such as those of truth and politics-free intellectual inquiry....[and] the Western canon... (Friedman and Narveson, 1995, p. vii).

The organisers and militants who push for political correctness usually reject the term, and present themselves as struggling for a multicultural, tolerant and diverse community. But, in practice, they are intolerant of any diversity which obstructs their goals, and often the only minority and non-Western cultures they extol are those which reject Western liberal-democratic civilisation. Their so-called *multiculturalism*, therefore, is a myth.

> The reality of culture is something that the ideological multiculturalists would despise if they knew what it was. The power of culture, especially the culture rooted in ancient traditions, is anathema to the actual goals and ideology of multiculturalism which does not seek an appreciation of other cultures but operates out of the wishful assumption that the unknown, obscure, neglected, subaltern cultures of the world are actually manifestations of a leftist ideology born out of the particular culture of American and European universities and existing practically no place else (Bernstein, p. 7).

Important parts of the multiculturalism of its radical-leftist advocates are the demands for extreme forms of affirmative action. These demands are not so much for the removal of barriers to the education, employment and promotion of women, people from ethnic minorities or other victims of adverse discrimination as for something quite different: using *affirmative action* as a code term for the achievement of an equality of outcome in which the members of the two sexes, and designated ethnic and other groups are to have educational places, employment, and positions of authority on the basis of their group's proportion of the population. A justified support for the more moderate of the movement's campaigns, its hatred of racism, and its recognising that liberties and rights may be of little help to people if their ethnicity and poverty makes them social pariahs has obscured for its liberal sympathisers the totalitarianism of the movement.[8] Yet the movement is totalitarian in at least four senses of the term.

First, its egalitarian objectives are both elusive and unlimited. Its militants may temporarily focus on specific grievances but, once successful or finding little enthusiasm and support, they speedily change their targets and immediate goals. The more power and influence they acquire, the more ambitious they become. Like the members of a Leninist vanguard party, the movement's activists utilise whatever grievances are at hand and can be moulded to their purposes. Second, the movement's militants are active in and try to subordinate to their objectives all accessible areas of political and social life, including political parties, churches, schools, universities and the communication and entertainment industries. Third, they try to totally suppress opposition and, by purging language of the words that are necessary for dissent, the very possibility of opposition to their views. In this respect, they resemble the promoters of Newspeak in the Oceania of George Orwell's *Nineteen Eighty-Four*. Fourth, by dispensing with the private-public distinction and regarding everything as political, all barriers to total political power are removed. Talk of rights by political-correctness enthusiasts, therefore, means not the rights which individuals hold against the state but the movement's goals and policies, dressed up as rights, which the state is pressed to enforce.

The character of political-correctness is exemplified in the stretching of the words *sexism* and *racism*. *Sexism* ceases to be confined to the behaviour of sexual predators, the allocation of social roles on the basis of a person's sex or the belief that sexual preferences justify adverse discrimination. The accusation of *sexism* may follow simply from chance remarks, mildly offensive jokes or similar indiscretions in an office, lecture room or anywhere else where the upholders of the desired orthodoxy are provoked. Likewise, people accused of *racism* are not necessarily advocates or supporters of racial supremacy, people who believe that some races are inherently superior to others and that their members are entitled to abuse, rule or exterminate those they regard as inferior. The accusation of racism threatens people who, without wishing to discriminate against anyone because of their different ethnicity, think that *race* is a meaningful category. Legislation is advocated not just to strengthen existing law when it fails to protect the rights of the victims of sexual discrimination and racial intolerance but to control the behaviour and, as far as possible, the thought of everyone.

Richard Bernstein, in his (1994) study of the American multicultural movement, has argued that American schools and universities

---

8 On the need to supplement formal, individual rights which are blind to the effects of racial intolerance and other forms of social discrimination, see Parekh (1994).

are being assailed by an army of ethnic-minority organisers, radical feminists and purported experts on non-sexist, non-racist, non-Western-biassed teaching and curriculum planning, all of whom share a revolutionary, counter-cultural ideology. At the same time, national and local government, the courts and industry are harassed by the demands of internal and external groups for affirmative action and the multicultural retraining of staff.

It is possible however that, despite the drive for political correctness being weaker outside of the United States, its repercussions will be worse in other nations. In democratic nations where parliamentary systems have no American-type separation of executive and legislative power, and where there are less judicial checks to political parties, as in Britain and the Scandinavian countries, political-correctness movements or movements with different goals but similar methods, should they capture parties capable of obtaining governmental power, may be an even greater danger. Even if the drive for political correctness disintegrates, is laughed out of existence or is halted in some other way, precedents have been set for new forms of intolerance. Needless to say, future illiberal movements may be those of the totalitarian right rather than the totalitarian left; they may be movements whose members hate and would love to crush political-correctness leftists as well as the liberals who, despite being among their main targets, compromise with them.

But a concern about actual and potential totalitarian-type movements and forces of the left and right is not the same as predicting their success. It is more probable that such movements will continue to surface yet fail to achieve the success they desire. The disruption and damage they cause to liberal democratic politics and culture, however, may be cumulative and severe. Likewise, acknowledging that there are corporate-capitalist, bureaucratic, technocratic and other oligarchic trends in modern democracies is not the same as believing that democracies will be unable to withstand them. A serious danger in technocratic and intolerant trends, however, is that socially interventionist governments and intolerant cultural movements will prove to be socially divisive, and that their main effect will be to make democratic nations increasingly ungovernable. They could produce, not a centralised corporate-capitalist, technocratic or quasi-totalitarian state but a new kind of feudalism in which, instead of turning to medieval lords, people seek security in unquestioned loyalties to financial, industrial, media or other corporations, government departments, political parties or parts of what has become known as the 'educational industry'. Such a postmodern feudalism could well be accompanied by the neo-tribalism which many observers (Schlesinger, 1992, for example) think will be the result of American and other multicultural, affirmative-action and other doctrines and programs to advance the interests of ethnic and other groups.

References

Bernstein, Richard (1994), *Dictatorship of Virtue: Multiculturalism and the Battle for America's Future*, Knopf, New York.
Bloom, Allan (1988), *The Closing of the American Mind*, 2nd edn, Penguin Books, London.
Burnham, James (1945), *The Managerial Revolution* [1941], 3rd edn, Penguin Books, Harmondsworth.
Burnham, James (1947), *The Struggle for the World*, Cape, London.
Burnham, James (1959), *Congress and the American Tradition*, Henry Regnery, Chicago.
Burnham, James (1965), *The Suicide of the West* [1964], 2nd edn, Cape, London.
Crosland, C.A.R., (1964), *The Future of Socialism* [1956], 2nd edn, Cape, London.
Drucker, Peter F. (1989), *The New Realities*, Harper and Row, New York.
D'Souza, Dinesh (1991), *Illiberal Education: The Politics of Race and Sex on Campus*, Free Pr., New York.
Dunant, Sarah (ed.) (1994), *The War of the Words: The Political Correctness Debate*, Virago, London.
Frances, Samuel T. (1984), *Power and History: the Political Thought of James Burnham*, Univ. Pr. of America, New York.
Friedman, Marilyn and Jan Narveson, (1995), *Political Correctness: For and Against*, Rowman and Littlefield, Lanham, Maryland.
Fukuyama, Francis (1989), 'The End of History?', *The National Interest*, No. 16, pp. 3-18.
Fukuyama, Francis (1990), 'The "End of History" Debate' [1989-90], *Dialogue*, No. 89, March.
Fukuyama, Francis (1992), *The End of History and the Last Man*, Hamish Hamilton, London.
Galbraith, John Kenneth (1972), *The New Industrial State* [1967], 2nd edn, Deutsch, London.
Huntford, Roland (1971), *The New Totalitarians*, Allen Lane, London.
Kimball, Roger (1990), *Tenured Radicals*, Harper and Row, New York.
Krugman, Paul, (1994), *Peddling Prosperity*, Norton, New York.
Lasch, Christopher (1995), *The Revolt of the Elites and the Betrayal of Democracy*, Norton, New York.
Loeb, Paul Rogat (1994), *Generation at the Crossroads*, Rutgers Univ. Pr., New Brunswick, N.J.
Meynaud, Jean (1968), *Technocracy* first Eng. edn, Faber and Faber, London.
Miller, Abraham H., (1993), 'Political Correctness and American Higher Education', *Politics*, vol. 13, No. 1, pp. 22-8.
Mills, C. Wright (1959), *The Power Elite* [1956], 2nd edn, Oxford Univ. Pr./Galaxy, New York.

Morrise, David (1993), 'Philosophical Errors of Political Correctness', *Politics*, vol. 13, No. 2, pp. 32-7.
Ortega y Gasset, Jose (1946), *Mission of the University* [1930], Routledge, London.
Ortega y Gasset, Jose (1961), *The Revolt of the Masses* [1930], 3rd Eng. edn, Allen and Unwin, London.
Paglia, Camille (1993), *Sex, Art, and American Culture*, 2nd edn, Viking/Penguin Books, London.
Paglia, Camille (1994), *Vamps and Tramps*, Viking/Penguin Books, London.
Pahl, R.E. and J.T. Winkler (1974), 'The Coming Corporatism', *New Society*, October 10th.
Parekh, Bhiku (1994), 'Cultural Diversity and Liberal Democracy', in David Beetham (ed.), *Defining and Measuring Democracy*, Sage, London.
Schlesinger Jr, Arthur M. (1992), *The Disuniting of America*, Norton, New York.
Shonfield, Andrew (1969), *Modern Capitalism: The Changing Balance of Public and Private Power*, 2nd edn, Oxford Univ. Pr., London.
Strachey, John (1956), *Contemporary Capitalism*, Gollancz, London.
Winkler, J.T. (1976), 'Corporatism', *European Journal of Sociology*, vol. 17, pp. 100-36.

11 Democratic Theory as Public Philosophy: Prospects and Problems

This chapter's reflections and conclusions on the many challenges to modern democratic government and to democratic theory as a public philosophy begin with the problems created by political parties. They turn to the type of press and electronic journalism which democracies require, the type they have, and the gap which separates them. They deal with the political problems generated by technology and the expectations it encourages, they emphasise the importance of culture, and they assess the extent to which it is possible to be optimistic about the future of democratic government and democratic theory as a public philosophy.

The Problem of Political Parties

Although it is over simple and misleading for modern democracy to be defined in formal terms as competition between political parties, the struggles for and the exercise of governmental power by political parties are the central empirical facts of current democratic politics. If, therefore, democracies are to be guided by public philosophic standards then their political parties must be the bearers of these standards - a task which makes them both the main hope for and the main obstacle to self government by and for citizens being a reality rather than a slogan.

    Opposed political parties, held together by shared interests and by loyalty to a leader or a cause, however, far from being a modern invention are as old as politics. Wherever there have been struggles to keep, capture or influence the centres of power in a society, be it anything from a small tribe to a large nation, there have been temporary if not permanent political parties. The courts of emperors, kings and high priests have all had their rival parties, as have ancient and later city states and republics, and the medieval parliaments of Europe. Although the main motives of most courtiers, notables and orators may have been power and privilege, many have also been driven by feelings of obligation, and the desire to achieve the respect of their peers and a place in the memory and historical records of their societies. But the political parties familiar to today's voters are little more than a century old. Apart from in Britain, where political parties trace their origins to the religious and political conflicts of the seventeenth century, most of the major parties of European and other nations are products of ideas and forces spawned by the French Revolution, and the subsequent social cleavages brought about by industrial and urban growth.

In Britain, the increased number of voters produced by the 1832 electoral reforms led to the formation of small constituency associations for the support of Tory and Whig members of and candidates for parliament. Later, at the end of the nineteenth century, these constituency associations federated to form the Conservative and Liberal Parties, both of which eventually had their annual conferences, paid officials, substantial extra-parliamentary memberships and central offices. But elsewhere in Europe, in North America, the British Commonwealth and other parts of the world, the formation of parties was less gradual. When parliamentary government was the product of a revolution, a national-liberation struggle or a negotiated settlement with an imperial power, parties were the products and sometimes the cause of the change. Their leaders were usually the people who had played a major part in creating the new constitutional and parliamentary systems, and party structures were designed to profit from the electoral arrangements of the new states.[1]

The impetus for parliamentary parties with large extra-parliamentary memberships and professional organisations, however, sometimes came not from foundation events but from the emergence of well organised socialist parties and labour movements. In the final decades of the nineteenth century, the Marxist Social Democratic Parties of Germany, Austria and other parts of Europe, whose popular support preceded their parliamentary representation, were the continent's first parties to acquire mass memberships, permanent organisations and internal party bureaucracies. A little later, in Britain and its dominions where Marxism had failed to take root, the trade unions provided the social base for non-Marxist labour parties. Prior to these parties, most political parties had consisted of little more than a parliamentary membership of aristocratic notables and their nominees, and a few constituency and national associates and followers. It was the competition from well organised social democratic and labour parties which impelled anti-socialist parties to follow suit in establishing and attracting members for extra-parliamentary organisations. Socialist attempts to mobilise industrial workers also encouraged, in the less industrialised nations East European, the formation of peasant parties, several of which obtained a share of governmental

---

1 For a detailed account of party formation in Britain, see McKenzie (1963). See also Beattie (1970). For political parties in the United States, Key, Jr (1964). For other types of party formation, Duverger (1972).

power. After the First World War and Russia's October, 1917, revolution, in Italy and Germany the Fascist and National Socialist parties capitalised on the fear of communism to obtain the support which enabled them to seize power and suppress opposition.

From 1945 to the 1970s, however, in nearly all parliamentary nations, including the restored democracies of Italy and Germany, despite the differences in the origins and rhetoric of parties, electoral competition for the support of middle-of-the-road voters led to the policies and platforms of the main right-wing and left-wing parties converging. Of the main parties, only the Communist Parties resisted this trend. By the 1970s, however, the loyalty to and the identification of voters with the long-established parties began to wane. New generations of voters were concerned with new issues; old social divisions gave way to new ones; governing parties had more difficult in keeping their election promises; and, in several nations, separatist, regional, environmentalist or other new parties became electoral forces. Voters became more volatile, election results more unpredictable, and the future of the older parties less certain.

Both similarities and dissimilarities are to be found in the history and character of the parties and party systems of present-day nations, with different electoral systems causing many of the variations. Thus, the simple-majority or first-past-the-post system of the United Kingdom consistently produces a predominantly two-party system. Conversely, the closer an electoral system is to proportional representation, with the percentage of a party's parliamentary representatives corresponding to its percentage of the national vote, the larger the number of parties it will foster, and the greater the likelihood of coalition government. Many electoral systems, however, combine simple-majority and proportional-representation devices. Second-election systems as in France, for example, produce similar results to a two-party system but with blocs of left- and right-wing parties rather than two giant parties competing for power.

By means of electoral engineering, therefore, nations can modify their party systems and to some extent their political culture. On this topic, Arend Lijphart has convincingly argued that, for nations with persistent and potentially violent religious, ethnic or other conflicts, social peace and stable government are best encouraged by an electoral system which prevents the party or parties of the larger social groups from possessing permanent parliamentary majorities. Such a system compels, if a peaceful politics is to be achieved, a consensus on limits and other essentials.[2] But,

---

2   Arend Lijphart's advocacy of 'consociational' (power-sharing) democracy is probably given its most systematic statement in *Democracy in Plural Societies* (1977). For classifications of party systems, see Sartori (1976); and for the relations between electoral and party systems, Lijphart et al (1994).

though the character of an electoral system can largely determine whether a nation has a multi- or a dual-party system in which factions within the large parties take the place of smaller parties, there are weightier factors which affect a nation's political culture, and make its democracy stable or unstable. Of greater importance is whether the parties are constrained by constitutional and public philosophic standards, a concern for all sections of the community, and a determination by a nation's population and its leaders to make their system of government work. Without such restraint and commitment, tinkering with or radically changing an electoral system is unlikely to suffice. The many failed democracies in South America, Africa, East Europe and other parts of the world, which have experimented with different electoral systems, attest to this fact.

But what are the fundamental or brute facts about twentieth-century political parties and their electoral and parliamentary combats which public philosophers, political scientists and anyone else who hopes to understand modern democratic politics must acknowledge? In answering this question it is helpful to turn to the work of public choice theorists which, since the 1960s, has produced fruitful and revealing hypotheses for explaining modern party politics, most of which have been confirmed rather than refuted by the evidence, even in the more mercurial electoral politics of the last quarter of the century.

The Public Choice View

Political parties, for public choice theorists, resemble large companies competing in an economic market, but with the opposed parties using their resources to obtain votes rather than profits, and with the purpose of their vote gathering being governmental power for their leading members, and the status, monetary rewards and other perks which go with it.[3] A party's parliamentary members 'treat policy purely as means to the attainment of their private ends, which they can reach only by being elected' (Downs, 1957, p. 28). Similarly, voters are said to be mainly motivated by self interest; they seek the maximum benefits from governments for the minimum cost and inconvenience. They are therefore more than pliant victims of party propaganda; as far as their information and knowledge permit, they vote for the parties that are likely to benefit them, and to have

---

3   The book which laid the foundations for public choice work on political parties and voting behaviour, and which continues to yield important insights, is Anthony Downs's, *An Economic Theory of Democracy* (1957). For summaries of later public choice work on political parties, see Tullock and Perlman (1976); and Mueller (1989), esp. Part III, 'Public Choice in a Representative Democracy'. See also the relevant essays in Buchanan and Tollison (1984).

policies which most comply with their notions of the best type of government. Public choice theorists regard this voting behaviour as rational, but by being *rational* they do not mean that voters are careful analysts of issues, diligent students of party election manifestoes and other political literature, regular newspaper readers or discriminating users of television. On the contrary, because one vote is of so little consequence in deciding elections, an intelligent and rational voter does not bother to master the details of electoral issues. He or she leaves this work to other voters. Moreover, neglecting what for most people is a tedious occupation may be done with impunity as parties will cater for the interests of apathetic voters, provided that their interests are shared with large numbers of other voters. And, if they are not, no matter how well informed the individual voter may be, political parties will probably ignore his or her interests.

Public choice theorists, by means of these somewhat cynical but in broad terms justified presumptions about current political practice have constructed several illuminating and well substantiated hypotheses about the party politics of democratic nations. First (my enumeration), the rhetoric and purported principles of a party and its leaders, and the images the public has of them are important as voters do not think only in narrowly economic terms. In most instances voters possess at least hazy ideas about the best types of government and society. Broad cultural changes therefore exert a strong influence on political parties, for, if they are to attract the necessary votes to govern, they must show that they are sympathetic to the views of large and influential groups of voters - hence the increased attention paid by politicians, during the past quarter of a century, to the demands of environmentalists, feminists, and ethnic and other minorities. Second, when parties are in office they try to buy votes for the least possible expense, preferably that of someone else - the tax payer. Third, unlike in two-party systems where parties will tend to resemble each other - the result of trying to capture the middle ground - in multi-party systems, parties, in order to attract loyal and constant support, will try to acquire distinct identities. But, fourth, even in multi-party legislatures, the parties will usually form two opposed blocs of government and opposition parties of roughly equal strength. A public choice explanation is that each

> party wants to have as many cabinet posts [and other spoils] as it can, and thus wants to let as small a number of additional parties into the government...and still secure a majority (Mueller, p. 223).

Fifth, it is rational and usual for political parties to make their promises and policies vague if not self-contradictory and incomprehensible. Obscurity is required because, if intentions and their implications are made clear, undecided voters are more likely to be repulsed than converted. It follows that, sixth, the interests of politicians and parties are opposed to those of voters. Whereas it is in the interest of parties to obscure issues, voters, in order to vote rationally, need clear, simple and reliable information. As a consequence, 'the more rational political parties are [in their pursuit of governmental power], the less rational voters must be, and vice versa' (Downs, p. 137). Seventh, as it is the most effective means for buying votes, governments cannot resist intervening in economic life, particularly when elections approach. It is for this reason that it has proved difficult to prevent increases in government expenditure, and that democratic governments find it difficult to maintain consistent economic policies. But, eighth, governments make some attempt to resist using economic policies for electoral purposes as electoral necessity also compels them to cultivate economic prosperity and growth. The drift towards governmental expansion and incoherent economic policies, which results from what is politically rational being economically irrational, therefore, is countered by the desirability of economic affluence.

Public choice theory implies that parties and politicians whose conduct corresponds to public choice hypotheses and discoveries about political behaviour are likely to achieve their goals. Conversely, politicians who consistently stand by their principles and conceptions of the public good, and who try to educate rather than flatter voters will find that high office eludes them. Machiavellian precepts are thus an inevitable product of public choice theory. In common with public philosophers, public choice theorists find gaps between democratic theory and practice, between the claims that sovereignty resides with citizens and that government is in their interests and the fact that most democratic nations have gigantic and intrusive governmental systems that are operated mainly for the benefit of political parties, their leaders, and the social groups they favour. But the responses of public philosophers and public-choice theorists to departures from democratic theory by democratic practice are usually different.

When public choice theorists prescribe cures for the ills caused by party politics, their main proposal has been that a more extensive market economy and society, and a contraction of governmental activity be achieved by novel constitutional, electoral and parliamentary constraints on governments. The problem is that, whatever the merits of these proposals, without major changes of a public philosophic kind to the political culture and practice of democratic nations, it is difficult to see how these proposals would either be adopted or, once adopted, made to work to the benefit of the community. But what exactly is the different public philosophic attitude to the problem of political parties?

The Public Philosophic Response

Democrats in the public philosophic tradition have resisted the undermining of democratic life by political parties and tried to further the potential of these parties to enhance it. In nineteenth century Britain, they followed Edmund Burke in distinguishing between political parties, the bearers of worthwhile political principles, and unprincipled factions. In the United States, they followed James Madison in seeing factions as the enemy, and the transforming of private into public interests as a primary purpose of representatives and their parties. It was this conception of a political party which made neo-Madisonians, in the 1830s, critical of the populist demagoguery and the construction of party machines by Andrew Jackson and other politicians. Jacksonian and other populists, it was held, made public power the instrument of sectional interests, in particular those of politicians who sought the material benefits of public offices for themselves and their supporters, and favourable legislation for the providers of campaign funds. From James Madison and Alexis de Tocqueville to T. H. Green and the New Liberals, the public philosophic view was that, by means of parliamentary and public debate, political parties should clarify issues, establish worthy and shared goals for national communities, and enable political conflicts to be settled peacefully and reasonably. Political parties should open political influence and careers to people to whom they had previously been closed. And they should give their members and followers a training in political limits. By means of their internal debates and procedures, as well as their participation in parliamentary and public debate, they should enable even the largest of democracies to have informed and responsible citizens rather than sullen and politically apathetic and/or aggressive masses. Political parties should provide democracies not only with governments, alternative governments and peaceful transitions of power but a citizenship culture, and representatives and voters who respected and were mutually responsive to each other.

Parties should provide leadership for a nation. Whether they were vehicles of reform and change or conservative supports for established institutions and practices, they should respect tradition while being open to reform and innovation. Their leaders should be statesmen who understood the culture of their nations, and both the worth and limitations of party members and voters. As leaders could achieve nothing without the support of their parties, they should be effective partisans for their party, forceful and persuasive in their advocacy of principles and policies; but they should never forget that the national interest, and the peace and progress of humanity came before electoral and parliamentary victories. For public philosophers, if democracy was to be a blessing rather than a curse, then crucial functions had to be performed and difficult balances achieved by political parties and their leaders.[4]

But nineteenth century hopes that political parties would strengthen a democratic politics and culture increasingly gave way to pessimism. By 1861, John Stuart Mill was disturbed by the effects of party politics in Britain, and in his *Considerations on Representative Government* (1993) he urged that, in order to retain sufficient independent members in the House of Commons to constrain the parties, there should be multiple votes by better-educated voters at elections, and the casting of votes in constituencies of the voter's choice. In 1902, Mosei Ostrogorski, in the first comprehensive study of modern political parties (1970), expressed the fears of many of liberal democracy's friends when he argued that political parties had become instruments for subordinating parliamentary government to alien and corrupt purposes. He accused parties of making parliamentary debate redundant and obstructing public debate, of creating unnecessary political and social divisions, and of causing political power to gravitate to the extra-parliamentary organisations of parties, and to the business companies and trade unions which provided their funds. Political parties, he thought, would also produce Caesar-like individuals who, even more than Gladstone and Disraeli, would dominate the politics of their nations. For Ostrogorski, political parties were destroying liberal democracy and replacing it with elected tyrannies (Ostrogorski, 1970; Barker and Howard-Johnston, 1975; and Pombeni, 1994). A decade later, the conclusion to Robert Michels's (1959) sociological classic on political parties was that they were subject to an 'iron law of oligarchy'. Basing his study on the pre-1914 German Social Democratic Party, which prided itself on its egalitarian, ultra-democratic organisation and principles, he argued that, in practice, party leaders and organisers were not accountable or even responsive to their party's rank and file; they used their position and control of the party's organisation to manipulate its members.

The post-1945, pluralist, arguments of Robert Dahl (1956) and other American behaviouralists, which were examined in Chapter 3, were to a large extent a response to the views of Ostrogorski and Michels. Dahl's contention was that the oligarchic internal organisation and politics of parties was irrelevant for democratic theory and practice so long as there was genuine competition between the parties and among the pressure groups of democratic nations. For Dahl and his co-thinkers, therefore, the

---

4   For examples of late-nineteenth- and early-twentieth-century public-philosophic conceptions of and hopes for political parties, see John Maccunn, *Ethics of Citizenship* (1894), Chapter 6, 'Party and Political Consistency'; and James Bryce, *The Hindrances to Good Citizenship* (1909), Chapter 3, 'Party Spirit as a Hindrance to Good Citizenship'. Bryce, however, is less optimistic than Maccunn.

decline in the importance of parliaments which concerned Ostrogorski, and the contempt for rank-and-file members and internal democracy emphasised by Michels were of little consequence. What counted was that party policies satisfy voters. Constraints on parties, politicians and pressure groups were expected to emerge, largely spontaneously, from their competition.

This was not so much an answer to as a failure to understand the questions raised by the critics of political parties. Ostrogorski, Michels and other critics had demonstrated that political parties were aggravating the paradox noted by Tocqueville: that, although political parties were a response to the lack of power felt by the peoples of large democratic nations, they would increase this helplessness. Ostrogorski, in fact, was so alarmed by the effects of disciplined parliamentary parties that he proposed that constitutional and legislative steps be taken to abolish them and to confine the membership of parliaments to independents. Needless to say, there are insurmountable obstacles to this remedy. It is illiberal and undemocratic to prevent people from associating together for legitimate political purposes; the proposal's implementation would require that parties abolish themselves; and it would be impossible to prevent parties of some kind re-emerging from cooperation among parliamentary 'independents' and their extra-parliamentary supporters.

Prospects

At the end of the twentieth century the problems which political parties create for democratic theory and practice remain; more disturbingly, questionable practices which once provoked concern are now taken for granted. They include the substituting of voter surveys, advertising and public-relations techniques for political debate; the systematic employment of the purveyors of these techniques, many of whom see little difference between marketing a political party and any other commodity; television's domination of election campaigns; meetings of parliamentary-party caucuses usurping parliamentary debate and decision making; co-operation between the members of legislatures and lobbyists; and the lobbyists and heads of financial and business companies having access to ministers or their representatives - a necessary practice but one which easily slips into a privileged treatment for the donors of party funds and experts in political blackmail. Not only has the main function of prime ministers and leaders of opposition parties become the winning of elections, a fact which their advisers, associates and party colleagues will not allow them to forget, but parliamentarians are, on general issues, little more than orchestrated spokespeople and voting puppets for their parties. If legislators in the United States have avoided the worst excesses of disciplined parties, it is at the cost of becoming dependent for campaign funds on local, state and national pressure groups. And if party politics have not altogether become the preserve of mediocrities, as predicted by Tocqueville, it is because they have attracted clever and energetic careerists, highly skilled in the techniques that take the place of rational persuasion - streamlined versions of the professional demagogues whom John Stuart Mill thought would be produced by the payment of parliamentarians.

Just over three decades ago in a study of contemporary history, Geoffrey Barraclough (1967) articulated the disquiet of public philosophic and other critics when he wrote that, in order to understand the political parties of democratic nations, distinctions must be made between those of nineteenth-century, bourgeois-individualist, democracy, in which power was exercised by parliamentary representatives, and post-bourgeois, 'mass democracies' in which political parties are integral parts of technocratic societies. Parliamentary democracy, Barraclough argued, had been reduced to a myth, a myth which masked the control of both the legislative and executive branches of government by disciplined parties on which there were few judicial or other constraints.

> Today, the British political scene is dominated by two great party oligarchies which have taken over and divided between them most of the sovereign powers Bagehot ascribed to the House of Commons. What we still think of as a parliamentary state has, in fact, become a party state, and the parties are now one of 'the most central and crucial of all the institutions of British government', as, indeed, of government everywhere (pp. 132-3).[5]

But political parties, for all their inadequacies and abuses of power perform necessary functions. They continue to provide governments, oppositions and peaceful transfers of power; they are one of the few remaining conduits between citizens and national centres of power; and, despite their centralisation and increasing inability to attract members, they still allow some serious competition between ideas, values and policies. In Austria, Belgium, West Germany and now a reunited Germany, and in other nations with histories of bitter religious and other conflicts, they have cooperated in multi-party systems to produce consensual and stable politics. They have also become places, it should be added, in which leaders and organisers who seek disciplined, election-oriented parties battle against not only rank-and-file purists who take a party's principles and rhetoric seriously but extremists and sectional interests who wish to capture a party

---

5   For a similar analysis of political parties to that of Barraclough (1967, Ch. 5, 'From Individualism to Mass Democracy'), see Moody, Jr (1983).

for their own ends. On the internal politics of both left-wing and right-wing parties, B. D. Graham (1993) has made the following apt comment. Parties

> provide one of the few remaining areas for self-expression and competition in societies whose institutions are increasingly subject to the rational-bureaucratic regulation of social and economic transactions. Unlike most organisations, a party will admit to membership anyone above a certain age who supports its objectives and is willing to pay a nominal fee....parties have kept alive the traditions of popular democracy, but their very openness does expose them to subversion from groups searching for a short cut to power or from a pressure group determined to cut a direct path to the party's policy-making bodies (p. 246).

Disputes between and within parties are far from being careful deliberations on the principles which should guide a nation. General elections often resemble a gigantic public auction, with party organisers and journalists concentrating on the rival clusters of promises, polling surveys, the popularity of the rival leaders, sexual or other scandals involving politicians, and the latest press releases. But whether the main responsibility for the abuses of democratic procedures is that of party leaders, parliamentarians and officials or of newspaper, radio and television journalism, neither political parties nor the media should be demonised. The root of the problem is cultural. If persuading voters and satisfying readers and viewers required something better, then politicians and journalists would hasten to provide it. Unless, therefore, there is an effective public philosophy and a democratic culture inspired by it, current party politics and democratic forms will produce not self-governing nations but old and new varieties of oligarchic rule and manipulated societies. Electoral competition will produce not governments that are accountable and responsive to citizens, whom they try to educate and whose interests they respect, but elected autocracies. Parliaments are likely to become even more like third-rate theatrical companies which no longer have an audience, and what remains of public life will become the preserve of the more media-conscious pressure groups.

More Problems: Journalism and the Media

The problem of whether political parties will advance or permanently damage democratic politics raises related questions about newspaper, television, radio and other journalism. Are democratic politics always to be treated as battles for power between political parties, with political journalism aping sporting journalism, or will political journalism, during and between elections, encourage serious public debate about issues and exhibit public philosophic standards? And will journalists act as mediators, transmitting the hopes and concerns of citizens to governments and political elites, and providing citizens with easily understood yet reliable information about political choices and their likely consequences? It is not altogether foolhardy to believe that positive answers to such questions are possible as the best political journalism has always performed these functions. In most democratic nations, there have been newspapers, including at times the popular tabloids, which have expressed public philosophic standards in their selection and presentation of news, and in their editorials and feature articles. So too have many radio and television news broadcasts, documentaries and discussion programs. Although the *media*, to use the catch-all word, are often held responsible for the trivialising of politics and the vulgarising of culture, they are as much a symptom as a cause. Their pursuit of growth, profits and mass markets impel newspapers and television to provide what is popular. If there were a more discriminating public, therefore, standards would be raised. This issue of the main cause of media irresponsibility, whether it is push or pull, however, is academic; the practical problem is that the media abet rather than resist the decay of public debate.

In both popular journalism and television reporting, simplifications are preferred to balanced and adequately detailed accounts and comments. Political issues are raised and dropped not because of their importance but their sensationalism. In the selection of news, the scandalous life of a politician is given a priority over more complex but more serious public scandals. What become public issues during and between elections are increasingly determined by the working arrangements which party leaders and their press agents have with newspaper and television journalists. In these relations, the media's power to publicise or ignore politicians, and to give them an honest and reliable or dishonest and cranky image is a trump card in their dealings with them.[6] In most democracies the media encourage a demagogic view of democracy in which public opinion, as interpreted and manipulated by the media, is considered paramount, and governments are expected to give majorities whatever they want. Moreover, not only is political news personalised and sensationalised but it is increasingly displaced by what is considered more likely to attract advertisers, readers and viewers: gossip and concocted stories about models, film and sports stars, and instant celebrities.

---

6   For revealing accounts by a UK insider of these relations, see Jones (1995). For further information, and for a carefully researched study of electoral and other political-party propaganda and campaigning, in Britain since 1945, see Rosenbaum (1997).

Television compounds most of these abuses, the result of its selection procedures on what is telecast; its capacity to highlight and distort; its enabling of millions of people to receive, simultaneously, graphic images; its being, for most people, their main if not only avenue to public affairs; and its culture of deception - the careful planning and presentation which gives the viewer the illusion of spontaneity and truth. In addition, the questioning techniques of television journalists and interviewers, when they confront politicians and other public figures, bring a utopian, politically holier-than-thou perspective into public life. This is a consequence of interviewers, without having clear and consistent positions which have to be defended or even remembered, being able, by means of persistent questioning and hectoring, to discredit policy makers and other political actors who are stuck with and responsible for their views and decisions - decisions which may be the unavoidable choice of a lesser evil. And problems are worsened by what was once the centralisation of television and other news, within nations, edging towards a more world-wide centralisation of international news sources, telecast material and ownership.

Reforms to counter the abuses of their freedom by the less responsible sections of the media would improve the political life of most democratic nations. The difficulty is that the media stifle the issue, condemn criticism and reform proposals as attacks on freedom of speech, and denigrate critics with charges of censorship, elitism and fuddy-duddyism. It is not surprising therefore that even leading government and opposition politicians are timid in the face of the media. Serious discussion of media reform, therefore, is permanently shelved. Significantly, in the United Kingdom in 1997, even the horrific death of Princess Diana, the public outrage over the hounding of the princess by the paparazzi, and a 'New Labour' government, purportedly intent on reform and with a record parliamentary majority, failed to produce any action. But what are the public philosophic standards which should guide media reform?

The public philosophic objective is that freedom of speech be secured for investigative journalism and other political and social inquiry, and the expression of opinion, but that the media realise that there is no absolute right which allows the dissemination of anything for which there is a market. Depraved tastes and idle curiosity do not have to be satisfied. The exposure of political, financial and other public scandals is different from the titillation of readers with the more salacious details of the private lives of politicians or anyone else. Similarly, there is a difference between questioning governments and politicians on policy issues, and breaking down walls of secrecy on the one hand, and, on the other, hounding anyone whose behaviour or views affront widespread prejudices and/or those of media pundits. Like all freedoms, freedom of speech has to be exercised responsibly, by media owners, managers, editors and journalists as well as by ordinary members of the public. As Walter Lippmann (1963) once wrote, the freedom possessed by journalists derives from the rights and duties of citizens: journalists simply 'do what every sovereign citizen is supposed to do but has not the time or interest to do for himself' (in Rossiter and Lare, p. 534).[7]

As with all freedom, if restraint is not voluntarily exercised, external constraints are required. No democracy should tamely accept, for example, practices that amount to the falsification of news and the harassing of politicians and other people whose only crime is offending the popular prejudices which journalists profess to share. It is no more an absolute right for the mass communications industry, which caters for the mind, to purvey anything it chooses than it is for medical and drug companies whose products cater for the body. It may be true that the dangers to a democracy from authoritarian governments and powerful private interests who wish to prevent inquiry and criticism are more serious than those of an unrestricted freedom for journalists, but that is a reason for jealously protecting a responsible press, television and radio freedom not for interpreting this freedom as a license to print, broadcast or telecast anything. Widening and strengthening the laws of libel - without restricting responsible political reports and comments - is one solution which strengthens civil society and the courts rather than governments. Another proposal worth more consideration than it has so far received is for codes of conduct for journalists to be backed by independent press ombudsmen and staff, subject to the courts, but with the authority to impose heavy fines and other penalties on journalists, editors, and media managers and proprietors.[8]

The oligopolist control of the media by a small number of proprietors, often with ambitions to be political giants as well as business tycoons, as occurs in many democracies, restricts the choice of consumers, and intimidates both government and opposition parties - though it would be less of a threat for Australian and some other democracies if there were less dislike of foreign ownership and competition, a nationalist prejudice which existing proprietors play on. But though there is often a strong case for laws to encourage greater competition, there are no legislative panaceas for either the control or character of the media. A flawed media, like an unprincipled party politics, is a chronic ailment for most democracies

---

7   The quotation is from one of Walter Lippmann's most thorough discussion of the responsibilities of political journalism, 'The Job of the Washington Correspondent', *The Atlantic Monthly*, January 1960, reprinted in Rossiter and Lare (1963).

8   For a summary of such a proposal for checks to the British media, in a report of a Parliamentary National Heritage Committee on Privacy and Media Intrusion, HMSO, London, 1993, and the predictable press hostility, see Culf (1993, p. 4).

which, at best, can be improved and prevented from becoming fatal for democratic life. What would be fatal, however, would be the continued ignoring of the media's abuse of mass-communication technology and the debasing of public standards.

At issue is the character of democratic politics, a politics to which the media are now a necessary and inescapable part. Irrespective of whether democrats appreciate, despise or are alarmed by mass communications, of which press and electronic journalism are the central part, democratic politics are inextricably tied to them. The media, even more than political parties and other voluntary political associations, are the main mediators between citizens and their legislative assemblies and governments. The media therefore will play a vital part in determining whether there are substantive democracies of responsible political actors and other citizens or formal democracies that provide a veneer for manipulated mass societies. Perhaps this is the question to which all serious discussion of the media must lead: whether mass communications must lead to mass societies. Are democracies to consist of people who are *citizens* in something more than the legalistic meaning of the word or are they to consist of ill-informed and resentful individuals, alienated from social ties and attached to no associations which contribute to political and other life - people who in crisis situations could be mobilised by anti-democratic political parties or other groups.[9]

To begin an assessment of the problems of and prospects for democratic nations by highlighting political parties and the media may be helpful but it is misleading unless some closely related phenomena are also considered. The power of centralised parties and the media, it should be remembered, would be less serious were it not for their technological resources. It is pertinent therefore to consider the role of some of the more relevant technologies in democratic societies, their dangers as well as their achievements, how they have changed the ways in which politics and the relations between politics and economics are perceived, and how they affect culture and political culture.

---

9   The idea that modern democracy tends to substitute mass attitudes and behaviour for citizenship standards goes back to Tocqueville (1968). In 1930 Ortega y Gasset (1961) placed it at the centre of his critique of contemporary democracies. For an attempt at giving it a more testable, political-science use, see Kornhauser (1960), and for a vigourous critique of most theorising about mass attitudes, and a denial that the United States of the 1950s was a mass society, see Bell (1962, 'America as a Mass Society...').

Technology, Excessive Expectations and Culture

Technology and Excessive Expectations

For previous ages economic activity, in the sense of the production and distribution of material goods, was seen as arising from necessity. It was the means for satisfying the fundamental needs of human beings for food, clothing and shelter, and those additional goods which made life more pleasant and fulfilling. Politics and the state were a product of the leisure and freedom which the satisfying of basic needs, at least for dominant and privileged classes, made possible. Economic activity provided the essential goods for human life, along with the luxuries demanded by human appetites when basic needs were satisfied; political life, by contrast, enabled the more moral and prudent of rulers, nobles and citizens to establish, by means of government and law, at least a modicum of social order, peace and acceptable conditions. Until the end of the eighteenth century, neither economics nor politics were given such grandiose aims as the abolition of poverty, and the achievement of universal material abundance and equal opportunities for all. Even the most idealist and ambitious of conceivable goals, outside of the imaginary societies of utopian writers, were more modest and achievable: improvements in government, trade and knowledge; and the establishing of the basic (natural) rights necessary for security. Economic activity, as political philosophers from Socrates to Hegel recognised, was a fundamental prerequisite for any human society - but it was not the chief end of life. It was the foundation for strong, well governed states and, as far as it was humanly possible, fulfilling lives for their members - originally for small minorities, later for larger numbers of people.

But beginning in the fifteenth and sixteenth centuries in Europe, and completed in nineteenth-and twentieth-century industrialised nations, this earlier conception of the relationship of economic activity to politics and culture was reversed. Politics and culture, including education, were made the servants of economic goals, principally the technological mastery of nature and, for all people, the overcoming of material scarcity. A part of this reversal consists of economic theory displacing both political science as the master science and a public-philosophic political theory as the guiding theory for government. In English speaking and other nations from the 1930s to the 1960s, it was the theories of Keynes and the Keynesians which performed this quasi-public-philosophic role; since the 1960s, however, Keynesianism has been on the defensive against the theories of Friedrich Hayek, Milton Friedman and other economic liberals.

The cause of the dominant position if no longer the prestige of economic theory, however, is not so much the vigour of economists in advancing their discipline as the fact that the political elites of modern democratic societies, with the tacit support of the public, have given a primacy to economic goals, a move favoured by both laissez-faire economists and their neo-Keynesian, technocratic and other antagonists. The dispute between these two parties is over means not ends: whether it is the market or governmental controls and direction which is the better instrument for achieving economic growth. But the background to and the other major cause of the subordination of politics to economics is modern technology.

It was technology which, in the nineteenth century, gave plausibility to the dream shared by liberals, socialists and other crusaders for progress that technical inventions would take the place of the slavery of the ancient world in providing a life of leisure, culture and active citizenship for all people.[10] If, today, the nineteenth century dream and faith in technology are held more cautiously and sceptically - the result of technology's contributions to massive population increases, horrendous weapons and wars of mass destruction, and its continual stimulation of new material wants and longings - they remain a basic part of contemporary culture.

Economic, political and military considerations all prevent modern states from withdrawing from technological competition; such abstinence would condemn their peoples to a lower standard of material life than those of their neighbours, weaken them militarily, and thus threaten their political sovereignty and independence. Democratic governments, therefore, find it impossible, even if they wished, to circumscribe technological progress and economic growth. Individuals may give a priority to other parts of life, but not nation states. A fundamental problem for modern democracies, therefore, is how they are to be self-governing, militarily defensible and economically prosperous without allowing technology and economics to swallow all other areas of life, including political life. Although there may be no halting of technological development in general, and though there can be no doubt about the many ways in which nineteenth and twentieth century technology has radically improved the standards and amenities of life, it does not follow that all technology is beneficial. It is a mistake to think that though technology has always been a feature of human life, and usually for the better, every technological development in medicine, education, genetic engineering and military and other affairs is desirable or irresistible. Some technology will worsen personal life and destabilise rather than improve social life, thus creating political problems. As far as there are solutions to these problems, therefore, they must begin not with the idea that there is

---

10 For a later, 1930s, restatement of this liberal and socialist dream, see Keynes (1972).

one big technological problem but with the realisation that there are many different problems to which different considerations apply.

Advances in technological knowledge and its applications, however, are difficult to query let alone combat because the goals of so many people are overwhelmingly economic and material. Technological growth would be slower and less destabilising if present day citizens were satisfied with, say, the material standard of life of the citizens of ancient Athens, the wealthiest of whom enjoyed living standards that were probably little better than those of an industrial worker or lower middle-class person in a late-nineteenth-century industrialised nation. But modern citizens, at least until a few years ago, have expected continual economic improvement. The main political problem caused by modern technology therefore is its stimulation of excessive economic and other expectations which no political party or government can satisfy.

The questions raised by modern technology and the demands for ever increasing material prosperity, however, are cultural rather than economic. How are excessive expectations to be restrained if there is to be an alternative to political coercion or continual disappointment if not turmoil? What kinds of life will the citizens and elites of modern democracies find acceptable if the satisfying of material hopes by technologically driven growth proves to be elusive? What assumptions, values, virtues and vices will constitute the culture of democratic peoples and shape their political attitudes if their expectations are frustrated?

Culture

Since Tocqueville, public philosophers have seen the culture of democratic nations as the main factor which determines their destinies. They have emphasised that whether or not governments, elites and citizens respond creatively to the challenges to their nations and to modern democratic civilisation will largely depend on their culture, and that their culture will evolve as a consequence of their choices and actions. Although public philosophers have understood that modern democracy is compatible with many different ways of life, their view has been that democracy is nevertheless a civilisation with a distinctive culture, basically liberal but with a fervour for equality. For the public philosophic tradition, although this democratic culture is far from perfect, it has the potential to produce governments that are more efficient and just than those of non-democratic regimes, and citizens who, in most instances, are superior in their resourcefulness, and their political and other qualities.

The fact that culture is a more evasive object of study than politics and economics does not affect its importance. Culture is pivotal for a society, for it is their culture which both moulds and expresses the character of a people, its elites and its government. Culture, as Marxists influenced by Antonio Gramsci remind us, is hegemonic, and, as T. S. Eliot saw so clearly, there 'is always more to it [culture] than we are conscious of; and it cannot be planned because it is always the unconscious background of all our planning' (1948, p. 94).[11]

Yet social causation is not one way, and the culture of a community is an effect as well as a cause of its political and economic life. But whatever the causal nexus between culture and the remaining areas of life, the beliefs, values and goals of the members of a community are politically crucial. Of central importance for today's democracies, therefore, are the family lives, and personal and wider social relations of their members; the formal and informal education provided by their schools, universities and other institutions; the influence exercised by the communications and entertainment industries, the churches and whatever organisations take the place of the churches; and, for societies subject to rapid change, the relations between the members of different generations. But what light does this consideration of culture cast upon the prospects for democratic societies, and how realistic is it to be optimistic about their future, and the future of democratic theory as a public philosophy?

Does Realism Allow Optimism?

Will the political actors and intellectuals who adhere to public philosophic standards be able to clarify and assist in successful confrontations with the political, economic and cultural challenges which face old, new and possible democracies in what is increasingly being called a *postmodern world*? This question and its reference to a *postmodern world* - a term which in addition to its other uses and connotations suggests that previous history is irrelevant to understanding current political issues - challenges one of Walter Lippmann's reasons for believing that a retrieval of an effective public philosophy was possible: that previous social achievements may again be repeated. But even without reference to the idea of a postmodern world, common sense suggests that a faith in such a retrieval may rapidly be becoming fatuous and utopian. Who seriously believes that it is possible to return to anything resembling ancient Athenian democracy, the Roman republic, the United States at its inception or late-Victorian and Edwardian Britain? But Lippmann's faith was not as foolish as this type of retort implies; his point was not that past social and political conditions could or should be restored but that, in new conditions, proven

---

11   Eliot also wrote that 'the effective culture is that which is directing the activity of those who are manipulating that which they call culture' (1948, p. 107).

principles could be rediscovered and again found to be effective. A similar view to Lippmann's is that of F. A. Hayek who, responding to the metaphor that clocks cannot be turned back, has observed that 'it expresses the fatalistic belief that we cannot learn from our mistakes, the most abject admission that we are incapable of using our intelligence' (1960, p. 284).

Additional grounds for believing that a revival and revitalising of democratic theory as a public philosophy is possible are to be found in the explanation which the Socrates of Plato's *Republic* (1992) offered for why justice sometimes triumphs over injustice, even when unjust people outnumber the just. Socrates's explanation was that just people were able to cooperate against the unjust whereas the unjust, as well as fighting against the just, fought among themselves. The same may be said about the public philosophy. Public spirited people who think in a public philosophic manner, despite their philosophic, religious and other differences, are able to cooperate against ideological apologists who cannot see beyond immediate conditions, against promoters of sectional interests, and against utopians. On the other hand, people who reject public philosophic standards compete among themselves. Because the purpose of democratic theory as a public philosophy is to protect and improve democratic government, all people who share these goals are able to discover public philosophic standards and to act together.

The fact that political foes are able to agree on common public philosophic principles and ends goes a long way in explaining, for example, how democracy in Germany took root after the failure of the Weimar Republic, and the devastation brought by National Socialist rule and military defeat; how democracy in France has survived the rise and fall of four republics; how British, Commonwealth, Scandinavian, Asian and other democracies have accomplished radical political and social changes by peaceful, parliamentary means; how democratic government in the United States has survived a bitter and destructive civil war, and a system of constitutional checks and balances which almost guarantees conflicts among its branches of government; and how South Africa has been able to take the first steps towards a multi-racial democracy. Sceptics who think that pragmatism and/or luck explain these and other democratic successes forget that even the most pragmatic and lucky of democratic politicians, when seeking solutions to serious and dangerous social and political problems, must look for precedents and principles which, because they are fundamental to democratic government and to a worthwhile human life, make agreement possible.

In periods of social and political crisis, therefore, it is to the public philosophy that even the most sceptical of democrats must turn. To the extent that democratic states are now endangered by global economic developments over which they have little control, the leakage of their sovereignty to transnational and internal regional governments, ethnic and other social cleavages, a drift towards oligarchic government and a totalitarian-type conformity, utopian political styles, aggressive pressure groups, opportunist political parties and politicians, an irresponsible journalism, the loss of confidence in and by schools and universities, the erosion of a citizenship culture, environmental disasters, finding appropriate responses to technological developments, and unemployment and the failure of public welfare services, it is to democratic theory as a public philosophy that people who seek solutions compatible with democratic politics must look. Although people who turn to this democratic theory and public philosophy will not find instant remedies, they will find guidance for understanding and responding to problems. Democratic theorists and other intellectuals, in fact, become public philosophers when they discard the utopian illusion that persistent difficulties can be reduced to problems with quick, tidy solutions. Similarly, they become public philosophers when they cease to believe that all that is required to cure the ills of a democracy is more democracy, with the democratic project interpreted not in a balanced and comprehensive manner but reduced to one or a small number of its many parts, be it equality, market and other freedoms, participation, authority or anything else.

Democratic theory as a public philosophy, as well as urging that opportunities be seized when there is support for radical but necessary reforms, enables despair to be held at bay in times of peril. As in more comfortable days it encourages political actors and citizens to think clearly about both opportunities and dangers, and about both the potential and the shortcomings of democratic life. As long as such a public philosophy survives, be it as no more than a stubborn resistance to managerial, majoritarian and other perversions of democracy, it will encourage calm thought and salutary action. It will encourage cooperation and keep alive the hopes of people drawn to it by means of small-circulation journals, electronic communication and whatever else is at hand in what could become little more than oases of genuine discussion and education. As long as the future falls short of some variant of George Orwell's *Nineteen Eighty-Four* image of a boot stamping on the human face forever, a public philosophy and a democratic revival based on it are possible.

But this is to border on the melodramatic. The main dangers to democratic government, democratic theory as a public philosophy, and constitutional, representative and other liberal-democratic principles are unlikely to come from their outright enemies of either the left or the right whose preference is for an undisguised despotism. Democracies are more likely to be damaged by two better-intentioned groups of people: by politicians, senior public servants and their advisers who, in their obsession with efficiency, and economic and technological growth, are blind to the erosion of democratic institutions, civil society and a citizenship culture; and by radicals who attach utopian styles of thought to what are otherwise worthy causes. Both groups make disappointment inevitable and foment a serious disenchantment if not a cynicism about democracy.

Against all the many dangers to democratic societies, the political thinkers and actors who are committed to and guided by the principles of democratic theory as a public philosophy will continue to warn and resist, and thus maintain a rich and wide-ranging tradition which offers something better than ideology and utopia. It is a tradition however which, because its relevant parts, their application and the courses of action they suggest always have to be thought out and decided on the basis of circumstances, provides no easy solutions. But it remains as the tradition which the leaders, elites and citizens of liberal democracies must preserve and revitalise if they wish to understand their civilisation, sustain their systems of government and the political cultures on which they rest, and realistically and firmly confront the problems, difficulties and dangers which, in old and new forms, are always a part of democratic life.

References

Barker, Rodney and Xenia Howard-Johnston (1975), 'The Politics and Political Ideas of Moisei Ostrogorski', *Political Studies*, vol 23, pp. 415-29.
Barraclough, Geoffrey (1967), *An Introduction to Contemporary History*, 2nd edn, Penguin Books, Harmondsworth.
Beattie, Alan (ed.) (1970), *English Party Politics, Volume I, 1660-1906*, Weidenfeld and Nicolson, London.
Bell, Daniel (1962), *The End of Ideology*, 2nd edn, Free Pr., New York.
Bryce, James (1909), *The Hindrances to Good Citizenship*, Yale Univ. Pr., New Haven.
Buchanan, James M. and Robert D. Tollison (eds) (1984), *The Theory of Public Choice - II*, Univ. of Michigan Pr., Ann Arbor.
Culf, Andrew (1993), 'Editors Scorn MPs' Proposed Press Safeguards', *Guardian Weekly*, April 4.
Dahl, Robert (1956), *A Preface to Democratic Theory*, The Univ. of Chicago Pr., Chicago.
Downs, Anthony (1957) *An Economic Theory of Democracy*, Harper and Row, New York.
Duverger, Maurice (1972), *Party Politics and Pressure Groups*, Crowell, New York.
The Economist (1997), 'Survey of the World Economy', September 20-26.
Eliot, T.S. (1948), *Notes Towards the Definition of Culture*, Faber and Faber, London.
Graham, B.D. (1993), *Representation and Party Politics: A Comparative Perspective*, Blackwell, Oxford.
Hayek, F.A. (1960), *The Constitution of Liberty*, Routledge, London.
Jones, Nicholas (1995), *Soundbites and Spin Doctors: How Politicians Manipulate the Media and Vice Versa*, Cassell, London.

Key Jr, V.O. (1964), *Politics, Parties, and Pressure Groups*, 5th edn, Crowell, New York.
Keynes, John Maynard (1972), 'Economic Possibilities for Our Grandchildren', in *The Collected Writings of John Maynard Keynes*, vol. 9, *Essays in Persuasion* [1931], Macmillan, London.
Kornhauser, William (1960), *The Politics of Mass Society*, 2nd edn, Routledge, London.
Lijphart, Arend (1977), *Democracy in Plural Societies*, Yale Univ. Pr., New Haven.
Lijphart, Arend et al, (1994), *Electoral Systems and Party Systems: A Study of Twenty-Six Democracies 1945-1990*, Oxford Univ. Pr., Oxford.
Maccunn, John (1894), *Ethics of Citizenship*, James Maclehose, Glascow.
McKenzie, Robert (1963), *British Political Parties*, 2nd edn, Heinemann/Mercury, London.
Michels, Robert (1959), *Political Parties* [1911], 2nd Eng. edn, Dover, New York.
Mill, John Stuart (1993), *Utilitarianism, On Liberty, Considerations on Representative Government, Remarks on Bentham's Philosophy*, (ed.) Geraint Williams, Dent/Everyman, London.
Moody Jr, Peter R. (1983), 'The Erosion of the Function of Political Parties in the Post-Liberal State', *Review of Politics*, vol. 45, pp. 254-79.
Mueller, Dennis C. (1989), *Public Choice II*, Cambridge Univ. Pr., Cambridge.
Ortega y Gasset, Jose (1961), *The Revolt of the Masses* [1930], 2nd Eng. edn, Allen and Unwin, London.
Ostrogorski, M. (1970), *Democracy and the Organization of Political Parties*, 2 vols [1902], reprinted, Haskell House Publishers, New York.
Plato, *The Republic* (1992), (ed.) Terence Irwin, 2nd edn, Dent/Everyman, London.
Pombeni, Paolo (1994), 'Starting in Reason, Ending in Passion: Bryce, Lowell, Ostrogorski and the Problem of Democracy', *The Historical Journal*, vol 37, pp. 319-41.
Rosenbaum, Martin (1997), *From Soapbox to Soundbite: Party Political Campaigning in Britain since 1945*, Macmillan, Basingstoke.
Rossiter, Clinton and James Lare (eds) (1963), *The Essential Lippmann: A Political Philosophy for Liberal Democracy*, Random House, New York.
Sartori, Giovanni (1976), *Parties and Party Systems: A Framework for Analysis*, Cambridge Univ. Pr., Cambridge.
Tocqueville, Alexis de (1968), *Democracy in America* [1835, 1840], 2 vols, (eds) J.P. Mayer and Max Lerner, 2nd edn, Collins/Fontana, n.p.
Tullock, Gordon and Morris Perlman (1976), *The Vote Motive: An Essay in the Economics of Politics...*, The Institute of Economic Affairs, London.

Bibliography

Adams, Larry L. (1977), *Walter Lippmann*, Twayne, Boston.
Albertoni, Ettore A. (1982), *Mosca and the Theory of Elitism*, Blackwell, Oxford.
Alexander, Peter and Roger Gill (eds) (1984), *Utopias*, Duckworth, London.
Almond, Gabriel A. and Sidney Verba (1963), *Civic Culture: Political Attitudes and Democracy in Five Nations*, Princeton Univ. Pr, Princeton, N.J.
Arblaster, Anthony (1984), *The Rise and Decline of Western Liberalism*, Blackwell, Oxford.
Arblaster, Anthony (1987), *Democracy*, Univ. of Minnesota Pr., Minneapolis.
Arblaster, Anthony and Steven Lukes (eds) (1971), *The Good Society: A Book of Readings*, Methuen, London.
Arendt, Hannah (1958), *The Human Condition*, Univ. of Chicago Pr., Chicago.
Arendt, Hannah (1961), *Between Past and Present*, Faber and Faber, London.
Arendt, Hannah (1972), *Crises of the Republic*, Harcourt Brace, New York.
Arendt, Hannah (1973), *On Revolution*, 3rd edn, Penguin Books, Harmondsworth.
Aristotle (1955), *The Ethics of Aristotle*, (ed.) J.A.K. Thomson, 2nd edn, Penguin Books, Harmondsworth.
Aristotle (1992), *The Politics*, (ed.) Trevor J. Saunders, 3rd edn, Penguin Books, London.
Auchincloss, Louis (1980), *The House of the Prophet*, Houghton Mifflin, Boston.
August, Eugene (1975), *John Stuart Mill: A Mind at Large*, Scribner, New York.
Bachrach, Peter (1969), *The Theory of Democratic Elitism: A Critique*, 2nd edn, Univ. of London Pr., London.
Bachrach, Peter and Morton S. Baratz (1962), 'The Two Faces of Power', *American Political Science Review*, vol. 56, pp. 942-52.
Baer, Michael A., Malcolm E. Jewel and Lee Sigelman (eds) (1991), *Political Science in America: Oral Histories of a Discipline*, Univ. Pr. of Kentucky, Lexington.
Barber, Benjamin R. (1984), *Strong Democracy: Participatory Politics for a New Age*, Univ. of California Pr., Berkeley.
Barker, Ernest (1918), *Greek Political Theory: Plato and His Predecessors*, Methuen, London.
Barker, Ernest (1937), *The Citizen's Choice*, Cambridge Univ. Pr., Cambridge.
Barker, Ernest (1942), *Reflections on Government*, Oxford Univ. Pr., London.
Barker, Ernest (1948a), *National Character* [1927], 4th edn, Methuen, London.
Barker, Ernest (1948b), *Traditions of Civility*, Cambridge Univ. Pr., Cambridge.
Barker, Ernest (1951), *Essays on Government* [1945], 2nd edn, Clarendon Pr., Oxford.

Barker, Ernest (1953), *Age and Youth*, Oxford Univ. Pr., London.
Barker, Ernest (1957), *Church, State and Education* [1930], 2nd edn, Univ. of Michigan Pr., Ann Arbor.
Barker, Ernest (1959), *The Political Thought of Plato and Aristotle* [1906], Russell and Russell, New York.
Barker, Ernest (1961), *Principles of Social and Political Theory* [1951], 2nd edn, Oxford Univ. Pr., Oxford.
Barker, Rodney and Xenia Howard-Johnston (1975), 'The Politics and Political Ideas of Moisei Ostrogorski', *Political Studies*, vol 23, pp. 415-29.
Barraclough, Geoffrey (1967), *An Introduction to Contemporary History*, 2nd edn, Penguin Books, Harmondsworth.
Barry, N.P. (1979), *Hayek's Social and Economic Philosophy*, Macmillan, London.
Barry, Norman P. (1987), *The New Right*, Croom Helm, London.
Bealey, Frank (1988), *Democracy in the Contemporary State*, Clarendon Pr., Oxford.
Beattie, Alan (ed.) (1970), *English Party Politics, Volume I, 1660-1906*, Weidenfeld and Nicolson, London.
Beer, Max (1957), *The General History of Socialism and Social Struggles*, Russell and Russell, New York.
Beetham, David (ed.) (1994), *Defining and Measuring Democracy*, Sage, London.
Beiner, Ronald (1983), *Political Judgement*, Methuen, London.
Bell, Daniel (1962), *The End of Ideology*, 2nd edn, Free Pr., New York.
Bellamy, Richard (1987), *Modern Italian Social Theory*, Polity Pr., Cambridge.
Bellamy, Richard (1992), *Liberalism and Modern Society*, Polity Pr., Cambridge.
Belz, Herman (1974), 'New Left Reverberations in the Academy', *Review of Politics*, vol. 36, 1974, pp. 265-83.
Benda, Julien (1969), *The Treason of the Intellectuals* [1927], 2nd Eng. edn, Norton, New York.
Benn, S.I. and R.S. Peters (1959), *Social Principles and the Democratic State*, Allen and Unwin, London.
Bentley, Arthur F. (1967), *The Process of Government* [1908], (ed.) Peter H. Odegard, Harvard Univ. Pr., Cambridge, Mass.
Berger, Fred R. (1984), *Happiness, Justice and Freedom: The Moral and Political Philosophy of John Stuart Mill*, Univ. of California Pr., Berkeley.
Berlin, Isaiah (1969), *Four Essays on Liberty*, Oxford Univ. Pr., Oxford.
Berlin, Isaiah (1990), *The Crooked Timber of Humanity*, John Murray, London.
Berlin, Isaiah and Bernard Williams (1994), 'Pluralism and Liberalism: a Reply', *Political Studies*, vol. 42, pp. 306-9.
Berns, Walter (1984), *In Defence of Liberal Democracy*, Gateway, Chicago.
Bernstein, Richard (1994), *Dictatorship of Virtue: Multiculturalism and the Battle for America's Future*, Knopf, New York.
Berry, Jeffrey M. (1989), *The Interest Group Society*, 2nd edn, Scott, Foresman, Glenview, Ill.

Bingham, June (1972), *Courage to Change: An Introduction to the Life and Thought of Reinhold Niebuhr*, 2nd edn, Scribner, New York.
Birch, Anthony H. (1993), *The Concepts and Theories of Modern Democracy*, Routledge, London.
Bloom, Allan (1988), *The Closing of the American Mind*, 2nd edn, Penguin Books, London.
Bloom, Allan (ed.) (1990), *Confronting the Constitution*, AEI [American Enterprise Institute], Washington D.C.
Bloom, Allan (1990), *Giants and Dwarfs: Essays 1960-1990*, Simon and Schuster, New York.
Blum, D. Steven (1984), *Walter Lippmann: Cosmopolitanism in the Century of Total War*, Cornell Univ. Pr., Ithaca.
Blum, John Morton (ed.) (1985), *Public Philosopher: Selected Letters of Walter Lippmann*, Ticknor and Fields, New York.
Bobbio, Norberto (1987), *The Future of Democracy*, (ed.) Richard Bellamy, Polity Pr., Cambridge.
Bosanquet, Bernard (1923), *The Philosophical Theory of the State* [1899], 4th edn, Macmillan, London.
Bottomore, T.B. (1966), *Elites and Society*, 2nd edn, Penguin Books, Harmondsworth.
Brecht, Arnold (1959) *Political Theory: The Foundations of Twentieth Century Political Thought*, Princeton Univ. Pr., Princeton, New Jersey.
Breitling, Rupert (1980), 'The Concept of Pluralism', in Stanislaw Ehrlich and Graham Wootton (eds), *Three Faces of Pluralism: Political, Economic and Religious*, Gower, London.
Brittan, Samuel (1975), *Participation Without Politics*, Institute of Economic Affairs, London.
Brittan, Samuel (1977), *The Economic Consequences of Democracy*, Temple Smith, London.
Brittan, Samuel (1988), *A Restatement of Economic Liberalism*, Macmillan, Basingstoke.
Bryce, James (1909), *The Hindrances to Good Citizenship*, Yale Univ. Pr., New Haven.
Buchanan, James M. and Robert D. Tollison (eds) (1984), *The Theory of Public Choice - II*, Univ. of Michigan Pr., Ann Arbor.
Buchanan, James M. and Gordon Tullock (1962), *The Calculus of Consent: Logical Foundations of Constitutional Democracy*, Univ. of Michigan Pr., Ann Arbor.
Burke, Edmund (1968), *Reflections on the Revolution in France* [1790], (ed.) Conor Cruise O'Brien, Penguin Books, Harmondsworth.
Burnham, James (1943), *The Machiavellians*, Putnam, London.
Burnham, James (1945), *The Managerial Revolution* [1941], 3rd edn, Penguin Books, Harmondsworth.

Burnham, James (1947), *The Struggle for the World*, Cape, London.
Burnham, James (1959), *Congress and the American Tradition*, Henry Regnery, Chicago.
Burnham, James (1965), *The Suicide of the West* [1964], 2nd edn, Cape, London.
Burnheim, John (1985), *Is Democracy Possible?: The Alternative to Electoral Politics*, Polity Pr., Cambridge.
Burns, J.H. (1969), 'J. S. Mill and Democracy, 1829-61', in J.B. Schneewind (ed.), *Mill: A Collection of Critical Essays*, 2nd edn, Macmillan, London.
Butler, Eamonn (1984), *Hayek's Contribution to the Political and Economic Thought of Our Time*, Temple Smith, London.
Cawson, Alan (1982), *Corporatism and Welfare*, Heinemann, London.
Cawson, Alan (1986), *Corporatism and Political Theory*, Blackwell, Oxford.
Ceaser, James W. (1990), *Liberal Democracy and Political Science*, John Hopkins Univ. Pr., Baltimore.
Chambers Twentieth Century Dictionary (1973), (ed.) A.M. Macdonald, 2nd edn, Chambers, Edinburgh.
Childs, Marquis and James Reston (eds) (1959), *Walter Lippmann and His Times*, Harcourt Brace, New York.
Churchill, Winston S. (1930), *My Early Life*, Thornton Butterworth, London.
Churchill, Winston Spencer (1973), *Liberalism and the Social Problem*, Haskell House, New York, a reprint of a 1909 edn.
Cigler, Allan J. and Burdett A. Loomis (eds) (1995), *Interest Group Politics*, 4th edn, CQ [Congressional Quarterly] Pr., Washington, D.C.
Cohn, Norman (1970), *The Pursuit of the Millenium*, 2nd edn, Temple Smith, London.
Cohn-Bendit, Gabriel and Daniel (1969), *Obsolete Communism: The Left Wing Alternative*, 2nd edn, Penguin Books, Harmondsworth.
Cole, G.D.H. (1920), *Guild Socialism Re-Stated*, Leonard Parsons, London.
Collini, Stefan (1979), *Liberalism and Sociology: L. T. Hobhouse and Political Argument in England, 1880-1914*, Cambridge Univ. Pr., Cambridge.
Connolly, William E. (ed.) (1969), *The Bias of Pluralism*, Atherton Pr., New York.
Cowling, Maurice (1963), *Mill and Liberalism*, Cambridge Univ. Pr., Cambridge.
Cranston, Maurice W. (ed.) (1970), *The New Left: Six Critical Essays*, Bodley Head, London.
Crick, Bernard (1959), *The American Science of Politics*, Routledge, London.
Crosland, C.A.R., (1964), *The Future of Socialism* [1956], 2nd edn, Cape, London.
Crouch, Colin (1983), 'Pluralism and the New Corporatism', *Political Studies*, vol. 31, pp. 452-60.
Crowder, George (1991), *Classical Anarchism: The Political Thought of Godwin, Proudhon, Bakunin and Kropotkin*, Clarendon Pr., Oxford.
Crowder, George (1994), 'Pluralism and Liberalism', *Political Studies*, vol. 42, pp. 293-305.
Crowder, George (1998), 'John Gray's Pluralist Critique of Liberalism', *Journal of*

Applied Philosophy, vol. 15, pp. 290-8.

Culf, Andrew (1993), 'Editors Scorn MPs' Proposed Press Safeguards', *Guardian Weekly*, April 4.

Dahl, Robert A. (1956), *Preface to Democratic Theory*, Univ. of Chicago Pr., Chicago.

Dahl, Robert A. (1970), *After the Revolution*, Yale Univ. Pr., New Haven.

Dahl, Robert A. (1986), *Democracy, Liberty and Equality*, Norwegian Univ. Pr., Oslo.

Dahl, Robert A. (1989), *Democracy and Its Critics*, Yale Univ. Pr., New Haven.

Daniels, Norman (ed.) (1975), *Reading Rawls*, Blackwell, Oxford.

Davis, J.C. (1984), 'The History of Utopia...', in Peter Alexander and Roger Gill (eds), *Utopias*, Duckworth, London.

The Dictionary of National Biography 1951-1960 (1971), (eds) E.T. Williams and Helen M. Palmer, Oxford Univ. Pr., Oxford.

Doering, Bernard E. (1983), *Jacques Maritain and the French Catholic Intellectuals*, Univ. of Notre Dame Pr., Notre Dame.

Douglass, R. Bruce and David Hollenbach (eds) (1994), *Catholicism and Liberalism: Contributions to American Public Philosophy*, Cambridge Univ. Pr., Cambridge.

Downs, Anthony (1957), *An Economic Theory of Democracy*, Harper and Row, New York.

Drescher, Seymour (1968a), *Dilemmas of Democracy: Tocqueville and Modernization*, Univ. of Pittsburgh Pr., Pittsburgh.

Drescher, Seymour (ed.) (1968b), *Tocqueville and Beaumont on Social Reform*, Harper and Row, New York.

Drucker, Peter F. (1989), *The New Realities*, Harper and Row, New York.

D'Souza, Dinesh (1991), *Illiberal Education: The Politics of Race and Sex on Campus*, Free Pr., New York.

Dunant, Sarah (ed.) (1994), *The War of the Words: The Political Correctness Debate*, Virago, London.

Duncan, Graeme (ed.) (1989), *Democracy and the Capitalist State*, Cambridge Univ. Pr., Cambridge.

Dunn, John (1974), 'Review Article: Democracy Unretrieved, or the Political Theory of Professor Macpherson', *British Journal of Political Science*, vol. 4, pp. 489-99.

Dunn, John (1979), *Western Political Theory in the Face of the Future*, Cambridge Univ. Pr., Cambridge.

Dunn, John (1990), *Interpreting Political Responsibility: Essays 1981-1989*, Polity Pr., Cambridge.

Dunn, John (ed) (1992), *Democracy: The Unfinished Journey 508 BC to AD 1993*, Oxford Univ. Pr., Oxford.

Duverger, Maurice (1972), *Party Politics and Pressure Groups*, Crowell, New York.

Dworkin, Ronald (1977), *Taking Rights Seriously*, Duckworth, London.
The Economist (1997), 'Survey of the World Economy', September 20-26.
Ehrlich, Stanislaw (1982), *Pluralism On and Off Course*, Pergamon Pr., Oxford.
Ehrlich, Stanislaw and Graham Wootton (eds) (1980), *Three Faces of Pluralism: Political, Economic and Religious*, Gower, London.
Eidelberg, Paul (1969), 'The Temptation of Herbert Marcuse', *Review of Politics*, vol. 31, pp. 442-58.
Eliot, T.S. (1948), *Notes Towards the Definition of Culture*, Faber and Faber, London.
Etzioni-Halevy, Eva (1989), *Fragile Democracy*, Transaction Publishers, New Brunswick.
Etzioni-Halevy, Eva (1993), *The Elite Connection: Problems and Potential of Western Democracy*, Polity Pr., Cambridge.
Evans, Joseph W. (ed.) (1963), *Jacques Maritain: The Man and His Achievement*, Sheed and Ward, New York.
Fachre, G. (1970), *The Promise of Reinhold Niebuhr*, Lippincott, Philadelphia.
Field, G. Lowell and John Higley (1980), *Elitism*, Routledge, London.
Finnis, John (1980), *Natural Law and Natural Rights*, Clarendon Pr., Oxford.
Fisher, Herbert (1924), *The Common Weal*, Clarendon Pr., Oxford.
Fox, Richard Wightman (1987), *Reinhold Niebuhr: A Biography*, 2nd edn, Harper and Row, San Francisco.
Frances, Samuel T. (1984), *Power and History: the Political Thought of James Burnham*, Univ. Pr. of America, New York.
Freeden, Michael (1978), *The New Liberalism: An Ideology of Social Reform*, Oxford Univ. Pr., Oxford.
Friedman, Marilyn and Jan Narveson, (1995), *Political Correctness: For and Against*, Rowman and Littlefield, Lanham, Md.
Friedman, Milton (1962), *Capitalism and Freedom*, Univ. of Chicago Pr.
Friedman, Milton and Rose (1980), *Free to Choose*, Harcourt Brace Jovanovich, New York.
Friedrich, Carl J. (1950), *Constitutional Government and Democracy: Theory and Practice in Europe and America* [1937], 4th edn, Blaisdell, New York.
Fukuyama, Francis (1989), 'The End of History?', *The National Interest*, No. 16, pp. 3-18.
Fukuyama, Francis (1990), 'The "End of History" Debate' [1989-90], *Dialogue*, No. 89, March.
Fukuyama, Francis (1992), *The End of History and the Last Man*, Hamish Hamilton, London.
Galbraith, John Kenneth (1972), *The New Industrial State* [1967], 2nd edn, Deutsch, London.
Galston, William A. (1980), *Justice and the Human Good*, Univ. of Chicago Pr., Chicago.
Galston, William (1982), 'Defending Liberalism', *American Political Science*

Review, vol. 76, pp. 621-9.
Garforth. F.W. (1980), *Educative Democracy*, Oxford Univ. Pr., Oxford.
Garson, G. David (1974), 'On the Origins of Interest-Group Theory', *American Political Science Review*, vol. 68, pp. 1505-19.
Georghegan, Vincent (1987), *Utopianism and Marxism*, Methuen, London.
Gerth, H.H. and C. Wright Mills (eds) (1970), *From Max Weber: Essays in Sociology* [1948], 2nd edn, Routledge, London.
Goldman, Emma (1969), *Anarchism and Other Essays* [1919], 3rd edn, reprinted, Dover, New York.
Goldstein, Doris S. (1975), *Trial of Faith: Religion and Politics in Tocqueville's Thought*, Elsevier, New York.
Gombin, Richard (1975), *The Origins of Modern Leftism*, Penguin Books, Harmondsworth.
Goodin, Robert E. (1995), *Utilitarianism as a Public Philosophy*, Cambridge Univ. Pr., Cambridge.
Goodin, Robert E. and Philip Pettit (eds) (1993), *A Companion to Contemporary Political Philosophy*, Blackwell, Oxford.
Gordon, Peter and John White (1979), *Philosophers as Educational Reformers*, Routledge, London.
Gould, Carol C. (1988), *Rethinking Democracy,* Cambridge Univ. Pr., Cambridge.
Graham, B.D. (1993), *Representation and Party Politics: A Comparative Perspective*, Blackwell, Oxford.
Gray, John (1994), *Beyond the New Right*, Routledge, London.
Gray, John (1995), *Isaiah Berlin*, Harper Collins, London.
Green, Philip (1985), *Retrieving Democracy: In Search of Civic Equality*, Methuen, London.
Green, T.H. (1964), *The Political Theory of T. H. Green*, (ed.) J.R. Rodman, Appleton-Century-Crofts, New York.
Green, T.H. (1986), *Lectures on the Principles of Political Obligation* [1882] *and Other Writings*, (eds) Paul Harris and John Morrow, Cambridge Univ. Pr., Cambridge.
Gutmann, Amy (1993), 'Democracy', in Robert E. Goodin and Philip Pettit (eds), *A Companion to Contemporary Political Philosophy*, Blackwell, Oxford.
Haldane, Richard Burdon (1928), *An Autobiography*, Hodder and Stoughton, London.
Halevy, Elie (1928), *The Growth of Philosophic Radicalism*, Faber and Faber, London.
Hamburger, Joseph (1965), *Intellectuals in Politics: John Stuart Mill and the Philosophic Radicals*, Yale Univ. Pr., New Haven.
Hamilton, Alexander, James Madison and John Jay (1971), *The Federalist* [1787-88], Dent/Everyman, London.
Harrison, R.J. (1980), *Pluralism and Corporatism: the Evolution of Modern Democracy*, Allen and Unwin, Winchester, Mass.

Hayek, Friedrich A. (1960), *The Constitution of Liberty*, Routledge, London.
Hayek, Friedrich A. (1973, 1976 and 1979), *Law, Legislation and Liberty*, 3 vols, Routledge, London.
Heater, Derek (1990), *The Civic Ideal in World History, Politics and Education*, Longman, London.
Heertje, Arnold (ed.) (1981), *Schumpeter's Vision: Capitalism, Socialism and Democracy after Forty Years*, Praeger, Eastbourne and New York.
Held, David (1987), *Models of Democracy*, Polity Pr., Cambridge.
Held, David (1989), *Political Theory and the Modern State*, Polity Pr., Cambridge.
Held, David (ed.) (1993). *Prospects for Democracy: North, South, East, West*, Polity Pr., Cambridge.
Hereth, Michael (1986), *Alexis de Tocqueville: Threats to Freedom in Democracy*, Duke Univ. Pr., Durham.
Higley, John (1992), 'Neo-Elite Theory and Democratic Doctrine: A Comment on Wintrop', *Australian Journal of Political Science*, vol. 27, pp. 522-6
Higley, John, Desley Deacon and Don Smart et al (1979), *Elites in Australia*, Routledge, London.
Himmelfarb, Gertrude (1974), *On Liberty and Liberalism: The Case of John Stuart Mill*, Knopf, New York.
Hindess, Barry (1997), 'Democracy and Disenchantment', *Australian Journal of Political Science*, vol. 32, pp. 79-92.
Hirst, Paul Q. (ed.) (1989), *The Pluralist Theory of the State: Selected Writings of G.D.H. Cole, J.N. Figgis, and H.J. Laski*, Routledge, London.
Hobhouse, L.T. (1904), *Democracy and Reaction*, Fisher Unwin, London.
Hobhouse, L.T. (1964), *Liberalism* [1911], 2nd edn, Oxford Univ. Pr., Oxford.
Hobson, J.A. (1902), *Imperialism*, Fisher Allen, London.
Hobson, J.A. (1976), *Confessions of an Economic Heretic*, 2nd edn, Harvester Pr., Brighton.
Holden, Barry (1974), *The Nature of Democracy*, Nelson, London.
Holden, Barry (1988), *Understanding Liberal Democracy*, Philip Allan, Oxford.
Huntford, Roland (1971), *The New Totalitarians*, Allen Lane, London.
Huxley, Aldous (1955), *Brave New World* [1932], Penguin Books, Harmondsworth.
Jacobs, Struan (1993), 'John Stuart Mill and the Tyranny of the Majority', *Australian Journal of Political Science*, vol. 28, 1993, pp. 306-21.
Jardin, Andre (1988), *Tocqueville: A Biography*, Peter Halban, London.
Jones, Henry (1905), *Social Responsibilities*, James Maclehose, Glascow.
Jones, Nicholas (1995), *Soundbites and Spin Doctors: How Politicians Manipulate the Media and Vice Versa*, Cassell, London.
Jordan, Grant (1990), 'The Pluralism of Pluralism: An Anti-theory', *Political Studies*, vol. 38, pp. 286-301.
Kariel, Henry S. (1961), *The Decline of American Pluralism*, Stanford Univ. Pr., Stanford.

Keller, Suzanne (1963), *Beyond the Ruling Class*, Random House, New York.
Keller, Suzanne (1968), 'Elites', *International Encyclopedia of the Social Sciences*, (ed.) David L. Sills, vol. 5.
Kelso, William Alton (1978), *American Democratic Theory: Pluralism and Its Critics*, Greenwood Pr., Westport.
Key Jr, V.O. (1964), *Politics, Parties, and Pressure Groups*, 5th edn, Crowell, New York.
Keynes, John Maynard (1972), *The Collected Writings of John Maynard Keynes*, vol 9, *Essays in Persuasion* [1931], Macmillan, London.
Kimball, Roger (1990), *Tenured Radicals*, Harper and Row, New York.
King, Preston (ed.) (1977), *The Study of Politics: A Collection of Inaugural Lectures*, Frank Cass, London.
Kolakowski, Leszek (1990), *Modernity on Endless Trial*, Univ. of Chicago Pr., Chicago.
Kornhauser, William (1960), *The Politics of Mass Society*, 2nd edn, Routledge, London.
Krugman, Paul (1994), *Peddling Prosperity*, Norton, New York.
Kuang Chuan Hsiao (1927), *Political Pluralism*, Kegan Paul, Trench, Trubner, London.
Kukathas, Chandran (1989), *Hayek and Modern Liberalism*, Oxford Univ. Pr., Oxford.
Kukathas, Chandran, David Lovell and William Maley (1990), *The Theory of Politics: An Australian Perspective*, Longman Cheshire, Melbourne.
Kukathas, Chandran and Philip Pettit (1990), *Rawls: A 'Theory of Justice'*, Stanford Univ. Pr., Stanford, Ca.
Kymlicka, Will (1990), *Contemporary Political Philosophy: An Introduction*, Clarendon Pr., Oxford.
Lasch, Christopher (1995), *The Revolt of the Elites and the Betrayal of Democracy*, Norton, New York.
Lasky, Melvin J. (1977), *Utopia and Revolution*, 2nd edn, Macmillan, London.
Levitas, Ruth (1990), *The Concept of Utopia*, Philip Allan, New York.
Lijphart, Arend (1977), *Democracy in Plural Societies*, Yale Univ. Pr., New Haven.
Lijphart, Arend et al, (1994), *Electoral Systems and Party Systems: A Study of Twenty-Six Democracies 1945-1990*, Oxford Univ. Pr., Oxford.
Lindsay, A.D. (1935), *The Essentials of Democracy* [1929], 2nd edn, Clarendon Pr., Oxford.
Lindsay, A.D. (1962), *The Modern Democratic State* [1943], 2nd edn, Oxford Univ. Pr., London.
Linz, Juan J. (1997), 'Democracy Today: An Agenda for Students of Democracy', *Scandinavian Political Studies*, vol. 20, pp. 115-32.
Lippmann, Walter (1925), *The Phantom Public*, Harcourt Brace, New York.
Lippmann, Walter (1929), *A Preface to Morals*, Macmillan, New York.

Lippmann, Walter (1943), *The Good Society* [1936], 3rd edn, Grosset and Dunlap, New York.
Lippmann, Walter (1955), *Essays in the Public Philosophy*, New American Library/Mentor, New York, a paperback edn of a Little, Brown, 1955, hardcover edn.
Lippmann, Walter (1960), *Public Opinion* [1922], 2nd edn, Macmillan, New York.
Lipset, Seymour Martin (ed.) (1995), *The Encyclopedia of Democracy*, 4 vols, Routledge, London.
Lipson, Leslie (1969) *The Democratic Civilization*, 2nd edn, Oxford Univ. Pr., London.
Lively, Jack (1962), *The Social and Political Thought of Alexis de Tocqueville*, Clarendon Pr., Oxford.
Lively, Jack (1975), *Democracy*, Blackwell, Oxford.
Locke, John (1993), *Two Treatises of Government* [1690], (ed.) Mark Goldie, Dent/Everyman, London
Loeb, Paul Rogat (1994), *Generation at the Crossroads*, Rutgers Univ. Pr., New Brunswick, N.J.
Lowi, Theodore J. (1979), *The End of Liberalism* [1969], 2nd edn, Norton, New York.
Lucas, J.R. (1980) *On Justice*, Clarendon Pr., Oxford.
Lukes, Steven (1974), *Power: A Radical View*, Macmillan, London.
Lukes, Steven (1977), *Essays in Social Theory*, Macmillan, London.
Lukes, Steven (1984), 'Marxism and Utopianism', in Peter Alexander and Roger Gill (eds), *Utopias*, Duckworth, London.
Lukes, Steven (1993), 'Five Fables about Human Rights', in Stephen Shute and Susan Hurley (eds), *On Human Rights*, Basic Books/Harper Collins, New York.
Luskin, John (1972), *Lippmann, Liberty and the Press*, Univ. of Alabama Pr., Alabama.
Maccunn, John (1894), *Ethics of Citizenship*, James Maclehose, Glascow.
MacIntyre, Alasdair (1970), *Marcuse*, Fontana/Collins, London.
Macpherson, C.B. (1966), *The Real World of Democracy*, Clarendon Press, Oxford.
Macpherson, C.B. (1973), *Democratic Theory: Essays in Retrieval*, Clarendon Pr., Oxford.
Macpherson, C.B. (1977), *The Life and Times of Liberal Democracy*, Oxford Univ. Pr., Oxford.
Macpherson, C.B. (1989), 'Do We Need a Theory of the State?', in Graeme Duncan (ed.), *Democracy and the Capitalist State*, Cambridge Univ. Pr., Cambridge.
Maddox, Graham (1986), 'The Christian Democracy of A. D. Lindsay', *Political Studies*, vol. 34, pp. 441-55.
Maddox, Graham (1986), 'Contours of a Democratic Polity', *Politics* (Canberra), vol. 21, No. 2, pp. 1-11.
Manent, Pierre (1996), *Tocqueville and the Nature of Democracy*, Rowman and

Littlefield, Lanham, Md.
Mannheim, Karl (1936), *Ideology and Utopia*, Routledge, London.
Mansbridge, Jane J. (1980), *Beyond Adversary Democracy*, Basic Books, New York
Manuel, Frank E. and Fritzie P. (1979), *Utopian Thought in the Western World*, Harvard Univ. Pr., Cambridge, Mass.
Maritain, Jacques (1945), *Christianity and Democracy*, Bles, London.
Maritain, Jacques (1953), *The Range of Reason*, Bles, London.
Maritain, Jacques (1955), *The Social and Political Philosophy of Jacques Maritain: Selected Writings*, (eds) Joseph W. Evans and Leo R. Ward, Sheed and Ward, New York.
Maritain, Jacques (1956), *Man and the State* [1951], 2nd edn, Univ. of Chicago Pr./Phoenix Books, Chicago.
Maritain, Jacques (1959), *The Degrees of Knowledge*, 2nd Eng. edn, Bles, London.
Maritain, Jacques (1966), *Challenges and Renewals*, (eds) Joseph W. Evans and Leo R. Ward, Univ. of Notre Dame Pr., Notre Dame.
Maritain, Jacques (1968), *The Peasant of the Garonne: An Old Layman Questions Himself about the Present Time*, Holt Rinehart and Winston, New York.
Maritain, Jacques (1972), *The Person and the Common Good* [1946], 3rd edn, Univ. of Notre Dame Pr., Notre Dame.
Maritain, Jacques (1975), *Reflections on America*, Scribner, New York.
Marshall, Geoffrey (1971), *Constitutional Theory*, Clarendon Pr., Oxford.
Marshall, T.H. and Tom Bottomore (1992), *Citizenship and Social Class*, Pluto Pr., London.
Mayer, J.P. (1960), *Alexis de Tocqueville: A Biographical Study in Political Science*, 2nd edn, Harper, New York.
Mayo, Henry B. (1960), *An Introduction to Democratic Theory*, Oxford Univ. Pr., New York.
Mazlish, Bruce (1975), *James and John Stuart Mill*, Hutchinson, London.
McCoy, C.A. and John Playford (eds) (1967), *Apolitical Politics*, Crowell, New York.
McIlwain, C.H. (1939), *Constitutionalism and the Changing World: Collected Papers*, Cambridge Univ. Pr., Cambridge.
McIlwain, Charles Howard (1947), *Constitutionalism: Ancient and Modern*, 2nd edn, Cornell Univ. Pr., Ithaca, N.Y.
McKenzie, Robert (1963), *British Political Parties*, 2nd edn, Heinemann/Mercury, London.
McLean, Iain (1987), *Public Choice: an Introduction*, Blackwell, Oxford.
Meisel, James H. (1958), *The Myth of the Ruling Class: Gaetano Mosca and the 'Elite'*, Univ. of Michigan Pr., Ann Arbor.
Meny, Yves (1990), *Government and Politics in Western Europe*, Oxford Univ. Pr., Oxford.
Merkley, Paul (1975), *Reinhold Niebuhr: A Political Account*, McGill-Queens

Univ., Pr., Montreal.
Meynaud, Jean (1968), *Technocracy*, Faber and Faber, London.
Michels, Robert (1959), *Political Parties* [1911], 2nd Eng. edn, Dover, New York.
Miliband, Ralph (1969), *The State in Capitalist Society*, Weidenfeld and Nicolson, London.
Mill, John Stuart (1964), *Autobiography* [1873], Foreword Asa Briggs, New American Library/Signet, New York.
Mill, John Stuart (1967), *Chapters on Socialism* [1879], in the *Collected Works of John Stuart Mill*, (ed.) J.M. Robson, vol 5, Univ. of Toronto Pr., Toronto.
Mill, John Stuart (1973), *Essays on Politics and Culture*, (ed.) Gertrude Himmelfarb, 3rd edn, Peter Smith, Gloucester, Mass.
Mill, John Stuart (1987), *Principles of Political Economy* [1848], new edn, (ed.) Sir William Ashley, Longmans, Green, London, 1909, reprinted Augustus M. Kelley, Fairfield, N.J.
Mill, John Stuart (1991), *On Liberty and Other Essays*, (ed.) John Gray, Oxford Univ. Pr., Oxford.
Mill, John Stuart (1993), *Utilitarianism, On Liberty, Considerations on Representative Government, Remarks on Bentham's Philosophy*, (ed.) Geraint Williams, Dent/Everyman, London.
Miller, Abraham H., (1993), 'Political Correctness and American Higher Education', *Politics*, vol. 13, No. 1, pp. 22-28.
Mills, C. Wright (1959), *The Power Elite* [1956], 2nd edn, Oxford Univ. Pr./Galaxy, New York.
Milne, A.J. (1962), *The Social Philosophy of English Idealism*, Allen and Unwin, London.
Mises, Ludwig von (1951), *Socialism: An Economic and Sociological Analysis* [1922], 4th Eng. edn, Yale Univ. Pr., New Haven.
Molnar, Thomas (1972), *Utopia: The Perennial Heresy*, Tom Stacey, London.
Moody Jr, Peter R. (1983), 'The Erosion of the Function of Political Parties in the Post-Liberal State', *Review of Politics*, vol. 45, pp. 254-79.
Morrise, David (1993), 'Philosophical Errors of Political Correctness', *Politics*, vol. 13, No. 2, pp. 32-7.
Mosca, Gaetano (1939), *The Ruling Class* [1923], first Eng. edn, McGraw Hill, New York.
Mosca, Gaetano (1972), *A Short History of Political Philosophy* [1937], first Eng. edn, Crowell, New York.
Mowat, Charles Lock (1961), *The Charity Organisation Society, 1869-1913*, Methuen, London.
Mueller, Dennis C. (1989), *Public Choice II*, Cambridge Univ. Pr., Cambridge.
Nicholls, D. (1974), *Three Varieties of Pluralism*, Macmillan, London.
Niebuhr, Reinhold (1941 and 1943), *The Nature and Destiny of Man: A Christian Interpretation*, 2 vols, Nisbet, London.
Niebuhr, Reinhold (1960), *The Children of Light and the Children of Darkness*

[1944], 2nd edn, Scribner, New York.
Niebuhr, Reinhold (1966), *Man's Nature and His Communities*, Bles, London.
Niebuhr, Reinhold (1986), *The Essential Reinhold Niebuhr*, (ed.) Robert McAfee Brown, Yale Univ. Pr., New Haven.
Niebuhr, Reinhold and Paul E. Sigmund (1969), *The Democratic Experience*, Pall Mall Pr., London.
Nisbet, Robert (1976), *Twilight of Authority*, Heinemann, London.
Niskanen Jr, William A. (1971), *Bureaucracy and Representative Government*, Aldine/Atherton, Chicago.
Novak, Michael (1981), 'The Economic System: the Evangelical Basis of a Social Market Economy', *Review of Politics*, vol. 43, pp. 355-80.
Nozick, Robert (1974), *Anarchy, State, and Utopia*, Basic Books, New York.
Oakeshott, Michael (1967), *Rationalism in Politics and Other Essays*, 2nd edn, Methuen, London.
Oglesby, Carl (ed.) (1969), *The New Left Reader*, Grove Press, New York.
Olson Jr, Mancur (1965), *The Logic of Collective Actions: Public Goods and the Theory of Groups*, Harvard Univ. Pr., Cambridge, Mass.
Olson, Mancur (1986), *The Rise and Decline of Nations*, Yale Univ. Pr., New Haven.
Ordeshook, Peter C. (1986), *Game Theory and Political Theory*, Cambridge Univ. Pr., Cambridge.
Orwell, George (1954), *Nineteen Eighty-Four* [1949], Penguin Books, Harmondsworth.
Ortega y Gasset, Jose (1946), *Mission of the University* [1930], first Eng. edn, Routledge, London.
Ortega y Gasset, Jose (1961), *The Revolt of the Masses* [1930], 3rd Eng. edn, Allen and Unwin, London.
Ostrogorski, M. (1970), *Democracy and the Organization of Political Parties*, 2 vols [1902], reprinted, Haskell House Publishers, New York.
Owen, John E. (1974), *L. T. Hobhouse: Sociologist*, Nelson, London.
Packe, Michael St. John (1954), *The Life of John Stuart Mill*, Secker and Warburg, London.
Paglia, Camille (1993), *Sex, Art, and American Culture*, 2nd edn, Viking/Penguin Books, London.
Paglia, Camille (1994), *Vamps and Tramps*, Viking/Penguin Books, London.
Pahl, R.E. and T.J Winkler (1974), 'The Coming Corporatism', *New Society*, Oct. 10.
Panitch, Leo (1981), 'Liberal Democracy and Socialist Democracy: The Antinomies of C. B. Macpherson', in *The Socialist Register 1981*, (eds) Ralph Miliband and John Saville, Merlin Pr., London.
Parekh, Bhiku (1993), 'The Cultural Particularity of Liberal Democracy', in David Held (ed.), *Prospects for Democracy*, Polity Pr., Cambridge.
Parekh, Bhiku (1994), 'Cultural Diversity and Liberal Democracy', in David

Beetham (ed.), *Defining and Measuring Democracy*, Sage, London.
Pareto, Vilfredo (1963), *The Mind and Society* [1916], 4 vols in 2, (ed.) A. Livingston, 2nd Eng. edn, Dover, New York.
Pareto, Vilfredo (1966), *Sociological Writings*, (ed.) S.E. Finer, Pall Mall Pr., London.
Parry, Geraint (1969), *Political Elites*, Allen and Unwin, London.
Passerin d'Entreves, A. (1951), *Natural Law*, Hutchinson, London.
Pateman, Carole (1970), *Participation in Democratic Theory*, Cambridge Univ. Pr., Cambridge.
Pennock, J. Roland (1979), *Democratic Political Theory*, Princeton Univ. Pr., Princeton, N.J.
Pickles, Dorothy (1971), *Democracy* [1970], 2nd edn, Methuen, London.
Pitkin, Hanna Fenichel (1969), *The Concept of Representation*, Univ. of California Pr., Berkeley.
Plamenatz, John (1963), *Man and Society: A Critical Examination of Some Important Social and Political Theories from Machiavelli to Marx*, 2 vols, Longman, London.
Plamenatz, John (1977), *Democracy and Illusion* [1973], 2nd edn, Longman, London.
Plamenatz, John (1993), *Man and Society: Political and Social Theories from Machiavelli to Marx*, 3 vols, Longman, London.
Plato, (1959), *Gorgias: A Revised Text with Introduction and Commentary*, (ed.) E.R. Dodds, Oxford Univ. Pr., Oxford.
Plato, *The Republic* (1992), (ed.) Terence Irwin, 2nd edn, Dent/Everyman, London.
Plumb, J.H. (1973), *The Death of the Past*, 2nd edn, Penguin Books, Harmondsworth.
Pombeni, Paolo (1994), 'Starting in Reason, Ending in Passion: Bryce, Lowell, Ostrogorski and the Problem of Democracy', *The Historical Journal*, vol 37, pp. 319-41.
Popper, Karl R. (1963), *Conjectures and Refutations*, Routledge, London.
Powers, Charles H. (1987), *Vilfredo Pareto*, Sage, Newbury Park.
Purcell Jr, Edward A. (1973), *The Crisis of Democratic Theory: Scientific Naturalism and the Problem of Value*, Univ. Pr. of Kentucky, Lexington.
Quinton, Anthony (1993), 'Conservatism', in Robert E. Goodin and Philip Pettit (eds), *A Companion to Contemporary Political Philosophy*, Blackwell, Oxford.
Rand, Ayn (1971), *The New Left: The Anti-Industrial Revolution*, New American Library/Signet, New York.
Rawls, John (1973), *A Theory of Justice* [1972], 2nd edn, Oxford Univ. Pr., Oxford.
Rawls, John (1993), *Political Liberalism*, Columbia Univ. Pr., New York.
Rejai, M. (ed.) (1967), *Democracy: The Contemporary Theories*, Atherton Pr., New York.
Richter, Melvin (1964), *The Politics of Conscience: T. H. Green and His Age*,

Weidenfeld and Nicolson, London.
Richter, Melvin (1968), 'Lindsay, A. D.', *International Encyclopedia of the Social Sciences*, (ed.) David L. Sills, vol. 9.
Riemer, Neal (1962), *The Revival of Democratic Theory*, Appleton-Century-Crofts/Meredith, New York.
Robson, J.M. (1968), *The Improvement of Mankind: The Social and Political Thought of John Stuart Mill*, Univ. of Toronto Pr., London.
Rosenbaum, Martin (1997), *From Soapbox to Soundbite: Party Political Campaigning in Britain since 1945*, Macmillan, Basingstoke.
Rossiter, Clinton and James Lare (eds) (1963), *The Essential Lippmann: A Political Philosophy for Liberal Democracy*, Random House, New York.
Roszak, Theodore (ed.) (1969), *The Dissenting Academy*, 3rd edn, Penguin Books, Harmondsworth.
Ruggiero, Guido de (1959), *The History of European Liberalism* [1927], 2nd edn, Beacon Pr., Boston.
Runciman, W.G. (1963), *Social Science and Political Theory*, Cambridge Univ. Pr., Cambridge.
Ryan, Alan (1974), *John Stuart Mill*, Routledge, London.
Samuel, Herbert (1902), *Liberalism; An Attempt to State the Principles and Proposals of Contemporary Liberalism in England*, Grant Richards, London.
Samuel, Viscount (1945), *Memoirs*, Cresset Pr., London.
Sandel, Michael J. (1996), *Democracy's Discontent: America in Search of a Public Philosophy*, Harvard Univ. Pr./Belknap Pr., Cambridge, Mass.
Sartori, Giovanni (1965), *Democratic Theory* [1958], 2nd Eng. edn, Praeger, New York.
Sartori, Giovanni (1976), *Parties and Party Systems: A Framework for Analysis*, Cambridge Univ. Pr., Cambridge.
Sartori, Giovanni (1987), *The Theory of Democracy Revisited*, 2 vols, Chatham House, New Jersey.
Schall, James V. (1998), *Jacques Maritain: The Philosopher in Society*, Rowman and Littlefield, Lanham, Md.
Schapsmeier, E. L. and F. H. (1969), *Walter Lippmann: Philosopher-Journalist*, Public Affairs Pr., Washington, D.C.
Schattschneider, E.E. (1960), *The Semisovereign People*, Holt, Rinehart and Winston, New York.
Schlesinger Jr, Arthur M. (1959), 'Walter Lippmann: The Intellectual v. Politics', in Marquis Childs and James Reston (eds), *Walter Lippmann and His Times*, Harcourt Brace, New York.
Schlesinger Jr, Arthur M. (1973), *The Imperial Presidency*, Houghton Mifflin, Boston.
Schlesinger Jr, Arthur M. (1992), *The Disuniting of America*, Norton, New York.
Schmitter, C. Philippe and Terry Lynn Karl (1991), 'What Democracy Is...and Is Not', *Journal of Democracy*, vol. 2, No. 3, pp. 75-88.

Schneewind, J.B. (ed.) (1969), *Mill: A Collection of Critical Essays*, 2nd edn, Macmillan, London.

Schumpeter, Joseph A. (1954), *Capitalism, Socialism and Democracy* [1942], 4th edn, Allen and Unwin, London.

Self, Peter (1993), *Government by the Market?: The Politics of Public Choice*, Macmillan, Basingstoke.

Semmel, Bernard (1984), *John Stuart Mill and the Pursuit of Virtue*, Yale Univ. Pr., New Haven.

Shatz, Marshall S. (ed.) (1972), *The Essential Works of Anarchism*, Quadrangle Books, New York.

Shklar, Judith (1957), *After Utopia: the Decline of Political Faith*, Princeton Univ. Pr., Princeton.

Shonfield, Andrew (1969), *Modern Capitalism: The Changing Balance of Public and Private Power*, 2nd edn, Oxford Univ. Pr., London.

Shute, Stephen and Susan Hurley (eds) (1993), *On Human Rights*, Basic Books/Harper Collins, New York.

Sigmund, P.E. (ed.) (1971), *Natural Law in Political Thought*, Winthrop, Cambridge, Mass.

Simon, Yves R. (1961), *Philosophy of Democratic Government* [1951], 2nd edn, Univ. of Chicago Pr./Phoenix Books, Chicago.

Simon, Yves R. (1962), *A General Theory of Authority*, Univ. of Notre Dame Pr., Notre Dame.

Simon, Yves R. (1965), *The Tradition of Natural Law*, (ed.) Vukan Kuic, Fordham Univ. Pr., New York.

Simon, Yves R. (1968), *Freedom and Community*, (ed.) Charles P. O'Donnell, Fordham Univ. Pr., New York.

Skorupski, John (1989), *John Stuart Mill*, Routledge, London.

Smith, Brooke Williams (1976), *Jacques Maritain: Antimodern or Ultramodern?*, Elsevier, New York.

Smith, Martin J. (1990), 'Pluralism, Reformed Pluralism and Neopluralism...', *Political Studies*, vol. 38, pp. 302-22.

Spitz, David (1949), *Patterns of Anti-Democratic Thought*, Macmillan, New York.

Stapleton, Julia (1989), 'The National Character of Ernest Barker's Political Science', *Political Studies*, vol. 37, pp. 171-87.

Stapleton, Julia (1994), *Englishness and the Study of Politics: The Social and Political Thought of Ernest Barker*, Cambridge Univ. Pr., Cambridge.

Statham Jr, E. Robert (1998), *The Constitution of Public Philosophy: Toward a Synthesis of Freedom and Responsibility in Postmodern America*, Univ. Pr. of America, Lanham.

Steel, Ronald (1980), *Walter Lippmann and the American Century*, Little, Brown, Boston.

Storing, Herbert J. (ed.) (1962), *Essays on the Scientific Study of Politics*, Holt, Rinehart and Winston, New York.

Strachey, John (1956), *Contemporary Capitalism*, Gollancz, London.
Strauss, Leo (1968), *Liberalism: Ancient and Modern*, Basic Books, New York, 1968.
Stretton, Hugh and Lionel Orchard (1994), *Public Goods, Public Enterprise, Public Choice: Theoretical Foundations for the Contemporary Attack on Government*, St. Martin's Pr./Macmillan, Basingstoke.
Sullivan, William M. (1986), *Reconstructing Public Philosophy*, Univ. of California Pr., Berkeley.
Summers, John, Dennis Woodward and Andrew Parkin (eds), (1990), *Government, Politics and Power in Australia*, 4th edn, Longman Cheshire, Melbourne.
Swedberg, Richard (1991), *Joseph A. Schumpeter: His Life and Work*, Polity Press, Cambridge.
Teodori, Massimo (ed.) (1970), *The New Left: A Documentary History*, Cape, London.
Thomas, William (1985), *Mill*, Oxford Univ. Pr., New York.
Thompson, Dennis F. (1970), *The Democratic Citizen: Social Science and Democratic Theory in the Twentieth Century*, Cambridge Univ. Pr., Cambridge.
Tocqueville, Alexis de (1959), *'The European Revolution' and Correspondence with Gobineau*, Doubleday/Anchor, Garden City, N.Y.
Tocqueville, Alexis de (1966), *The Ancien Regime and the French Revolution* [1856], Collins/Fontana, n.p.
Tocqueville, Alexis de (1968), *Democracy in America* [1835, 1840], 2 vols, (eds) J.P Mayer and Max Lerner, 2nd edn, Collins/Fontana, n.p.
Tocqueville, Alexis de (1970), *Recollections* [1893], Macdonald, London.
Truman, David B. (1971), *The Governmental Process* [1951], 2nd edn, Knopf, New York.
Tucker, Robert C. (1972), *The Marx-Engels Reader*, Norton, New York.
Tucker, Robert C. (1981), *Politics as Leadership*, Univ. of Missouri Pr., Columbia.
Tullock, Gordon and Morris Perlman (1976), *The Vote Motive: An Essay in the Economics of Politics*, Institute of Economic Affairs, London.
Vincent, Andrew and Raymond Plant (1984), *Philosophy, Politics and Citizenship: The Life and Thought of the British Idealists*, Blackwell, Oxford.
Voegelin, Eric (1974), 'Liberalism and Its History', *Review of Politics*, vol. 36, pp. 504-19.
Walker, Geoffrey de (1988), *The Rule of Law: Foundation of Constitutional Democracy*, Melbourne Univ. Pr., Melbourne.
Walzer, Michael (1980), *Radical Principles*, Basic Books, New York.
Walzer, Michael (1983), *Spheres of Justice: A Defense of Pluralism and Equality*, Basic Books, New York.
Watt, E.D. (1982), *Authority*, Croom Helm, London.
Weber, Max (1970), 'The Vocation of Politics' [1919], in H. H. Girth and C. Wright Mills (eds), *From Max Weber: Essays in Sociology*, 2nd edn, Routledge, London.

Webster's New Collegiate Dictionary (1977), (ed.) Henry Bosley Woolf, 5th edn, Merriam, Springfield, Mass.

Weinstein, Leo (1962), 'The Group Approach: Arthur F. Bentley', in Herbert J. Storing (ed.), *Essays on the Scientific Study of Politics*, Holt, Rinehart and Winston, New York.

Wellborn, Charles (1969), *Twentieth Century Pilgrimage: Walter Lippmann and the Public Philosophy*, Louisiana State Univ Pr., Baton Rouge.

Wheare, K.C. (1964), *Modern Constitutions*, 3rd edn, Oxford Univ. Pr., London.

Whelan, Frederick G. (1982), 'Justice: Classical and Christian', *Political Theory*, vol. 10, pp. 435-60.

Wieler, Peter (1982), *The New Liberalism*, Garland, New York.

Wiggershaus, Rolf (1994), *The Frankfurt School: Its History, Theories and Political Significance* [1986], first Eng. edn, MIT Pr., Cambridge, Mass.

Williamson, Peter J. (1985), *Varieties of Corporatism*, Cambridge Univ. Pr., Cambridge.

Williamson, Peter J. (1989), *Corporatism in Perspective*, Sage, London.

Winkler, T.J. (1976), 'Corporatism', *European Journal of Sociology*, vol. 17, pp. 100-36.

Wintrop, Norman (ed.) (1983), *Liberal Democratic Theory and Its Critics*, Croom Helm, London.

Wintrop, Norman (1992), 'Elite-Theory and Neo-Elite Theory Understandings of Democracy: An Analysis and Criticism', *Australian Journal of Political Science*, vol. 27, pp. 464-77.

Wintrop, Norman (1993), 'Fukuyama's Challenge to Leftists', *Quadrant*, June.

Wollheim, Richard (1958), 'Democracy', *Journal of the History of Ideas*, vol. 19, pp. 225-42.

Wood, Ellen Meikins (1981), 'Liberal Democracy and Capitalist Hegemony...', in *The Socialist Register 1981*, (eds) Ralph Miliband and John Saville, Merlin Pr., London.

Wright, Benjamin F. (1973), *Five Public Philosophies of Walter Lippmann*, Univ. of Texas Pr., Austin.

Yack, Bernard (1986), *The Longing for Total Revolution: Philosophic Sources of Social Discontent from Rousseau to Marx and Nietzsche*, Princeton Univ. Pr., Princeton.

Yack, Bernard (1993), *The Problems of a Political Animal: Community, Justice and Conflict in Aristotelean Political Thought*, Univ. of California Pr., Berkeley.

Young, Nigel (1977), *An Infantile Disorder?: The Crisis and Decline of the New Left*, Routledge, London.

Zetterbaum, Marvin (1967), *Tocqueville and the Problem of Democracy*, Stanford Univ. Pr., Stanford, Ca.

Index

abstract political thought 64, 88-9
affirmative action 211-12, 239-41
Albertoni, E. 38-9, 42
anarchism, 29-30, 76, 76n, 86-7, 185
Aquinas, St T. 99, 167, 173, 179
Arblaster, A. 4n, 10, 83-6, 89
Arendt, H. 92n
Aristotle 6, 49, 92, 97, 111, 124, 151, 179, 203, 208-13 *passim*
Asia, 227, 263
Asquith, H.H. 140
associations 128, 156
Augustine, St 181, 181n
Augustinian realism
  see Niebuhr, R.
Austin, J. 49
Australia 41, 258
Austria 227, 253
authority 26, 133, 176-80
  see also leadership
autonomy, personal
  see freedom

Bachrach, P. 82-3, 85, 86, 184
Bagehot, W. 253
Bakunin, M. 86
Barber, B.R. 10, 77, 89-91.
Barker, E. 150-1, 157-61, 162, 167
Barraclough, G. 253
Barrot, O. 123
Beaumont, G. de 123
behaviourism and the behavioural revolution
  see political science, behavioural
Belgium, 253
Benn, S.I. 162-5, 167, 201-2, 213-14
Bentham, J. 18, 55, 131, 134, 162, 182, 185-6
Benthamism, 7, 20, 49, 55, 134, 140
  see also utility and utilitarianism
Bentley, A.F. 51
Berlin, I. 16, 73, 73n

Bernstein, R. 239, 240-1
Blackstone, W. 100, 106-7, 115
Bloom, A. 207
Bosanquet, B. 140, 142n
Bottomore, T.B. 44n
Britain
  see United Kingdom
Brittan, S. 58-9, 59n
Bryce J. 141
Buchanan, J.M. 215
bureaucracy and bureaucratic government 40, 45, 49-50, 58, 132, 145, 179, 207, 234, 236-8
  see also managerial revolution and society; public servants and services
Burke, E. 64, 89, 250
Burnham, J. 40-41, 43n, 231-3
Burnheim, J. 86, 89

Callicles 203
Campbell-Bannerman, H. 140
capitalism 85, 91, 129, 154-5, 173-4, 224, 231
  see also economics and economic issues; globalisation; liberalism, laissez-faire; socialism v. capitalism
capitalism, corporate 226-8
  see also corporatism and corporate theory
China 223, 231
Christianity and the Christian churches 127-9, 143-4, 151, 169-73
  see also Judeo-Christianity
Churchill, W.S. 92, 92n, 97, 141, 149, 190, 217-18
citizens and citizenship 3-4, 7, 25-6, 29, 50, 113, 157, 170-1, 261
  virtues of 42-3, 113, 132-4, 142-5, 152, 250, 257-8
  see also obligations, political; rights; toleration; voting responsibilities and behaviour

civilisation 35, 223-4
  see also culture
civilisation, Western 105-6, 120, 123-3, 162, 202-3, 203n
Civil Rights movement, 78-9
civil services
  see public servants and services
civil society 25, 36-40 passim, 45, 50, 55, 201, 257
  see also private-public distinction
classes and ruling classes
  see interests, sectional; political and ruling classes
Clinton, B. (W.J.) 227n
Coke, E. 99, 115
Cold War 232
Cole, G.D.H. 83
Coleridge, S.T. 132, 139
common good 19-20, 24, 57, 63, 65n, 68, 135, 145, 164, 177-8, 199-200, 208, 214-15
  see also justice
communications
  see journalism; media, the; public discussion
communism 79, 83, 161, 224, 246
  see also Marxism and Marxist Leninism; Soviet Union; totalitarianism
communitarianism 5
communities 7, 79, 82, 178-9
Comte, A. 132
consent and consensus 7, 33, 106-7, 152-3, 246-7
conservatism 34-35, 57, 60, 84, 139, 164, 224-5, 236
Conservative Party, UK 135, 245, 246
constitutions and constitutionalism 4, 53, 112, 117, 128, 153, 189, 191-2, 200-1
contractual relations 155, 178-9
corporations, business 59, 82, 228-29, 229-30
corporatism and corporate theory 45, 57, 59-60, 59n, 226-7
  see also capitalism, corporate; totalitarianism, Swedish
Crosland, C.A.R. 229, 230-1, 232, 233

culture 39-40, 78, 125-8, 153-4, 239, 248, 254, 255, 259, 260-2
  see also civilisation; masses and mass society; materialism, cultural; multiculturalism; political culture; secularism
Czechoslovakia 79

Dahl, R.A. 51, 61, 83, 185, 251-2
  Democracy and Its Critics, 63-8
  Preface to Democratic Theory, 51-7, 65-68
Davis, J.C. 72-3
de Gaulle, C. 79, 175, 217-18
de Klerk, F.W. 217-18
democracy 4-6, 9, 13, 15-18, 38-44, 52-7, 81, 119, 135-8
  ancient 21, 25, 64, 124, 213, 218, 222-3
  and elites 26, 28-34, 36-44. 88, 103, 113, 184-93 passim, 197, 223, 225-6, 229-30, 232-3, 234, 236
  and the problem of evil 171-2, 180-4
  and the public philosophy 175, 230-1
  as end of history 10-11, 197, 222-6
  conditions for 16, 22-4, 38-9, 132, 160-1, 183, 202
  corporate-capitalist 226-8
  dangers of 34-6, 122-3, 125, 131, 219
  definitions of 2, 15-16, 18-22, 124-5, 144, 163, 164, 189
  participatory and populist 20, 43, 52, 53-4, 58, 62-3, 65-8, 80-7, 187
  prospects 37-8, 44-5, 261-5
  revisionist theories 18-24, 185, 187
  technocratic and managerial 227-33
  threats to 25-6, 101-3, 112-17, 143-5, 179-80, 192-3, 227-8, 230-41 passim, 249, 251-4, 263-5
  totalitarian 233-41
  see also constitutions and constitutionalism; democratic-elite theory; democratic elitism; democratic theory as public philosophy; formalist democratic theory; liberalism and democracy; representation and representative democracy; utopian democratic theory

democracy, procedural
  see formalist democratic theory
democratic-elite theory 44n, 184-93
  see also democratic elitism; elites and elite theory
democratic elitism 82-3, 184
  see also democratic elite theory; elites and elite theory
democratic theory
  see democracy, revisionist theories; democratic-elite theory; democratic elitism; democratic theory as public philosophy; formalist democratic theory; utopian democratic theory
democratic theory as public philosophy vii-viii, 1-6, 92-3, 119, 124, 187-93 *passim*, 193-4, 199-202
  and political parties 250-2
  cooperation with political philosophy and the sciences 6, 212-17
  cultivating prudence 193, 217-19
  finding the mean, 139, 190-1, 200, 209-12
  promoting justice 202-9
  prospects 230-1, 261-5
  see also Benn, S.I.; Lippmann, W.; Maritain, J.; mean, idea of; Mill, J.S.; New Liberals; Niebuhr, R.; Peters, R.S.; Plamenatz, J.; political parties, public philosophic response; political judgement; public philosophy; Sartori, G.; Simon Y.R.; Tocqueville, A. de
Dewey, J. 4, 102, 182
Diana, Princess of Wales 256
Disraeli, B. 251
Douglass, R.B. 8
Downs, A. 247-8
Drucker, P.F. 229-31, 232, 233
Dunn, J. ix, 13, 218-19
duties
  see obligations, political; rights
Dworkin, R. 207

East Europe 152
economics and economic issues 87, 138-9, 190-1, 217n, 249, 259-61
  see also Keynesian economic management; liberalism, laissez-faire; pressure groups and pressure group politics; socialism v. capitalism
education 76-7, 87, 113-14, 138-9, 142-4, 192, 234, 235-6, 239-41
Egypt 78
elections and electoral systems 36-7, 128, 245-8, 254
Eliot, T.S. 262, 262n
elites and elite theory 21-4, 28-30, 44-6, 59, 88, 178n, 184-93 *passim*, 223, 225-6, 229-33 *passim*, 260
  neo-elite theory 28, 30, 38-44
  see also authority; democracy and elites; democratic-elite theory; democratic elitism; leadership; political and ruling classes
end of history
  see democracy as end of history
Engels, F. 74-5, 80
environment and environmentalism 139, 211-12, 224-5, 248
equality and egalitarianism 2-3, 64-7, 82-3, 86-7, 125, 130, 163, 204-7
ethics
  see morals and moral theory
Etzioni-Halevy, E. 38-40, 42
Europe
  see Social Democratic Parties, European; Tocqueville on Europe
evil
  see democracy and the problem of evil

Fascism 32, 161, 224, 246
  see also National Socialism, German
Federalists, the 52-4
feminism 139, 211-12, 224-5, 248
Field, G.L. 43
First World War 101, 140, 246
Fisher, H.A.L. 142
formalist democratic theory vii-viii, 1-6, 149
  democracy as competitive political leaderships 18-24
  democracy as integrated elites 28, 38-43
  democracy as parliaments and elections 15-18

democracy as political and social pluralism 51-7, 62-7
objections to vii-viii, 24-6, 38-40, 43-6, 57-61
France 79, 123-4, 246, 263
French Revolution 245
Franco, F. 175
Freedom, 34-6, 50, 64-5, 119, 161, 204-8 *passim*, 259
and responsibility 110-11, 141-2, 163, 202, 256-7
Freud, S. and Freudian theory 80, 101
Friedman, M. 260
Fukuyama, F. 10-11, 197, 222-6

Galbraith, J.K. 228-233 *passim*
Galston, W. 208
Georghegan, V. 75
Germany 58, 178, 227, 231, 251, 253, 263
see also National Socialism, German
Gladstone, W.E. 251
globalisation 211-12, 263-4
Goodin, R.E. 7
Gould, C.C. 10, 88-9
government
see bureaucracy and bureaucratic government; democracy; oligarchy and oligarchic government; overloaded government; parliaments and parliamentary government; state, the
Graham, B.D. 254
Gramsci, A. 80, 262
Gray, J. 3n
Greece, classical 141, 157, 261
see also democracy, ancient
Green, P. 10, 86-7, 89
Green political issues
see environment and environmentalism
Green, T.H. 10, 42, 81, 120, 140, 144, 149, 153, 201, 206, 250
groups,
see associations; communities; interests, sectional; pluralism, political and social; pressure groups and pressure-group politics
Gutmann, A. 5

Haldane, R.B. 141
Hamilton, A. 52
happiness 77, 109-11, 130-1, 140, 259
see also human nature; morals and moral theory; utility and utilitarianism
Havel, V. 149, 217-18
Hayek, F.A. 191-2, 259-60, 263
Hegel, G.W.F. and Hegelianism 144, 206, 139-40, 223-4, 259
see also left-Hegelianism
Held, D. 5
higher law
see natural law theory
Higley, J. 40-4
Hirst, P.Q. 48
history, concept and discipline of 77, 214, 225-6
see also democracy as end of history; philosophy of history
Hitler, A. 49, 117, 119, 178, 232, 234
Hobbes, T. and Hobbesian thought 152, 162, 171, 201
Hobhouse, L.T. 42, 140-1, 144-5
Hobson, J.A. 140-1
Hollenbach, D. 8
House, E.M. (Colonel) 100
human nature 19-21, 32, 35, 77, 109-11, 119, 130-1, 140, 151-2, 180-2
see also happiness; morals and moral theory
Hume, D. 84
Hungary 78, 231
Huntford, R. 235, 236-8
Huxley, A. 45, 73, 237, 238

ideology and ideological bias vii-viii, 1-2, 32, 38, 52, 55-7 *passim*, 60-1, 67, 82, 206
ideological democratic theory
see formalist democratic theory
impartiality
see justice
imperialism and empire 143, 145
industrialisation 49-50
see also technology
instrumental rationality 216
intellectuals 3-4, 45, 78-81 *passim*, 134, 155, 172, 177, 206, 262

interest, general, national and public
    see common good
interests, sectional 17, 25, 31, 51, 52, 60
    see also pluralism, political and social;
        pressure groups and pressure-group
        politics
international relations 118, 126, 143
    see also Cold War; imperialism and
        empire; nations and nationalism
Islam 224
Italy 31, 32, 35, 37, 231
    see also Fascism

Jackson, A. 53, 123, 250
Jacobinism, concept of 105, 116-17, 119
James, W. 100, 109-10
Japan 58
Jay, J. 52
Jefferson, T. 102, 217-18
Johnson, L.B. 100
journalism 78, 87, 100-1, 213, 255-9
    see also Lippmann on journalism;
        media, the
Jowett B. 150
Judeo-Christianity 108, 157, 173, 174
    see also Christianity and the Christian
        churches
justice 65n, 135, 163-4, 182, 199-204,
    263
    Barker's theory of 157-60, 203-4, 208-9
    challenges to Rawls 207-8
    Rawls's theory 204-7
    see also common good; rights; utility
        and utilitarianism

Kant, I. and Kantian thought 139-40
    see also left-Kantianism
Karl, T.L. 17n
Keller, S. 40-1
Kelso, W.A. 62-3, 68
Kennedy, J.F. 100
Keynes, J.M. 97, 112, 259
Keynesian economic management 112,
    119, 162, 229
King, M.L. 78
knowledge workers 229-31
Kolakowski, L. 118
Korsch, K. 80

Kropotkin, P. A. 86, 92-3
Krugman, P. 217n, 227n
Kymlicka, W. 207

Labour Party, UK 140, 145, 246, 256
Lasch, C. 42, 197, 236
Laski, H. 50
last man, the 225
law and legislation 58, 112, 117, 152-3,
    158-60, 167, 199, 241, 357-8
    differences between 191-2
leadership 21-6 passim, 33-7 passim, 52,
    79, 101, 113-14, 125-6, 133, 160,
    165, 177, 186-7, 245, 250-1
    see also authority; political judgement
left Hegelianism 77, 92
left-Kantianism 77
Lenin, V.I. 80
Levitas, R. 72n, 75
liberalism 43, 50, 80-5 passim, 110, 117,
    120, 152-3, 173, 183, 189-90, 208,
    260
    and democracy 4-, 31, 34-5, 189, 211,
        224
    laissez-faire 2-3, 111-12, 138-9, 144,
        215, 224-5
    see also constitutions and
        constitutionalism; freedom; Green,
        T.H.; Hobhouse, L.T.; Mill, J.S.;
        rights; Tocqueville, A. de; toleration
Liberal Party, UK 135, 140, 245
libertarianism 2-3
    see also liberalism, laissez-faire
liberty
    see freedom
Lijphart, A. 246-7
Lindsay, A.D. 8n, 150-6, 162, 163, 167,
    211
Lippmann, W. ix, 2, 7-10, passim, 99-
    104, 149-50, 170, 180, 211-14
    passim, 262-3
    as democratic theorist and public
        philosopher 109-19
    on journalism 102, 113-15, 257
    on the public philosophy 7, 8, 104-9,
        199-200
Lipson, L. 9n
Lloyd George, D. 141
Locke, J. 162, 201

Louis Napoleon 124
Louis Philippe 123
Lowi, T.J. 59n
Lucas, J.R. 208
Lukacs, G. 80
Lukes, S. 75, 83-6

McCarthy, J.R. 117
Machiavelli, N. and Machiavellianism 13, 172, 183, 215-16
McIlwain, C.H. 97, 214
McLean, I. 215
Macpherson, C.B. 4-5, 10, 80-1, 83, 85, 86, 89
Madison, J. 52-4, 57, 102, 217-18, 235, 250
majorities and majoritarianism 53, 55, 115-17, 131, 137, 143, 190, 200, 255-6
  see also minorities; popular sovereignty
managerial revolution and society 40-1, 231-3
  see also technocracy
Mandela, N. 217-18
Mannheim, K. 1-2, 77
Manuel, F.E. and F.P. 74n, 80
Mao Zedong 49, 234
Marcuse, H. 80
Maritain, J. 167, 168-76, 179, 180, 201, 211
Marx, K. 74-5, 81, 86, 89-90, 92, 93
Marxism and Marxist-Leninism 29-30, 40, 73-6, 79-81, 182, 185, 231
  see also neo-Marxism
Masaryk, T. 149
masses and mass societies 52-3, 126-7, 144, 235-6, 258, 258n
materialism, cultural 106
  see also secularism
Mayo, H.B. 15-18, 66-7
mean, idea of 10, 111-12, 118-19, 139, 190-1, 200, 209-12
media, the 128-9, 234, 237, 255-9
  television 115, 252, 255-6
  see also journalism
Meynaud, J. 228
Michels, R. 185, 251-2

millenarianism and secular millenarianism 72-3, 74-8
Mill, J. 18, 131, 185
Mill, J.S. 4, 10, 18, 29, 34, 81, 99, 120, 123, 131-2, 139-40, 145, 149, 162, 185, 200, 206, 213-14
  on capitalism and socialism 138-40, 200, 211
  on history and culture 132-5, 144, 235
  on representative government 42-3, 83, 122, 130-1, 134-8, 156, 164, 251, 253
Mills, C.W. 40-1, 229, 233
minorities 16, 53, 55, 61-2, 137, 249
  see also majorities and majoritarianism; rights
Mises, L. von 75
Molnar, T. 13, 72n
morals and moral theory 76-7, 82-5, 129, 141-5 passim, 160, 163, 167-8, 170-1, 174n, 211
  see also happiness; human nature; utility and utilitarianism
More, St T. 72
Mosca, G. 28, 30, 34-8, 42, 45, 135, 185
multiculturalism 239-41
Mussolini, B. 101, 232

National socialism, German 161, 224, 246, 263
  see also Fascism; totalitarianism
nations and nationalism 145, 152, 157-8, 260
  see also international relations; state, the
natural law theory 7, 99-100, 103, 105-9, 117-18, 167-8, 183, 202
  see also Maritain, J.; morals and moral theory; Simon, Y.R.
Nehru, J. 149
Neo-Marxism 73-80 *passim*
  see also Marxism and Marxist-Leninism; New Left
New Deal 102-3, 112, 120, 232
New Left vii, 5, 7, 10, 60-1, 67n, 78-80, 185, 238
New Liberalism 122, 139-45, 150, 154, 163, 201-2, 250

see also Barker, E.; Green, T.H.;
    Hobhouse, L.T.; Lindsay, A.D.
New Right 57-9, 207, 215
    see also public choice theory;
    libertarianism
Niebuhr, R. 167, 180-4, 211, 216
Nietzsche, F. 73, 225
Novak, M. 174
Nozick, R. 207-8

obligations, political 142-5, 159-60, 199
    see also citizens and citizenship;
    rights; toleration; voting
    responsibilities and behaviour
oligarchy and oligarchic government 25,
    28, 31-2, 41, 44-6, 154, 216-17,
    227-8, 232
    see also managerial revolution and
    society; technocracy
Olson, Jr, M. 58, 59n
Ordeshook, P.C. 214
Ortega y Gasset, J. 235-6
Orwell, G. 45, 49, 73, 240, 264
Ostrogorski, M. 251-2
overloaded government 58, 192
    see also pressure groups and pressure-
    group politics

Pahl, R.E. 227n
Papen, F. von 178
Parekh, B. 4n, 8n
Pareto, V. 21, 28-34, 42, 185
parliaments and parliamentary
    government 15-18, 23, 31-3, 97,
    135-8, 241, 250-3
    see also political parties;
    representation and representative
    democracy
Pateman, C. 10, 83, 85, 86, 89
pedlars of prosperity, 217n
Peters, R.S. 162-5, 167, 201-2, 213-14
philosophy 6, 16, 90-1, 117, 162, 175
    epistemology 90-1
    teleology 210
    see also morals and moral theory;
    philosophy of history; political
    philosophy; positivism; rationality
    and reason; relativism, value

philosophy of history 130-1, 144, 176,
    223-4
    see also history, concept and discipline
    of
Pickles, D. 15-18, 65, 67
Plamenatz, J. 20-1, 167, 184-7, 213-14
Plato 6, 73, 99, 124, 203, 206, 213, 263
Plumb, J.H. 214n
pluralism, meta-ethical
    see relativism, value
pluralism, political and social 3-4, 48,
    51-7, 62-7, 108
    legal and classical 49-51, 158
    see also Dahl, R.A.; interests,
    sectional; pressure groups and
    pressure-group politics
political and ruling classes 23, 30, 31-8,
    44-5, 177-8, 228, 232-3
    see also capitalism, corporate; elites
    and elite theory; managerial
    revolution and society
political correctness 235, 238-41
political culture 113-16, 125-8, 246-7
    see also culture
political judgement 174-5, 210
    see also prudence; realism, political;
    state craft
political parties 11, 16, 17, 23, 40-1, 60,
    119-20, 128, 135, 156, 161, 234,
    244, 255, 258
    elections and electoral systems 128,
    245-8 *passim*
    origins and history 244-6, 253-4
    prospects 252-4
    public choice view 247-50
    public philosophic response 250-2
    see also voting responsibilities and
    behaviour
political philosophy 6, 212-3
political science 259
    behavioural vii, 13, 22, 48, 51-7, 60,
    68, 186, 251-2
    see also positivism
Popper, K.R. 72n
popular sovereignty 53-4, 64, 66-7, 82-3,
    85
    see also majorities and
    majoritarianism; sovereignty

populism
    see democracy, participatory and populist
positivism 53, 106, 162, 188
postmodernism 10-11, 203, 262-3
praxis 73-8, 89-91
pressure groups and pressure-group politics 54-6, 58-9, 68, 192
    see also pluralism, political and social
private property and property rights 53, 66-7, 82-3, 106-7, 207-8
    see also rights
private-public distinction 240
    see also civil society
Proudhon, P.J. 86
prudence 143-4, 216, 218-19
    see also political judgement
psychology
    see Freud, S. and Freudian theory; human nature
public choice theory 58, 214-16
    see also political parties, public choice view
public discussion 134, 137, 143, 155-6, 165, 199, 219, 250
    see also journalism; rhetoric
public opinion 16, 102, 255-6
public philosophy 1-2, 6-9, 99-100, 104-9, 165, 170, 230-1, 259
    see also democratic theory as public philosophy
public policy 216-17
public servants and services 23, 35-6, 58, 62-3, 113
    see also bureaucracy and bureaucratic government
public welfare 59, 129, 142, 201, 264

Quinton, A. 89

racism 62, 240
rationality and reason 19-20, 163, 248, 249
    see also philosophy
Rawls, J. 204-7
    see also justice
Reagan, R. 226, 227n
realism, political 72-3, 84, 180-4, 216
    see also prudence

Reformation 108
relativism, value 19, 106-8 *passim*, 162, 167, 203, 205-6, 210-11
    and democracy 66, 115-16, 134, 159, 190
    and utopianism 73, 83-5, 89-90
representation and representative democracy 4, 50, 57, 86, 135-8, 185, 200-1, 241, 250-3
    see also democracy; Mill, J.S. on representative government
Republican Party, US 236
republican traditions 5-9 *passim*, 25
    see also citizens and citizenship
rhetoric 33-4, 67, 149, 248
    see also ideology and ideological bias; public discussion
Riemer, N. 218
rights 54, 62, 66, 91, 170-1, 201-2, 240
    see also constitutions and constitutionalism; justice; natural law theory; obligations, political; private property and property rights
Roosevelt, F.D. 100, 102-3, 112
Roosevelt, T. 100
Rousseau, J.-J. 18, 20, 83, 171, 185
Ruggiero, G. de 4n
rule of law
    see constitutions and constitutionalism; law and legislation
Russia 223, 231
    Russian Revolution 32, 231, 246
    see also Soviet Union

Samuel, H. 141
Sandel, M.J. 8-9
Santayana, G. 100, 109-10
Sartori, G. 77, 167, 184, 187-93, 201, 211, 213-14
Schattschneider, E.E. 60-1
Schlesinger, Jr, A.M. 241
Schmitter, C.P. 17n
Schumpeter, J.A. VII, 18-24, 28, 30, 45, 52, 62, 67, 71, 83, 185
science 155, 167
    see also social sciences; technology
Scott, C.P. 140
Second World War 149, 231

secularism, 108, 127
  see also materialism, cultural;
    millenarianism and secular
    millenarianism
Selden, J. 115
sexism 240
sexual relations 237
Shklar, J. 72n
Shonfield, A. 227n
Simon, Y.R. 167, 168, 176-80, 202
Smith, A. 182
social democracy
  see Social Democratic Parties,
    European; socialism, democratic
Social Democratic Parties, European
  236-8, 245, 251
socialism 5, 31, 36, 50, 66, 74-5, 79, 182,
  224-5, 231, 260
  and utopianism 2-3, 71, 79-85 *passim*
  democratic 78, 154-5, 163, 228-9
  guild 5, 50
  v. capitalism 111-12, 138-9, 200, 211
  see also Marxism and Marxist
    Leninism
social sciences 57, 213-14
  see also economics and economic
    issues; history, concept and
    discipline of; political science;
    public policy
society
  see associations; civil society;
    communities; masses and mass
    societies; state, the
Socrates 203, 213, 259, 263
South Africa 223, 263
sovereignty 49-51, 153, 171
  see also popular sovereignty
Soviet Union 10, 236
  see also communism; Russia
Spitz, D. 30
Stalin, J. 49, 119, 232, 234
Stapleton, J. 160
state, the 21-2, 140, 145, 154, 154n, 157,
  163, 179, 201-2, 259-60
  see also bureaucracy and bureaucratic
    government; constitutions and
    constitutionalism; democracy; law
    and legislation; nations and
    nationalism; sovereignty; state craft

state craft 113-14, 160, 250-1
  see also leadership; political
    judgement
statesmanship
  see state craft
Statham, Jr., E.R. 8
Strachey, J. 229, 230-1, 232, 233
Strauss, L. and Straussian political
  thought 8, 13, 60, 60n
  see also Bloom, A.; Statham, Jr., E.R.
Sullivan, W.M. 7
summum bonum 208
  see also common good
Sweden, 235
  see also totalitarianism, Swedish
Switzerland, 31
syndicalism 5, 83

technocracy 192, 216-17, 227-33 *passim*
  see also bureaucracy and bureaucratic
    government; managerial revolution
    and society; oligarchy and
    oligarchic government
technology 155, 229-30
  and excessive expectations 259-61
  see also industrialisation; science
Thatcher, M. 226
Thomism and neo-Thomism 167-8
  see also natural law theory
Thrasymachus 203
Tocqueville, A. de 4, 9, 9n, 10, 29, 34,
  42, 45, 99, 139, 143, 149, 172, 211
  Democracy in America 122-30, 132,
    192, 219, 250-3 *passim*, 261
  on Europe 122-4, 127-30 *passim*
toleration 3-4, 23-4
Tories
  see Conservative Party, UK
totalitarianism 41, 49, 233-5, 239-41
  routes to totalitarian democracy 235-
    41
  Swedish 236-8
Toynbee, A. 140
trade unions 45, 59, 154-5, 173-4, 226,
  245
traditionalism
  see conservatism
tragic dimensions to life 73, 76, 182,
  182n

Truman, D.B. 51-2
Tullock, G. 215

United Kingdom 31, 85, 115, 117, 132, 135-8, 140, 152, 162, 244-5, 263
  parliamentary government 23, 97, 135-8, 241
  traditions and culture 142-3, 152
  see also Conservative Party, UK; Labour Party, UK; Liberal Party, UK
United States 8, 78-9, 118-23 passim, 173-4, 215, 231-2
  system of government 48, 52-7 passim, 80, 106, 115, 238-41, 263
  traditions and culture 42, 48, 52-7 passim, 80, 106, 115, 238-41, 263
  see also New Deal; Republican Party, US; Tocqueville, *Democracy in America*
utility and utilitarianism 7, 134-5, 139, 145
  see also Bentham, J.; Benthamism; Mill, J.; Mill, J.S.
utopia 1-2, 13, 72-3
utopian democratic theory vii-viii, 1-6 passim, 16-17, 30, 71, 78, 80-87, 149, 188
  objections to 16-17, 87-93
utopianism 2-3, 14, 43, 67-8, 71-4, 78-85 passim, 89-90, 206-7, 264
  see also Jacobinism, concept of; millenarianism and secular millenarianism; praxis

virtue, political
  see citizens and citizenship; prudence; toleration
voting responsibilities and behaviour 19-20, 23, 107-8, 136-7, 143, 161, 247-8

Wallas, G. 100
Walzer, M. 208
Weber, M. 21, 73, 174n
West Germany
  see Germany
Whelan, F.G. 203n
Wilson, W. 100, 149
Winkler, J.T. 227n
Wollheim, R. 17
Wood, E.M. 81
Wright, B.F. 103

Yack, B. 76, 77
Yugoslavia 189